CONFLICT ON
MOUNT LEBANON

Alternative Histories: Narratives from the Middle East and Mediterranean

Series Editor: Sargon Donabed

This series provides a forum for exchange on a myriad of alternative histories of marginalised communities and individuals in the Near and Middle East and Mediterranean, and those of Middle Eastern or Mediterranean heritage. It also highlights thematic issues relating to various native peoples and their narratives and – with particular contemporary relevance – explore encounters with the notion of 'other' within societies. Often moving beyond the conventional state-centred and dominant monolithic approach, or reinterpreting previously accepted stories, books in the series examine and explain themes from inter-communal relations, environment, health and society, and explore ethnic, communal, racial, linguistic and religious developments, in addition to geopolitics.

Editorial Advisory Board

Professor Ali Banuazizi
Dr Aryo Makko
Professor Laura Robson
Professor Paul Rowe
Professor Hannibal Travis

Books in the Series (Published and Forthcoming)

Sayfo: An Account of the Assyrian Genocide
'Abd al-Masih Nu'man of Qarabash
translated and annotated by Michael Abdalla and Łukasz Kiczko

Tunisia's Andalusians: The Cultural Identity of a North African Minority
Marta Dominguez Diaz

Palestinian Citizens of Israel: A History Through Fiction, 1948–2010
Manar Makhoul

Armenians Beyond Diaspora: Making Lebanon their Own
Tsolin Nalbantian

Conflict on Mount Lebanon: The Druze, the Maronites and Collective Memory
Makram Rabah

The Art of Minorities: Cultural Representation in Museums of the Middle East and North Africa
Edited by Virginie Rey

Shi'a Minorities in the Contemporary World: Migration, Transnationalism and Multilocality
Edited by Oliver Scharbrodt and Yafa Shanneik

Protestants, Gender and the Arab Renaissance in Late Ottoman Syria
Deanna Ferree Womack

www.edinburghuniversitypress.com/series/ahnme

CONFLICT ON MOUNT LEBANON

THE DRUZE, THE MARONITES AND COLLECTIVE MEMORY

Makram Rabah

EDINBURGH
University Press

Edinburgh University Press is one of the leading university presses in the UK. We publish academic books and journals in our selected subject areas across the humanities and social sciences, combining cutting-edge scholarship with high editorial and production values to produce academic works of lasting importance. For more information visit our website: edinburghuniversitypress.com

© Makram Rabah, 2020, 2022

Edinburgh University Press Ltd
The Tun – Holyrood Road
12 (2f) Jackson's Entry
Edinburgh EH8 8PJ

First published in hardback by Edinburgh University Press 2020

Typeset in 11/15 Adobe Garamond by
Servis Filmsetting Ltd, Stockport, Cheshire,

A CIP record for this book is available from the British Library

ISBN 978 1 4744 7417 7 (hardback)
ISBN 978 1 4744 7418 4 (paperback)
ISBN 978 1 4744 7419 1 (webready PDF)
ISBN 978 1 4744 7420 7 (epub)

The right of the contributors to be identified as authors of this work has been asserted in accordance with the Copyright, Designs and Patents Act 1988 and the Copyright and Related Rights Regulations 2003 (SI No. 2498).

CONTENTS

List of Figures	viii
Note on Transliteration and Style	xi
Acknowledgements	xii
Map: Operation Peace for Gallilee	xviii
Introduction	1
1 Studying the Druze–Maronite Conflict through the Prism of Collective Memory and Oral History	7
History vs Memory	9
Sources and Methodology of Oral History	11
Paul Andary Shot Twice	13
The Curious Case of Ghanam Tarabay	16
The Trope of Oral History	20
The Shah of Baʿabda Meets Salazar	21
Bashir: The Series	24
The Progressive Socalist Party's Oral History Project	25
The Council for Druze Studies and Development	27
The Permanent Bureau for Druze Associations	28

2 The Druze and the Maronites: Perceptions of the Other   35
   The Druze: Frontier Warriors and Feudal Lords   36
   Unity in Variety   43
   A Recipe for Disaster   45
   Emir Bashir vs Sheikh Bashir   47
   The Maronites: Lebanon, a Refuge   51
   The Maronites Go West   55
   The Maronites and the Eastern Question   58
   The Birth of the Lebanese Nation   63

3 The Communal Centres of Power and Elements of Collective Identity   77
   The Custodians of Identity   79
   The Warrior Monks   82
   The Kaslik Research Committee   86
   The Kataeb: In the Service of Lebanon   91
   The Druze Way   94
   Lost Druze History   96
   Druze: Blood Brothers across Generations   98
   O Brother, Where Art Thou?   101
   Wise vs Ignorant   102
   Druze Oneness through Time and Space   106
   Progressive Socialism Meets the Druze   108
   The '1958 Generation'   114
   The Slaying of Na'im Moghabghab   119

4 The Road to Conflict   130
   Harb al-Jabal: 1982–3   130
   The Rise of Bashir Gemayel   136
   Unity at Gunpoint   139
   Zahle: Victory in Defeat   143
   The Alliance of Minorities Resurrected   147
   The Likud Party and Bashir   149
   The End of the Affair: The Killing of Kamal Joumblatt   151
   Preparing for War   153
   The Missed Opportunity   155
   Crossing the Rubicon: Operation Snowball   160

5 The Point of No Return	167
Reclaiming our Rightful Place	168
Bashir vs Walid	174
The Battle of Qoubbei' al-Krayeh: The First Spark	176
You're Back? . . . We Have to Fight	178
The Assassination of Bashir	186
Long Live the King	190
6 The War of Others vs Druze–Maronite Collective Animosity	198
The Israeli Tide Shifts	198
The Druze Follow-up Commission	201
The Unification of the Druze	210
The Battle of Mtolleh	219
7 History Meets the Battlefield	230
The Maronite Via Dolorosa	230
General Beaufort Resurrected	232
The Faustian Deal Revoked	234
The Druze Canton	235
Israel Exits the Inferno	237
The Lebanese Army: One Last Try	240
The Battle of Bhamdoun	243
The Siege of Deir al-Qamar	252
The Maronite Exodus	254
8 Post-conflict Rehashing and the Preservation of Collective Memory	262
Collecting the Collective	262
The Story of a Hero Called Charbel	263
Zajal Harb al-Jabal	276
Bashir . . . We have Returned	284
Conclusion	291
Post-war Lebanon: The Quest for Reconciliation	291
Appendix: Table of Interviews	301
Bibliography	303
Index	314

FIGURES

1.1	Paul Andary	14
1.2	Ghanem Tarabay holding the PSP banner at a local rally	17
1.3	PSP credential of Ghanem Tarabay	19
3.1	Jocelyn Khoueiry	85
3.2	Bashir Gemayel greeting Bulus Naʿaman	87
3.3	Pierre Gemayel, founder of al-Kataeb, surrounded by members of his party	92
3.4	Al-Kataeb parade, 1937	93
3.5	Sheikh al-ʿAql Muhammad Abu-Shaqra of the Joumblatti faction Kamal Joumblatt and Sheikh al-ʿAql Ali Abdul Latif of the Yazbaki faction	104
3.6	PSP rally in Barouk, March 1951	109
3.7	Unveiling of the statue of Fakhr al-Din in Baakline	111
3.8	Kamal Joumblatt in his home in Moukhtara	114
3.9	Yasser Arafat, Chairman of the PLO, with Kamal Joumblatt	115
3.10	Kamal Joumblatt with his rebel fighters in Moukhtara, 1958	118
3.11	Majid Arslan and Naʿim Moghabghab	121
3.12	Zalfa Chamoun, Camille Chamoun, Majid Arslan and Naʿim Moghabghab	122

4.1	Kamal Joumblatt with his driver and bodyguard	133
4.2	Kamal Jumblatt's car riddled with bullet holes	134
4.3	Walid Joumblatt at the funeral of his father	135
4.4	Kamal Joumblatt identity cards and a picture of his son, damaged by bullets	135
4.5	Bashir Gemayel	138
4.6	Walid Joumblatt	140
4.7	Bashir Gemayel, Camille Chamoun and Pierre Gemayel	141
4.8	Returning from Zahle	146
4.9	Ariel Sharon, Bashir Gemayel and Lieutenant General Rafael Eitan	150
4.10	Bashir Gemayel meeting with Lieutenant General Rafael Eitan	151
4.11	Assad to Joumblatt: 'How much you resemble your father!'	153
4.12	PSP cadets at the military academy, 1978	156
4.13	Sharon to Bashir: 'We rearrange the northern border by launching a major military operation . . .'	162
5.1	Naji Butrus addressing his troops before their Shuf incursion	169
5.2	Bashir Gemayel, President Elias Sarkis and Walid Joumblatt	175
5.3	The first and only meeting between Bashir Gemayel and Walid Joumblatt	175
5.4	Massoud 'Poussy' Achkar and Fadi Frem	180
5.5	The Beirut Defense Unit	180
5.6	Mir Majid welcoming Bashir Gemayel into his home in Aley	184
5.7	Faisal Arslan, Bashir's Druze partner	184
5.8	Charles Malik, Bashir Gemayel and Faisal Arslan, following the tallying of votes	185
5.9	Bashir Gemayel in his last photograph, at the Monastery of the Holy Cross	188
5.10	Amin Gemayel, Pierre Gemayel and Bashir Gemayel	192
6.1	Farid Hamada	209
6.2	Akram Shehayab, Anwar al-Fatayri, Raja Harb, Sharif Fayyad and Hisham Nasreddine	214
6.3	Fouad Abu-Nadir	220
6.4	The al-Saddam unit, fashioned after the elite Israeli unit Sayeret Matkal	221

7.1	PSP map of the Battle of Bhamdoun	246
7.2	PSP tanks rolling into Bhamdoun, 3 September 1983	246
7.3	LF fighters manning a 14.5 anti-aircraft gun	247
7.4	LF Infantry heading into battle	247
7.5	Druze sheikh working his land armed with an AK-47	248
7.6	LF fighter praying to a statute of St Charbel	249
7.7	Druze cleric fighting with the *Quwwat Abu-Ibrahim*	257
8.1	Charbel addresses priest who resembles Abbot Bulus Na'aman	265
8.2	Keyrouz Barkat receiving the Medal of Zahle	267
8.3	Charbel is studying history when his comrade calls him: 'Charbel, come on . . .'	268
8.4	Comrade: 'Brother, put aside the history books . . .'	269
8.5	'Any gun that is yielded by a non-believer . . .'	270
8.6	Scenes from different episodes of *The Story of Charbel*	271
8.7	The killer and the warrior	272
8.8	Bashir Gemayel visiting the front lines	273
8.9	Medal of the Mountain, issued by the LF in 1983	274
8.10	Taleh Hamdan, with the PSP flag and pictures	280
8.11	'Son of the Mountains'	283
8.12	Walid Joumblatt saluting his troops	286
8.13	Walid Joumblatt lighting the torch	286
8.14	Walid Joumblatt flanked by Raja Harb, Anwar al-Fatayri and Sharif Fayyad	287
8.15	'Bashir . . . We have returned'	288

NOTE ON TRANSLITERATION AND STYLE

For Arabic-language transcription, I have relied on the style guide of the *International Journal of Middle East Studies* (IJMES). The names of places and people will therefore lack diacritical marks except *hamza* and *cayn*. For citation purposes, I have followed the *Chicago Manual of Style, 16th edition*.

In many cases, I have deliberately deviated from the IJMES transliteration system and followed the names as used by their owners, such as Joumblatt instead of Junblatt, while I have utilised the common usage assigned by the Lebanese government to place names.

ACKNOWLEDGEMENTS

Journeys, at least the ones worthwhile, are seldom ones which are taken alone.

First and foremost, my late Mou'allam Kamal Salibi whom we lost in September 2011 was with me every step of the way, even after he departed. Each time I sat down to write or edit, his voice would accompany me, criticising, suggesting or praising, as he had done while I sat at his dining table writing my Master's thesis.

For me and many others, Kamal Salibi was not merely a teacher, but also an inspiration as well as a model of how one should always question many of the essential truths we take for granted. The many hours I have spent in his home and on his balcony, I hope, have made me a better person and put me on a path towards intellectual discovery.

Over my brief career, I have received a number of titles and degrees, but perhaps the one I cherish most was given to me by Salibi, as he used to refer to me as his grand-student, having studied under his star pupil, my mentor and friend Abdul Rahim Abu-Husayn. From the first day I met Prof. Abu-Husayn at the door of College Hall, he granted me all the privileges of a son. His many fatherly reprimands throughout the years were a constant reminder to never allow my activist lifestyle to interfere with my academic progress.

Perhaps more importantly, Prof. Abu-Husayn, as the primary authority on Ottoman Lebanon, has provided the field with many of the building blocks that shape my current study and helped develop the revisionist school of Lebanese history, to which I proudly belong.

My gratitude also goes out to my thesis adviser and mentor at Georgetown University, Prof. Osama Abi-Mershid, who nurtured me throughout my years on the hilltop. Since my first visit to his office, Prof. Abi-Mershid's door has always been open to me, despite his busy schedule and his many responsibilities. His course suggestions and recommendations outside my field of study have enriched my knowledge and opened up many comparative fields where I would not have ventured on my own.

Special thanks go to Prof. Yvonne Haddad who so kindly accepted to serve on my thesis committee and whose comments and feedback have significantly enriched my study.

Fourteen years ago, I was offered a position as research assistant for an American professor from Boston, writing a book about the history of AUB. Little did I know that my encounter with Betty Anderson would lead to years of friendship. Accepting to serve as one of my thesis readers, Prof. Anderson gave me spot-on comments and edits and pointed out both flaws and strengths of my thesis; she also suggested possible ways to develop and improve my work. For this I will always be grateful.

I would also like to thank HE PM Saad al-Hariri, a fellow Hoya, who upon the good offices of a dear friend, Ms Elena Anouti, offered me a full scholarship from the Hariri Foundation in the USA, which made it possible to pursue my doctorate. I would also like to thank Mr Rafic Bizri, the director of the Hariri Foundation, and Dr David Thompson, my adviser, for their care and guidance. Thank you, Elena.

My utmost gratitude goes to the people who so kindly accepted to be interviewed for this study. The countless hours I spent interviewing them went beyond merely sharing copious amounts of beverages and food, and listening to their most intimate tales – stories of death, murder, pride, and remorse; stories of a lost youth and childhood. By allowing me into their memories, these brave individuals in more than one way shaped my understanding and analysis of the conflict on both sides involved. While I do acknowledge all of the interviewees' contributions, I would like to specifically thank Ghanem Tarabay, a brave soul whose dedication to his cause and his people never ceases to amaze me.

I would also like to thank MP Walid Joumblatt, President of the Progressive Socialist Party of Lebanon, who gave me unrestricted access to the PSP Oral History Project, which proved extremely valuable for my work. I would also like to thank the Director of Dar al-Takadoumi, the late Mr Mahmoud Safi, and his staff for facilitating my research as well as supplying me with all sources relevant to this study. I would also like to acknowledge the friendship and help of Monika Borgmann and Lokman Slim, as well as the UMAM Documentation and Research who have always provided me with logistical and scholarly support and allowed me to be part of their family. Thanks are equally due to the kind people and entities who provided me with the pictures to this book, MP Nadim Bashir Gemayel, the Bashir Gemayel Foundation, the Lebanese Forces, Walid Fayyad, Wassim Jabre, Abbas Tarabay, Tarek Ghassan Moghabghab, the PSP archives and Maison Du Future.

I cannot thank enough my parents, Ghassan and Nabila, and my brother Rami for the never-ending love and the support they have lent me during the many challenges I encountered. My father, retired Judge and Law Professor Ghassan Rabah, a man of principle and justice, has always stood as my pillar and a constant reminder that ethics and values still do exist in a world that is governed by might rather than right.

I owe a great debt of gratitude to my mother Nabila whose large heart and worrisome nature is the paradigm of motherly love. I owe a great debt of gratitude to my brother Rami who still hopes one day to sell off my books to make more room in our shared bedroom. Hopefully, when this thesis becomes a book you will have to read it.

I am truly saddened that Kamal Abdul-Rahim Abu-Husayn who meticulously and lovingly helped to edit this work is no longer with us to share in my humble achievement. Kamal – who shares the name of his grandfather, the late Kamal Salibi – left us suddenly on 28 October 2018. A talented and kind soul, he will be remembered every time I hold this book. You are deeply missed, Kamoul.

Many who know me are aware of my difficult character; the stress and pressures of life and all that comes with it have been made bearable by the love and care of my partner, Rasha. Her love and her eyes have always kept watch over me at the most difficult of times. For this, I pledge my love and life.

As time passes, I have become ever more appreciative of friends, especially those who proved that true friendship is indeed a rare commodity.

Thanks is due to Sami Saab, Omar Slim, Zeina Ghosn, Siso, Wassim Jaber, Nadine and Bassam Abu-Shakra, Teymour and Diana Joumblatt, Tony Haikal, Tarek Hassan, Enass Khansa, Eli Khoury, Elie Khayat, Nadim Shehadi, Abbas Tarabay, Walid Fayyad, Michel Farha, Siso and many more whose names I have failed to list here.

I also owe thanks to my comrade-in-arms, Husam Raja Harb, a brother and friend who has always had my back; to him I owe never-ending love, trust and my unwavering friendship.

While I acknowledge the collective credit and recognition to all persons listed above, the shortcomings of this study are my sole responsibility.

وَقَدْ يَنْبُتُ الْمَرْعىَ عَلَى دِمَنِ الثَّرَى
وَتَبْقَى حَزَازاتُ النُّفوسِ كما هِيّا

زفر بن الحارث

Grass will regrow on a blood-soaked pasture
While the rancour of souls remains unchanged

Zafar bin Hareth

In Memory of my Mouʻallam
Kamal Salibi (1929–2011)

and

his namesake Kamal Abu-Husayn (1979–2018)

and to the longevity of my Friend and Mentor
Abdul-Rahim Abu-Husayn

Operation Peace for Galilee – Israeli Invasion of Lebanon, 1982 (Maison du Future).

INTRODUCTION

This study is an attempt to gauge the impact that collective memory had on determining the course and nature of the 1982 conflict between the Druze and the Maronite communities on Mount Lebanon in what came to be called the War of the Mountain (*Harb al-Jabal*). This stretch of land running parallel to the Mediterranean Sea in the west and adjacent to the Anti-Lebanon mountain range in the east, is home to the Druze and the Maronites, the founding communities of modern Lebanon; they clashed on more than one occasion over the past two centuries, earning them a reputation of fierce archnemesis. Here, I will attempt to reconstruct, perhaps for the first time, the events of the 1982 war within the framework of collective remembrance. In doing so, I hope to achieve a better understanding of the conflict, as well as of the consequences it had on the two communities and beyond, most importantly the post-war reconciliation process. This understanding, then, may also be applicable to other communal conflicts in the country and to the region as a whole.

On the morning of 13 April 1975, unknown assailants opened fire on a Maronite Church in the Christian suburbs of Beirut, killing three people, among them the bodyguard of Pierre Gemayel, the founder of the Lebanese Kataeb (Phalangist) Party, Lebanon's leading Maronite party. An outspoken opponent of the Palestinian armed presence in Lebanon, Gemayel was attending the consecration of this church, and this context took this incident to a new dimension. In retaliation, members of the Kataeb Party ambushed a bus transporting people returning from a commemorative event in the Palestinian refugee camp of Tal al-Za'atar.[1] This ambush on a spring Sunday morning constituted, as Walid Khalidi would later call it, 'the Sarajevo' that ignited the war.[2] Khalidi's analogy to describe the direct cause for the outbreak of the war has not been shared by the majority of scholars, who believe that the roots of this conflict predated 1975, and even the existence of the Lebanese state.

The Lebanese Civil War (1975–90) has been studied extensively by historians, anthropologists, political scientist, health scientists and many others. Of course, it was also closely and extensively covered by journalists. Their efforts yielded various interpretations to explain and understand the underlying structural causes of this war that ultimately led to the destruction of a country previously held up as an economic and political success-story. However, my extensive field research led me to the conclusion that the War of the Mountain has never been addressed or analysed on its own; rather, it has been incorporated into the master narrative of the different schools of thought that govern Lebanese Civil War Studies. Such an approach has obscured the distinctive nature of this chapter of the war – a war that was not merely a continuation of earlier conflicts, or a prelude to later confrontations. Many of the scholarly works on the civil war place major responsibility on the Palestinian factor and the presence of the Palestine Liberation Organisation (PLO), which after 1969 had moved its centre of operations almost exclusively to Lebanon. This approach either tends to totally exclude and excuse or make only passing reference to the war's local dimensions, which perhaps had a much greater or at least equal share in the responsibility. A remarkable example of this trend is Farid Khazen's *The Breakdown of the State in Lebanon, 1967–1976*. This work has taken such an approach even a step further, as it has placed the blame almost exclusively on the PLO and their Lebanese allies for challenging and weakening the authority of the Lebanese state, thus paving the way for the conflict to erupt.[3]

A variant of this interpretation adopts the notion that Lebanon was an arena for regional and Cold War conflicts, and that the Lebanese had no real say in the subsequent events. Ghassan Tuwayni's *Une Guerre Pour Les Autres* constitutes an eloquent example.[4] A structural analysis of the Lebanese system has been undertaken by what may be referred to as the Marxist school of interpretation. Fawwaz Traboulsi's *A History of Modern Lebanon* and Salim Nasr's 'Backdrop to Civil War: The Crisis of Lebanese Capitalism' argue that the Lebanese economy, which promoted unmitigated capitalism, paved the way for the migrant Lebanese working class to channel their syndical demands via the Palestinian revolution and other, similar venues.[5] According to the Marxists, this fact, together with the failure of the traditional political class to reform and adjust to the ever-changing realities of Lebanon and the region, was the main reason for the collapse of the state. The most common and widely circulated reading, however, concerns the confessional and sectarian nature of the Lebanese political system, which divided the country along confessional lines. These divisions did not recognise class or social mobility, and this was coupled with each sect's alliance with a foreign power to protect and support its share in the state and its economy. As a result, Lebanon was exposed to recurrent rounds of violence, as in the events of 1958 and 1975–89. Writing at the end of the war, Kamal Salibi has summed up the main problems of the Lebanese political system and the essence of the conflict; in his *A House of Many Mansions: A History of Lebanon Reconsidered*, he has stressed that most of the conflicts between these groups were waged over each group's interpretation of Lebanese history, which at one stage or another were linked to a certain political project.[6]

I argue that these interpretations have largely been skewed due to their neglect of history and collective memory; they have viewed the conflict through the lens of contemporary affairs, such as state structure, Cold War politics and class struggle. Hence, my approach will incorporate both new sources and new methodologies, particularly oral history. This will make it possible to reconstruct the War of the Mountain and offer a more in-depth understanding of this event, especially as it relates to the two Lebanese founding communities. This deeper understanding will then hopefully contribute to post-war reconciliation, which remains pending. Thus far, the writing of a narrative of the War of the Mountain and the events that led up to it has never been attempted, at least not within scholarly circles. Telling the story, or perhaps stories, of the many men and women who participated in these events, or simply suffered as a consequence, is a valuable contribution to the field of Lebanese historical scholarship – especially when it can help expose the intrinsic motives that led to this conflict.

This book will extensively utilise oral history in some of its sections, in order to explore how collective memory has shaped the conflict between the two communities. I have interviewed a number of informants from both (within and outside) the Druze community (particularly the Progressive Socialist Party) and the Maronite community (especially the Kataeb Party), who have been involved in or witnessed the conflict. I asked these and other informants about how their respective communities have recalled previous encounters. Therefore, part of my work will deal with the question of employing oral history in historical research, and the challenges and advantages that this tool can present to Lebanese history and beyond.

I have also used primary source documents (political party literature and propaganda), including oral history interviews, as well as the secondary literature available in the Jafet Library at the American University of Beirut, at Saint Joseph University and the Lebanese National Archives, to reconstruct the events of the War of the Mountain and its ramifications. Furthermore, I will examine the history of both communities – how they have evolved and interacted with each other on Mount Lebanon as early as in the eighteenth century, so as to uncover any recurrent patterns in their history. A deeper understanding of the two community's perceptions of themselves and each other will shed more light on the background of the 1982 conflict. Therefore, this study will also be relevant for the exploration of earlier conflicts between these two communities, primarily of 1840–5, 1860 and 1958, which still echo very clearly in their collective memories, rhetoric and literary production.

Subsequently, I will illustrate how the centres of power within each of the two communities have been actively working to maintain their communities' somewhat unified collective memories and perceptions. While my focus appears to be on the 'collective', in no way do I intend to neglect or sideline individual agency or the relevance of individual memory.

Rather, my work openly challenges the essential facts that both the Druze and the Maronites take for granted – namely, that they are a primordial social fabric organically formed over time. As the following chapter will demonstrate, the process of creating the collective entails the active involvement and agency of these communities' centres of power, which create and maintain these memory frameworks. Therefore, before delving into this aspect and in order to properly frame my work, I will present the different schools of thought in memory studies, beginning with Maurice Halbwachs and his subsequent supporters and critics. This will be followed by two examples of active agents as used by the centres of power to promote a collective identity as well as to recast, adjust and modify the respective communities' memories of themselves, as well as of 'the other'. In the Maronite context, *Al-Masiraa'*, the official publication of the Lebanese Forces (Maronite), published *The Story of a Hero called Charbel*, a weekly illustrated cartoon written in colloquial Lebanese dialect. In contrast, the Druze utilised the works of the prominent strophic poet Taleh Hamdan, which abound with examples of what the Druze centres of power wanted their community to remember concerning their archnemesis (the Maronites) and the *Harb al-Jabal*.

The modern history of Mount Lebanon began in the seventeenth century, when the Maronites migrated from its northern to its southern district. This history involves an elaborate tale of many chapters, some of which are still waiting to be told. While my work focuses on certain episodes of conflict between the Druze and the Maronites, this should not deny the fact that these two founding Lebanese communities have worked together and coexisted for much longer periods of time. It is essentially these dynamics of conflict and accord that came to define the strained relationship between these two groups and that consequently contributed in one way or another to the War of the Mountain and its subsequent events.

While the Druze and the Maronite, at least at present, are not in a state of open warfare or hostility, both communities retain their collective memory weapons to be deployed when needed, much like all other Lebanese groups. The following pages will explore the history of this conflict, while using collective memory as a lens to better understand an important event that has shaped the history of modern Lebanon and continues to do so until this day.

Notes

1. Kamal Salibi, *Crossroads to Civil War: Lebanon, 1958–1976* (Delmar: Caravan Books, 1976), 98. Consequently, all the passengers on board, except for the driver, were massacred. The Kataeb claimed that the passengers (mostly Palestinians) had been armed; however, this claim was never substantiated.

2. Walid Khalidi, *Conflict and Violence in Lebanon: Confrontation in the Middle East* (Cambridge, MA: Center for International Affairs, Harvard University, 1979), 47.
3. Farid Khazen, *The Breakdown of the State in Lebanon, 1967–1976* (Cambridge, MA: Harvard University Press, 2000).
4. Ghassan Tuwayni, *Une guerre pour les autres* (Paris: J. C. Lattes, 1985).
5. Fawwaz Traboulsi, *A History of Modern Lebanon* (London: Pluto Press, 2007), 115; Salim Nasr, 'Backdrop to Civil War: The Crisis of Lebanese Capitalism', *MERIP Reports* 73 (1978): 3.
6. Kamal Salibi, *A House of Many Mansions: The History of Lebanon Reconsidered* (London: I. B. Tauris, 1988), 200.

1

STUDYING THE DRUZE–MARONITE CONFLICT THROUGH THE PRISM OF COLLECTIVE MEMORY AND ORAL HISTORY

The many attempts to document and explore the history of the Lebanese Civil War (1975–90) have thus far relied heavily, not to say exclusively, on written archival sources. Virtually no attention has been paid to non-orthodox sources, such as collective memory and oral history. These untapped sources can go beyond the obvious utilitarian function of merely offering new facts pertaining to the conflict overall; they can play a more important role, especially within the context of the War of the Mountain and the events that transpired between the Druze and the Maronites in the summer of 1982. Accordingly, as this study will argue, the central significance of historical remembrance for both the Druze and the Maronites places oral history and collective memory at the crux of the motives that facilitated polarisation and eventually led to war. Consequently, the framing of these motives and the interplay between collective memory and oral history requires a clear understanding of the theoretical concepts of collective memory, as well as the advantages and limitations of oral history, as utilised throughout this study.

The concept 'collective memory' first appeared in 1902 in the writings of Hugo von Hofmannsthal. However, it was not until Maurice Halbwachs published his book *The Social Frameworks of Memory* in 1925, followed by his main work entitled *On Collective Memory*, that this concept gained currency and became well-established in the social sciences.[1] Halbwachs, an apprentice of Emile Durkheim, has stated that memories are both public and shareable and that memory is a product of individual remembrance within a group, rather than a subjective endeavor. By shifting the unit of analysis from the individual alone to the individual within his or her social group, Halbwachs challenged the Freudian model that reigned supreme at the time.

According to the Halbwachsian model, memory is transmitted by both individuals and members of groups; therefore, 'there are as many collective memories in a society as there are social groups'.[2] Halbwachs has furthermore placed individuals within the different frameworks imposed on them by their group, be they society or family, or anything else between these two ends of the spectrum. This is clear for Halbwachs who has emphatically asserted the following:

> It is in society that people normally acquire their memories. It is also in society that they recall, recognize, and localize their memories ... It is in this sense that there exists a collective memory and social frameworks for memory; it is to the degree that our individual thought places itself in these frameworks and participates in this memory that it is capable of the act of recollection.[3]

It follows that the process of remembering and forgetting is regulated by the interests, goals and practices of the group; essentially, the memories that one retains of the past are filtered through the medium of the group. Therefore, the fluidity of memory makes the past exclusively dependent on the present context and in effect renders futile the attempt to determine what really happened in the past.

Despite Halbwachs's novel ideas, sociologists and researchers did not embrace his work until much later.[4] While some researchers adopted the Halbwachsian interpretation of collective memory, others found his analysis to be fraught with problems. One of the major criticisms levelled at Halbwachs has posited that his approach removes individual agency from remembrance and elevates the group to an overpowering entity. Frederic Bartlett, deemed the father of modern memory studies, has criticised Halbwachs, claiming that not groups, but rather individuals in groups have memories. However,

Bartlett has agreed with Halbwachs on the importance of the group for harnessing individual memory, affirming that 'social organisations give a persistent framework into which all detailed recall must fit, and it very powerfully influences both the manner and the matter of recall'.[5] In contrast, Barry Schwartz has criticised Halbwachs for overstating changes in the memory process, which ultimately make the past somewhat more vague than it really is. According to Schwartz, there exists a dialectical relation between the past and the present, and memory can be understood through that lens of 'continuities in our perception of the past across time and to the way that these perceptions are maintained in the face of social change'.[6] It must be emphasised that such continuities in perception abound within the Druze and Maronite historical psyche, as the subsequent chapters will illustrate.

History vs Memory

The most significant criticism against memory studies arose from within the field of history. Starting in the nineteenth century, historiographical scholarship moved towards anchoring the study of history within a more scientific framework; commonly referred to as the German school, this scholarly approach sought objectivity in historical writing and relied heavily on written primary sources.[7] Naturally, this excluded memory from playing any role in the newly founded historical profession. Historians frowned upon unwritten forms, especially memory, which they claimed to be distorted by a number of factors; hence, memory came to be labeled as ahistorical.[8] However, the somewhat recent debate on memory vs history has taken a different turn. The prominent French historian Pierre Nora has regarded memory as the archenemy of history. According to Nora, 'memory remains in a permanent evolution and is unconscious of its successive deformations, vulnerable to manipulation'; history, on the other hand, 'is an intellectual secular production, calls for analysis and criticism . . . history is suspicious of memory, and its true mission is to suppress and destroy it'.[9] Peter Novick, another critic of the Halbwachsian discourse, has stripped collective memory of its historical relevance with the following argument:

> To understand something historically is to be aware of its complexity, to have sufficient detachment to see it from multiple perspectives, to accept

the ambiguities, including moral ambiguities, of protagonists' motives and behavior. Collective memory simplifies; sees events from a single, committed perspective; is impatient with ambiguities of any kind; reduces events to mythic archetypes.[10]

Dismissing the so-called 'noble dream' of objectivity in historical research, Novick has stressed the following important dimension of collective memory, as it relates to forging a common identity for the group: 'Collective memory is understood to express some eternal or essential truth about the group, usually tragic. A memory, once established, comes to define that eternal truth, and, along with it, an eternal identity, for the members of the group'.[11]

It is exactly these eternal or essential truths that make collective memory problematic in the context of the Druze–Maronite encounter, as 'the memorializing of tragedies or perhaps victories won against ones' group will most probably lead to engendering hostile feeling'.[12] Moreover, as this study will demonstrate, when collective memory is left to develop in an exclusionary manner within a divided society such as that of Lebanon, it can prevent post-war reconciliation and perhaps reignite dormant hostilities. This was the case in 1860, 1958 and 1975–90. The War of the Mountain is perhaps the best case in point.

While I prefer here to use of the term 'collective memory', rather than terms such as social memory or memory cultures,[13] my approach to the realm of memory does not adopt a strict Halbwachsian model. I rather subscribe to the notion that, although memory is framed by the group (in Lebanon's case, the religious sect or the tribe), individuals are still the vessels in which the act of remembrance occurs, even if these individuals identify with a certain group. Amos Funkenstein has squarely placed the individual in the middle of this debate:

> Consciousness and memory can only be realized by an individual who acts, is aware, and remembers. Just as a nation cannot eat or dance, neither can it speak or remember. Remembering is a mental act, and therefore it is absolutely and completely personal.[14]

While the individual, as opposed to a group, does indeed remember, the meanings of these memories are interpreted or recast by the group to serve a certain purpose. Another reason for my adoption of this term lies in the fact that the concept of collective memory, or its Arabic translation *al-dhākirah al-jamāʿīyah*, resonates more with the subjects of my oral history interviews. The very term in Arabic assigns a major role to memory. Hence, coining and using a different phrase would have alienated or disenchanted my interviewees. While the plain word 'memory' presents its own challenges, using it in conjunction with oral interviews presents even further challenges and complications for the writing of history. At the same time, it reveals new vantage points for analysis and offers new insights.

Sources and Methodology of Oral History

In his memoirs, the distinguished yet controversial historian Bernard Lewis has sketched out the duties and prerogatives of a historian. To Lewis, history is unequivocally 'an approach that is free from both inherited attitudes and imposed constraints, where one follows evidence wherever it leads, where one starts a piece of research without a prescribed or in any way predetermined result'.[15] Almost all attempts at writing history have theoretically endorsed Lewis's answer to the question 'why study history?' Yet, some have gone so far as to believe that a type of ultimate universal truth is attainable. This school of thought has not come to dominate the profession, at least not at the time of the writing of this book. Historians have become more and more aware that their craft, as Marc Bloch has stressed, in fact consists not of a synthesis of the past, but rather of observation and analyses of past events, grounded in documentation and traces of evidence which are at times 'forced to speak'.[16] This spirit, as embodied by Bloch, has become the foundation of modern historical scholarship.

Lewis's remarks, however, leave one pondering several issues. Most importantly, if the evidence which historians deal with is incomplete, is it permissible to look outside the traditional sources available for supplementary evidence and documentation? Lewis, a medievalist, came from a generation of scholars who equated evidence with textuality – evidence was to be found in the primary sources held in state archives and libraries, kept under lock and key by archivists and librarians.

The sources used in this project range from the more traditional to previously untapped ones. These primarily, but not exclusively, consist of oral history and both Druze and Maronite party publications. In using them, I aspire to uncover the symbiosis between individuals and group memory and to reveal aspects of those stories that otherwise remain suppressed or simply untold. Alessandro Portelli, a pioneer in the field of oral history, has elaborated on the uniqueness of this approach:

> The first thing that makes oral history different, therefore, is that it tells us less about events as such than about their meaning. This does not imply that oral history has no factual interest; interviews often reveal unknown events or unknown aspects of known events, and always cast new light on unexplored sides of the daily life of the non-hegemonic classes.[17]

Oral history has rarely been used in works dealing with the Lebanese Civil War. Most of the recent work dealing with memory studies, such as that by Lucia Volk and Sune Haugbolle, do so based on an anthropological approach that relies on ethnography, a cousin of oral history.[18] Furthermore, all the relevant studies to some extent discuss post-war Lebanon but rarely explore the conflict and the role of memory in it, focusing on post-war implications rather than the events of the conflict.

The centrality of memory to oral history adds to the criticism launched against it as being flawed and unreliable. Nevertheless, collective memory is always at play when interviewing informants; in fact, it is this encounter between group and individual memory that adds to our understanding of what really happened and, most importantly, what it meant to people then and in hindsight. Furthermore, to use Portelli's words, 'the credibility of oral sources is a different credibility', because within this exercise 'what informants believe is indeed a historical fact just as much as what "really happened"'.[19] Therefore, instead of viewing collective memory as tainting the individual's remembrance process, historians can use orality to study encounters between the two.

These encounters between collective memory and the individual's remembrance process are best understood when keeping in mind that most of what oral historians receive from their subjects is in narrative form. The narrative aspect of this process renders the quest for accuracy somewhat more elusive. Oral historians do not merely ask their subjects to remember events and their implications. More accurately, oral history in a sense involves the reconstruction of past experiences, rather than simply retrieving them from the 'database' commonly referred to as memory. To every question, the narrator responds based on what s/he remembers and, more importantly, based on what her/his present predisposition dictates. Elizabeth Tonkin's work *Narrating Our Pasts: The Social Construction of Oral History* underscores this point.[20] Having conducted extensive research on oral tradition and oral history in Liberia, Tonkin has concluded that much of what we remember and relate to others is mediated through the dynamics that bond the teller and the listener. Tonkin has described this process as follows:

> The social contexts of oral histories include the additional condition that their tellers must intersect with a palpable audience at a particular moment in time and space. What they choose to say is affected by those conditions, which also mean that they get immediate feedback.[21]

She goes on to describe how these narrations are in constant flux:

> The narrators and listeners connected by this contingency are thereby caught at a certain stage of their lives; they have also been formed inescapably by their own personal pasts to date. These factors influence the narration whether or not it is autobiographical; tellers are constructing retrospective accounts for audience with different time scales, and they may adjust their own narrations to the memories and understanding of their listeners.[22]

This is not meant to demote the reliability of oral sources; however, Tonkin's point supports the claim that oral history accounts are far more important than just presenting us with factual (or in some cases erroneous) accounts. Consequently, in the case of the Druze–Maronite relationship oral history can serve as a tool to investigate and reconstruct a certain historical event or occasion. Yet, these oral accounts are much more indicative of changes and continuities across groups and boundaries. Paul Andary's interview is a case in point, as the informant's testimony has been shaped by his own evolution, as well as the person asking the questions (in this case, myself).

Paul Andary Shot Twice

When I interviewed Paul Andary, the Second-in-Command of the Lebanese Forces (LF) of the Jabal district during the War of the Mountain, I made a point of putting the question to him in direct and clear terms: In how far

Figure 1.1 Paul Andary (LF Archives).

were the events of the 1860 civil war between the Druze and the Maronites instrumental for shaping his own psyche and that of his comrades? In response, Andary was clear in dismissing any connection whatsoever between the 1860 and the 1982 events.[23] Yet, an examination of Andary's memoirs *Al-Jabal: Haqīqah lā Tarḥam* (The Mountain: A Ruthless Reality) published immediately after the War of the Mountain proves otherwise.

For example, he described his entry at the head of an LF contingent into the town of Deir al-Qamar in the following way: 'its *saray* [palace] which had remained unchanged since the dawn of the 1860 massacre . . . imprinted on its walls are the shadows of the [Druze] attackers, with their striped robes and black trousers'.[24] By choosing to open his book with a tale of the massacres that the Druze committed against the Christian inhabitants of Deir al-Qamar in 1860, Andary fused the two episodes, of 1860 and 1983, and inserted himself and his Maronite cohorts in their midst, thus forming an uninterrupted link transcending both space and time. However, Andary has recently published an English translation of his memoirs. An examination of the cover of both editions indicates that Andary has become increasingly circumspect of any statement or act that would insult the present-day allies of the LF and the Druze PSP. Interestingly, Andary's English-language book cover and title – *War of the Mountain: Israelis, Christians and Druze in the 1983 Mount Lebanon Conflict Through the Eyes of a Lebanese Forces Fighter* – does not resonate with the same tone as the Arabic version, which reflects a bitter animosity between the Maronites and the Druze.[25] In his English translation, Andary rather wanted to portray that Lebanon's problems can be externalised and virtually blamed on the Syrians and the Israelis. Andary's somewhat mild answers to my interview in 2010 might have been affected by his awareness of the interviewer's – that is, my – identity as a Druze, originally hailing from the area that saw much of the fighting.

This relates perfectly to the observations made by Paul Thompson, a pioneer in the field of oral history:

> ... neither contemporary nor historical evidence is a direct reflection of physical facts or behavior. Facts and events are reported in a way which gives them social meaning. The information provided by interview evidence of relatively recent events, or current situations, can be assumed to lie somewhere between the actual social behavior and the social expectations or norms of the time. With interviews which go back further, there is the added possibility of distortions influenced by subsequent changes in values and norms, which may perhaps quite unconsciously alter perceptions. With time we would expect this danger to grow.[26]

Andary, therefore, was not being deceitful in his answers; rather, his answers should be viewed as part of an evolution that he himself and perhaps his community have undergone. Furthermore, had I limited myself to Andary's book, I would have missed the opportunity to explore this aspect, which sheds light on collective memory formation – in other words, how collective memory is constantly rehashed to conform to current requirements, whether personal or communal in nature.

However, neither Tonkin's remarks nor Andary's example should lead one to believe that the narrative nature of oral history renders it unreliable and incapable of reconstructing the past accurately, as textual archives do.

The work of Alice and Howard Hoffman has illustrated how, despite the narrative aspect and the interplay between personal and social memory, oral history can still produce accurate accounts when cross-referenced with written records.[27] Hoffman, who had fought in World War II, was interviewed by his wife Alice on numerous occasions over a period of ten years. This experiment revealed that the transcripts of all these interviews were to a large extent identical to events as they had been recorded by the US Army. Most importantly, the Hoffmans concluded that 'it is possible for memory to achieve an archival quality if it is sufficiently rehearsed unconsciously or consciously shortly after the experience it documents'.[28]

There also exists the eternal claim that man by nature is forgetful and that events experienced cannot be accurately recalled, especially if these encounters are distant, or if they involve a traumatic experience. The nature of the topic at hand – namely, warfare – is highly charged with traumatic experiences, as almost every single one of my interviewees either lost loved ones, was seriously injured, or killed another human being in the course of the war. Still, this does not necessarily mean that we need to discard the information obtained from the informants; instead, we should critically evaluate this source, just as scholars would with any other document, so as not to misinterpret the information or drastically add to the traumatic experience.

While poor recall may affect oral history, historians have recourse to a wide array of tools to jog the memory. This is exactly why historians who use oral sources allow their informants to speak about themselves at length – to grease the machine of memory, so to speak. Coincidentally, many of my interviews started with a short informal conversation about the informant's personal life and then continued with questions directly related to their role in the war or the events surrounding it. However, despite the many strides achieved in the field of memory studies, both empirical and theoretical, human memory continues to baffle and amaze.

The Curious Case of Ghanam Tarabay

One of my primary informants, Ghanem Tarabay – a commander in the Progressive Socialist Party (PSP) militia who lost his father and several cousins during the Battle of Qoubbe'i between the LF and the PSP, one of the first military engagements in the summer of 1982 – took me on a tour of the

Figure 1.2 Ghanem Tarabay holding the PSP banner at a local rally (PSP Archives).

actual battleground and narrated the events of that battle, which lasted for a full seven days. He vividly described everything, including how his father had mocked him when he ordered his men to stay in their positions, just seconds before a bullet ended his father's life. However, almost a year after my first interview with him, Tarabay told me that his maternal uncle later reminded him of an episode of which he personally had no recollection whatsoever. Tarabay's uncle told him how they both took his father's dead body and had to make the long drive back to their village to avoid enemy roadblocks. Furthermore, his uncle added how the soldiers at the Syrian Army checkpoint, fully aware that Ghanem was transporting his deceased father in the back of the vehicle, performed the official military honours reserved for fallen Syrian soldiers. To this day, Ghanem insists that he cannot remember any of these details recalled by his uncle; moreover, he cannot even remember that he himself buried his father. This perplexing episode underscores both the volatility of oral accounts and the availability of corrective measures. It also points to untold stories. Had I not interviewed Ghanem in 2010, he would not have discussed the topic with his uncle and thus retrieved the story; it would have remained buried next to his late father.

Much of what Ghanem experienced in terms of loss and repression of memory is an extremely common occurrence, to varying degrees dependent on the intensity of the relevant event. The seven sins of memory, as Harvard Psychologist Daniel Schacter has called them, explain the elusive nature of memory, as well as how its loss or involuntary remembrance can have affect peoples' lives.[29] According to Schacter, these sins are the main reasons for the malfunction of memory, and 'just like the ancient deadly sins, the memory sins occur frequently in every daily life and can have serious consequences for all of us'.[30] Schacter has divided these seven sins into two main groups: sins of omission and sins of commission. Sins of omission (transience, absent-mindedness and blocking) account for forgetfulness, while sins of commission (misattribution, suggestibility, bias and persistence) are responsible for flawed or unwanted memories. However, these 'seven deadly sins' do not adequately explain the repression of of Ghanem's memory. Sins of omission are instances where one might forget a number or name, but certainly not the death of a loved one. Furthermore, while sins of commission – in particular, the sin of persistence which involves repeatedly recalling traumatic and disturbing memories – can lead to psychological problems especially for individuals involved in combat, Ghanem did not suffer from persistent memories, but a total lack of memory. As early as after World War I, such mental disorders, previously referred to as shell-shock and now as Post Traumatic Stress Disorder (PTSD), have been the focus of mental health experts and social scientists.[31] However, an examination of the existing literature on memory loss makes it somewhat difficult to place Ghanem's case within the existing groupings of amnesia.[32] In most cases of combat-related memory loss, the memories lie dormant within the person and lead to dissociative amnesia, which impedes one's ability to remember for a time-span ranging from a few hours to longer periods.

Still, this does not apply to the case under investigation, for a number of reasons. Ghanem had never suffered from memory loss, other than the incident reported. My hours of interviews and sporadic conversations over an extended period, as well as the consistency and vividness of most of the information he provided, attests to this fact. More importantly, Ghanem

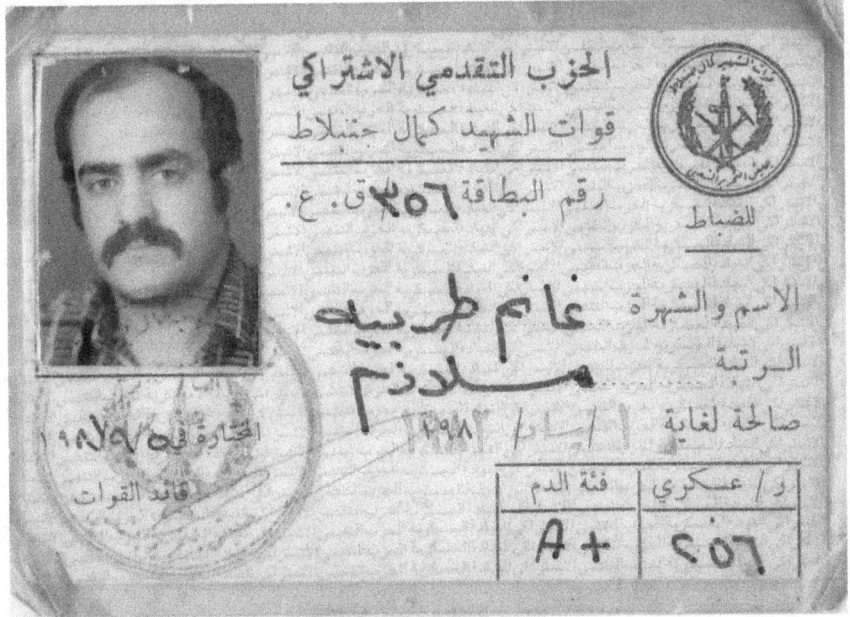

Figure 1.3 PSP credential of Ghanem Tarabay, ranked Lieutenant (PSP Archives).

remembers the actual traumatic experience, the battle and the death of his father and cousins, down to the smallest detail, but he lacks any recollection of the funeral proceedings that ensued. Ghanem's case remains one of many that continue to baffle scholars in their quest to gain a better understanding of memory and its mechanisms. It also became one of the many occasions on which I had to re-examine my conclusions while conducting research.

An additional challenge I encountered is the generational gap, which at times impeded my ability to understand my interlocutors' somewhat difficult idiomatic language. For example, Ghanem told me how his school principal used to tell him about the decline of the Druze with the following line: 'The Druze became weak the day they stopped sealing their windows with rocks during the wintertime'.[33] This quote did not resonate with me at first, apparently because it was a reference completely alien to me, but not to Ghanem and his cohorts. This obstacle, however, is easy to overcome: As I did so on that occasion, researchers should ask their informants to elaborate on generational or local idioms to be able to follow the narrator. When asked about the meaning of this expression, Ghanem explained that in the past the dwellings of the Druze did not feature windowpanes; thus, in winter they had to use makeshift wood or rocks to block themselves from the cold and wild animals. Therefore, 'the real degeneration of Druze power started when they abandoned their old ways and decided to embrace the modern way of life'.[34] Among other old ways that have been abandoned count the celebrated and much-cited Druze cohesion and solidarity. Of course, the point of the anecdote here is not only architectural, but also underlines the Khaldunian concept of *'asabiyyah* or group temperament, which withers away when the people or the tribe abandon their old ways. This concept is essential for understanding the Druze's self-perception as a proud warrior clan, as the following chapter will elaborate. Much of the Druze rhetoric and literature produced before and during the conflict reiterated Ibn Khaldun's *'asabiyyah* to serve a long-term strategic goal, as well as a more immediate tactical one, such as military mobilisation.

The Trope of Oral History

Many critics also claim that oral history is essentially unverifiable, because it is grounded in personal stories, in contrast to textual evidence, which usually can be cross-checked. Although oral historians heavily rely on oral sources, like all scholars, they nevertheless utilise textual sources including archival documents, newspapers, songs, films and so on. Without these sources, oral historians cannot prepare for interviews, nor can they critically evaluate what informants tell them. The claim that oral accounts are unverifiable is therefore inaccurate. While at times incidents cannot be traced back to textual evidence, this does not mean that the actual event did not occur.

By forming a bond of trust with their informants, oral historians often find personal archives, which the informant so far has been reluctant to share with anyone else. This is exactly what happened when I asked the former Minister of Public Works, Ghazi al-Aridi, about the archive of the Voice of the Mountain, the PSP wartime radio station. Generally believed to have been destroyed after the end of the war, Aridi, the former director of the station, enthusiastically shared the contents of this archive, which he keeps locked up. Thus, even though oral historians are perceived as bypassing textual evidence, their activities in fact only enhance the scope and diversity of their sources. As a consquence, previously unheard voices and experiences become central and can assist historians in redrafting or perhaps discovering new aspects of many previously taken-for-granted issues. My research on the War of the Mountain is a case in point. Portelli has forcefully summarised this shift which oral history was able to accomplish:

> The task and theme of oral history – an art dealing with the individual in social and historical context – is to explore this distance and this bond, to search out the memories in the private, enclosed spaces of houses and kitchens – to connect them to history and in turn force history to listen to them.[35]

Yet, oral history is still struggling to attain the same recognition that written archival documents, incomplete and full of gaps as they are, have achieved. At best, academia has acknowledged that oral sources are supplementary in nature and should be combined with written sources to add more depth and insight to a historian's work.[36] Hence, it is natural for historians to prefer the textual explanation of an event, if it is contradicted by oral testimony. This approach, however, can prove to be a slippery slope.

The Shah of Ba'abda Meets Salazar

Usually, historians practise great caution when analysing written evidence, ranging from speeches over newspaper articles and meeting minutes to radio broadcasts. However, based on the oral history work I have conducted thus far, I argue that despite being properly documented and verified, these written documents or broadcasts are unreliable and, at times, quite misleading.

For instance, in the archive of the radio station Voice of the Mountain (VOM, active 1984–90), the Druze PSP Radio, one can come across a repeated reference to the then President of the Republic Amin Gemayel as the Shah or Salazar of Ba'abda. Ba'abda is a reference to the site of the Lebanese Presidential Palace, while the two titles are a derogatory set of terms to indicate the despotic nature of the PSP's political Maronite opponent – the first refers to the Iranian Shah who was deposed during the Islamic Revolution in 1979, and the second to Antonio Salazar, the autocratic Portuguese Prime Minister who held office for thirty-six years. The Salazar incident, as I will call it, indicates how archives are constantly manipulated and should not necessarily be given primacy over oral sources.

During one of the radio station's daily broadcasts, the newscaster interrupted the usual program to read out a letter that the station had received from the family of the deceased Portuguese dictator Antonio Salazar. In this letter, the Salazar family demanded that the radio station immediately cease using their father's and their name to refer to Gemayel. The letter said that Gemayel could not be compared to a man as great as Salazar. A historian who comes across this segment in the course of research must track down the actual letter in the station's archive. Upon investigation, a historian would be able to see that this letter was indeed mailed to the station and had all the necessary credentials of a 'real' document; however, utilising oral history methods to verify or explain this specific event leads to a different conclusion.

Upon interviewing Ghazi al-Aridi, the former head of the VOM, I was presented with a different version of the Salazar incident. Ghazi al-Aridi recounted that they were fully aware that Gemayel would feel offended by these remarks, which the station constantly used in its news segments and commentaries. Therefore, he and a few of his colleagues decided to play a practical joke on the air. After drafting the content of the above-mentioned letter, Aridi instructed one of his staff members to mail it to the radio station. A few days later, Aridi's secretary brought him this letter, to which he responded in a serious manner, requesting that it be aired *verbatim* immediately.[37] While Aridi may have regarded this incident as practical joke, a historian writing many years later and with access to either the textual or the audio evidence, but not both, might perceive this incident differently, resulting in unforeseeable consequences. This exemplifies that oral history should not be viewed as ancillary and merely complementary to already existing textual evidence, but as an autonomous tool that can be utilised to study and document past events in the historian's attempt to reach a kind of truth – or, in the case of the Lebanese Civil War, truths.

The study of civil wars has been a challenging and elusive task for scholars. In the case of Lebanon, historians have approached the civil war as fueled primarily by economic, regional, or sectarian impulses. Even Marxist accounts, which have used class as a unit of analysis, have not ventured beyond the group, nor have they looked at individuals beyond their class affiliation. Moreover, the different theoretical approaches notwithstanding, scholars have over and over relied on the same sources, never venturing outside the realm of textuality. These textual primary sources, however, are problematic, for two main reasons: First, proper state archives or similar entities are virtually non-existent, and the collections that the state claims to possess are housed in an abandoned warehouse where they remain un-catalogued, with the as of yet unfulfilled promise that they will be digitised and made available to the public. Moreover, most of what remains of this archive has miraculously survived fifteen years of bombings and looting, which has left us with a fragmented, if not unusable archive. Most of the political parties' archives have experienced a similar fate, and what is left of them has over the years been amassed by universities and research centres, or in some cases private collectors.

The second reason has to do with the most accessible archives, which consist of the newspapers and periodicals published by the Lebanese and non-Lebanese (Palestinian, Syrian) factions. *Al-Anbaa'* (PSP), *Al-Masiraa'* (LF) and *Al-'Amal* (Phalangist) are some of the periodicals I have used in my work on the Druze and the Maronites. Yet, these periodicals, like most primary sources dealing with the Lebanese Civil War, are problematic because they are partisan in nature and address local and sometime internal matters that are usually difficult to infer from the text. An example of this would be *Al-'Amal* and *Al-Masiraa'*, both published by the Maronite factions. The former was the official mouthpiece of the Phalangist Party, while the latter served as mouthpiece for their militia, the Lebanese Forces (LF).[38] These two factions were bitter rivals, especially after the death of Bashir Gemayel in 1982, and the majority of the contents published revolved around this feud. This fact could not be deduced from a traditional examination of both publications, but through my oral history informants, as many of them pointed out or elaborated on the background or the motive of a certain document or article I encountered in the archives. Many of the articles in either publication did not carry the author's name, and when they did, it was usually a pen name. It is also difficult to locate these publications, because most of them ceased operations after the end of the war. The many books, pamphlets and visual material published by the above-mentioned parties or by individuals espousing a certain political ideology were not released by an official publishing house; thus, obtaining them can prove a difficult task at times. This was the case with Andary's book, which only became readily available after the Syrian army withdrew from Lebanon in 2005.

Throughout the research for and writing of this book, I have conducted many interviews, for either brief or extended periods of time. Each of the interviewees shared with me, to varying degrees, their personal experiences and their involvement in the events in question. Furthermore, some of the oral history sources I use here are not my own, but the product of various projects conducting over many years. Some of these projects were partisan in nature and toed the line with a certain collective memory of either the Maronite LF or the Druze PSP.

Bashir: The Series

Shortly after the assassination of Bashir Gemayel in 1982, his wife Solange and a few of his close associates founded the Bashir Gemayel Foundation (BGF) with the aims of preserving his legacy and documenting his brief but meteoric career. The BGF went on to produce a series of publications and organise various activities around the time of the annual commemoration of Bashir's assassination.

In 2012, the BGF collaborated with Mercury Media, a Lebanese online media platform, to produce a five-part series about the life and political career of Bashir Gemayel.[39] In addition to the conventional sources that the filmmakers consulted – such as books, newspaper articles and Bashir's speeches – the production team interviewed and filmed thirty-nine individuals who had intimate knowledge of Bashir as a man and as a militant politician.[40] The scope of these interviews included his immediate family members, such as his brother and sisters, his personal assistant, his party comrades, and members of his militia with whom he had worked closely until his assassination. Given that this film series had been commissioned by the BGF, the interviews were edited and inserted throughout the cinematic series to sanctify Bashir and his actions.

Nevertheless, in their entirety these interviews exceed the series' aim to reveal more about the era and shed light on the events that led to the War of the Mountain and the subsequent period. The majority of these interviews were conducted with members of Bashir's inner circle, who since 1980 had worked closely with him in his bid to be elected president.[41] This circle met almost daily, and their discussions were transcribed by the group's secretary, Antoine Najm, whom I later interviewed.[42] My interviews also included other group members not featured in the documentary. While these interviews were conducted almost twenty-nine years after the fact, the interviewees provided a fairly consistent and lucid narrative that corresponds to much of the textual sources I used throughout my research. However, this highlights the limitations of these interviews, in addition to the fact that they were conducted with an obvious aim in mind. A cross-examination of the full transcripts and the segments that the producers used for the final released series clearly reveals how the BGF wanted to adhere to the Maronite collective identity that Bashir Gemayel had moulded and upheld through his rhetoric and actions. Their bias notwithstanding, these interviews still retain their historical relevance and are extremely useful, especially when juxtaposed to similar literature from the Druze side.

The Progressive Socialist Party's Oral History Project

Another important source I employed in the course of my research is the Progressive Socialist Party's Oral History Project, a collection of interviews conducted by the PSP with its senior leadership, military commanders, soldiers, Druze clerics, allies from other parties, civil society activists, families of fallen soldiers and the public at large.[43] The collection contains hundreds of hours of audio interviews conducted between 1983 and 1984, which were transcribed between 2000 and 2005.[44] As a whole, the collection is meticulously transcribed and properly indexed, as the header of each page features the interview number, the number of the tape from which it was transcribed and the date of the transcription. Each interview opens with a small introduction by the interviewer, during which they brief the subject about the purpose of this project and request that the interviewee talk about their upbringing, education, siblings, spouse and professional career. The interviewer then asks the subject to speak about their political or military involvement in the recent events, as well as their personal encounters with the enemy – in this case, the Israelis and the LF. It is noticeable that, with high-ranking or senior individuals, the interviewer does not feature prominently, as the interviewee is left to direct the interview as they wish, a luxury not afforded to junior or less educated interviewees. Overall, the interviews provide an overall picture of the Druze psyche, or at least that of the Joumblatti faction, concerning the War of the Mountain. Nevertheless, like all oral history interviews, they are not without their limitations and challenges.

One of these limitations is technical in nature. Given that these interviews were transcribed sixteen years after they had been conducted, they have been vulnerable to some of the glitches that usually accompany the transcription process. The transcribers were not aware of some of the information and thus were unable to add marginal comments about the events discussed; in some cases, they simply misunderstood references to names and places.[45] Hence, reading these interviews requires extensive knowledge of the events discussed for the reader to understand some of the informants' references, such as geographical locations and the casual or careless mention of localised events.

This project, commissioned by Walid Joumblatt directly after the War of the Mountain in 1984, seemingly sought to document the period before the Israeli invasion in 1982 and the subsequent events, culminating in a series of bloody clashes between the Druze and the Maronites. The reasons for undertaking this documentation are several, and they vary according to many of the people I interviewed. The popular explanation behind this project has stressed the military nature of these interviews: They could serve to teach the PSP militia about the errors they had committed and thus help them to avoid any future debacle, especially given that the war was still far from over, despite the recent Druze victory. This claim may be substantiated by the fact that many of the interviews provide a detailed description of the battles and the preparations for the ultimate showdown with the Maronite militia. Additionally, the range of these interviews included all rank and file of the Druze militia – from the top military commanders, over the less senior members, to the platoon and squadron leaders.[46] Yet, the apparent reason for this oral history project goes beyond this somewhat simplistic, utilitarian military aim, since it features as part of a bigger project that Walid Joumblatt seemed to have envisioned at that stage of his political career.

These interviews are, in fact, part of a more comprehensive project that Joumblatt hoped to achieve – that is, to rewrite or purify Lebanon's history from the fallacies that the Maronite political establishment and its historians have propagated over the years, virtually erasing the Druze's role in the establishment of modern Lebanon. Coincidentally, these interviews are extremely charged with the Druze's own understanding of their regions' history dating back to the eleventh century and even earlier. The depth or sophistication of these historical claims and analogies usually depend on the informants' age, educational background and proximity to the decision-making process within the Druze community. Overall, nearly all the interviewees adhere to a strict interpretation of the Druze past and at times also their future. Ultimately, these interviews were intended to act as a repository for future Druze and non-Druze scholars to consult when documenting the War of the Mountain and other events, with the goal to rewrite a 'genuine' history of Lebanon, which naturally should be more compatible with Joumblatt's own view of Lebanese history.

The Council for Druze Studies and Development

The fact that Joumblatt revived an already existing think-tank almost concurrently with the PSP's Oral History Project and thus established another entity to pursue this endeavour adds to the validity of the above-mentioned claim. The Council for Druze Studies and Development (CDSD), established in 1977, brought together a number of predominantly Druze scholars – such as Sami Makarem, Abbas Abu Salah and Abbas al-Halabi – whose writings would provide a counter-narrative to the Maronite accounts of Lebanese history. Both before and after the War of the Mountain, many of their projects and publications centred on promoting Druze history and heritage while serving a larger Druze project.

At a congress held in Beirut in 1980 for representatives of the Druze diaspora, Sami Makarem, Professor of Arabic Literature, Islamic Thought and Sufism at the American University of Beirut (AUB), in his capacity as chairperson set out the main aims of the CDSD:

- Collect, publish and translate Druze works.
- Produce films and documentaries about the Druze that particularly target the Druze diaspora.
- Establishment of a Druze university, which would prepare professionals capable of teaching the Druze about their faith and history.
- Founding a permanent exhibit for Druze arts and crafts.

- Creating a Druze library that would hold all works published about the Druze
- Setting up youth clubs in the diaspora for young people to meet, and prohibiting marriage outside the sect.[47]

In due course, most of these aims of the CDSD were addressed, albeit to varying degrees of success. The council was able to produce a series of studies and publications whose goal was to re-examine the history of Lebanon as written by the Maronites, which willfully erased the role played by the Druze and portrayed the Lebanese past as an exclusively Maronite affair.

One such publication was the joint work of AUB professors Abbas Abu Salah and Sami Makarem, entitled *Tārīkh al-Muwaḥḥidīn al-Durūz al-Siyāsī fī al-Mashriq al-ʿArabī* (Political History of the Unitarian Druze in the Arab East).[48] The book's cover depicts a Druze warrior on horseback brandishing a sword and surrounded by the five colours of the Druze; according to its publisher (CDSD), the work intends to cover 'the political history of the Druze in a scientific manner using primary sources, more specifically Druze manuscripts, which historians have yet to make use of'.[49] The introduction goes on to elaborate the purpose of this work and its ultimate aim – that is, to 'remind the Druze of their true heritage, which has been distorted by some historians, either out of malice or simple negligence, so the Druze can be aware of their national duty and to renounce any side loyalties which could harm the state's national structure'.[50]

The Permanent Bureau for Druze Associations

The second entity established to support Joumblatt's vision consisted of the Permanent Bureau for Druze Associations (PBDA). Founded at the end of 1982,[51] the PBDA was a parallel organisation that served a more immediate goal than the CDSD. The PBDA had no far-reaching aims, nor did it hope to rewrite the history of the Druze. Its newsletter, which appeared almost daily between January 1983 and December 1986, reveals that its main aim was to counter the propaganda generated by the right-wing Maronite media. The PSP never acknowledged the PBDA as an entity organically linked either to itself or to Joumblatt; rather, it was presented as an independent initiative by several leading Druze public figures and non-governmental organisations.

Al-Anbaa', the PSP's official mouthpiece, went so far as to affirm the PBDA's autonomy with an article praising what it called 'the Phenomena of the PBDA', claiming that it was a populist movement countering Maronite false claims about the ongoing war in the mountains.[52]

While the PBDA unequivocally restricted its membership to non-party affiliates,[53] all participants in this entity, in one way or another, adhered to the PSP/Joumblatti view of the ongoing conflict. Rajeh Naim, the editor of the PBDA newsletter, had never been a card-carrying member of the PSP; however, he previously had served as head of the media office for the Lebanese National Movement (LNM), which after Kamal Joumblatt's assassination elected his son Walid as its chairman.[54] The publication that Naim issued was clearly skewed towards the PSP and the Joumblatt clan, as it explicitly criticised and discredited any faction or person trying to defend the Maronite/LF's point of view. Raja Naim recalled the establishment of the PBDA as a spontaneous response to the imminent danger that the Druze faced after the Israeli invasion and the LF's entry into southern Mount Lebanon. He also emphasised that 'much of the actions of the PBDA was of a defensive rather than offensive nature and an attempt to correct the deliberate misinformation of the Christian media outlets against the Druze'.[55]

While this publication did not produce much original content, except for an occasional column by its editor, most of it took the form of press clippings from local, regional and international publications; the selection of these clippings in itself was a statement. They can be broadly placed into four main categories. The first category comprised articles that condemn the LF and the Maronites, usually by quoting from articles in Maronite publications supportive of their goal to spread fear among the Druze. The second category consisted of articles highlighting the activities of Druze notables unfavoured by the mainstream Druze consensus, which the PSP and its subsidiaries represented. The articles of this second category were cleverly laid out adjacent to the first category, to suggest to the reader that these two groups were secretly conspiring, thus discrediting them in the eyes of the Druze public. The third category of articles mainly focused on defending acts of violence committed by the Druze, which were explained as a legitimate use of force triggered solely by the aggression of the LF militias invading their lands.[56] The fourth category included articles and communiqués that reported on the activities of the PBDA, such as visits to the president of the republic or his prime minister and other branches of government, as well as the occasional press conference, all geared towards bolstering public opinion for the Druze cause. The newsletter had '250 daily subscribers as well as a wide circulation which targeted the Druze diaspora reaching as far as Africa, Europe, Brazil and the United States to such entities as the American Druze Society, as well as others'.[57] I will refrain here from elaborating further on these various publications and oral history projects and the role they played in the course of the conflict, as these will receive more extensive treatment in the following chapter on Druze and Maronite collective perceptions of themselves and each other.

Despite all the complications that accompany institutionally commissioned projects – such as *Bashir: The Series*, the PSP's Oral History Project, and the CDSD's and the PBDA's activities – which might void its objectivity, it is exactly this trait that renders them useful, at least for the purposes of this study. For example, the framework of remembrance that Walid Joumblatt wished to create for the Druze can be reconstructed by using these interviews and publications and by further elaborating on the collective memory formation of this group and potentially also of their Maronite opponents.

Several attempts at writing the history of the civil war and its post-war implications have fallen victim to the obsession with historical truth, as propagated by the warring factions. It is precisely for this reason that oral history can salvage and revive scholarship on the civil war, which began to fade away as early as in the second half of the 1990s. In this respect, oral history can serve two purposes: First, it can shed more light on earlier episodes already analysed based on traditional textual sources. Second, and most importantly, oral history can be used as to heal old wounds.

It is within these parameters that oral history projects about the Lebanese Civil War and particularly my own project about the War of the Mountain can investigate these memories of past conflicts, not with the intention of proving who stood on the right side of history, but of fostering an atmosphere of dialogue. The informants of these projects can publicly endorse this dialogue, by breaking the silence that has dominated post-war Lebanon. The various stories and publications of the warring factions were often framed to explain and justify their positions, or to merely justify some of their actions; therefore, the writing of a new narrative grounded on oral sources may be called a corrective process. Perhaps, by trying to write a narrative of the War of the Mountain, Lebanese attics may one day be properly swept, to use Salibi's words, paving the way for a country that embraces its past as well as its present.[58]

Notes

1. Lee Klein Kerwin, 'On the Emergence of Memory in Historical Discourse', *Representations* 69 (2000 = Special Issue: Grounds for Remembering), 127.
2. Halbwachs, as quoted in *The Role of Memory in Ethnic Conflict*, ed. Ed Cairns and Micheál Roe (New York: Palgrave Macmillan, 2003), 11.
3. Ibid., 38.
4. Ibid., 12.
5. Bartlett, as quoted in James V. Wertsch, 'Collective Memory', in *Memory in Mind and Culture*, ed. Pascal Boyer and James Wertsch (Cambridge: Cambridge University Press, 2009), 118–19.
6. Schwartz, as quoted in Patrick Devine Wright, 'A Theoretical Overview of Memory and Conflict', in *The Role of Memory in Ethnic Conflict*, ed. Cairns and Roe, 12.
7. Frederick Beiser. *The German Historicist Tradition* (Oxford: Oxford University Press, 2011), 253.
8. Georg Iggers, 'The Role of Professional Historical Scholarship in the Creation and Distortion of Memory', in *Historical Perspectives on Memory*, ed. Anne Ollila (Helsinki: Hakapaino Oy, 1999), 55.
9. Nora, as quoted in James V. Wertsch, 'Collective Memory', in *Memory in Mind and Culture*, ed. Boyer and Wertsch, 125.
10. Peter Novick, *The Holocaust in American Life* (Boston: Houghton Mifflin, 1999), 3–4; Peter Novick, *That Noble Dream: The 'Objectivity Question' and the American Historical Profession.* (Cambridge: Cambridge University Press, 2007).
11. Novick, as quoted in James V. Wertsch, 'Collective Memory', 126.
12. Graig Blatz and Michael Ross, 'Historical Memories', in *Memory in Mind and Culture*, ed. Pascal Boyer and James V. Wertsch (New York: Cambridge University Press, 2009), 230.
13. Some authors, such as Frentress and Wickham, have opted to use the term social memory rather than collective memory, despite their acknowledgment that at times this usage might apply to Halbwachs' collective memory as such. James Fentress and Chris Wickham, *Social Memory* (Oxford: Blackwell, 1992).

14. Amos Funkenstein, 'Collective Memory and Historical Consciousness,' *History & Memory* 1, no. 1 (1989), 6.
15. Bernard Lewis and Buntzie Ellis Churchill, *Notes on a Century: Reflections of a Middle East Historian* (New York: Viking, 2012), 136.
16. Paul Ricoeur, *History and Truth*, trans. and intr. by Charles A. Kelbley (Evanston: Northwestern University Press, 1965), 23–4.
17. Alessandro Portelli, 'On the Peculiarities of Oral History', *History Workshop* 12 (1981): 99.
18. Lucia Volk, *Memorials and Martyrs in Modern Lebanon* (Bloomington: Indiana University Press, 2010); Sune Haugbolle, *War and Memory in Lebanon* (New York: Cambridge University Press, 2010).
19. Portelli, 'On the Peculiarities of Oral History', 100.
20. Elizabeth Tonkin, *Narrating Our Pasts: The Social Construction of Oral History* (Cambridge: Cambridge University Press, 1992).
21. Ibid., 38.
22. Ibid., 66.
23. Interview with Paul Andary, Adma, Lebanon, January 2010.
24. Paul Andary, *Al-Jabal: Ḥaqīqah lā Tarḥam* [The Mountain: A Ruthless Reality] ([n. p.], 1983), 59.
25. The original Arabic title of the book was *Al-Jabal: Ḥaqīqah lā Tarḥam* (The Mountain: A Ruthless Reality). Paul Andary and Rani Geha, *War of the Mountain: Israelis, Christians and Druze in the 1983 Mount Lebanon Conflict Through the Eyes of a Lebanese Forces Fighter* (CreateSpace Independent Publishing Platform, 2012).
26. Thompson, *The Voice of the Past*, 129
27. Alice Hoffman and Howard S. Hoffman, *Archives of Memory: A Soldier Recalls World War II* (Lexington: University Press of Kentucky, 1990).
28. Alice M. Hoffman and Howard S. Hoffman, 'Memory Theory: Personal and Social', in *Thinking About Oral History: Theories and Applications*, ed. Thomas L. Charlton, Lois E. Myers and Rebecca Sharpless (Lanham: Altamira Press, 2008), 39.
29. David Schacter. *The Seven Sins of Memory* (Boston: Houghton Mifflin, 2001).
30. Ibid., 4.
31. Peter Leese, *Shell Shock: Traumatic Neurosis and the British Soldiers of the First World War* (New York: Palgrave, 2002).
32. Theodore Kiersch, 'Amnesia: A Clinical Study of Ninety-Eight Cases', *The American Journal of Psychiatry* 119, no. 1 (1962): 57–60.

33. Interview with Ghanem Tarabay, Qoubbei', Lebanon, 23 June 2013.
34. Ibid.
35. Portelli, *The Battle of Valle Giulia*, viii.
36. Barbara Allen and William Lynwood Montell, *From Memory to History: Using Oral Sources in Local Historical Research* (Nashville: American Association for State and Local History, 1981), 15.
37. Interview with Ghazi al-Aridi, Beirut, Lebanon, 8 July 2016.
38. I interviewed the editors-in-chief of both publications, Joseph Abu Khalil (*Al-'Amal*) and Elie Khayat (*Al-Masiraa*).
39. *Bashir: The Series* was released on 4 September 2016, the date of Bashir's assassination.
40. Eli Khoury, CEO of the Quantum Group, the owner of Mercury Media, gave me unrestricted access to this collection.
41. This group will be discussed in detail in the subsequent chapters.
42. These minutes still survive with some of the members of this group; I had the chance to view some of their contents.
43. This collection is closed to the public. It is housed in *Dar al-Takadoumi*, the PSP's official publishing house and archive, in Moukhtara, the Joumblatt's ancestral village.
44. These interviews are available in audio format on cassette tapes and have been fully transcribed by hand, by the staff of Dar al-Takadoumi, as indicated in the index sheet of the collection. There remain almost fourteen audio cassettes that have not been transcribed, mostly containing interviews with fighters from the Maten region (south of Mount Lebanon). These interviews were made available to me after I requested permission from Walid Joumblatt.
45. The staff at *Dar al-Takadoumi* confirmed this claim, as all their staff who transcribed these interviews were too young to remember or participate in the War of the Mountain. Furthermore, these transcribers were given strict instructions to write down these interviews *verbatim*, without any comments or additions.
46. Platoons usually consist of two squads, with one squad composed of eight to twelve soldiers.
47. http://tayhid.ba7r.org/t64p25-topic, accessed 12 May 2016.
48. Abbas Abu Salah, *Tārīkh al-Muwaḥḥidīn al-Durūz al-Siyāsī fī al-Mashriq al-ʿArabī*)Beirut: Manshūrāt al-Majlis al-Durzī lil-Buḥūth wa-al-Inmā', 1980).
49. Ibid.
50. Ibid., 10.

51. There exists no official date for the launch of this bureau; however, its newsletter appeared in January 1983, which implies that it had to be created by the end of the preceding year.
52. *Al-Anbaa'*, 31 January 1983.
53. Halim Takiedinne (senior Druze religious judge), Nadia Noueihad (writer), Sami Abdul Baki (Professor of Engineering at AUB), Afif Khodar (contractor), Abbas al-Halabi (banker), Issam Naiman (journalist), Siham Saab Khodar, Shawki Ghraizi (physician), Marwan Hamada (journalist) and Rajeh Naim (journalist).
54. Bernard Reich, *Political Leaders of the Contemporary Middle East and North Africa: A Biographical Dictionary* (New York: Greenwood Press, 1990), 291.
55. Interview with Rajeh Naim, Beirut, Lebanon, 24 May 2016.
56. PBDF Newsletter, 31 January 1983.
57. Interview with Rajeh Naim, Beirut, Lebanon, 24 May 2016.
58. Salibi, *House of Many Mansions*, 234.

2

THE DRUZE AND THE MARONITES: PERCEPTIONS OF THE OTHER

To be able to relate to both Druze and Maronite collective identity, it is necessary to properly understand the rich and controversial past on which both communities draw to construct a historical narrative that frames their understanding of themselves and the 'other'. This chapter will trace the historical evolution of both the Druze and Maronites while paying close attention to those events that directly contributed to forming a sense of collective identity across both space and time. Druze–Maronite enmity was not an abrupt development and may not be explained as simply sectarian in origin, nor can it be attributed to the advent of imperialism, or the failure of the *Tanzimat* to modernise the Ottoman Empire and enable it to resist the meddling of the great European powers in its affairs.[1] While enmity certainly played a role in the eruption of violence and hostility, the situation is far more complex, and its origins can be traced back to the seventeenth century. Prior to the establishment of Greater Lebanon in 1920, the Druze and the Maronites constituted the majority of the inhabitants of Mount Lebanon. According to Kamal Salibi, the history of Lebanon until then 'essentially involves a Maronite-Druze story in which other Lebanese communities played only marginal roles, if any'.[2] The fact that the Druze and the Maronites perceived themselves as the creators or proprietors of Lebanon made them embark on a historic feud, with each side trying to prove that Lebanon was exclusively their own creation, thus subordinating the other side. Therefore, this conflict is perhaps better understood, as Salibi has framed it, as 'a conflict between two tribes flying distinct historical flags with no common vision of their past'.[3]

These two distinct historical banners can be summarised as two broad perceptions: The Druze have perceived themselves as descendants of a proud warrior clan, brought to this land from Arabia to fend off the attacks of the Byzantines and their associates, and later the Crusaders. While the Maronites believe that they are native to this land and trace their ancestry back to the early Semitic peoples, more often than not they underscore this fact to merely distinguish themselves from the Muslim Arabs who invaded Syria in the seventh century AD. As a matter of fact, the Maronites make irreconcilable claims about their descent and the nature of their nation. Thus, they claim to be a melting pot of different ancient civilisations (the Arameans, Akkadians and Canaanites) who inhabited the Lebanese coast and mountains and transformed it into a refuge from oppressive Muslim invaders. They also claim that the Maronites were none other than the *Jarajimah* who protected this refuge and valiantly defended Christianity against the invading Muslim hordes. However, after their defeat in the seventh century, the Maronites out of necessity forged an alliance with the Druze, who in turn wanted to maintain a certain autonomy from the Sunni Caliphate.

The Druze: Frontier Warriors and Feudal Lords

The Druze – or, as they prefer to call themselves, *Ahl al-Tawḥīd* (People of Unitarianism) or *al-Muwaḥḥidūn* (Unitarians) – are a heterodox offshoot of Ismaʿili Islam, who trace their faith to the movement of the Fatimid Caliph al-Hakim (996–1021) and his minister Hamza bin ʿAli.[4] The Druze trace their descent to the confederation of Islamic-Arab tribes of the Taym, Lakhim, Tay, Tamim, Jandal and Taglib, who were brought to the *Bilād al-Shām* (the Syrian coast) by the Abbasid Caliph Abu Jaʿafar al-Mansur from different part of the Arabian peninsula to fend off the attacks of the Byzantines and their associates, known as the Mardaites or the *Jarajimah*. With the beginning of the Crusades in the eleventh century, these tribes gained prominence, as they became the first line of defence against the invaders.[5] The Druze-born

Shakib Arslan, a man with a well-founded claim to scholarship and highly regarded by both the Druze and Sunnis, claims direct descent from these early frontier warriors hailing from the Lakhmid tribes of southern Iraq. According to him, 1,500 Lakhmid cavalrymen joined the armies of Khalid Ibn al-Walid in the seventh century to conquer Syria under the banner of Islam.[6] During the reign of al-Mansur in the eighth century, the threat posed by the Byzantines and their agents, the Mardaites, who had fortified themselves in the mountainous regions and disrupted the spread of Islam, needed to be addressed.[7] Hence, al-Mansur devised a strategy to populate the vacant area adjacent to the Mardaite region so as to contain and defeat their forces. For this purpose, the caliph summoned two of the Lakhmid emirs (princes), Munzar and Arslan, 'who exhibited fervor towards this plan, and thus the caliph commanded them to settle in the depopulated mountain of Beirut and he bestowed upon them land and the required documents and urged them to depart'.[8] While a number of other sources corroborate parts of this narrative, the areas where the ancestors of the Druze settled were not entirely vacant, as the Umayyad caliphate had dispatched tribes from the Syrian hinterland to the coast.[9] The first wave of Lakhmids were later joined by other tribes from different regions of the Islamic caliphate, possibly to join in the defence of the frontier against the continuous Byzantine attacks on the Syrian coastal lands.[10]

Kamal Joumblatt, the Druze chieftain and founder of the PSP, makes this abundantly clear in many of his writings. In a book published posthumously, Joumblatt has boasted of the Druze claim that they regard themselves as the rightful lords and true defenders of Lebanon:

> The German [Karl] Baedeker claims that our house [in Moukhtara] was built on the site of an old Crusader castle. The Joumblatt family once possessed all the lands of Aley up to the Shuf. The great Druze families owned all the big estates from the Kisrwan frontier [in the north] to the Jezzine [in the south] and beyond, from the sea to the Syrian frontier and, at one time, even to the outskirts of Damascus.[11]

The peripheral location and military nature of their charge gave these tribes a *quasi*-autonomous status, which depended on the success of the task assigned to them and their relationship with the central authority. It is perhaps this fact, as well as the decline of the Abbasid state following the death of the tenth caliph, al-Mutawakkil, that led to some of these tribes adopting the heterodox Islamic movements prevalent at the time – such as the Isma'ili, Qarmatian, Alawite and Hashashin sects. By the ninth century, Shi'ism in its different variants came to dominate most of Syria, including the areas that the ancestors of the Druze now proclaimed home.[12] Among these religious currents were the *Qaramita*, an offshoot of the Isma'ili doctrine, which according to Kamal Salibi were 'possibly an unsophisticated rural offshoot of the [Isma'ili] movement with a largely Bedouin and *'ashā'air* (tribal) following'.[13] As a movement, the Qarmatians started in Kufa (Iraq) and later spread to different parts of the region, including Greater Syria. The Qarmatians essentially adopted a brand of revolutionary socialism, refusing to acknowledge the imamate of the Fatimid caliphs and challenging their authority throughout the Muslim realm. In 971 AD, following a series of defeats, the Fatimid army commanded by the famous general Jawhar al-Siqilli faced off against Qarmatian forces in Ramla, defeating the latter.[14] This led to the eventual retreat of the Qarmatians and their downfall on the Syrian political scene. As a result, the Qarmatian tribes were soon incorporated into a similar radical movement that emerged within the Fatimid religious establishment.

After defeating the Ikhshidids in 969 AD, the Fatimid caliphate, originally founded in North Africa, moved its seat of power to Egypt.[15] The Fatimids, who subscribed to the Isma'ili faith, considered the caliph or the Imam to be infallible and only guided by the will of God, much like other, similar heterodox Muslim Imamate groups. However, it was during the reign of the sixth Fatimid caliph, al-Hakim bi-Amr-Allah, that the status of the Imam was elevated to an unprecedented level.[16] It was around the figure of the eccentric and vacillating al-Hakim that a movement of Persian and Turcoman immigrants declared al-Hakim's divinity. Hamza bin 'Ali, a central figure in this new movement, declared al-Hakim to be 'no mere imam like his predecessors, but the living manifestation of the unity of the Godhead, ultimate and transcendental'.[17] The party of al-Hakim, a religious as well as political movement, did not strike roots in Egypt and soon petered out with the disappearance and possible murder of al-Hakim. However, it was among the Qarmatian tribes in Syria, who were already receptive to similar preachings, that this cult was to gain new followers. By embracing the teachings of

Hamza and his missionaries, the Druze as a religious community were born; as they themselves believe, they have remained unchanged ever since. This static nature of the sect was further enhanced by the fact that in 1043 AD the Druze (*tawhid*) *daʿwa* (calling) was finally sealed off to outsiders. From that point onwards, the Druze became 'a self-contained society: no missionary activity, no proselytism, no public performance of rituals, no places for open collective worship, and no marriage outside the community'.[18]

These neophyte Druze tribes experienced their first real challenge with the arrival of the First Crusade in 1098 AD. Under the leadership of the Buhturid clan, the tribes settled in the Gharb region overlooking the coast and in one way or another resisted the Crusader armies. Initially, these tribes refrained from confronting the superior Frankish forces and instead let them pass unscathed on their quest to capture Jerusalem.[19] The fall of Beirut in 1110 AD led to the defeat of the Buhturids, who had to fully retreat to the Gharb region on the coast. However, this retreat did not spare them the wrath of the Crusaders who invaded the Druze areas in an attempt to prevent any future threats to the coast which they now controlled. However, the Druze have deliberately chosen not to acknowledge several episodes in their history involving the Crusaders, at least in the modern era. As the Crusaders controlled the coast, their relationship with their enemies involved not only resistance, but also collaboration. While the Druze, at least in recent times, have emphasised their resistance towards the foreign invaders and the valiant role they played throughout that period, they completely deny that they had cordial relations with the Franks, or possibly collaborated with them. An examination of one of the few surviving works of Druze history of the time, Salih ibn Yahya's *Tārīkh Bayrūt* clearly implicates the Buhturids as collaborators with the Crusaders.[20] A prominent fifteenth-century Buhturid emir, Salih ibn Yahya alluded to the role that his family played in appeasing as well as confronting the Crusaders who were occupying the Lebanese coast. It is perhaps interesting to note that this Buhturid emir saw no shame in this act, as he mentioned these episodes without providing any comment or justification. Kamal Salibi, one of the editors of *Tārīkh Bayrūt*, has remarked:

> The lords of Beirut and Sidon were always willing to pay well for Buhturid's good will, and the Buhturids often found it necessary as well as profitable

to come to terms with them, although their raison d'être was to fight the Franks and to block their advance in the region. At the same time, the Buhturids were anxious to show their masters in Damascus that they were performing their duties with pious zeal, lest subsidy and support be withdrawn and punishment follow.[21]

However, these maneuvers, as Salibi calls them, never reached an extent that would have justified officially regarding the Druze as standing in the Crusaders' service. This on-the-fence tactic was also adopted by the Buhturids under the Mamluks and has since then become a hallmark of Druze political behaviour. When it became obvious to the Buhturid emirs that a clash between the Mongols and the Mamluks was imminent, during the Battle of 'Ayn Jalut the family decided to divide its ranks in a remarkable feat of *realpolitik*. Salih ibn Yahya, a crack-archer who fought with the Mamluk army of Sultan Qutuz, unashamedly reported the decision of his family who:

> held counsel together and agreed that [the latter] would leave and join the Egyptian army while [the former] would stay with the Mongols in Damascus ... and the man on the side of the victors [a third prince who stayed with the Franks] would intercede for his comrade and for the country.[22]

This Buhturid gamble paid off after the Mamluk victory: Overall, the family continued to enjoy the sultans' favour. During the later Mamluk era, the Buhturids were officially inducted into the Mamluks army as officers within the *halqa* corps (cavalry). One of them even attained the prestigious rank of Emir of Forty: He had to maintain forty horsemen and could have a military band to go along with his men.[23] Part of their duty was to serve with the *darak* (guard) force assigned to protect Beirut and the coast from the Crusader raids and to maintain security and order.[24] While this new arrangement greatly reduced their administrative power, as well as their previous *iqta* (tax farming) concessions, their access to Beirut with its flourishing port and spice trade made some of the emirs exorbitantly rich.[25]

By 1517, the Buhturids' good fortune was about to end. The Ottoman conquest of Syria in 1516 and the defeat of the Mamluks whom the Buhturids had chosen to support left them defeated, with no chance of making a transition into the Ottoman power structure. The downfall of the Buhturids gave rise to another Druze family who under the Ottomans would rule Mount Lebanon for the next two centuries. The Maʿanids, who were related to the Buhturids, rose to prominence during the early Ottoman years and assumed leadership of the local government. While some historians, both Druze and Maronite, have maintained that the Maʿanids were natural heirs to their Buhturid cousins and that their new position was in fact a reward for their support of the Ottoman conquest of Syria, this claim does not hold any water when properly examined. Kamal Salibi has maintained that this alleged succession is a later invention of the Shihabi emirs, who were related to the Maʿanids by marriage, and their circle, who wanted to 'provide the Shihab regime in Lebanon as the successor of the Maʿanid regime, with an Ottoman legitimacy dating back to the time of the conquest'.[26] In fact, a more thorough examination of these allegations leads to the conclusion that the Druze transition from Mamluk to Ottoman rule was certainly not as smooth as previously assumed.

In his various works on Druze and Ottoman Lebanon, Abdul Rahim Abu-Husayn, using the Ottoman archives as well as regional primary sources, has painted a rather different historical picture of the Druze-Ottoman encounter. While the Druze like to maintain their image as a warrior society loyal to the Muslim Ottoman authority, the reality was somewhat different. In 1518, shortly after the Ottomans took over Syria, a number of Druze chiefs joined the rebellion of Nasir al-Din ibn al-Hanash, which amounted to little more than a desperate last attempt at a Mamluk counter-revolution.[27] However, this Druze mutiny, and the others that followed, went beyond the typical struggle among Muslim factions vying for power. The Druze chiefs seemingly did not want to lose out on the profits of the lucrative trade with the Italian merchant-republics of Venice and later Tuscany via the Beirut port.[28] For the next few decades, the Druze used weapons smuggled from the Venetian base in Cyprus to challenge the Ottoman authorities and seize every opportunity to rise in mutiny.[29] As Salibi has pointed out, it is no coincidence that the Arabic name for musket (*bunduqiyya*) corresponds to the Arabic name for the city of Venice.[30] By getting their hands on an abundant supply of weapons superior to those used by the Ottomans, the Druze proved to be a handful.[31]

The Ottomans did not back away from this challenge and dispatched numerous punitive campaigns against the Druze. This period of 'long rebellion', as Abu-Husayn has branded it, led to the destruction of many Druze villages and the death of many of their men. Over time, this would have dire consequences on the community, as it greatly reduced its numbers and its ability to maintain a viable peace-time economy. At the time, contemporary chroniclers such as Ibn Tulun spoke of loads of Druze heads brought to Damascus and paraded in public to underscore the Druze defeat and the great lengths to which the Ottomans were willing to go to suppress any rebellion.[32] Furthermore, the Ottomans used the Druze scriptures (which the Druze hold secretive), captured during their campaigns, to underscore the heresy of their sect. This was meant to justify their excessive use of force and to set a deterrent example for other potential rebels. Despite this tactic, the Ottoman punitive actions against the Druze were never religiously motived, something that the Druze refuse to acknowledge. The Druze have preferred to maintain that the calamities that have befallen them over time (some claim that the Druze were butchered seven times) all occurred due to their faith, rather than as a consequence of their earthly or political choices.[33] Furthermore, many different tales and Lebanese school textbooks relegate this period of rebellion and the violent and unprovoked manner in which the Ottomans reacted as the outcome of false claims and allegations hurled by the Maʿanid opponents.[34] The claim that Ibrahim Pasha's 1585 attack against the Druze was a response to a Maʿanid emir falsely accusing the Druze of robbing a tax convoy has been proven incorrect.[35] Abu-Husayn has maintained that this tax convoy was never robbed, but in fact reached its intended destination in Istanbul, and that the money was deposited in the state treasury, according to Ottoman records.[36] This expedition, like many others before it, was therefore dispatched to punish the Druze for their continued insubordination, and not as a response to a single infraction. The many Ottoman reports on the matter underscore this point: In an order to the *beylerbeyi* (governor) of Damascus and other related letters, no mention is made of the tax convoy incident; instead, it stresses the rebellious nature of the Druze against the Ottomans and issues instructions to neutralise them:

> The person known as Korkmaz ibn Maʿin [Maʿan], of the Druze community (*taife*), is a rebellious chieftain (*mukaddem-i asi*). He has gathered [around him] miscreants from the Druze community and done harm and

mischief (*mefsedet*) in the sancak of Safad in my divinely guarded territory (*memalik-i mahruse*). The people of the area have requested that you march against the aforesaid community where it is gathered. I have commanded, upon the arrival [of this order], that you march against the aforesaid community with extreme circumspection.[37]

Starting in the sixteenth century, the ascent of the Safavids gave rise to the hope that the great glories of the Persian Empire would once again be resurrected.[38] The Safavids' adoption of Twelver Shi'ism pitted them against their Sunni Ottoman rival. However, it would be wrong to assume that this contention was sectarian in nature; rather, religion served both sides as a tool used in a political rivalry that persists to this day. In 1590, during the height of the Safavid-Ottoman conflict, Fakhr al-Din Ma'an, Korkmaz's son, was appointed administrator of the Sanjak of Sidon-Beirut. In the hope of curbing Safavid penetration into this region, the Ottomans sanctioned this young emir's return to power. Using both brains and brawn, Fakhr al-Din would do exactly that, by destroying the Shi'ite Harfush emirs of the Beqa'a region in eastern Lebanon. The Harfush, who traditionally had been in Ottoman service, had switched sides and were trying to expand their area to integrate the predominately Shi'ite Jabal 'Amil region to the south.[39] Fakhr al-Din's success in responding to the Safavid threat once again returned the Druze to their original status as warriors in the service of Islam, albeit momentarily.

Unity in Variety

Much of the Druze rhetoric and self-perception underscores the unity of the community, to such an extent that pluralism within is often suppressed and transformed into one single dimension. However, a closer examination of the Druze as a political community reveals a complex and diverse reality that is very different from what the Druze like to maintain. Throughout their history, the Druze were led by a number of prominent families whose leadership status fluctuated depending on their relationship to the central Islamic authority, as well as to each other.[40] Since settling in the area in the eighth century, these families have divided themselves according to the Qaysi-Yemeni divide which governed the tribes' political structure at the time. This feud, which started in the early years of Islam, divided the Arab tribes into a northern Qaysi faction and a southern Yemeni faction and over time would evolve to include other non-Muslim Arab tribes.[41] This feud survived intact well into the nineteenth century in different parts of the Levant, especially in Syria. According to Jane Hathaway, 'under the Ottomans Lebanon above all was riven by Qaysi-Yemeni rivalry' which led to serious tensions between the antagonists.[42] Naturally, the Druze were the main driving force behind this feud, at least until the seventeenth century. This divide, however, ran across traditional sectarian lines and included Druze and Christians alike. Ultimately, these tensions erupted into a civil war *en miniature* in the famous Battle of 'Ayn Dara in 1711, which ended with the final defeat and downfall of the Yemeni faction headed by the 'Alam al-Dins, who regarded themselves as the rightful successors to Ahmad Ma'an, the last Ma'anid Emir.[43]

While the Qaysi-Yemeni divide was indeed crucial for the events unfolding on Mount Lebanon, another divide of equal or greater importance came to define the political history of the Druze. The Joumblatti-Yazbaki feud was a predominately Druze affair which pitted against each other two factions – one faction led by Sheikh Joumblatt against a second faction led by Sheikh Yazbak bin 'Abd al-Salam, the father-in-law of Fakhr al-Din Ma'an.[44] Many scholars view this feud as a post-1711 development, which essentially replaced the Qaysi-Yemeni division and was rooted and utilised in the ensuing Shihabi succession struggle.[45] Important as this feud was within the Shihabi context, it certainly constituted an earlier phenomenon that had developed already under the reign of Fakhr al-Din, almost a century earlier. Based on a careful examination of the contemporaneous chronicles of Fakhr al-Din, Abu-Husayn has confirmed that 'the division among the Druzes between Junblati [Joumblatti] and Yazbaki factions was already a fact of Druze political life in the Shuf during the times of Fakhr al-Din Ma'an long before the time of the Shihabs, in the mid-eighteenth century, when it is commonly believed to have developed'.[46] Regardless of the birthdate of or reason behind this feud, it is certain fact that the political history of the Druze community has since then been shaped by two factions in a state of constant rivalry, with both groups uniting to defend the community when needed. This union, which at times would suspend Joumblatti-Yazbaki factionalism, was usually a response to any kind of external threat against the Druze – for instance, the 1860 and 1982–3 wars against the Maronites are a case in point.

A Recipe for Disaster

In itself, the valiant warrior image that the Druze have perpetuated for themselves was not sufficient to cause conflict and civil strife with other local communities. Only a challenge constituting an anti-thesis to the Druze self-perception and posing an existential threat (or a threat perceived as such) could do so and cause the whole community to radicalise and mobilise. At least in the Druze's perception, such a threat materialised in the form of the Maronites who, through a series of events, by the eighteenth century had become the real masters of what was formerly the Druze lands *par excellence*.

The Druze image of their Maronite neighbours on Mount Lebanon, as it is imprinted into their collective memory, is that of lowly peasants brought in to perform chores unbefitting of warriors. According to the Druze, the Maronite migration to the southern part of Mount Lebanon began in the seventeenth century, with the encouragement and under the protection of the 'Great Prince Fakhr al-Din Ma'an', to meet certain economic demands, as the Druze, as 'warrior-aristocratic rulers, relied heavily on the Maronites who turned out to be diligent farmers and obedient subjects'.[47] While Christian immigration to Mount Lebanon was indeed sanctioned and encouraged by Fakhr al-Din, this was never due to his largesse; rather, it was a response to economic and political needs. The successive Ottoman punitive campaigns against the rebellious Druze had affected the latter's demographic presence in the southern part of Mount Lebanon, to such an extent that the Druze did not have enough manpower to farm the land and carry out other economic activities.

The earliest clashes between the Druze and the Ottoman forces of the governor of Damascus, Khurram Pasha, in 1523 led to the deaths of hundreds of Druze and 'the burning of 43 Druze villages including the village of Baruk', the seat of the Ma'anids at the time.[48] The subsequent waves of Ottoman military campaigns to punish the Druze and the extended duration and magnitude of these clashes ensured that the Druze incurred heavy and unrecoverable losses. Thus, Fakhr al-Din out of pure necessity encouraged the Christians of the northern parts to settle in his area to provide labour for farming the Druze lands. The tolerance that Fakhr al-Din exhibited towards the new arrivals was twofold in character. First, it was only natural for the Druze to make these outsiders feel at home and thus allow them to build churches, especially if they expected them to be productive labourers. Second, they were confident that the Christians had no real prospect of converting any of the Druze to Christianity, mainly because of their strong tribal structure. Moreover, their status as Christians precluded the possibility that they would ever pose a threat to their Druze masters' rule, as the Ottoman authorities always preferred to appoint a Muslim ruler to administer the land.

Later on, Fakhr al-Din's strong relations with the Italian merchant republics of Venice and Tuscany, as well as his contact with the Papacy, made this policy of tolerance somewhat expedient for him, perhaps even constituting a condition set by his Christian allies. These historical details do not figure prominently in the Druze's modern psyche, as the Druze insist on emphasising the agrarian nature of the Christian immigration. Many of my Druze interviewees made this abundantly clear, and at times they went so far as to use the image of the Christian peasant in slanderous terms. The Druze insist on branding these Maronite migrants as *sanay'ayha* (people who mainly work with their hands, lowly professions that involve manual and unskilled labor), a belittling term at best. One female informant, a graduate of the American University of Beirut and native of the city of Aley, insisted that the Christians have always been peasants and that the Druze the princes and warriors of Mount Lebanon. When I pointed out the fact that the Druze community had also been agrarian and that life in the past required all people to farm their lands, she refused to acknowledge this fact and responded mockingly: 'Shut up, shut up, and go read your history'.[49] Such a clearly condescending tone about the Maronites espoused by fairly educated Druze has shaped the relationship between the two sides, leaving the Maronites feeling somewhat betrayed.

Over the centuries, the Christian subjects, through the Maronite Church, developed relations with different foreign missionaries operating in the Ottoman Empire. Subsequently, these missionaries encouraged the Maronites to rebel against their Druze overlords and to curtail and abolish Druze feudalism. According to the Druze collective psyche, the Maronite Church supported Bashir Shihabi II (known among the Druze as the Red Prince), who turned against his former ally, Sheikh Bashir Joumblatt.[50] The Shihabs were outsiders to Mount Lebanon, as they inhabited the Wadi al-Tayim region and were related to the Ma'anids through the female linage.

After the death of the last Ma'anid emir in 1697, the Druze notables chose the Shihabs to manage their cousins' estates.[51]

This tale of Shihabi succession has been incorporated by most Lebanese scholars and the public at large, both Maronite and Druze, into the master narrative of the country's past, as it empowers both factions. The Druze can thus claim that they as a political faction were capable of appointing a new *multazim* (tax farmer), while the Maronites can also boast that their rule was fully legitimate and achieved through a sort of democratic vote. This peculiar transition from a Druze to a Sunni feudal lord almost alien to the region was a compromise for the Druze chieftains who were divided among themselves over the succession. According to Abu-Husayn, none of the local Druze tribal chiefs wished to concede even nominal precedence to any of the other Druze tribal chiefs, as this would upset the delicate balance of power. A tax concession of this magnitude would certainly do so, as it would bestow on its recipient superior moral standing and possibly considerable wealth. Hence, instead of keeping the position as an exclusively Druze preserve, the Druze notables preferred to give it to the Shihabs who had no local constituency and thus no chance of affecting the power balance, or so they thought.[52]

Emir Bashir vs Sheikh Bashir

Originally Sunni, the Shihabs began to convert to Christianity in the second half of the eighteenth century. It was not long before the different factions of the Shihabs started to compete for power, as they allied themselves with either the Joumblatti or Yazbaki faction to outmaneuver both Maronite and Druze contenders. In 1788, with the help of the Joumblatti party led by the powerful Sheikh Bashir Joumblatt, Bashir II (Shihab) was appointed to rule the Lebanese Emirate, replacing his uncle Emir Youssef Shihab. Following a short period of instability, Bashir II was able to assert himself as a powerful ruler capable of intervening in the internal affairs of the different communities, including the Druze. By the nineteenth century, the Druze had been furthered weakened by several factors, primarily the infighting between the Yazbaki and the Joumblatti. By allying himself with Emir Bashir II Shihab, Bashir Joumblatt was able to crush his Druze opponents; something that would in the long run prove detrimental to the Druze, and perhaps to the Maronites as well.

The rise of the Ottoman ruler of Egypt, Muhammad 'Ali Pasha, in 1831 and his increasing intervention in the affairs of the Levant had dire consequences on Mount Lebanon. Muhammad 'Ali's political and financial backing of Emir Bashir II enabled him to assert himself as the paramount ruler of *Jabal Lubnan*.[53] Emir Bashir II proceeded to put a heavy financial burden on the feudal lords and treated them with utter condescension, particularly his former ally, Bashir Joumblatt. As the popular story goes, Emir Bashir II was receiving a number of Druze notables, among them Sheikh Bashir, in his newly built mansion in Beit al-Din, which must have cost an exorbitant sum. During this reception, he declared: 'Sheikh Bashir, the mountain is not big enough to accommodate two Bashirs'. To this Sheikh Bashir arrogantly replied: 'That might be true, however, whoever feels uncomfortable can leave'.[54] This probably imaginary encounter is an indication of how the Druze have perceived this confrontation: as mere jealousy between the two parties, rather than a calculated grab for power and dominance. In response to the Emir Bashir II's challenge, Bashir Joumblatt appealed to the Yazbaki factions whose numbers and support were insufficient to defeat the powerful emir. The final military confrontation between the two Bashirs in 1825 ended with the defeat of Joumblatt and his Yazbaki allies, who were arrested by the governor of Damascus and handed over to the governor of Acre. Upon the insistence of Emir Bashir II, both Sheikh Bashir Joumblatt and the head of the Yazbaki faction, Sheikh Amin al-Imad, were later executed.

Given that most political feuds ended with bloodshed, this episode may have seemed quite ordinary at the time. Yet, the slaying of Sheikh Bashir was an entirely different matter. Bashir Joumblatt was revered by the Druze as one of their most important political leaders. *Amud al-Sama* (the pillar of heaven), as he was called by his supporters, was known to maintain a pious lifestyle and to abide by the dress code of the Druze clerics.[55] In his important work on the families of Mount Lebanon, Tannus al-Shidyaq has underscored the exalted status of Sheikh Bashir. Shidyaq, a Maronite who worked for the Shihab family, has described Bashir as follows:

> of medium height, soft-bodied, handsome with a dark complexion, dignified, wise, balanced, chivalrous, brave, gallant, generous, forgiving, just, forthcoming, protective, extremely wealthy in money as well as followers,

defender of the land, known as the pillar of heaven. He distributed in one year 650,000 piasters to all the poor in the land. He erected bridges and repaired roads, and during his times temples [churches] became plentiful, and peace and stability prevailed, earning him a reputation throughout the lands.[56]

Sheikh Bashir's personal attributes and his symbolic status transformed his death into a watershed moment in the history of Druze–Maronite relations. Kamal Salibi has described this act by Emir Bashir II as follows:

> A last blow to Druze political dominance in the country; the Druze never forgave him for it. Weakened and leaderless, they henceforth ceased to cooperate wholeheartedly in the affairs of the Emirate and awaited the opportunity for revenge. The Christian Shihab, it is true, had crushed the Druze Janblat [Joumblatt] not because he was Druze, but because he was a powerful political rival. The Druze, however, were to remember the incident differently; and Bashir's subsequent policy was to make them look upon him more and more as a Christian enemy to their community.[57]

The events following the execution of Bashir Joumblatt only reinforced for the Druze the notion that Emir Bashir II was truly seeking to destroy them. The Egyptian conquest of Syria by Ibrahim Pasha, son of Muhammad 'Ali, and the subsequent war with the Ottomans further estranged the Druze who preferred to side against the Egyptians, because of their support of Emir Bashir II. In the fall of 1837, the Druze of Hawran rebelled against the Egyptians' decision to disarm them and to conscript more Druze into their army. The Druze of Hawran were soon joined by their coreligionists from the Shuf and Wadi al-Tayim. Initially successful in their rebellion, the Druze were eventually defeated by the 20,000 troops that Ibrahim Pasha personally commanded. Among these were 4,000 Christian troops commanded by Emir Bashir II's son Khalil.[58] The fact that Emir Bashir II had been born a Maronite, after his father had converted from Sunni Islam to Christianity, also complicated things even more, as the Druze perceived his quest for power as driven by sectarian motives.[59] The alliance that Bashir had established with the Maronite Church reinforced the sectarian fears of the Druze and further drove them to rebellion

The Druze never forgave the Maronites' betrayal and collaboration with the Egyptians; they perceived these acts as threat not only to their feudal status, but also to their existence as a community. Consequently, the 1841 defeat of the Egyptians by the Anglo-Turkish forces resulted in Emir Bashir II being overthrown and exiled. For the next two decades, Mount Lebanon was a scene of bitter feuds and skirmishes between the Druze and the Maronites, which in 1860 finally erupted into a full-scale civil war. During that time, Sa'id, son of the slain Sheikh Bashir Joumblatt, emerged as leader of his community, ready to avenge his father. In the following lines, Leila Fawaz gives a vivid description of the setting on the eve of the war:

> The continued absence of a strong government, coupled with Druze–Maronite frustrated ambitions, was a recipe for disaster. Any social unrest could trigger warfare within communities and between them, and opportunities for generating unrest were clearly not lacking.[60]

Moreover, the Ottomans' desire to discipline the Maronites for their treacherous collaboration with the Egyptians allowed the well-organised Druze forces to destroy major Christian villages and towns. Consequently, under the united leadership of the Joumblatti and Yazbaki factions the Druze massacred the inhabitants of three of the largest Christian towns: Deir al-Qamar, Zahle and Hasbaya. A contemporary Druze chronicler admitted that his coreligionists would not spare the life of any adult male, even if he pleaded for mercy. The Druze raiding parties entered villages, killed their male inhabitants and then proceeded to systemically loot homes and shops, setting them ablaze.[61]

The civil strife ended with the arrival of the French navy in Beirut, which imposed a cease-fire and stationed garrisons across the country. Although the Druze had gained a military victory, they were not successful in capitalising on this victory. The French intervened on behalf of the Maronites and demanded that the Ottoman authorities arrest the perpetrators of the heinous crimes. Thus, Sa'id Joumblatt and other leading Druze notables were imprisoned and later exiled. Joumblatt's death while incarcerated even further increased the hatred that the Druze already harboured towards the Maronites. According to the Druze historical narrative, the Maronites forced the six major powers at the time – France, Britain, Russia, Austria, Prussia and the Ottoman Empire – to abolish the old feudal system and in its place install an administrative council (*mutasarrifiya*).⁶² The council gave the Maronites ultimate control over Mount Lebanon, deprived the Druze of their feudal status and transformed this communal space into an exclusively Maronite homeland.⁶³ The new arrangement allocated the governorship to a non-Muslim Ottoman administrator; four of the twelve seats on the council were allotted to the Maronites, three to the Druze, two to the Greek-Orthodox, one to the Catholic, one to the Sunni and one to the Shi'ite community. Furthermore, the first Ottoman *mutasarrıf* (governor) favoured the Maronites by creating the post of a deputy *mutasarrıf* and granting it to them, even further disenfranchising the Druze.⁶⁴

The Maronites: Lebanon, a Refuge

While the Druze have perceived themselves as gallant warriors in the service of Islam, the Maronites have seen their country and their existence from a wholly different perspective. The Maronites believe that they are native to this land, tracing their ancestry back to the early Semitic peoples. The Maronites have claimed that their nation was primordial, even predating Christianity, as these civilisations were 'forged on the lands of Lebanon into one people, which were called the Phoenicians, and these Phoenicians in turn adopted Christianity and became the Maronites'.⁶⁵ The emphasis on this Phoenician tradition rests the following assumptions: First, the Maronites have always existed in Lebanon, even before the arrival of Christianity. Second, the Lebanese – like their seafaring ancestors, the Phoenicians – were civilised entrepreneurs with no connection to the nomadic tribal traditions of Arabia. Moreover, this Lebanese nation was always protected by its brave and organised armies, known as the Mardaites and the *Jarajimah*.

According to Maronite tradition, the *Jarajimah* defended the nation from the invasions of the Muslims, starting with the Islamic conquest in the seventh century AD. These 'Lebanese Mardaites', as Daw has called them, made possible the establishment of a refuge for people persecuted by the Muslims and newly colonised Arab tribes, the precursors of the Druze. After the Druze had settled in Lebanon, rather than engage in open warfare with them, the Maronites opted for a peaceful alliance. According to Walid Phares, an advisor to US President Donald Trump during his candidacy, this historical settlement was mutually beneficial. On one hand, the Druze needed the labour provided by the Maronites to maintain their agrarian economy; on the other hand, the Maronites endured until the time to reclaim their rights had come.[66] To achieve their goal, the Maronites employed certain tactics. They continued to support the Lebanese entity against outside forces (mainly Islam) and supported the Druze sect within this entity, while at the same time trying to convert the Druze emir to Christianity. When all these elements aligned during the reign of the Shihabs, the Maronites reclaimed what was rightfully theirs; however, in a last desperate attempt to maintain their feudal status, the Druze committed the massacres of 1860.

The Maronites' insistence on tracing their ancestry back to this warrior community is perhaps better understood when juxtaposed against the Druze's view of them. While the Druze look down on Christians as pitiful peasants, the Maronites deny this heritage and instead assert that this was the status of other Christian communities. Furthermore, they insist on linking their past to that of the Maradites, who originally hailed from Anatolia, so as to assert and emphasise that they have no links whatsoever to the Arabs. This claim to a Mardaite lineage was propagated by two prominent Maronites historians, Jibra'il bin al-Qilai, the Maronite Bishop of Cyprus in the fifteenth century, and the Maronite Patriarch Istfan al-Duwayhi in the seventeenth century. Ibn al-Qilai was the first to establish that the Maronites – or *Sha'b Marun*, the people of Saint Marun – date back to the sixth century AD and were descendants of the 'kings and heroes amongst them, who defended the mountains and the coastlands. From the heights of the mountains, their valiant chiefs would descend together with their men as a torrential fall of rain to rout Muslim invaders whenever they attacked'.[67]

Building on this, Duwayhi in the seventeenth century went even further to assert that Youhana Marun, the first patriarch of the Maronite Church, was of 'Mardaite princely descent and his mother a Frankish princess of the Carolingian line'.[68] The Maronites' flight from Byzantine persecution to their mountain refuge in Lebanon was facilitated by a certain Ibrahim, the nephew of the patriarch who was 'a valiant Mardaite warrior that secured the withdrawal of his uncle and his faithful followers to the safety of Mount Lebanon'.[69] Within this framework, the image that the Maronites want to preserve for themselves, according to Salibi, possesses the following characteristics:

Warlike instincts and skills which preserved them in Mount Lebanon as a free and defiant Christian people in their Islamic surroundings. Was it not the same valour inherited from their Mardaite forebears that made them also rise in the defence of the True Apostolic Faith of Rome against the wicked schisms and heresies of the East, to deserve in the end the supreme compliment paid to them by no less a person than the pope himself: that they were, truly, a rose among the thorns?[70]

Incontrovertible as these claims may seem, especially coming from a prominent Maronite cleric such as Duwayhi, their authenticity is easily challenged.

The Maronite doctrines of the 'Mountain Refuge' (*Asile du Liban*), the 'Resurrection of the Phoenician Nation' and their Mardaite connection are clear examples of how collective memory is fabricated and moulded over time to serve a present political project. The roots of the first two doctrines (*Asile du Liban* and Phoenicia) are to be found not in prehistoric records or on archeological sites, but in the modern scholarship of the Jesuit priest Henri Lammens. Lammens formulated the idea that Lebanon stood apart from the rest of the Syrian lands because of its terrain and distinct past. This rugged terrain provided shelter to all the dissidents and the oppressed who sought to escape the wrath of a central authority, while Lebanon's prehistoric past explained the country's uniqueness.[71] In addition, the Maronite political establishment, represented by notable Maronite families and the rising bourgeoisie, adopted this doctrine of *Asile du Liban* and transformed it into their ideological flagship. This 'consortium' of powerful Christian businessmen wanted to reinstate the image of Lebanon as a continuation of the Phoenician merchant republic.[72] They considered that a Phoenician legacy would firmly distinguish them from the Arab-Muslim countries surrounding them. However, according to Salibi, the refuge theory, as reproduced by the Maronites in the twentieth century, disregards several important points.[73]

First, the Maronites had fled from the Syrian hinterland to Lebanon because of Byzantine persecution rather than the tyranny of the Muslim rule. Second, it assumes that the Islamic Empire never established control over Mount Lebanon, a point easily falsified when subjected to proper historical examination. As early as in the time of Caliph Mu'awiyah (d. 680), the Islamic Empire had been established in nearly all parts of Mount Lebanon, and the periods that followed were no different, as the Muslim central authority could always enforce its will on the peripheries when needed. Mount Lebanon was no exception. Most importantly, Salibi has stressed the fact that most of the tribes that existed in this so-called 'refuge', including the Maronites, were ethnically Arab as early as in the third century AD. Furthermore, when these tribes adopted the Islamic faith, they did so peacefully and chose to convert to heterodox Islam, mainly the Druze faith and Shi'ism. This was not a direct result of the Islamic conquest, nor of persecution by a central Muslim state. Therefore, contrary to the Maronite notion, the ancestors of the Lebanese did not flee any persecution, and their arrival in the region of present-day Lebanon was contemporaneous with the Islamic conquest.[74]

According to Salibi, the doctrine of the Maronites' Phoenician legacy is easy to debunk. While the Maronites' primary reason for the resurrection of Phoenicia was to stand apart from the Arabs, in reality the Phoenicians were originally from Arabia. The origin of the word Phoenicia can be traced to the Greek word Phoenix, literally meaning 'date palm'.[75] The Greeks named these seafaring people 'date-eaters' because they used to consume dates on their long voyages. Date palms are more abundant on the Arabian Peninsula and not commonly grown along the Syrian coast. Salibi has pointed out that the Maronites consciously dismissed Herodotus, the Father of History, who traced the Phoenicians' Arab origins and instead preferred to promote their own interpretation. The Maronite myth served a far greater goal: By claiming that the Lebanese were in fact the inventors of the modern alphabet, which the Greeks later adopted, 'the whole human culture owed the Lebanese a great debt'.[76] However, Salibi has concluded that any similarities between the Phoenicians and the Lebanese might be justified by the mere fact that they both share the same geographic location, rather than the same historic legacy.

The purported Mardaite-Maronite link, however, appears even easier to debunk. A gesture to distinguish themselves genealogically from the Arabs, this claim is contradicted by Maronite history. According to Salibi, Duwayhi himself provided evidence that negates the non-Arab roots of the Maronites. In his book on the origins of the Maronites, Duwayhi has mentioned that the Maronites of Aqura in the north of Lebanon were 'divided into Qaysi (north Arab) and Yemenite (south Arab) factions, much as other tribal Arabs in Syria were'.[77] Furthermore, the Khazens, the Maronite lords of the Kisrwan region and the allies of Fakhr al-Din, were members of the Qaysi party. It is highly unlikely that the Qaysi-Yemeni faction would have entertained allowing any person or family to join its ranks, if their Arab lineage had been questionable.

The Maronites Go West

In the end, the Maronite attempt to build connections to a non-Arab or Western entity was achieved, not through prehistoric or an imagined ancestry, but through links to the First Crusade. The Crusader-Maronite encounter in the spring of 1099 was a watershed moment for the Maronites, not only politically, but also in terms of religion. Salibi has gone so far as to consider this juncture as a transformational event: 'were it not for the Crusades the Maronites might very well have remained the fossil peasant community which the Franks found in Mount Lebanon in the last year of the eleventh century'.[78] When the Crusaders arrived on the Lebanese coast, the Maronites were among the first communities to welcome them with jubilation and offer their services as guides.[79] William of Tyre, the Crusader chronicler and archbishop of Tyre, documented this early contact:

> High up on the lofty range of Lebanon, whose towering summits rise far above those cities on the east which I have just mentioned, lived certain Syrian Christians. These people had come down to offer their congratulations to the pilgrims and to pay them their tribute of brotherly affection. Since they were well-acquainted with the country all about, the leaders called these people and consulted with them, as experienced men, about the safest and easiest way to Jerusalem. In all good faith the Syrians carefully considered the advantages and all the lengths of the various routes leading thither and finally recommended the shore road as the most direct.[80]

Naturally, the Maronite association with the Crusaders persisted for the next two centuries, until the Mamluks were finally able to evict them from the Lebanese coast.[81] With this removal also came the Mamluk reprisal for the Maronite collaboration with the Crusaders; consequently, the status of the Maronite community greatly diminished. The persecution of Maronites experienced its peak in 1367, with the execution of Patriarch Jibra'il of Hjula, whom the Mamluks burnt at the stake. The Crusades, however, set the Maronites on a course that no military defeat could divert – namely, the Maronite Church's union with Rome. The Maronite-Crusader connection and the special privileges that the Maronites had enjoyed under Frankish rule encouraged the former to shed their Monothelitism and embrace Roman orthodoxy. Prior to this leap, the Maronite Church had been part of the Eastern doctrine of Monothelitism, which Rome branded as heretical. This doctrine professed that Jesus Christ had two natures but one will, while the Roman-Catholic Church maintained that Christ had two wills, one human and one divine.[82] The Maronites, and especially the clergy who received their religious training in Rome, have tried to maintain that they had never been part of this heresy, but that they had always been believers in Roman orthodoxy.[83] In a book published by the Maronite League (*al-Mawarina*), Antoine Khoury Harb has stated that 'the Maronites were the only eastern Christians that remained loyal to the Holy See, which explains why they were joyful and welcoming of the Crusades'.[84] However, this claim is challenged by many Maronite works indicating that the Maronites adopted Monothelitism before and during the early encounters with the Franks.[85]

Although the Maronite Church willfully entered a union with Rome in 1180, this was not the case with all Maronites, as some rejected this union by all means possible. These anti-union elements went as far as 'attacking the Uniate churches and monasteries, beating, mutilating, and sometimes killing Uniate priests, monks, bishops and abbots'.[86] These challenges increased with the entry of other Monophysite Christian factions – that is, factions believing in Jesus possessing one divine nature – into Mount Lebanon, primarily the Jacobites whose preaching was effective and greatly embarrassed the Uniate Maronites.[87] According to Matti Moosa, much of the scrambling of the Maronites to prove their Roman Orthodoxy goes beyond merely denying their Monothelitism; they also attempt to hide the fact that they were Jacobites or adherents of Syrian Orthodoxy.[88] Dissecting the literature of the Maronite Church and their contemporaries, Moosa has confirmed that 'the Maronites had been Syrian Orthodox "Jacobites" before they were forced to adopt Monothelitism in the formula promoted by Heraclius, and that after becoming Monothelites they separated themselves from Syrian Orthodox "Jacobites" and seized many of their church buildings and monasteries'.[89] Moosa has furthermore debunked Henri Lammens's and others' assertions that the Maronites are the descendants of the war-like Mardaites, demonstrating that these are 'historically false' and 'a construction of modern writers who cannot support their claims with any historical evidence'.[90]

Over the next few centuries, relations between Rome and the Maronites were in flux, as the so-called orthodoxy of the Maronites was doubted and deemed unworthy of papal patronage. In the fifteenth century, Catholic missionaries, specifically the Franciscan order, helped the Maronites to finally seal the debate over the orthodoxy of their community.[91] This order provided religious guidance and training to the Maronite clergy and at the same time lobbied on their behalf with Rome. Finally convinced that investing time and effort in the Maronites was a worthwhile eneavour, the Papacy in 1584 established the Maronite college, an institution which has remained in operation to this day. The college, supervised by the Jesuits, welcomed 'students [who] soon arrived from the Orient to be immersed in Latin theology and liturgy as well as devotion to the Church of Rome'.[92] Thee institution graduated a number of leading Maronite clerics who later assumed various positions within the church, ranging from the office of the patriarch to lesser posts. The college's graduates included Patriarch Istfan al-Duwayhi and Bishop Jibra'il bin al-Qilai, who, in addition to fulfilling their ecclesiastic duties, authored important works on the history of their community.[93] The final cementing of the union with Rome in the sixteenth century not only provided the Maronites with an institutional backbone, but also gave them political patronage and protection from the West, something that would prove vital for the Maronites in the centuries to come. The Franco-Ottoman rapprochement starting in the sixteenth century allowed France to proclaim itself as protector of the Catholics in the Levant.[94] Since the Maronites were Catholic, this protection was naturally also extended to them, and they enthusiastically embraced this advantage. In 1715, Patriarch Jacob IV Awad stated that the Maronites have 'no refugee, no salvation, outside the throne of France and its representative in the Levant'.[95]

An important aspect of this political patronage was the Maronites' opportunity to benefit from the religious and secular education made available by the missionaries dispatched to the Levant – for example, by the Jesuits.[96] This education gave the Maronites an advantage over the Druze who did not really possess any schools that could have taught them about foreign languages or other applied knowledge. In the sixteenth century, despite their dwindling numbers, the Druze were still politically dominant, but came to rely on the Christians as intermediaries with the West, especially in commercial affairs. This naturally empowered the Christians who soon came to be important brokers for the leading commodity at the time – that is, silk. According to Salibi, the Christians held a sort of monopoly over the different stages of the silk production process, from 'the peasants, to the moneylenders, to the intermediaries, brokers to the local markets and the merchants that exported to Europe'.[97] The estranged Druze thus felt that the Maronites, once upon a time their clients, had now surpassed them, and this made them resentful.

The Maronites and the Eastern Question

The successive Ottoman-Russian wars and the many setback suffered by the Ottomans enabled the major European powers of the time to take a more active role in the empire's affairs.[98] This Western intervention reflected itself in the 'Eastern Question', concerning how to divide the Ottoman territories after the empire's demise, as well as the fate of the Christians residing on these territories. Consequently, the Maronites, who by the seventeenth century had assumed power following the Shihabi succession, were beneficiaries of this forceful Western intervention in the region, as it gave them the international support needed to maintain a Christian-dominated Mount Lebanon. The Maronite Church, having secured its liturgical and doctrinal connection with Rome, began to assume a more active role in governing Mount Lebanon. During the reign of Emir Bashir II, the support of the church proved decisive in the confrontation against Sheikh Bashir and the Druze.[99] This was partly why the Druze progressively started to demonise the church and its clerics as the main instigators of hatred against the Druze. Further buttressing this notion was the role that the church later played in the peasant revolts against the feudal lords, both Maronite and Druze. The peasant revolt started in Kisrwan, the predominantly Maronite northern part of Mount Lebanon, in 1859. It was a response to the high-handed policies of the feudal sheikhs. Consequently, groups of Christian peasants congregated and organised themselves as a protest movement pledging to defend each other from the yoke and likely retaliation of these sheikhs.[100] This dissident movement gradually gained momentum and spilled over to different parts of the mountain, including the southern Druze–Maronite part. Under the

Qaimaqamiyya system set up in 1845, a Druze governor administrated the southern sector, while the northern sector was under the jurisdiction of a Maronite local notable. The Druze therefore perceived the spread of the revolt into their regions as a sectarian ploy to further weaken and ultimately dominate them. The fact that the church had implicitly empowered these commoners to rise against the feudal sheikhs further aggravated the situation. Yehoshua Porath, in his study of the 'The Peasant Revolt of 1858–1861 in Kisrwan', has described the principal role of the Maronite church as such:

> Sharpening communal conflict in 1841 gave the Church its first great opportunity to exert its influence on the Christian peasants. The Maronite Patriarch called for unity under the leadership of the people's representatives, in contrast with the long tradition according to which the shaykhs and amirs were the sole leaders. From then on the Church did not cease to interfere in political issues.[101]

The head of the church at the time, Patriarch Bulus Mas'ad, as well as several leading clerics, hailed from modest backgrounds and were thus naturally predisposed to support the commoners rather than the sheikhs. Regardless of the reasons behind this grassroots revolt, or the motives of the church at that stage, they indeed played a major role in exacerbating an already tense relationship between the Druze and the Maronites; along with other factors, they paved the way for a full-scale civil war.

The fighting between the Druze and Maronites started in the early summer of 1860 and momentarily spread to Damascus. The Maronites were driven primarily by economic factors. The Ottoman authorities did not immediately intervene to stop the atrocities but remained neutral, and at times the Christians accused them of supporting the Druze in committing their massacres. Leila Fawwaz's *An Occasion for War* has detailed the different reasons behind the local Ottoman authorities' incompetence, or perhaps even complicity in the events of 1860, but she has also confirmed that 'some of them [the Ottomans] believed that at least in the early phases massacres attributed to them [Druze] were really victories over an aggressor who had been equally armed and equally bellicose'.[102]

Yet, the Maronites and their French patrons felt differently and were adamant to restore the imbalance caused by the debacle. The French also wanted to perform their duty as protectors of the Maronites. Consequently, after a series of diplomatic acts between the European powers and the Ottomans, the French Emperor Napoleon III dispatched a European expeditionary force, half of which was French. These troops were under the command of the seasoned General Charles de Beaufort, who during the Syrian campaign had served as chief-of-staff for Ibrahim Pasha of Egypt and thus was familiar with the complexities of the region.[103] Landing after the events had already transpired, Beaufort had a set of directives, primarily to restore law and order, and to return the displaced Christians to their towns and villages. More importantly, Emperor Napoleon's orders to his general were to 'catch, judge and punish the guilty, return to the Christians their confiscated goods, disarm the Druzes, and force on them reparations as indemnity to the victims of the insurrection'.[104] These objectives were never openly announced; instead, the French took the moral high ground and declared that their mission was to bring justice and provide humanitarian aid to the victims of Mount Lebanon. Napoleon personally addressed his troops before their departure to the Levant:

> Soldiers, you are departing for Syria, and France happily salutes an expedition which has one purpose only, that of making the rights of justice and humanity triumph. For you are not going in order to wage war against any nation but to help the Sultan bring back to obedience subjects blinded by a fanaticism from another century. You will do your duty in this far away land rich in memories, and you will show yourself the dignified children of these heroes who gloriously brought the banner of Christ to that land.[105]

The French were largely successful in carrying out their agenda: punishing the Druze and making them pay for the damages. Many of the leading Druze feudal sheikhs lost land, money, their freedom and even their lives. The French quest for vengeance, however, was curbed by the British who had assumed the role of guardians of the Druze, similar to that of the French for the Maronites. The British played an instrumental role in protecting the Druze, especially against some of the haphazard verdicts of the extraordinary tribunals set up in Beirut and Moukhtara to judge the accused Druze.[106] One issue, for instance, was some Christian moneylenders' request to immediately collect the debts of the deceased Sa'id Joumblatt, Sheikh Bashir's son, who had borrowed money to pay for the Druze war efforts. These lenders, with the help of the church, requested that the French confiscate and auction off the Joumblatt estate, including their family palace in Moukhtara. This was averted by the British who rented the Palace of Moukhtara for the British Syrian School, which was part of the 'Lebanon Schools' administered by the Lebanese Protestants.[107] This maneuver saved the palace, which constituted a symbol of Druze political power and legacy of the once powerful clan, from the greed of the lenders until the Joumblatts would be wealthy enough to once again acquire and administer their estate.[108] Certainly, the Druze took the attempt to confiscate the Moukhtara Palace as ample proof of the Maronite's exclusionary policy.

Following the success of the punitive expedition and the evacuation of troops, the French hoped to reinforce the Maronites' status by attempting to reinstate a Shihabi Christian governor on Mount Lebanon.[109] This proposal was unequivocally rejected by both the British and the Ottomans, who after a process of arduous negotiations with the rest of the European powers hammered out a new governance structure for Mount Lebanon. On 9 June 1861, the ambassadors of the five great powers to the Porte and the Ottoman Empire signed the *Règlement et protocole, relatifs à la réorganisation du Mont Liban,* which gave the mountain an autonomous governance status with an elected administrative council supervised by an Ottoman Christian (non-Muslim) governor. The *Mutasarrifiya*, as it came to be known, was divided into six districts, each with a fairly homogenuous sectarian makeup. Each of these districts had an elaborate electoral hierarchy, which ultimately delegated one or more representatives to the administrative council. In addition to putting together the nucleus of a relatively modern state, the *Mutasarrifiya* instituted two main practices that became pillars of Lebanese politics: sectarianism and foreign intervention.

While the Ottomans officially retained power over Mount Lebanon, after 1860 the great Europeans powers were given certain roles in the affairs of this newly born entity. John Spagnolo, however, has considered these claims as being an 'over-simplification' of a more intricate process whereby the Ottomans certainly kept the upper hand, while the great powers' prerogatives were restricted to merely 'influencing the appointment of the governor and then only if they acted together'.[110] Spagnolo's remarks might be conceptually true, especially since the Ottoman government exercised full sovereignty through the governor and other parts of the administration; however, in the psyche of the Lebanese – both Christian and Druze – the *Mutasarrifiya* was unequivocally directed by the great powers. This would lead these two congregations, as well as others who settled in Lebanon after the collapse of the Ottoman Empire, to further develop relationships with the respective foreign powers – an act that would prove to be a source of both stability and volatility.

The second practice, which had existed before but now became codified, was the sectarian division of the country, as the six districts reflected a sectarian reality caused by the changing demographics. Thus, at that time it was possible to elect people to office based on their sectarian rather than their tribal or political affiliation. However, to imply that sectarianism was a foreign introduction and that the culture of sectarianism was caused by Ottoman experimentation with modernity, forced upon them by pressure from the West, is inaccurate. The politics of Mount Lebanon, as this chapter has thus far demonstrated, experienced various stages, from the Qaysi-Yemeni split to the Joumblatti-Yazbaki rivalry. The outwardly sectarian Druze–Maronite clashes that followed are better understood through the lens of politics, rather than of religious animosity brought about by a number of factors, including western intervention.

The Druze perceived the creation of *al-Mutasarrifiya* as a Maronite triumph, as the intervention of France enabled the latter to achieve what they had failed to gain on the battlefield. However, this view contradicted reality, as the Maronites themselves perceived this arrangement as a political setback and not a victory on the path towards their political project. The Maronite Church, according to Carol Hakim, was extremely disgruntled about the new regime, which installed a non-Maronite governor to rule over a predominately Maronite mountain.[111] The Maronite Patriarch Bulus Mas'ad, believed to be the main instigator of the anti-feudal peasant revolt a few years earlier, voiced his objection to this new governance structure, which placed the Maronites, who outnumbered all the other communities combined, on the same footing and prevented them from ruling themselves (see Table 2.1).

Mas'ad called on the French to 'restore to us [the Maronites] our ancient rights' by sanctioning the appointment of a native Maronite *mutasarrif* (governor), someone with the profile of Yusuf Beik Karam, a powerful north-

Table 2.1 Ottoman population of Mount Lebanon, 1830–1914. From Kemal H. Karpat, *Ottoman Population, 1830–1914* (Madison: University of Wisconsin Press, 1985), quoted from Youssef Choueiri, *Breaking the Cycle: Civil Wars in Lebanon* (London: Stacey International, 2007), 24.

Maronites	242,308 (58.4 %)
Druze	47,290 (11.4 %)
Greek-Orthodox	52,356 (12.6 %)
Greek-Catholic	31,936 (7.7 %)
Shi'ite	23,413 (5.7%)
Sunni	14,529 (3.5%)
Other	2,968 (0.7%)
Total	414,800

ern notable and hero of the 1860 war with the Druze.[112] According to Mas'ad, only by correcting this injustice and allowing for majority rule 'which, at present, is the fundamental principle of the civil Constitutions of all the civilised countries' could a more practical form of governance be achieved.[113] Despite their disappointment, the Maronites cooperated with the Ottoman authorities throughout the existence of *al-Mutasarrifiya*. The only somewhat serious challenge to the Ottomans over *al-Mutasarrifiya* came in 1866, with the rebellion of Yusuf Karam, who had been exiled two years earlier. Karam had hoped that, by opposing the Ottoman governor Daud Pasha, he could prove that this non-native bureaucrat was incapable of carrying out his duties and thus possibly replace him instead. Yusuf Karam's false sense of entitlement and his extreme reliance on France, in addition to other local factors, led to his defeat and eventual exile to France. Bulus Mas'ad, who by extension was equally defeated, also realised that the great powers, and France in particular, would not intervene to aid the Maronites; therefore, it was prudent and wise to accept the reality of Daud Pasha's governorship.[114] Although the Maronites failed to restore a Shihabi-like rule, they nevertheless were able to plant the seeds of a Maronite homeland, which over time would acquire an ideological structure to help the Maronites reclaim what they considered to be rightfully theirs.

The Birth of the Lebanese Nation

As Ottoman rule was weakening, a group of young men educated in a secular fashion, all graduates of the Jesuit University in Beirut (USJ), provided the ideological framework for a Maronite homeland. These students had studied under the leading scholars of USJ's School of Oriental Studies. The school housed a number of renowned scholars of Religion, Semitic languages, Near Eastern History, Archeology and Geography, such as Henri Lammens, Louis Jalabert, Sebastian and Louis Ronzavelle and Louis Cheiko.[115] Although these scholars altogether were of equal academic importance, Henri Lammens perhaps had the greatest impact on the course of the Lebanese nationalist project. While writing his book on the history of Syria, entitled *Le Syrie: Précis historique*, Lammens concluded that Lebanon was a Mountain Refuge (*Asile du Liban*) detached from the Syrian coast by virtue of its geography.[116] Coincidentally, Lammens's work appeared in 1921, one year after the declaration of *Grand Liban*.[117] Lammens' students were mostly scions of the leading Christians families renowned for their involvement in mercantile activities; the names of families such as Chiha, Pharaoun, Corm, Fattal and Tayan became synonymous with Western trade as much as Lebanese nationalist discourses.

Charles Corm was one such student of Lammens; he was a poster-child for these merchant families and a founding figure of Lebanese nationalist thought. After graduating from the Jesuit University in 1911, Corm came to be the kingpin of the automotive distribution industry, as the exclusive representative of the Ford Motor Company in Syria and Lebanon. He was often referred to by the Lebanese as 'Mr Ford', which he detested.[118] Corm, who only wrote in French, established around him a network of intellectuals and businessmen who produced a wide array of literature exclusively promoting Lebanon's Phoenician legacy. Along with other prominent individuals, such as Yusuf al-Sawda and Albert Naccache, Corm established the Society of Young Phoenicians, which acted as a think-tank for the Lebanese nationalists. On the pages of *La Revue Phénicienne*, the society's official publication, Corm focused on the notion that the Lebanese were members of a distinct race which had survived over the course of the centuries. This notion, however, had major implications: Membership in the Lebanese nation entailed relinquishing any recognition of the partial Muslim legacy of the country. Therefore, the adoption of race as a pillar in Corm's national dogma excluded the non-Christian population, practically more than half of the Lebanese. The only official Lebanese census, conducted in 1932 under the French Mandate, recognised the Christians as majority of the population, a deliberate mistake. To this day, the resulting numbers remain a bone of contention because the inaccurate census gave the Maronites more power within the confessional system codified in the constitution.[119] Corm apparently was not interested in offering his Muslim 'compatriots' an inclusionist vision of the nation. In his famed work of poetry, *La Montagne Inspirée* (The Inspired Mountain), Corm has explicitly stated the racial and the religious elements of his brand of nationalism in addressing the Muslims:

> My Muslim brother, understand my frankness: I am the real Lebanon, sincere and churchgoing; All the more Lebanese that my faith symbolizes the heart of a pelican. If my fervor is attached to the dogmas of the Church, it is because in my eyes it is the universality; because I cannot believe in a god that divides the immense humanity.[120]

Throughout this work, Corm religiously reiterated the notion that the Phoenician race and its civilisation has been carried forth by the Lebanese Christians, the rightful inheritors of the land. Furthermore, he stressed the importance of the Phoenician language:

> It is that we were only at the gable of history, before becoming Muslims or Christians, we were only a people united in the same glory, and, in evolving, we should at least, by the fact of one faith all the more praiseworthy, love ourselves like in the Era when we were pagans! [. . .] language of my country, tell us our history, tell our children that in all that seems to humiliate, that they can be proud to have been in glory, in glories by the thousands! Language of my country, give us confidence, make us still believe in ourselves and in our ancestors, protect for us our place, and protect our audience at the table of the gods![121]

Corm's overly anti-Arab sentiments even led him to contemplate an alliance which the Zionists in Palestine, something that would surely have enraged the Lebanese Muslims. Corm believed that both the Jews and the Maronites were suffering from the same plight, due to the century-long Muslim tyranny; therefore, it was natural for these two minorities to strike a strategic alliance. Consequently, Corm drew his inspiration from the biblical alliance between King Hiram I (980–947 BC), the alleged father of the Lebanese, and King Solomon of Israel, so as to form:

A common front against their principal enemy and that is the Muslim Arab proclaiming pan-Arabism. [The Muslim danger forced] Christian Lebanon to find 'partners in fate' and among them is the Jewish community in Palestine and Zionism in general . . . the Jews and the Lebanese must find a way to mutual understanding and regular relations and we are ready for this.[122]

Despite some of the Maronite community's fervour for Corm's line of thinking, the Maronite political leadership did not want to alienate the Arabs, especially at a time when the Jewish project was still in its infancy and its success still uncertain. During the 1975 civil war, however, many of the ideologues who promoted a Maronite-Israeli rapprochement looked towards Corm's works for inspiration.

One of Corm's fellow travellers, perhaps equally influenced by Lammens, was Bulus Nujaym. Nujaym's seminal work *La Question du Liban* had appeared in 1908 under his pen name M. Jouplain.[123] Written during his stint in Paris, while finishing his doctorate in Law and Political Science, it hints that Nujaym harboured political aspirations; hence, he did not wish to damage his career by setting his name on a publication that the Ottomans might construe as a call to secede and that thus would land him in trouble. It is no coincidence that this book, with its Lebanese nationalist tone, was written almost concurrently with the revolution of the Young Turks who demanded constitutional reform and introduced their own brand of Turkish nationalism.[124] Nujaym's work marks a change of mood towards *al-Mutasarrifiya*, which for the author was 'a stepping-stone towards real independence, which would someday be achieved with the help of Europe'.[125] This indispensable stepping-stone had in fact prepared Lebanon for its eventual sovereignty. Moreover, Nujaym's work presented a vivid Lebanese past as well as future, beginning with the Muslim conquest and tracing the events on Mount Lebanon to the present – that is, 1908. This historical account encouraged Christians to join the Maronite homeland, if they choose so, by sharing in 'the national and patriotic sentiment, transcending former religious divisions and solely preoccupied with future development and prosperity'.[126]

Najm's education and work in local government made it clear to him that Mount Lebanon was not viable with its current borders, due to objective economic realities such as lack of access to seaports and scarcity of arable land. According to Nujaym, these realities would lead to the destruction of the mountain, unless it were given 'new land by expanding its territory'.[127] For Nujaym, the expansion of the current *Mutasarrifiya* would merely mean a return to the Lebanon of Fakhr al-Din, rather than a new construction. This proposal was in fact an inclusionary proposal that would introduce new groups alien to the sectarian fabric of Mount Lebanon. With an annexation of the coastal cities – Beirut, Saida and Tripoli – and the Beqa'a Valley, the Muslim population of these lands would join the Maronite and the Druze in their mountain refuge. This quest for expansion, even though driven by necessity rather than pure altruism, exhibited a good understanding of the reality of the country and the surrounding region. Including Muslims in the newly expanded territory would help to protect Lebanon from the surrounding hostile Muslim environment, especially if the Lebanese Muslims truly became part of this Maronite homeland. The terrible humanitarian conditions and the famine that ensued across Mount Lebanon during World War I reaffirmed the need to expand Lebanese territories, especially if a repetition of such events was to be averted in the future.[128]

The end of World War I and the collapse of the Ottoman Empire turned the idea of a Maronite homeland into reality. The Lebanese delegates to the Paris Peace Conference, resulting in the Treaty of Versailles, in 1919 all advocated, in one way or another, a Maronite homeland with extended borders, very similar to the borders specified by Lammens and Nujaym. The two delegations headed by Daoud 'Ammun, a member of *al-Mutasarrifiya*'s Administrative Council, and the Maronite Patriarch Elias Hoayek, respectively, met with many stake-holders to convey the wishes of the Lebanese to form a separate Christian entity apart from the Arab world around it.[129] Most of the individuals involved in the lobbying with the French and other participants at the Paris Peace Conference were ideologically committed, albeit to varying extent, to the notion of a Greater Lebanon and its Phoenician heritage. The memorandum that Hoayek submitted on behalf of the Lebanese to the peace conference on 23 October 1919 clearly underscores the Maronite *zeitgeist*:

> Lebanon's independence, as it was declared and as it was conceived by the near majority of the Lebanese, is not only an independence stemming from the

collapse of Ottoman authority! It is, above all, a complete independence vis-à-vis any Arab state that might come into being in Syria... Some have, through an abusive manipulation of language, sought to confound Lebanon with Syria. This is a grave error. Without even having to summon their Phoenician ancestors, it is quite evident that the Lebanese have always constituted a distinct national entity, separate from the groupings surrounding it, whether in terms of language, moral principles, affinities, or Western culture.[130]

Eleven months later, on 1 September 1920, the representatives of the different Lebanese communities listened to the French High Commissioner General Henri Gouraud as he brought the Maronites' dream of a Greater Lebanon to fruition. As if reading from an article from *La Revue Phénicienne*, Gouraud proclaimed the establishment of a political entity that conformed to the aspirations and demands of the Maronite elite, including the Maronite Church. France, which under the provisions of the Sykes-Picot Agreement of 1916 received Syria and Lebanon, found it convenient and practical to award the Maronites their own homeland. Gouraud affirmed that this entity indeed was to be 'a single nation, rooted in its past', a range of 'majestic mountains, [. . .] impregnable stronghold of [Lebanon's] faith and freedom', and a 'mythical sea, which has been witness to the triremes of Phoenicia [and which] transported through the world [Lebanon's] subtle, skillful, and eloquent [Phoenician] forefathers.[131]

The creation of Greater Lebanon was truly a feat of great importance to the Maronites and an equally resounding defeat for the Druze, as they lost their status as the second largest community on Mount Lebanon. The Druze, who had gradually lost the reins of power after the demise of the Ma'anids, suddenly found themselves alienated by a system that did not celebrate their historical legacy and merely gave them a proportional share corresponding to their meager demographic reality. Meir Zamir has stated that the Druze all of a sudden found themselves replaced by the Sunnis, who after 1943 agreed to partition Lebanon among themselves according to the National Pact and thus left the Druze completely alienated.[132] Decades after Lebanon had gained its independence from the French Mandate, Walid Joumblatt still harboured the sentiment that the Maronites had betrayed the Druze, a sentiment he would sustain until his conflict with the Maronites in 1982.[133]

In 1980 – upon the good offices of the Director of Army Intelligence, Colonel Johnny Abdu – Joseph Abu Khalil, Editor-in-Chief of the newspaper *Al-'Amal* and a close associate of Bashir Gemayel, met Walid Joumblatt over dinner for the first time. Abu Khalil, a Maronite from Beit al-Din in the Shuf Mountain(s), was on a mission to convince the young Druze leader of the validity of Bashir Gemayel's plan for Lebanon and to possibly reconcile the two kingpins.[134] Abu Khalil addressed Joumblatt by emphasising 'the unity of Mount Lebanon and the importance of a Christian-Druze alliance under the patronage of the state which would pave the way for the rise of a strong central state capable of gradually reclaiming its sovereignty', but was surprised by the aloof response he received. Joumblatt's telling response to this utopic alliance was: 'Why didn't you [the Maronites] do so in 1943, when you ignored the political reality of the mountain and you went through with a settlement that contradicts this reality or at best is unharmonious with it?'[135] This same sentiment was shared by other Druze as well; Saleh Zahreddine, Professor of History at Lebanese University, is a case in point. In an interview conducted in 1984, Zahreddine saw 'the national pact as a sectarian compromise whose disastrous implications are still felt to this day'.[136]

However, this sentiment was not shared by the majority of the Druze community, as the Yazbaki faction under Emir Majid Arslan continued to support the traditional Maronite elite until 1983, when the clashes grew into a full-scale civil war between the two communities.[137] But it is equally important to bear in mind that the Maronite-Druze relationship within Greater Lebanon and even after 1943 was not always contentious in nature; rather, it experiences phases of appeasement during which both parties were working together. Yet, the fact that the Maronites from 1920 onwards were strategically placed within the state apparatus, including the bureaucracy and the armed forces, placed them at the helm, while all other sects (including the Druze) had to assume secondary roles within the new state structure. This Maronite political establishment, referred to as *al-Maruniyah al-Siyasiyah*, dominated Lebanon, but still incorporated Muslim and Druze elements. However, the bond between these individuals consisted of economic interests rather than a common political vision. Fawwaz Traboulsi, writing on the economic and political elite following independence, has remarked that among these thirty families of oligarchs, the ratio was '24 Christian families (nine Maronites, seven Greek Catholic, one Latin, one Protestant, four Greek Orthodox and one Armenian), to six Muslim (four Sunni, one Shiite and one Druze)', which clearly indicates the Christians' hegemony in all matters of state.[138]

These two contradictory Druze and Maronite readings of history, which both groups formulated over time, as this section demonstrates, had extremely negative ramifications: Each community identified itself in opposition to the other, with no chance of both political projects being able to coexist or reconcile beyond short spells. These charter myths, which validate certain powers structures, as Bronislaw Malinowski has argued, 'cannot be sober dispassionate history, since it is always made ad hoc to fulfil a certain sociological function, to glorify a certain group, or to justify an anomalous status'.[139] Therefore, when the Druze and the Maronite myths collided, the consequences were dire, since for one myth to exist, the other must be destroyed; neither community left within their identity construct any room to entertain the other.

Notes

1. Ussama Makdisi, *The Culture of Sectarianism: Community, History, and Violence in Nineteenth-Century Ottoman Lebanon* (Berkeley: University of California Press, 2000).
2. Salibi, *House of Many Mansions*, 231.
3. Ibid., 18.
4. Marshall G. S. Hodgson, 'Al-Darazî and Ḥamza in the Origin of the Druze Religion', *Journal of the American Oriental Society* 82, no. 1 (1962), 6–20.
5. *Al-Jabal: Difa'an 'an al-Woujoud wal Karamah* [The Mountain: In Defense of our Existence and Dignity], published by the Civil Administration in the Shuf (Moukhtara: Dar al-Takadoumiya, April 1984), 19; Abbas Abu Salah and Sami Makarem, *Tārīkh al-Muwaḥḥidīn al-Durūz al-Siyāsī fī al-Mashriq al-ʿArabī* (Beirut: Manshūrāt al-Majlis al-Durzī lil-Buḥūth wa-al-Inmā', 1980), 20.
6. Abu Salah and Makarem, *Tārīkh al-Muwaḥḥidīn al-Durūz*, 27.
7. Ibid.
8. Tannus al-Shidyaq, *Akhbār al-Aʿyān fī Jabal Lubnān* (Beirut: Lebanese University Publications, 1970), Part 2, 278.
9. Kamal Salibi, 'The Buhturids of the Garb: Mediaeval Lords of Beirut and of Southern Lebanon', *Arabica* 8 (1961), 74–97.

10. Abbas Abu Saleh believes that the influx of these tribes (Abdul Malak, Bani Fawaris, Abdallah and Hilal) went beyond the mere military explanation and hints at the possibility that these groups might have migrated due to political factors. Abu Salah and Makarem, *Tārīkh al-Muwaḥḥidīn al-Durūz*, 29. See also Salibi, 'The Buhturids of the Garb'.
11. Kamal Joumblatt and Philippe Lapousterle, *I Speak for Lebanon* (London: Zed Press, 1982), 31.
12. Kamal Salibi, *Syria under Islam, 634–1097*, 2nd ed. (Beirut: Dar Nelson, 2009), 43.
13. Ibid., 45.
14. Abu Salah and Makarem, *Tārīkh al-Muwaḥḥidīn al-Durūz*, 42. Salibi, *Syria under Islam*, 82.
15. Marshall Hodgson, *The Venture of Islam: Conscience and History in a World Civilization* (Chicago: University of Chicago Press, 1974), vol. 2, 18.
16. Paul Walker, *Caliph of Cairo: Al-Hakim Bi-Amr Allah, 996–1021* (Cairo: American University in Cairo Press, 2009).
17. Salibi, *Syria under Islam*, 102.
18. Fuad Khuri, *Being a Druze* (London: Druze Heritage Foundation, 2004), 26.
19. Abu Salah and Makarem, *Tārīkh al-Muwaḥḥidīn al-Durūz*, 98.
20. Ṣāliḥ ibn Yaḥyá, Kamal S. Salibi and Francis Hours, *Tārīkh Bayrūt, wa-Huwa Akhbār al-Salaf min Dhurriyat Buḥtur ibn ʿAlī Amīr al-Gharb bi-Bayrūt* (Bayrūt: Dār al-Mashraf, 1969).
21. Salibi, 'The Buhturids of the Garb', 6.
22. Ibid., 65.
23. Nejla Abu Izzeddin, *The Druzes: A New Study of Their History, Faith, and Society* (Leiden: Brill, 1993), 161. For details about this body, see 'Ḥalḳa', *Encyclopedia of Islam*, 2nd ed.
24. Ibid., 162.
25. Salibi, *House of Many Mansions*, 122.
26. Ibid., 124.
27. Abdul Rahim Abu-Husayn, 'Rebellion, Myth-Making and Nation-Building: Lebanon from an Ottoman Mountain Iltizam to a Nation State', *Studia Culturae Islamica* 97 (Tokyo: ILCAA, Tokyo University of Foreign Studies, 2009), 8.
28. Abu-Husayn, *The View from Istanbul: Lebanon and the Druze Emirate in the Ottoman Chancery Documents, 1546–1711* (London: I. B. Tauris; Oxford: Centre for Lebanese Studies, 2004), 17–18.

29. Ibid., 19.
30. Salibi, *House of Many Mansions*, 125.
31. Abu-Husayn, 'Rebellion, Myth-Making and Nation-Building', 15.
32. Abu-Husayn, *The View from Istanbul*, 15.
33. Interview with Raja Naim, Beirut, Lebanon, 24 May 2016. Naim was one of many who used this line when asked about the Druze and their history.
34. Abu Salah and Makarem, *Tārīkh al-Muwaḥḥidīn al-Durūz*, 133. Like many others, Abu Saleh considered that the Ottoman campaign was an unjust act prompted on the instigation of the enemies of the Druze.
35. Abdul-Rahman Abu-Husayn, 'The Ottoman Invasion of the Shuf in 1585: A Reconsideration,' *Al-Abhath* 33 (1985), 16.
36. MD 53, No. 724, 11 Safar 993/12 February 1585. Order to the *beylerbeyi* of Damascus. Ottoman chancellery document, as translated in Abu-Husayn, *The View from Istanbul*, 17.
37. Ibid., 34.
38. Adel Allouche, *The Origins and Development of the Ottoman-Safavid Conflict, 906–962/1500–1555* (Berlin: Klaus Schwarz, 1983), 146.
39. Salibi, *House of Many Mansions*, 126.
40. These families included the Arslans, Joumblatts, Abu Nakad, Imad, Talhouks, Abd al-Maliks, Abu Harmouch and el-Eid Abi-Lama.
41. Jane Hathaway, *A Tale of Two Factions: Myth, Memory, and Identity in Ottoman Egypt and Yemen* (Albany: State University of New York, 2003), 32.
42. Ibid., 33.
43. Ibid., 34.
44. Abdul-Rahim Abu-Husayn, 'The Junblats and the Janbulads: A Case of Mistaken identity,' in *Acta Viennensia Ottamanica*, ed. Markus Köhbach et al. (Vienna: Selbstverlag des Institutes für Orientalistik, 1999).
45. William Harris, *Lebanon: A History, 600–2011* (New York: Oxford University Press, 2012), 119. Introduction to Mikhail Mishaqah and Wheeler Thackston, *Murder, Mayhem, Pillage and Plunder: The History of Lebanon in the 18th and 19th centuries by Mikhayil Mishaqa*, trans. from the Arabic by W. M. Thackston Jr (Albany: State University of New York Press, 1988), 7.
46. Abu-Husayn, 'The Junblats and the Janbulads', 6.
47. *Al-Jabal: Difa'an 'an al-Woujoud wal Karamah*, 21.
48. Abu-Husayn, 'The Ottoman Invasion of the Shuf in 1585', 17.
49. Interview with AA, 14 October 2014.

50. Salibi, *House of Many Mansions*, 67.
51. Abu-Husayn indicates that the Ottoman archives do not give any reference to this election by the local Druze factions. Abu-Husayn, *The View from Istanbul*, 9; Abu-Husayn, 'The Shihab Succession (1697): A Reconsideration', *Archive Orientalni, Supplementa VIII* (1998).
52. Abu-Husayn, 'The Shihab Succession', 11.
53. Caesar Farah, *The Politics of Interventionism in Ottoman Lebanon, 1830–1861* (Oxford: Centre for Lebanese Studies, 2000), 740.
54. 'Izzat Ṣafi, *Ṭarīq al-Mukhtārah Zaman Kamāl Junblāṭ* (Beirut: Dar Nahar, 2007), 22.
55. It has not been confirmed that Bashir Joumblatt was a cleric, but he was famous for his piety and highly respected by the Druze religious class.
56. Tannous al-Shidyaq, *Kitab Akhbar al-A'yan fi Jabal Lubnan* (Beirut: Lebanese University Publications, 1970), 150. Translation mine.
57. Salibi, *Modern History of Lebanon*, 27.
58. Ibid., 34–8.
59. Salibi, *House of Many Mansions*, 109.
60. Leila Fawaz, *An Occasion for War: Civil Conflict in Lebanon and Damascus in 1860* (London: I. B Tauris, 1994), 30.
61. Abu Shakara, *Al-Hrakat fi Lubnan*, as quoted in Fawaz, *An Occasion for War*, 72.
62. Engin Akarli, *The Long Peace: Ottoman Lebanon, 1861–1920* (Berkeley: University of California Press, 1993).
63. *Al-Jabal: Difa'an 'an al-Woujoud wal Karamah*, 23–4.
64. Akarli, *The Long Peace*, 83.
65. Butrus Daw, *Tarīkh al-Mawārinah al-Dīnī wa-al-Sīyāsī wa-al-Haḍārī* (Beirut: Dār al-Nahār, 1977), vol. 3, 171.
66. Walid Phares, 'The Historical Background of the War of the Mountains', *Al-Masiraa'* 4 (1984), 51.
67. Salibi, *House of Many Mansions*, 78.
68. Ibid., 83.
69. Ibid., 84.
70. Ibid., 85.
71. Salibi, *House of Many Mansions*, 131.
72. Fawwaz Traboulsi, *A History of Modern Lebanon* (London: Pluto Press, 2007), 115.
73. Salibi, *House of Many Mansions*, 136.

74. Ibid., 148.
75. Phoenix dactylifera.
76. Ibid., 173.
77. Ibid., 85.
78. Kamal Salibi. 'The Maronites of Lebanon under Frankish and Mamluk Rule (1099–1516)', *Arabica* 4 (1957), 288.
79. Kenneth Setton, *A History of the Crusades* (Madison: University of Wisconsin Press, 1969).
80. William of Tyre, as quoted in Salibi, 'The Maronites of Lebanon', 290–1.
81. The Crusader Kingdom of Tripoli fell in 1289.
82. Salibi, *House of Many Mansions*, 6.
83. Matti Moosa, *The Maronites in History* (Syracuse: Syracuse University Press, 1986), 195.
84. Anṭwān Khūrī Ḥarb, *Al-Mawārinah: Tārīkh wa-Thawābit* ([Beirut]: Al-Rābiṭah al-Mārūnīyah, 1998), 82.
85. Kamal Salibi, *Maronite Historians of Medieval Lebanon, with a Preface by Bernard Lewis* (Beirut: Paris Naufal, 1959), 44–5.
86. Kamal Salibi, 'The Maronite Church in the Middle Ages and Its Union with Rome', *Oriens Christianus* 42 (1958), 95.
87. John Joseph, *Muslim-Christian Relations and Inter-Christian Rivalries in the Middle East: The Case of the Jacobites in an Age of Transition* (Albany: State University of New York Press, 1984), 110.
88. Moosa, *The Maronites*, i.
89. Ibid., 177.
90. Ibid., 193.
91. Salibi, 'The Maronite Church in the Middle Ages', 99–100.
92. Charles Frazee, *Catholics and Sultans: The Church and the Ottoman Empire, 1453–1923* (London: Cambridge University Press, 1983), 138–9.
93. See page 52. See also Abdulrazzak Patel, *The Arab Nahdah: The Making of the Intellectual and Humanist Movement* (Edinburgh: University Publishing Online, 2013). <http://universitypublishingonline.org/edinburgh/ebook.jsf?bid=CBO9780748677900>
94. Kenneth Setton, *The Papacy and the Levant, 1204–1571* (Philadelphia: American Philosophical Society, 1976), vol. 3, 401.
95. Christopher M. Andrew and A. S. Kanya-Forstner, *The Climax of French Imperial Expansion, 1914–1924* (Palo Alto: Stanford University Press, 1981), 40.

96. Frazee, *Catholics and Sultans*, 141.
97. Salibi, *House of Many Mansions*, 105.
98. France, Britain, Prussia, Austria, and Russia.
99. Akarli, *The Long Peace*, 86.
100. Yehoshua Porath, 'The Peasant Revolt of 1858–1861 in Kisrawan', *Asian and African Studies Annual* 2 (1966), 77–157.
101. Ibid., 134–5.
102. Fawaz, *An Occasion for War*, 207.
103. Davide Rodogno, *Against Massacre: Humanitarian Interventions in the Ottoman Empire, 1815–1914: The Emergence of a European Concept and International Practice* (Princeton: Princeton University Press, 2012), 106.
104. Fawaz, *An Occasion for War*, 114.
105. As quoted in Fawaz, *An Occasion for War*, 115.
106. Rodogno, *Against Massacre*, 112.
107. For a full history of these schools, see Abdul Rahim Abu-Husayn, 'The "Lebanon Schools" (1853–1873): A Local Venture in Rural Education', in *The Syrian Land: Processes of Integration and Fragmentation: Bilād Al-Shām from the 18th to the 20th Century*, ed. Thomas Philipp and Birgit Schaebler (Stuttgart: F. Steiner, 1998), 205–20.
108. Kamal Salibi, *Ṭāir ᶜalá Sindiyānah: Mudhakkirāt* ('Ammān: Dār al-Shurūq, 2002), 25.
109. John P. Spagnolo, *France and Ottoman Lebanon* (London: Ithaca Press, 1977), 36.
110. Ibid., 46–7.
111. Carol Hakim, *The Origins of the Lebanese National Idea, 1840–1920* (Berkeley: University of California Press, 2013), 101.
112. Hakim, *Origins of the Lebanese National Idea*, 108.
113. Ibid., 105.
114. Ibid., 117–18.
115. Asher Kaufman, *Reviving Phoenicia: The Search for Identity in Lebanon* (London: I. B. Tauris, 2004), 31.
116. Salibi, *House of Many Mansions*, 131.
117. Lammens' works have been discussed in the previous chapter.
118. Asher Kaufman, '"Tell Us Our History": Charles Corm, Mount Lebanon and Lebanese Nationalism', *Middle Eastern Studies* 40 (2004), 5.
119. Rania Maktabi, 'The Lebanese Census of 1932 Revisited: Who are the Lebanese?' *British Journal of Middle Eastern Studies* 26, no. 2 (1999): 219–41.

120. As translated by Kaufman, 'Tell Us Our History', 25.
121. Ibid.
122. Corm, as quoted in Laura Zittrain Eisenberg, *Lebanon in the Early Zionist Imagination, 1900–1948* (Detroit: Wayne State University Press, 1994), 64.
123. Bulus Najm, *La Question du Liban: Étude d'histoire diplomatique et de droit international* (Paris: A. Rousseau, 1908).
124. For more details on the Young Turks and the Arabs, see Hasan Kayalı, *Arabs and Young Turks: Ottomanism, Arabism and Islamism in the Ottoman Empire, 1908–1918* (Berkeley: University of California Press, 1997).
125. Kais Firro, *Inventing Lebanon: Nationalism and the State Under the Mandate* (London: I. B. Tauris, 2003), 17.
126. Hakim, *Origins of the Lebanese National Idea*, 190.
127. Ibid., 192.
128. For more information on the famine during World War I, see Leila Tarazi Fawaz, *A Land of Aching Hearts: The Middle East in the Great War* (Cambridge, MA: Harvard University Press, 2014).
129. Patriarch Hoayek dispatched a third delegation in February 1920, headed by Abdallah Khuri.
130. Hoayek's memorandum, as quoted and translated in Franck Salameh, *Language, Memory, and Identity in the Middle East: The Case for Lebanon* (Lanham: Lexington Books, 2010), 91.
131. Gouraud, as quoted and translated in Franck Salameh, *Language, Memory, and Identity in the Middle East*, 93.
132. Meir Zamir, *The Formation of Modern Lebanon* (Ithaca: Cornell University Press, 1988), 25.
133. Joseph Abou Khalil, *Qiṣṣat al-Mawārinah fī al-Ḥarb: Sīrah Dhātīyah* (Bayrūt: Sharikat al-Maṭbūʻāt lil-Tawzīʻ wa-al-Nashr, 1990), 145.
134. Ibid.
135. Ibid., 155. Translation mine.
136. Interview with Saleh Zahreddine, Druze Oral History Project, 18 July 1984. Interview number 1100.
137. For a detailed account of the Druze relationship with the Lebanese state, see Yusri Hazran, *The Druze Community and the Lebanese State: Between Confrontation and Reconciliation* (London: Routledge, 2014).
138. Traboulsi, *History of Modern Lebanon*, 115.
139. Bronislaw Malinowski and Robert Redfield, *Magic, Science and Religion: And Other Essays* (Garden City: Doubleday, 1954), 102.

3

THE COMMUNAL CENTRES OF POWER AND ELEMENTS OF COLLECTIVE IDENTITY

In his famous lecture 'What is a Nation' (1882), Ernest Renan laid out what he believed were the main pillars of a nation. Renan systematically dissected the existing misperceptions *vis-à-vis* nationalism by clearly affirming that 'Man is a slave neither of his race nor his language, nor of his religion, nor of the course of rivers nor of the direction taken by mountain chains. A large aggregate of men, healthy in mind and warm of heart, creates the kind of moral conscience which we call a nation'.[1] According to Renan, the main and perhaps only prerequisite for a nation is the collective will of the people, while all other claims are nothing but mere myth. Renan emphasised that 'a nation is a soul, a spiritual principle. Two things which, properly speaking, are really one and the same constitute this soul, this spiritual principle. One is the past, the other is the present'.[2] Most of the modern experiments at nation-building hoped to accommodate or create a common heritage for people occupying the same terrain, in the hope that this constructed model could serve as the nation's building block. More often than not, this process was carried out by the state or its auxiliary agencies, which produced a wide range of cultural products (history books, anthems, anniversaries and statues) to act as 'glue' for the citizens of the same state. At least in theory, these groups were expected to shed their communal identities over the course of time, or to simply incorporate them into the meta-narrative crafted by the authoritative centres of power, mainly the state. In the case of the Druze and the Maronites, these communal identities were preserved through a number of organic institutions which either created, propagated, or remolded the past to serve the groups' immediate or strategic goals.

In the fall of 1860, Renan arrived on the shores of Lebanon as a member of a scientific mission attached to the French forces dispatched by Emperor Napoleon III to end to the civil war raging between the Druze and the Maronites. During his stay, Renan conducted several archeological excavations that unearthed Phoenician and other Semitic inscriptions and artifacts. After his return to France, Renan published the findings resulting from his stay in the Levant in a book entitled *Mission de Phénicie*.[3] Renan's work greatly helped to popularise the Phoenician past of Lebanon in the West and beyond, especially since these claims were packaged in scientific garb and by a scholar of great acclaim. However, it is perhaps paradoxical that Renan, who emphasised collective will as essential to the rise of any nation, lent his support to one Lebanese faction over another, thus making the process of an all-encompassing Lebanese nationalist project even more elusive. Be that as it may, Renan's remarks about statehood and the soul of a nation (both past and present) beg the following question: How could the Maronites and the Druze, each with their own distinct soul, exist in the same body? More importantly, how could these two souls resist the many attempts to domesticate them and forge them into a nation? The present chapter will explore how both the Druze and the Maronites were able to keep their respective collective identities fairly intact, and which centres of interest were responsible for the preservation of these conflicting identities over an extended period of time.

According to Michael Johnson, the Maronite combatants of 1975 and the following years 'might have thought they remembered the appalling events of 1860; however, there is no indication that there was an unbroken line of communal fear and hatred from 1860 to 1975'.[4] In light of this study's findings, it seems that both the Druze and the Maronite communities maintained a more or less unbroken, or perhaps fabricated bond with an imagined or real past, which each community used to serve its political project. Each community's collective memory is transmitted through two mediums: either socially by intra-group interaction, or instrumentally through active agents. In this case, these active agents comprised the Maronite Church and its subsidiary institutions, and the Druze religious and political leadership who utilised cultural tools to mould and distribute these memories.[5] Such cultural tools range from story-telling and ritual performances to paintings, architecture, monuments, language, music, photos and film; over time, these create sites of memory (especially monuments, archives, cemeteries, museums and the like). These sites represent arenas where a group can 'recollect knowledge(s) of the past and convey and sustain it by a circulation of signs that calls attention to its own logic of inclusion, exclusion, and selective in completeness'.[6]

The Custodians of Identity

As early as in the seventeenth century, the Maronite Church embodied the Maronite political project that defined Lebanon as a homeland for the Christians of the East. The church's union with Rome in the twelfth century greatly empowered its clergy and augmented the resources at its disposal, offering a religious as well as political backbone. However, local forces within the church, mainly the Monastic Orders (the Lebanese Maronite Order, the Carmelite Order, and the Antonine Maronite Order) played a key role in moulding and, more importantly, preserving a Maronite identity. While all these orders have equally contributed to the Maronite community, it is the Lebanese Maronite Order that takes a leading position, in its religious as well as socio-economic capacity.[7]

This institution, as its history indicates, was not created on the initiative of the church, but established and developed against its will. In 1695, three young Maronite monks – Jibra'il Hawwa, Abdallah Qaraali and Joseph (Yusuf) al-Bite, all scions of leading Aleppan merchant families – moved to Mount Lebanon and commenced to explore the monasteries in the region so as to establish a new monastic order. They wanted to apply clear-cut rules and regulations for monastic life, which until that time had tended to follow earlier monastic traditions and practices without structure or institution to guide and supervise their activities. Following an arduous process, which involved a tug-of-war with the church, the order finally received the seal of approval from Patriarch Istfan al-Duwayhi. At a later stage, in 1770, this new order split into an Aleppan and a Lebanese branch. The Lebanese branch – the *baladiyah*, meaning 'homegrown' or 'local order' – slowly established itself as a socio-economic powerhouse, as it gradually started to replace the Maronite nobility in many aspects of the local economy. The powerful families of tax-farmers, appointed by the local government or the Ottoman authorities, saw their economic resources dwindling, especially during the reign of Emir Bashir II, and thus had to hand over to the orders some of the monasteries they had subsidised. Richard van Leeuwen's *Notables and Clergy in Mount Lebanon* has traced the financial and political rise of these monastic orders, which through a series of agreements with local feudal families, such as the Khazens, as well as their adoption of efficient administration succeeded in significantly expanding their real-estate portfolio.[8] Having been born out of the intention to see change within the Maronite Church, the monastic order was naturally inclined to support any movement that promoted reform. The order's chance to further advance its reformist goals came in 1736, with what was referred to as the Lebanese Council (*al-Majma' al-Lubnani*). The Lebanese Council was the first in a series of measures taken by the Vatican to strengthen the orthodoxy of the Maronite Church. At the top of its agenda, this synod sought the introduction of a number of structural changes in the church hierarchy, especially at the senior level, as well as the adoption of regulations that would delimit the influence of lay notables in the internal workings of the church.[9] The Lebanese Order was fully supportive of the council's decision to give more weight to commoners and clerics that hailed from humble backgrounds, allowing them to participate in affairs formerly restricted to a privileged few. In his book *A Concise History of the Lebanese Maronite Order*, Father Youssef Mahfouz, a member of the Lebanese Order, has depicted the tension between the monks and the traditional Maronite clergy on the eve of 1736. Although writing in 1969, Mahfouz lashed out at the traditional Maronite clerics who had:

> received their education in the college in Rome and were lost and sometimes pompous, because of the fact they have acquired from the West a mentality which clearly clashes with the mentality of their countrymen, and they [clerics] were unable to reconcile these two mentalities. The Maronite people live in utter minimalism while only few of them are governed by pretentiousness and the tyranny of their leaders.

Mahfouz, however, distinguished the monastic orders from the traditional church structure; he has stated:

> It [the Lebanese Order] was the only organization which could have been entrusted with carrying out a set of reforms throughout the Maronite community, mainly because all its members were unified and enlisted in serving a common good no matter what difficulties they would confront or regardless of the price they had to pay.[10]

The Lebanese Order's zeal to see this council succeed went as far as contributing to the expenses of the synod 6,000 piasters, a small fortune by the standards of the time.[11] Quite interestingly, the anti-council faction supported by the notables went out of their way to derail the task of the papal emissary, in an effort to keep matters as they were. The gradual adoption of the decisions of the synod was a victory for the monks over the traditional clergy, and the beginning of a democratisation process within the church. This process was felt throughout the next century, and in the end allowed a cleric of lower social rank, such as Bulus Mas'ad, to be elected head of the church.

An equally important accomplishment of the 1736 synod was the adoption of mandatory education for all Maronites, male or female, a measure which over time gave them a palpable advantage over the Druze. The synod dictated:

> teachers ... to abide by the public order rules, to teach the youngsters in schools the principles of reading and writing in Syriac and in Arabic, then to teach them the psalms, then the mass service book and the daily prayers, then the New Testament. In case the students prove to have exceptional capacities for learning, teachers have to inculcate to them Syriac and Arabic grammars then the melody science, calculation, and later on to promote them to higher studies. Higher studies encompass rhetoric, poetry writing, philosophy, topography, arithmetic, cosmology and other mathematical sciences. It gathers law principles, Gospel explanations, conceptual and literary theology, and any important and relevant matters they find necessary for them to accept the sacraments, and to hold rituals and celebrations.[12]

To accomplish these goals, the synod ordered each parish to set up a school to carry out this educational mission, as:

leaders of dioceses, towns and villages, farms and convents, individually and collectively, to cooperate and work hand in hand to promote this important and useful work. It invited bishops and priests, heads of monasteries and convents, to work on putting a teacher where needed, to write down the names of the youngsters at the age of learning, and to force their parents to take them to schools whether they liked it or not. In case the family was poor and needy, it asked the monasteries or the local church to provide for them either through their own wealth or through collecting alms on Sundays. As for the teacher fees, a part was to be paid by the church or the monastery (provided the teacher is not one of the fathers or monks) and the remaining was to be paid by the parents.[13]

The Lebanese Order would pursue these directives with remarkable vigour and dedication, setting up an impressive network of schools across Lebanon, reaching as far as Cyprus, Akka and Latakia. These schools offered the 'Maronite people' an education that ranged from literacy and simple arithmetic courses, to more advanced degrees equivalent to the modern high school diploma. By 1950, after the founding of Holy Spirit University in Kaslik, the order had at its disposal a fully functioning educational system and curriculum, from primary education to more advanced university degrees. Many of these monastic institutions also included printing presses that produced and disseminated publications of both religious and secular nature, which allowed the monks to further extend their reach.[14] This educational expansion led by the order greatly empowered the Maronite community, so that by the mid-seventeenth century the Maronites became the main interlocutors with the West on all matters pertaining to commerce, primarily the silk trade.[15]

The Warrior Monks

The role of these monastic orders went beyond merely educating the youth, as they were also crucial in forging a collective identity within the community. As custodians of Maronite identity, they also played a crucial role in militarising the Maronite youth, especially in the years leading up to the civil war in 1975. Tanyous Nujaym has confirmed that the Lebanese Monastic Order helped in moulding Maronite identity on several levels. First, through . . .

its elaborate organisational structure and its vast and rich property and its pioneering role, second as an entity that preserves authenticity and the legacy of the community ... Third by ensuring the full commitment [of the Maronites] to Catholicism while still preserving their own [Lebanese] identity. Finally, and most importantly, a model for preserving the Maronite existence the special Lebanese status and propagating the uniqueness of Lebanon.[16]

In brief, these monks, through their unmediated daily interaction with their congregation, used different mediums to disseminate their creed which was completely aligned with the Maronite political project. Many of the combatants of the Christian militia during the civil war of 1975–90, especially the younger crowd, looked at the traditional church authority with apathy and saw them as distant and far removed from their hopes and aspirations. Patriarch Anthony Khoraish (1975–86), with 'his namby-pamby pro-Palestinian' attitude, was overshadowed by the heads of the monastic order. Charbel Kassis (1974–80) and Bulus Na'aman (1980–6), superiors of the order, with their hands-on approach, were far more popular and influential than the patriarch, as their rhetoric and actions were more in sync with the mood of the Maronite commoners.[17] The Muslims and the Leftists equally detested these monks, as they regarded them as the main instigators of hatred, as well as the financiers behind the weapons purchased for the Christian militias. This last accusation was confirmed by Na'aman, when he related to me a verbal altercation he had had with Yasser Arafat (PLO Chairman) and Salah Khalaf (Abu Iyad), a senior PLO official.

Khalaf, who had joined Yasser Arafat at one of his many meetings, as a joke asked Na'aman to donate the 4.5 million LBP he had collected from his last fundraising trip abroad (to be used for weapons purchases) to the PLO, which, as Arafat added, were also to be used to purchase land in Palestine. Na'aman responded coolly to the challenge: 'So you know, the Lebanese Resistance has collected fifteen, not only four million LBP, and we have enough money to buy both land and weapons, and let me remind you it was you, not us, who sold their land [to the Jews]'.[18] Kassis was equally confrontational in his own public statements, as he confirmed that 'monks are existentially and organically linked to the people . . . and in order to defend himself, every Christian has the right to be trained to handle weapons'.[19] Therefore, the order saw it prudent to encourage its monks to participate in combat and to allow the Christine militias to use its property and monasteries for logistics and weapon storage.[20] The Druze later used this last action during and after the battles in 1983 to vindicate their looting and demolition of many churches and monasteries. The monk's warrior-like stance, as well as their die-hard commitment to their cause, made Kamal Joumblatt remark in his usual sarcastic fashion: 'The tonsured heads of Lebanese monks give off a golden halo'.[21] The hatred towards these clerics was equally shared by common Druze folk – my maternal grandmother is a case in point. Years after the end of the war, she cautioned me as a teenager never to donate money to any church, because 'this money would be used to buy weapons to kill us [Druze]'.

Despite being 'relatively unsophisticated students of simpler stock than the middle-class boys and girls who attended USJ or AUB', as Johnathan Randal has described them, the students who graduated from these monastic institutions shared a palpable fervour for the above-mentioned Maronite myth.[22] Jocelyn Khoueiry, the commander of the *Nizamiyat* (the female fighting division of the Lebanese Forces), was a student of theology at Kaslik University and soon became a poster-child and promoter of her community's ideology. A member of the Kataeb, Khoueiry had gained fame after a picture of her in a tank top and shooting her AK-47 appeared in the local and international press. Speaking to a group of women in Souk al-Gharb, a village in the region of Aley, in 1983, Khoueiry clearly broadcast the Maronite collective identity:

> What we are experiencing today goes back well before the eight years of war, but it is rather a piece of a larger chain of events which go back 1400 years, ever since the Islamic conquest, specifically after the Battle of al-Yarmouk in 636. Some of the Christians fearing persecution went to the mountain and have survived there ever since. The people of this mountain have resisted for the last 1400 years, because they have chosen the hard course. They refused to leave and to live the life of a *Dhimmi*, so they stood their grounds and fought . . . In 1860, the Druze through trickery infil-

Figure 3.1 Jocelyn Khoueiry (LF Archives).

trated Deir al-Qamar. We will not butcher them as they did because Jesus taught us to sacrifice and to endure but to also defend our church when it is in danger. We should understand that from today, we should always be vigilant so as to avoid the trickery and deception of the Druze who have been conspiring since 1860.[23]

Notably, during most of her interviews and political activities, Khoueiry visibly wore a crucifix, and her rhetoric and manners greatly resembled those of the clergy. Monk Butrus Daw has claimed that women like Khoueiry can be traced back to the Phoenician goddess Astarte, whose female offspring – among them Jocelyn – were defending the Maronite nation by fighting in the civil war.[24]

The monks also lent their unwavering support to Bashir Gemayel, who by 1980 had become the uncontested leader of his community. Within the Lebanese Front – a hodgepodge of Christians, intellectuals, political parties, and militias – the Order of Monks represented by their father superior lobbied for Bashir's vision, a vision that more often than not clashed with that of the other members of the front.[25] The monks did not restrain their fascination with Bashir, who stood apart from the rest of the Christin political elite; similar to the monks, he was closer to the people and able to speak their language. Bulus Na'aman, branded by many as Bashir's ideological godfather, in 2012 explained this whole-hearted political support for Bashir:

> We were convinced that Bashir was the man of the hour, because he was able to fully impose his personality and leadership talent and patriotism. We never had a doubt that we will not be able to build a country on the bases of democracy, humanism and freedom unless if it is done by someone as brave as Bashir. We all supported him because we knew that he will rid the country of all its problems [PLO and Syrian forces].[26]

This sober political statement, however, does not reflect the emotional attachment that the monks had formed with Bashir, especially at the height of his power. Explaining to Syrian President Hafez al-Assad what Bashir meant to him, Na'aman went so far as to portray the young leader 'not [as] Pierre Gemayel's son, but the son of all the injustice that the Christians of the Middle East had suffered over the centuries'.[27]

The Kaslik Research Committee

Bashir on his part reciprocated the monks' admiration, as he further entrusted them with a number of missions that included mediation with other Maronite factions, as well as the PLO and their Lebanese Muslim allies. The rela-

Figure 3.2 Bashir Gemayel greeting Bulus Naʿaman; in the background, the former Lebanese Foreign Minister Charles Malik (BGF).

tionship between the order and this 'maverick leader' was institutionalised through the activities of the Kaslik Research Committee (KRC), an assembly of prominent Christian intellectuals who endorsed the 'Lebanese Idea', as propagated by Charles Corm and his associates.[28] This think-tank housed an imposing line-up of over a hundred individuals who played influential roles in a number of educational and political institutions.[29] Bashir was first introduced to this group in 1977; according to Naʿaman, there was an immediate intellectual chemistry between the members and Bashir, whom the former saw as 'an honest Lebanese willing to fully defend his country'.[30] The KRC had initially started as a subsidiary to the Lebanese Front, a coalition of Christian parties formed at the beginning of the civil war, but the rapid rise of Bashir brought the KRC closer to his ideological sphere, with some of its members becoming close confidantes and members of his inner circle. The KRC published numerous books and booklets, and organised conferences and roundtables, all with the declared intention of endorsing Lebanon as a refuge for the minorities of the Middle East against the yoke of Islam. Above all, it intended to lend support to the Lebanese Resistance, as embodied by Bashir Gemayel.[31]

The mobilising and propaganda activities of the KRC played a fundamental role in the Maronites' war efforts; however, its real contribution went beyond merely providing ideological support to Bashir or justification for his actions. The KRC gave the young warlord the much-needed ideological depth and strategic planning, which he had lacked earlier in his career. The younger son of the Kataeb Party's founder, Bashir had gained a fierce reputation of being willing to engage in bare-knuckle confrontations when needed. In comparison to his older brother Amin, who by Lebanese standards was a typical white-collar politician, he was politically restrained. For Bashir to make a transition from warrior to statesman, he desperately needed the endorsement of the KRC's members, whose reputation and experience granted him legitimacy. In addition to empowering Bashir, the KRC, as Theodore Hanf has put it, 'was coming up with radical solutions to fundamental questions on the future of the Christian communities in Lebanon',[32] which became more pressing as the civil war progressed, especially after 1976, with the entrance of the Syrian army into Lebanon and the ensuing events.

Perhaps one of these pressing questions was the following. How could the Christians survive in a predominately Muslim environment, with the demographic advantage clearly tilting towards the Muslim side? This demographic reality was exacerbated by a more dangerous call for reform and secularisation, championed by the Muslims and Leftist parties supporting the PLO. The Lebanese National Movement (LNM), headed by Kamal Joumblatt, demanded the abolition of the sectarian system that gave the Maronites privileges and unmediated access to the resources of the Lebanese state. One of the radical responses that the KRC offered to counter the LNM's demands was the adoption of new system of governance that would entertain a broad spectrum of options – ranging from decentralisation over full-scale federalism to the partition of Lebanon into self-governing districts. While many Christian intellectuals had implicitly endorsed federalism as a viable solution for Lebanon beforehand, no one had discussed it in public, apart from the occasional scholarly publication. Diplomat and judge Antoine Fatal and lawyer Musa Prince, a member of Chamoun's National Liberal Party, brought forth a detailed program that proposed a mixture of confederalism and federalism, with the intention of preserving the unity and diversity of Lebanon.[33] However, the Lebanese Front's position on this matter, at least at the beginning of the conflict, was never well defined, and they never openly asked for 'all-out federalism'. The Lebanese Front, which included old-school politicians, stressed the need for constitutional reform, but also repeatedly made it a point to demand the unity of Lebanon under the provisions of the 1943 pact. The Maronite psyche had always entertained a federalist option, or a return to the pre-1920 *Petit Liban*, which would give the Christians a clear demographic superiority, as well as the ability to resist any attempts to absorb them into their Muslim surroundings.

In January of 1977, at one of the well-known conferences held at al-Bir Monastery, Camille Chamoun, former President of the Lebanese Republic, made his position on federalism extremely clear. In his typical manner, Chamoun declared to a room full of Christian leaders and intellectuals:[34]

> The Christian, who for the last 1,400 years considers Lebanon his home, is terrified for his future and for Lebanon as a national entity. This is the first premise, and the last premise, to remove from the Muslim mind the idea that they might possibly control the fate of Lebanon now and in the future. Removing the fear that the Christians and the greed that the Muslims have is the beginning to reach[ing] a solution. Any return to the 1943 formula, coupled with any minor altercation would lead to more fighting, where we [Christians] will have to stoop to their level and implement our point of view by force, and to pay taxes on their [the Muslims'] behalf and to pay for public works and projects conducted in their areas, without them even showing gratitude. We have to all agree to cooperate and to live together in amity and this can be achieved by adopting a new political of governance. In my opinion, I suggest confederalism, because we just cannot live with them and to grant them their demands which will persevere until they are rid of us. I am willing to endorse any plan that takes such a [confederate] direction.[35]

Chamoun's blunt and clearly condescending manner towards the Muslims reflected his own frustration with the Lebanese political system and his realisation that the privileged status of the Maronites was perhaps a thing of the past. This projection of inferiority led to a spreading phobia. The Maronites saw themselves being transformed into *dhimmi* subjects with no legal or social rights of any kind.

This *dhimmi* status refers to the treatment given to the Jews and Christians conquered by the early Muslim armies, according to which those people classified in the Qur'an as 'People of the Book' are given protection in exchange for a *jizyah* (head tax). In return, *dhimmis* were expected to abide by a set of rules, such as abstaining from wearing certain colours in public and on the streets giving the right of way to Muslims.[36] The Maronites, however, had never been subjected to such mental or physical abuse, because technically they had never lived under direct Muslim rule; in their own admission, under the Druze emirate their status had been that of a privileged community. Nevertheless, at that time the Maronite establishment's rhetoric underscored the *dhimmi* fate that would await the Christians if the Palestinians or their allies were to triumph. Many of the rumours circulating at the beginning of the conflicts between the Christians militias, the PLO and their allies included talk of deporting the entire Maronite population to North America on board of ships, as part of a bigger conspiracy engineered by Henry Kissinger, the US Secretary of State, to install the Palestinians in their place.[37] While there existed no evidence of such a conspiracy, the tone of many Maronite politicians and intellectuals in their speeches and publications reminded their constituency of what would be at stake if the Maronites lost the war. Bashir Gemayel forcefully declared that the real fight of the Lebanese Christians was to have a 'country where we can live without bowing our heads to the ground, a place where nobody can come and tell us "Wear a turban or die" as they did during the rule by the Turks'.[38] Bulus Na'aman went even further, branding Islam as a religion essentially incapable of tolerating anything distinct from it:

> Islam is a system with totalitarian demands on all aspects of society ... if there is any provision for people of a different faith, then it is only in a subordinate position. Islam is not backwards compared to Christianity, as many believe. It is simply different, its character prevents it changing. An Islam that accepted a secular society will no longer be Islam.[39]

The publications of the KRC and its members also took a similar stance. Writing under the pen name Amin Naji, Antoine Najm's *Lan Na'isha*

Dhimmiyyīn (We Will Not Live as *Dhimmis*) detailed why it was not possible for the Lebanese to continue operating under the 1943 pact. Doing so would only lead to the inevitable – that is, Muslims persecuting and ultimately dominating Christians.[40] Najm unequivocally declared that, as Christians, we 'do not agree to be *dhimmi*s, or second class citizens, where they enjoyed perhaps the best conditions in their material life and in terms of reproduction, [. . .] but [where] their effective rights are lower than those of their fellow Muslims'.[41] A school teacher by profession and originally from Qartaba in the Byblos region of Mount Lebanon, Najm had grown up in the predominately Muslim city of Tripoli where his father was employed. Still a charming and candid person in his eighties, Najm recalled how his father in the marketplace got into a fistfight with a Muslim because the latter had yelled at his father to use the side of the road closer to the gutter, since he himself, as a Muslim, had the right of way.[42] This naturally enraged Najm's father, who proceeded to assault the man who disrespected him for being a non-Muslim.[43]

The Arab debacle in the 1967 war with Israel was also an eye-opener for Najm. At that time, Najm was teaching in a public school, and as the news about the Arab's shocking defeat broke, Najm's Muslim colleagues stopped talking to him, suddenly and without any provocation. Najm admitted that the episode troubled him greatly, as he truly never considered himself anti-Arab; however, his Muslim fellow teachers assumed that he was, simply because of his Maronite identity. In addition to other factors, these personal experiences confirmed to Najm that now, more than ever, a reconsideration of the 'Lebanese Formula' constituted the only salvation for the Christians. Consequently, Najm's political career and nearly all of his writings, especially after the outbreak of the civil war, revolved around devising a federal solution for the Lebanese problem, earning him the title 'Philosopher of Lebanese Federalism'. Paradoxically, Najm was a senior member of the Kataeb and the head of its 'Creed Branch', responsible for instructing members in party doctrine and ideology.

The Kataeb: In the Service of Lebanon

Founded in 1936 and fashioned after the European fascist movements of the time, the Kataeb was a social democratic party with essentially unpretentious goals. Its founder was Pierre Gemayel, a pharmacist and avid football player.

Figure 3.3 Pierre Gemayel, founder of al-Kataeb, surrounded by members of his party (Wassim Jabre).

Writing about the party in the early stages of the civil war, Frank Stoakes has seen the Kataeb as a 'builder, surrogate and defender of the [Lebanese] State'.[44] Stoakes's fascination with the Kataeb partially stemmed from his shadowing some of its senior members and his visits to their para-military training camps. According to Stoakes, the Kataeb's existential aim was 'the preservation of the state and the advancement of society, and the second is subordinate to the first; without the state there can be no progress'.[45] In 1943, the Kataeb adopted the phrase 'in the service of Lebanon' as its main mantra and was one of the main factions that, along with its Muslim equivalent, the al-Najada Party, took to the streets for what is popularly referred to as the 'battle of Lebanese independence'. Following this brief anti-French revolt, the al-Kataeb unreservedly supported the 1943 national pact and the simple power-sharing arrangement which clearly privileged the Maronites over the rest of all other Lebanese. This pro-pact stance became part and parcel of much of the party's politics and actions well into the civil war.

Although being a founding member of the Lebanese Front, which at times issued innumerable anti-pact statements, Pierre Gemayel and his party's old guard always underscored the intransience of the National Pact. Joseph Abu Khalil, a close confidant of both Pierre and Bashir Gemayel, confirmed that at a certain point Bashir opposed his father concerning the National Pact, which Pierre until 'his last breath fully embraced'.[46] Therefore, despite what Andre Sleiman has called the 'Grand Debate' about the abolition of the National Pact and the adoption of federalism, within the Kataeb the party establishment – which coincidentally included Pierre's older son Amin –

Figure 3.4 Al-Kataeb parade, 1937 (Wassim Jabre).

nipped federalism in the bud and prevented Bashir from incorporating it into the mainstream doctrine.⁴⁷

For this anti-pact or federalist tendency to develop beyond mere rhetoric, there needed to exist an intellectual incubator that could help this movement grow, something that was not possible within the conservative setting of the Kataeb's structure. The KRC was precisely the incubator that the Maronite identity needed: There, one could try out and discuss ideas that previously would have been considered treason, at least from the perspective of the Lebanese Muslims who shunned the West and viewed it as an enemy of the Arabs and a friend to Israel. It is noteworthy that after 1978 the KRC republished some of the studies promoting federalism written before or at the beginning of the civil war (1975) and then published under an alias or anonymously, but this time under the name of the author. One such publication was Fouad Ephrem al-Boustani's *Le Problème du Liban*, which Holy Spirit University republished in 1978.⁴⁸ Furthermore, many leading Kataeb members, including Bashir Gemayel and Antoine Najm, were able to flaunt their federalist aspirations without contradicting the pro-pact party to which they officially belonged, thanks to their involvement with the KRC.

More importantly, by offering the logistical and intellectual scaffolding for this project, the Lebanese Order of Monks gave Bashir and his team the ability to disseminate these ideas beyond the Maronite intellectual elite. While Maronite collective identity is influenced by many entities and factors, such as education and class structures, it was these institutions that radicalised the Maronites and placed them in stark opposition to other Lebanese communities. As will be demonstrated below, this recasting and strengthening of collective perceptions also applied to the Druze community, but through different vehicles, conveyances and centres of power.

The Druze Way

As a faith, the Druze are an extremely introverted group that allows neither proselytising nor intermarriage. When the movement started under the Fatimid Caliph al-Hakim, it was essentially a missionary endeavour that dispatched hundreds of preachers to different regions of the caliphate, including present-day Lebanon. Following the disappearance and possible murder of al-Hakim, the members of his movement underwent a period of persecution or *mihna*, which lasted for seven years.[49] In 1043, the door of the *da'wa* (calling) was permanently sealed, as the Druze themselves call it, and no new initiates were permitted to become part of this movement. This sense of exclusivity led the Druze to see themselves as a chosen folk blessed enough to belong to a family that embraced the call for *tawhid*. In addition, the Druze are expected to practise endogamy to strengthen social cohesion; therefore, the Druze who deviate from this norm are weakening this eternal bond and are shunned, religiously and socially. Such an expulsion can range as far as the extreme measure of excommunicating the violator and refusing to bury their corpse in a Druze cemetery, where Druze clerics usually administered the last rites during the burial ceremony. Any Druze who strays from the communal and religious consensus will find themselves ostracised and denied the privileges and protection awarded by their clan. The Druze go even further by asserting that, for someone to be a Druze, both parents have to be Druze. Consequently, anyone born from a Druze father and a non-Druze mother can never be fully recognised as Druze and thus never be treated as equal. A child born to a Druze father, but from a non-Druze mother, can never attain the full rank of a Druze.[50]

Politically, the Druze perceive that their community's strength resides in their unwavering unity and cohesiveness, especially when faced with external challenges. The fact that the Druze were a heterodox minority not exceeding a number of 750,000 worldwide made unity a central theme within the community.[51] After the fall of the Ottoman Empire, the Druze who were spread out across the Levant played an important role in the formation of the new nation-states – that is, Syria, Lebanon and, to a lesser extent, Palestine-Israel. Although the Druze worldwide share a common bond, their political decision-making processes have always been directed by the community's current interests. In 1925, the Druze of Syria under the leadership of Sultan Pasha al-Atrash took up arms against the French mandate. The Great Syrian Revolt that ensued spread to other parts of Syria and lasted until 1927. Across the border, however, the majority of the Druze of Lebanon, contrary to custom, did not come to the aid of their Syrian Druze brethren and preferred to maintain their pro-French standing. In 1921, the decision to appease and collaborate with the French mandate cost Fouad Joumblatt (Kamal's father), who served as administrator of the Shuf district, his life. Local Druze rivals known for their Arab nationalist fervour, led by Shakib Wahab, ambushed and fatally wounded him in the 'Ainbal Valley, in the district of Shuf.[52]

While the Druze have always maintained unity in the face of danger, their political history bears witness to bitter rivalries between the different factions competing for wealth and power, a struggle that eventually weakened the Druze. At least sine the seventeenth century, the Druze have been traditionally divided into two main political factions: the Joumblatti and the Yazbaki, headed by the houses of Joumblatt and Arslan, respectively.[53] Consequently, the majority of the Druze 'aligned themselves with either one side or the other, as dictated by their interests at any particular time'.[54] The Druze as a society are a highly stratified group: Class plays an important role in their daily lives, as social mobility within the sect is not entirely impossible, but fairly difficult to achieve. Leading the Druze are local notables or sheikhs who draw their authority from their historic status, as well as from their ability to lead and protect the group and cater to its needs. These needs are met partially with the funds generated by the sheikhs' tax farming, or out of their own pocket, if needed. In his book *Being a Druze*, Fouad Khuri has remarked how the Druze, unlike other Lebanese groups, have stuck to their traditional leadership, even when the latter were unable to deliver on these clientelistic services. However, Khuri has also confirmed, full of admiration, that these sheikhs in return exhibited 'steadfastness and persistence, in the face of the socio-economic changes that swept, as they still do, throughout Druze society'.[55] These notables have maintained a direct relationship with their constituency, which also extends to any non-Druze who pledge allegiance to their household, something that is usually passed on through generations. Most of the Druze interviewees claiming allegiance to the Joumblatt house made it clear that their family ties to the *Dar al-Moukhtara* (Palace of Moukhtara) go back centuries and that at least one or more of their ancestors fought and spilled blood under the Joumblatt's banner.

Lost Druze History

The Druze, as a community, do not rely on written sources to learn about their past or to propagate their group identity. They primarily employ communal structures, as well as socio-religious elements to facilitate their group's memory formation process. While the Maronites have produced copious works of history documenting their political and social evolution, the Druze have faltered on this front. The only two surviving works by Druze authors are Salih bin Yahya's *Tārīkh Bayrūt* and Ibn Sabat's *Ṣidq al-Akhbār*, both of which are limited due to a partial view of Druze history.[56] In the end, the Maronites authored most of the primary sources on the Druze, as demonstrated in the earlier chapters. However, according to the Druze, these works are skewed, as they only served the Maronite political project and sidelined the Druze's contribution to the founding of modern Lebanon.

It is perplexing why the Druze, for all their valour and military victories, have fallen short in terms of recording their history. Rajeh Naim has claimed that the Druze were too preoccupied with their military conquests and operations and did not bother to write down their own history and exploits, as they considered record-keeping a secondary task.[57] Yet, such an explanation seems too simplistic and even unlikely, as different Druze leaders employed an elaborate administrative hierarchy and people capable of recording events in the minutest detail. One may presume that the series of Ottoman punitive campaigns not only killed a large number of Druze, but also destroyed the records that the Druze kept along with their holy religious letters (*Rasa'il al-*

Hikma). Possibly, among the various religious scrolls that Ibn Tulun claimed to have been captured by the Ottomans, there existed works of history similar to the two that survived.[58]

The lack of written sources has forced the Druze to rely heavily on oral tradition to preserve the socio-political legacy of their ancestors. Much of the stories of Druze lineage, valour and supposed religious persecution are perpetuated through oral traditions which, at least for the Druze, carry equal or greater weight than written sources. This oral transmission is naturally regulated by various centres of power within the group, in order to ensure that such traditions are always in line with the community's collective memory.

Issam Aintrazi (Abu Said), the military commander of the PSP in Beirut, has confirmed that, while growing up in his Druze surroundings, oral tradition was infinitely more influential for his historical perception than the textbooks he used to read in school.[59] Aintrazi, who holds an MA in History from the State University of New York, has stressed the impact of the Druze familial sphere on the formation of his own adolescent perception of the world. Born in 1953, Abu Said grew up in Beirut and found it difficult to adjust to the various schools he was forced to attend. This was partially because his classmates would at times bully him for being a Druze, until his mother finally decided to move him to a Druze-owned school in Choueifat. Aintrazi said that other members of his community were also victims of bullying, which consequently led them to be more cohesive and look to their sect for moral and physical protection. According to Aintrazi:

> while in school we were taught that Emir Bashir al-Shihabi was a Lebanese hero, in our community he was a dog and a villain, they never taught us anything about Sheikh Bashir, but as children we would listen to the grownups talk amongst each other and thus learnt the true history of the Druze, from one generation to the other.[60]

This was equally true of the 1860 Druze–Maronite clashes, as the history books that Aintrazi read at school dealt with these events from a pro-Maronite vantage point, depicting the Druze as aggressors and the Maronites as hapless victims – something that Druze oral tradition rejected. Abu Said admitted that, although he was too young to remember the events of 1958, he and his Druze friends used to listen to his brother-in-law, who had fought in the revolution, talk about his exploits, prompting their generation to 'wish we had gotten the chance to fight in defense of the Druze'.[61]

Druze: Blood Brothers across Generations

In addition to these oral traditions, there exists a set of socio-religious practices and beliefs as building blocks for creating a feeling of group solidarity or *'asabiyyah*. When viewed through an Ibn Khaldunian lens, the social and political evolution of the group reveals how Druze solidarity or *'asabiyyah* did not wane despite the community's evolution. On the contrary, the tribal structure remained virtually intact, regardless of whether the Druze were at their zenith of power during the reign of Fakhr al-Din or at a disadvantage under the reign of the Bashir II.[62] According to Ibn Khaldun, the strongest form of *'asabiyyah* or group solidarity is that of kinship or blood ties. This strong fraternal bond between the Druze, which at times transcends geography, is achieved due to the interaction of various social and religious elements – primarily their intrinsic belief in reincarnation, which ultimately unites them as one big family. The belief in the perpetual nature of the soul and its constant movement from one vessel to another occupies a central place in the Druze sect's socio-religious creed. Contrary to the conventional interpretation of life after death in Islam, the Druze believe that, after the body perishes, the soul simply migrates to another body.[63] For the Druze, death is therefore just the decay of the present vessel or garment, which will simply be exchanged for a newer one; therefore, the Druze refers to the act of reincarnation as *taqammus*, derived from *qammis*, meaning 'shirt'.[64]

Beyond its spiritual and religious implications, reincarnation plays an important role for creating a single bloodline, which all Druze share, regardless of space and time. This perceived lineage is usually cemented by intermarriages and births which welcome new persons into groups that call themselves clans, tribes or families. This blood tie may weaken and disappear due to natural death or marriage outside the group; however, in the case of the Druze it remains intact because of their belief in reincarnation, which ensures that this blood bond is never lost, even posthumously. According to the Druze, reincarnation is a global phenomenon that happens to all human beings, but not all religions are willing to entertain the validity of this elementary system. Fuad Khuri has poignantly stated, 'I am yet to meet to a

Druze, young or old, educated or uneducated, male or female, rich or poor who publically or privately casts doubt on his or her belief in reincarnation'.[65]

The Druze firmly believe that the soul of any Druze or *muwahid*, regardless of their social status or level of piety, is exclusively reincarnated in the body of a newborn Druze. In practical terms, a Druze born from a Druze father and mother is part of a circle, which is 'never altered by marriage, conversion or death'.[66] According to this system, all Druze are brothers in a former, present or future life because they are 'born into each other's houses'. This belief in reincarnation is disseminated within the community through different channels, but perhaps the most salient vehicle is the phenomenon known as *nutuq*. *Nutuq* means 'to speak' in Arabic and involves a child recalling their past life in detail and with an adult's assertiveness. This usually involves specifics concerning their former life, family, career and even the way they met their death. This common, yet baffling phenomenon does not happen to all Druze, but to individuals who perished in a sudden and tragic manner.[67] People who died in combat, were murdered or killed in work accidents are most likely to experience this ritual of recall, which is always oral and public. Parents of children who experience *nutuq* encourage this process by tracking down the families of the child's past life and consequently establishing a familial relationship. Many of the Druze I interviewed volunteered the information that they remembered their past life. Imad al-Awr, who participated in the War of the Mountain in 1983, stated that in his former life he had been shot in the chest in the village of Kfar Nabrakh in 1958. Imad vividly recalled the weapon he was carrying, the identity of the family members who were fighting alongside him and feeling the bullet that killed him as it entered his body.[68]

In his written testimony on the matter of reincarnation and Druze politics, Fawaz Dalal from the town of Rashaya has also narrated with great lucidity and conviction the interplay between his two lives in the context of the events of 1958 and 1982. Dalal, a high school teacher holding a Doctorate in History and Political Science, has written:

> One of those days, I was one of the people who took part in the 1958 revolution, alongside the great leader Kamal Joumblatt. Our fight was against what we called the reactionary Lebanese current which was part of the

Baghdad Pact . . . at that stage my intellectual capacity did not permit me to understand the implications of that era, nor to join the struggle out of pure conviction; however, I was one of the first to join the revolution because of my sectarian or tribal affiliation which manifested itself in the party [PSP], a journey which ended with my martyrdom. Coincidentally I was reborn in the village [Rashaya] of my former military commander, but in a family that did not share my past-life political convictions.[69]

Dalal recalled how his many encounters with his former commander 'would transport them both back to a different place, time and event' and how the former 'would validate many of the stories the young boy would share with him'.[70] As a young man, Dalal converted his anti-Joumblatti family to supporters of Kamal Joumblatt and the PSP, which he himself had joined officially. In 1982, Dalal fought with the National Resistance Movement against the invading Israeli army and their Lebanese allies. His mesmerising account of the War of the Mountain is a resounding example of how reincarnation allows the Druze to maintain an uninterrupted link across time and space:

In the painful events which occurred on Mount Lebanon, I found myself yet again going back in time twenty years, as if I was a son of that land, this land was my land and its people my people. During those events, I still recall the cries of the fighters on the various fronts. 'Here are the martyrs of 1958 fighting you but with new bodies and different names', and also another famous motto at the time: ' Why would we care if we die, we will come back in twenty years and bear arms to fight you for the same reasons and goals'.

Regardless of the stance one takes on the issue of reincarnation, whether scientific or spiritual, it is beyond doubt that the Druze consider the matter with great seriousness and place memory at the crux of their beliefs. According to a story that one of my informants told me, a child in the Shuf Mountain revealed that in his past life he had been murdered by an individual whom he identified by name. His past-life family had always assumed that their son had died in an accident and thus not suspected any foul play. Once the child convinced the past-life father of the slaying and its circumstances, the father avenged his murdered son by killing the perpetrator. This perplexing moral and judicial aspect of this tale leaves one pondering the question, to what ends are the Druze willing to go, to protect one another?

O Brother, Where Art Thou?

This fraternal relationship obliges all Druze to offer care and aid to any other Druze, as if they were immediate family members. Consequently, being a Druze involves maintaining this belief in reincarnation, as well as in other precepts of the faith in one's daily practices. While they do consider themselves a sect within Islam, the Druze do not fully practice the five pillars of Islam – that is, the profession of faith, daily prayer, *zakat* (almsgiving), fasting and pilgrimage. Instead, the Druze subscribe to a more elaborate seven-pillar code that combines both tribal and religious elements:

- Truthfulness in intent and of the tongue (*sidiq al-lisan*)
- Safeguarding brothers and sisters (*hifiz al-ikhwan*)
- Renunciation of idolatry and paganism
- Repudiation of the devil and all forces of evil
- Belief in *tawhid* of the Lord in every age and stage
- Acceptance of God's divine acts, whatever they may be
- Submission to God's divine will in private and in public[71]

Unity and fraternity are thus clearly embedded within the seven pillars of the Druze faith, and to lie or to refuse aid to a fellow Druze is a cardinal sin that leads one to lose membership in this exclusive society. Therefore, it is very common for a Druze from a different region or even a different country to rush to the aid of another Druze whom they have never met before. *Ya gheirt al-din*, the customary call used to evoke camaraderie, is enough to awaken the tribal feelings of the most secular and educated Druzes. The Druze of Lebanon fervently evoked this eternal bond in 1983 during their conflict with the Maronites. Druze from different classes, professions, regions and countries (such as Syria and Israel) rushed to the aid of their brethren, defying the political realities of the time. Chapter 6 will elaborate on this brotherly bond, with a particular focus on the role played by the Druze of Israel, whose aid to the Lebanese Druze proved to be instrumental.

Wise vs Ignorant

Despite the profound effect of reincarnation on the collective identity of the Druze and the binding function it performs, another element is still needed to ensure the propagation of the belief. This function is carried out by the Druze clerics known as *ajawid*, whose role is to guard customs and traditions, and to regulate and mediate the exchange of memories. These *ajawid* maintain that all Druze are brothers and therefore bound by a sacred oath of allegiance to this real or imagined family. Unlike the Christian Church, the Druze ecclesiastical body is not divided in an institutional or clear-cut manner. The Druze faith and religious scriptures are exclusively restricted to individuals who have been initiated into the faith, commonly referred to as *'uqqal* (wise men), while the rest fall into a category known as *al-juhhal* (the ignorant). Upon reaching adulthood, a Druze may 'ask for his religion' or to join this class of *'uqqal*, but to take such a step, according to Anis Obeid, involves adhering to 'strict rules of conduct in personal and private life and to remain under continuous peer review and scrutiny'.[72] Naturally, embracing such a life of piety includes practising temperance and shunning almost all earthly pleasures, such as smoking, consuming alcohol and overindulging at the dinner table. Learning the Druze religion greatly differs from the Christian and Islamic traditions, as the Druze faith greatly differs from any official religious schools with somewhat rigid structures. The Druze do not utilise any institutions such as the Maronite college discussed above, or al-Azhar in Cairo, the bastion of Islamic learning. Instead, learning the Druze religion involves a mentor-disciple relationship: A learned sheikh allows the novice to study under him, either by way of individual tutoring, or by joining the sheikh's circle of learning.[73] The only form of religious schooling exists in the Khalwat al-Bayada, a religious retreat in Hasbaya, in south Lebanon. The Khalwat al-Bayada, which I have visited, act as a hermitage and venue for initiates to receive religious tutoring from one or more of the learned clerics on its grounds.

Although lacking a clear religious curriculum, the Khalwat al-Bayada have played a key role in educating the Druze, as well as fortifying the bond between the *'uqqal*, who in turn go on to interact with the non-initiates and fortify their sense of belonging to the Druze community. Particularly interesting is the fact that the Khalwat al-Bayada's influence is not only restricted to the Lebanese Druze but has also played an important role in enhancing the collective nature of the Druze of the entire region and beyond. The founding of the state of Israel in 1948 precluded the Druze on its territory from crossing the border into Lebanon and from openly engaging with their Lebanese Druze brethren. However, this would radically change after the 1982 invasion and occupation of south Lebanon, as the Israeli Druze became frequent visitors and even residents of the religious seminary of Khalwat al-Bayada. The head of the Druze community in Israel, Sheikh Amin Tarif, made frequent visits to the seminary, met with its custodians and maintained with them a working relationship that culminated in Tarif's inauguration of a wing for Israeli Druze religious scholars.[74]

Promotion within the ranks of the *'uqqal* is not determined solely by the level of learning, but also by the degree of piety and commitment to the values and essence of *tawhid* that one exhibits in their daily interactions with other Druze. The most virtuous among these *'uqqal*, distinguishable by their rounded turban (*mukalwas*), are usually very few in number; at any given time, throughout the entire Levant their number has never exceeded ten.[75] Few as they may be, these clerics are the effective custodians of the sects' spiritual affairs, and while they refrain from meddling in politics, in times of crisis they have a decisive say about how the Druze should react. In 1983, the *mukalwas* clerics Abu Hassan Aref Halawi (Lebanon) and Abu Youssef Amin Tarif (Palestine) expanded their customarily spiritual position to a blatantly political one, all for the sake of protecting their coreligionists. These sheikhs usually do not issue public statements, but instead make their wishes known to visitors who seek their advice.

The active involvement of the Druze clerics in the political affairs of the community involves the *sheikh al-'aql*, who gets to wear a spiritual as well as a political hat. Historically, this institution was part and parcel of Druze political factionalism, with the Yazbaki and Joumblatti factions selecting their own sheikh for a lifetime appointment. The *sheikh al-'aql* is expected to conform to the will of the party that appointed him. The *mashyakhat al-'aql* as an institution can be traced to Sayid Abdallah al-Tanukhi, a fifteenth-century Druze religious reformer and member of the Buhturids, who ruled over the Druze at that time. Extremely revered by the Druze, Sayid Abdallah established many

Figure 3.5 *Sheikh al-'Aql* Muhammad Abu-Shaqra of the Joumblatti faction (second from left), Kamal Joumblatt and *Sheikh al-'Aql* Ali Abdul Latif of the Yazbaki faction (Sheikh Ali Abdul Latif).

of the religious legal structures and practices that survive to this day. The role of the *sheikh al-'aql* as the paramount religious authority has changed over time, to become more supportive of the political factions and the strong feudal lords that led them. In her study 'Shaykh al-'Aql and the Druze of Mount Lebanon', Judith Harik has observed the opposite of what many assume – that is, the *mashaykhat al-'aql* has contributed to the instability and feuds between the different Druze, which ultimately led to the overall weakening of the Druze political status.[76] After 1943, the Lebanese state officially recognised the dual status of both sheikhs, who legally became salaried employees of the state and attached to the Office of the Prime Minister. In 1970, with the passing of Rashid Hamada, the Yazbaki *sheikh al-'aql*, both factions agreed to unite the post under the incumbent Joumblatti sheikh, Muhammad Abu-Shaqra. Abu-Shaqra's assertive and confrontational nature proved a versatile asset to the Druze, especially in the civil war beginning in 1975.

The unification of the post of *sheikh al-'aql* allowed the Druze religious establishment to broaden its influence, as it was no longer restricted by the Joumblatti-Yazbaki divide. By that time, Kamal Joumblatt had practically overshadowed Majid Arslan, the head of the Yazbaki faction, due to many local and regional factors. Compared to Joumblatt's progressive brand, Arslan was somewhat of a traditional politician having neither a formal education nor any interest in politics beyond the clientelistic system he occupied. In 1971, with the support of Kamal Joumblatt, a number of Druze clerics launched a fundraising campaign to establish an association that would provide educational and health services to the people of the Shuf.[77] Consequently, the al-Irfan Unitarian Foundation set up a network of schools and clinics that spread across all areas inhabited by the Druze, with an estimated student body of 6,000.

Al-Irfan's curriculum, with its good academic track record, did not include any Druze religious instructions, as none of the students had reached the age of adulthood, a prerequisite for religious initiation. Despite their laymen's status, Irfan students did receive religious training anchored in the Qur'an as well as the Abrahamic tradition, but never in a manner that allowed them to claim Druze initiate status. In the course entitled *Al-Tarbiya al-Tawhidiya* (Unitarian Education), they were told the stories of different prophets in the Old Testament, stories from the Qur'an and advice on how to be a good Druze. Certainly, much of the religious and secular knowledge that these boys and girls received clearly resonated with the Druze collective identity. As a Druze foundation, al-Irfan naturally taught its students the history of Lebanon from the perspective of the Druze, which contributed to a widening gap between them and their Christian neighbours. Coincidentallly, after 1984, the civil administration that the PSP set up to replace the Lebanese state published its own history and civics textbooks. Effectively, all schools in the areas controlled by the PSP were obliged to use these books, which triggered a process of rewriting a proper history of Lebanon, very similar to what the CDSD did, as discussed above.

The sheikhs' involvement in the affairs of their community extended to all levels, as their commitment to the protection of their brethren had no limits and transcended the civilian sphere. In times of war, these men of religion actively participated in combat, providing the regular Druze fighters with motivation and vigour whenever needed, and with sorely needed numbers on the battlefield. During the War of the Mountain, these Druze clerics formed a military order known as *Quwwat Abu Ibrahim* (Forces of Abu Ibrahim), in reference to Isma'il bin Muhammad al-Tamimi, the brother-in-law of Hamza bin 'Ali, one of the five key figures in the Druze tradition.[78] Apart from their psychological effect, this fighting outfit struck decisive blows due to its ability to completely disregard some of the political restrictions that the Joumblatti faction faced, such as the relationship with the Syrian regime and their own unmasked hostility towards the state of Israel. The mere presence of these fighting clerics, in khaki versions of their traditional uniforms and skullcaps, boosted the morale of the other Druze non-initiates and gave the ongoing conflict a religious fervour.

Druze Oneness through Time and Space

One of the essential truths that most Druze hold dear is the fact that, regardless of temporal and spatial constraints, all Druze are a united entity and can always count on each other when danger lurks, especially in matters related to the survival of the sect. This feeling of unity was more or less a product of the socio-religious factors and elements used by the centres of power to erase many of the lines that divided the Druze across the Levant.

While cohesion is indeed an overall feature of the Druze, its history and composition reflect factional and clannish traits which pitted the Druze against each other in *quasi* civil wars, the War of the Mountain being one of them. Thus, there exist in their history many examples that contradict their meta-narrative downplaying diversity and underscoring cohesion. This also applies to the Lebanese Druze relationship with their coreligionists in both Syria and Israel, as there exists the assumption that the Druze of Syria and Israel are identical to their Lebanese brethren. This overarching generalisation is not entirely unwarranted, since the Druze of Syria and Israel do share the same socio-religious values, especially the above-mentioned seven pillars including the protection of their brethren (*hifiz al-ikhwan*) wherever they are to be found. However, as members of the nation-states that they helped establish, the Druze were not totally immune to the Zionist and the Baathist projects in Israel and Syria, respectively. Kais Firro has maintained that the Druze were able to resist Israel's many attempts to subjugate them, but they had to adopt a 'neo-particularism made to fit the reality of the Jewish state', thus setting themselves apart from their Palestinian Muslim milieu.[79]

Although the Druze never fully integrated into the Israeli political system, many of them were actively involved in Israeli politics and became an integral part of the Israeli armed forces, especially after 1956, when they first accepted conscription – a move that over time allowed them to acquire senior command positions. While more emphasis has been placed on their role in the Israeli armed forces, they also participated in the Israeli political process almost since the state's inception. Sheikh Salah Hassan Hanifes was the first ever Druze Knesset member, having been elected in 1951 and again in 1955, staying in office until his retirement from politics in 1959.[80] Hanifes, a native of the village of Shefa-'Amr in northern Galilee, was sent to the Khalwat al-Bayada to receive his religious training, but had to return abruptly after his father was gunned down by Palestinian rebels in 1939.[81] Consequently, together with other leading figures of his community (such as Labib Abu Rukun and Yusuf al-'Aysami), Hanifes used his relationship with the Jewish agency to convince many coreligionists to refrain from joining the Palestinian rebels; this relationship would live on with the rise of the state of Israel in 1948.[82]

Scholars and the public at large have debated and sometimes even tried to justify Druze collaboration with Israel based on a number of opposing points of views; still, the relationships of the Druze of Israel to their anti-Zionist Druze brothers in the neighbouring country was never damaged over their support for or opposition to the state of Israel. While the Druze of Lebanon or Syria, whether by choice or convenience, adopted Arab nationalism, they never actively sought to frame the Druze of Israel as collaborators and turncoats. These continued good relations would later allow them to come to their brethrens' aid, as the subsequent chapters will demonstrate.

Progressive Socialism Meets the Druze

In 1949, Kamal Joumblatt founded the Progressive Socialist Party (PSP), which, despite its secular inclusive doctrine, came to be a vessel for the Joumblatti faction and predominately championed by the Druze. At the apex of his career, Joumblatt endeared himself to a broad Lebanese and Arab audience as a genuine and committed reformer; however, the party itself was never able to outgrow its Druze base. Farid al-Khazen has seen Joumblatt as a paradoxical character driven by a combination of opportunism, moralism, sectarianism and socialism, despite his impressive credentials and grand schemes for reform.[83]

Born in 1917, Kamal Joumblatt was brought up by his mother Nazira Joumblatt, who had to assume family leadership after the murder of her husband Fouad. Educated at the Aintoura Lazarist School and later the Sorbonne in France, where he studied psychology and sociology, Joumblatt returned to Lebanon in 1939, after the outbreak of World War II, and pursued a degree in Law. In the course of his studies in France, Joumblatt fell under the spell of progressive thinkers such as Rousseau, Saint Simon and Teilhard de Chardin; in the hope of modernising the Lebanese political system, he brought their thinking back home with him.[84] Following a period of conventional political activity, which included a ministerial appointment and two terms in parliament, Joumblatt departed from the conventional role into which he was born. In 1949, over afternoon tea, a group of intellectuals, businessmen and middle-class professionals, including Joumblatt, founded the Progressive Socialist Party. It sought to champion the interests of the workers based on a non-Marxist model, its ultimate aim being identical to its motto of 'Free Citizen and Happy People'.[85] It is interesting to note that the PSP flag, which Joumblatt himself designed, depicts a blue globe with a pen and a pick axe in its centre against a red background. Red was the official colour of the Qaysi faction that had dominated the politics of Mount Lebanon in the seventeenth and eighteenth centuries. Joumblatt and the other founding members believed that reform could be achieved gradually, by collaborating with like-minded individuals within the Lebanese system and especially the members of the Maronite elite. This would have been the same elite with whom he had grown up and then attended school as well as university.

Figure 3.6 PSP Rally in Barouk in March 1951 to announce the electoral list for the upcoming parliamentary elections (PSP Archives).

In 1952, the Popular Socialist Front, a coalition of reformist individuals from across the sectarian spectrum and led by Kamal Joumblatt, defied the first post-independence President of the Republic, Bishara al-Khuri, who had violated the constitution by extending his own mandate, a mandate marred by corruption and cronyism.[86] Following a period of peaceful protests, the Socialist Front was able to depose Khuri and replace him with a member of its own, Camille Chamoun. As publicised at the time, Chamoun had received Joumblatt's endorsement, after he had pledged that his term would be used to champion the reform platform set forth by the Popular Socialist Front.

Joumblatt and Chamoun's understanding soon fell apart, and their once friendly relationship transformed into bitter animosity, especially when Chamoun started to challenge Joumblatt in the traditionally Druze areas of the Shuf. This rivalry finally came to a head after Chamoun rigged the 1957 parliamentary elections to oust all of his main rivals, including Joumblatt. Chamoun was successful in doing so because he controlled all key junctures of the Lebanese state and furthermore had styled himself as an ally of the West, able to stand up to the impending threat of Gamal Abdul Nasser of

Egypt.[87] By securing enough votes in parliament, Chamoun could amend the constitution to renew his term, which was originally set as a six-year non-renewable term. The Druze perceived this as another episode of treason, as it brought back memories of Bashir II's betrayal of Bashir Joumblatt in the nineteenth century. In the Druze mind, what Camille Chamoun perpetrated was identical to what had happened a century earlier. Furthermore, the fact that Chamoun hailed from Deir al-Qamar, which the Druze had destroyed in 1860, provided both sects with ample material to bolster their collective memory of enmity.[88] Regional developments – such as the union between Egypt and Syria and the fall of the pro-Western Iraqi Monarchy – redistributed the regional political balances and finally led to the outbreak of violence in Lebanon. The landing of the US Marines shortly thereafter ended the battles between the warring factions. However, the two main parties at the heart of the conflict – namely, the Druze and the Maronites – viewed these events as just another chapter in their collective memory of conflicts, as I will demonstrate below.

The events of 1958 forced Joumblatt to reconsider his early beliefs, as he discarded all illusions that the Maronite political establishment would treat him as an equal. Under Joumblatt's watchful eyes, the PSP became a supporter of the Pan-Arab and Third World liberation movements. The 1967 Arab debacle and the rise of the Palestinian Revolution saw Joumblatt and his party become one of the most important Arab allies within the Lebanese political system. Yusri Hazran has confirmed that, 'by 1969 (Cairo Agreement), Junblatt had become the Palestinian Resistance Organization's most faithful ally'; in his new post as Interior Minister, he assumed the role of mediator between the PLO and the Lebanese state.[89] More importantly, the PSP became a venue where the Druze historical banner received positive reinforcement in serving the party as well as the clan's short- and long-terms goals. From a Druze perspective, the Arab nationalist, anti-Western line that the PSP incorporated into its creed was a perfect fit for the Druze collective self-perception as protectors of the land, be it against the West or its local Lebanese collaborators. The drive for reform that Joumblatt steered also fell perfectly in line with the Druze's longing to regain their original status within the Lebanese political system, a status that they had lost in 1920, after the annexation of the Sunni areas to Mount Lebanon. Joumblatt's

Figure 3.7 Unveiling of the statue of Fakhr al-Din in Baakline (PSP Archives).

disenchantment was obvious in many of his statements and articles in which he expressed his frustration with the confessional system.

In summer of 1975, the Lebanese state unveiled a statue of Fakhr al-Din in his hometown of Baakline. Joumblatt refrained from attending and used this occasion to remind the establishment of the inequalities within the system:

> There is a significant difference between the Lebanon of today and the authentic historical Lebanon. The Lebanon today does not represent the historical heritage or national unity which Fakhr al-Din embodied, and we, the authentic Lebanese, feel foreign in a confessional system.[90]

It is no coincidence that in 1983, shortly after the end of the fighting against the Maronites, this same statue was destroyed with a charge of explosives. While no side officially claimed responsibility for this act, Walid Joumblatt never shied away from expressing his discontent over how the Maronites 'abducted' the historical figure of Fakhr al-Din to incorporate him into their own myth.[91] Much of what father Kamal and son Walid Joumblatt shared in their discontent about the hegemony of the Maronites was also shared by other, non-Druze Muslims who, despite their numerical majority, were forced to assume a secondary role. An attack on a sectarian entity such as the Maronite political establishment could indeed be seen as a demand for reform, as it ultimately aspired to establish a modern secular state, something that Joumblatt had placed at the top of his socialist agenda, at least after 1958. However, what stands out as a purely Druze feature is the tone which Joumblatt, and consequently the PSP supporters, used to describe the Maronites, reflecting obvious hatred and seemingly primordial condescension. Kamal Joumblatt made these sentiments abundantly clear when he described the Maronites as follows:

> Good scribes, authors, historians and poets as well as workers, traders and laborers, but they had never been more than that. The [French] Mandate handed them complete political power on a plate, a gift that they did not deserve, as they themselves have demonstrated. Druses have a saying: Maronites make poor governors, for they lack both the feeling and the tradition of government.[92]

The aggressive and escalating attitude with which Joumblatt expressed himself was partly due to his frustration with the rigidity of his opponents, but it was also directly proportional to the rise of the Palestinian Revolution and its increasing popularity among the Muslims of Lebanon.

Following the events of Black September in 1970, which pitted the Jordanian army against the PLO and resulted in the latter's expulsion from Jordan, Lebanon became the PLO's last remaining base of operations. This led to an upsurge in the PLO's political and military presence in different regions of Lebanon, especially the areas along the border with Palestine. As leader of the Leftist Lebanese National Movement and Secretary-General of the Arab Front for the Support of the Palestinian Revolution, Joumblatt was aware of the impact that the PLO's presence had on the Maronites; therefore, he tried to use the PLO as a vehicle to advance some of his legitimate demands, if necessary by force. Joumblatt's maneuver backfired, as the Maronites perceived it as part of a wider plot to displace them from their lands and settle the Palestinians in their place. Thirty years after the beginning of the war, Bulus Naʿaman spoke of the fears that his community experienced at that time:

> The Palestinian project at the time seemed to us to be swinging between two options, either using Lebanon as a permanent base for the liberation of Palestine, or making Lebanon a surrogate country for the Palestinians. Furthermore, the plan of the [Lebanese] National Movement reeked of deep-seeded hatred and meant to settle old scores, some of which go back to before the foundation of Greater Lebanon in 1920, to the time of the feud between Emir Bashir II and Sheikh Bashir Joumblatt. This was clear to us, as Kamal Joumblatt, president of the Progressive Socialist Party, declared: we will eradicate the plot of the great [Bashir II] Shihabi who during his reign exiled Sheikh Bashir [Joumblatt] and advanced the Maronites at the expense of the Druze.[93]

Be that as it may, the Druze as a community were highly influenced by the PSP, as a secular entity that empowered them, as an avant-gardist group willing to embrace change and as a proud warrior community indigenous to the land. Through its Joumblatti leadership under Kamal and later Walid, the party drew the same parameters that others centres of power within the community had used to define Druze identity. While other political parties – such as the Nazi-style Syrian Socialist Nationalist Party (SSNP) and the Lebanese Communist Party – were active among the Druze at large, none had the legitimacy or the appeal as the PSP under the leadership of its charismatic Socialist lords.

Kamal Joumblatt's transformation early in his career, from a traditional Lebanese politician espousing the Phoenician image of Lebanon into a pan-Arab and internationalist figure, fit perfectly well with the Druze's self-depiction and the historical banner highlighted in Chapter 7. Consequently, Joumblatt was now able to appeal to more members of the Druze community, not merely his immediate Joumblatti power base who would

Figure 3.8 Kamal Joumblatt in his home in Moukhtara (PSP Archives).

have followed him anyhow, regardless of ideology or political principles. According to Yusri Hazran, the end of the 1960s saw Joumblatt transform into 'a leader of regional proportions and [he] received prizes from the Soviet Union and the People's Republic of China and people began to relate to him as a world leader'.[94] By championing Arab nationalism and the Palestinian cause, Joumblatt not only conformed to the Druze political heritage, but also helped his people gain further prominence, which allowed them to rise above the remaining Lebanese communities, and perhaps even beyond. Moreover, Joumblatt's charisma and political clout caused many young men and women, and especially those born after 1943, to look to him for mentorship and inspiration.

The '1958 Generation'

One of the major outcomes of the 1958 conflict was perhaps a generation of young men and women who saw in the 1958 crisis sufficient proof that coexistence was no longer possible within the current political system. In 1958, the majority of those who constituted the cadres of the different militias in 1975, and even more so in 1982, had been around the age of ten, and

Figure 3.9 Yasser Arafat, Chairman of the PLO, with Kamal Joumblatt (PSP Archives).

they recalled this event as an important juncture in the subsequent civil war. Subsequently, this '1958 Generation' did not endorse *al-Mithaq al-Watani* (the National Pact) that had been forged among the founders of the 1943 republic.[95] The Muslims (the Druze, Sunnis and Shi'ites) found the pact inequitable because it gave the Maronite minority unrestricted control over the country. By contrast, the Maronites saw that their Christian homeland was threatened by various factors and therefore no longer sustainable under the provisions of the pact.

Bashir Gemayel and Walid Joumblatt had been born in 1947 and 1949, respectively, and both were typical of their generation. The anti-National Pact sentiment was a central theme in Bashir Gemayel's political rhetoric; he made it clear that 'the 1943 formula has been buried and we have placed a tombstone on the grave, and we have stationed a guard [over this grave] so it will not be resurrected'.[96] Many of Bashir's opponents used his disdain for the pact to paint him as endorsing a racist vision that ultimately refused to acknowledge Lebanese Muslims as equals. Antoine Najm, however, has confirmed this not to be true; although Bashir had never been fully exposed to the Muslims of the country, he never saw Lebanon as a purely Maronite homeland, especially towards the end of his career, as he made his final bid towards the presidency.[97] In the preface of his book *Dawlat Lubnan al-Ittihadiya* (The Federal State of Lebanon), Najm has clarified his claim, as he opens his book with 'we are pro-Pact but not pro-Formula'.[98] Najm has stated:

> We are with the [National] Pact because it endorses Christian-Muslim coexistence in the free state of Lebanon within its internationally recognized borders. This coexistence is steadfast; to us, it is ingrained in our liberal nature and our belief in dialogue as we are committed towards fortifying, defending and removing any obstacle standing in its way.[99]

However, according to Najm, the main problem rested in the formula that hindered the pact's implementation:

> We are against the '1943 formula' or the legal and constitutional implementation framework of this pact, which is a variant. Despite the Muslim refusal of this formula since independence, it has continued to serve the

pact, which made it a threat to the pact itself. The pact can only be served through a system which ensures the presence of both Christian and Muslim groups in such a way that their freedom and development can be preserved, in geographical, institutional security and cultural frameworks that allow them to have a final say in their fundamental affairs.[100]

Bashir's contempt of the state and the 1943 formula, together with his wish to abolish it, amounted to an obsession, at least at the beginning of his career. Most of his speeches between 1979 and 1982 purposely debunked the so-called 'successful formula of coexistence and pluralism' which its proponents had tried to pass off as a modern state. Bashir was clear in declaring that this formula was outdated:

> The new stage dictates that all Lebanese should come together but not under the desolate stale 1943 pact. We will not accept to go back to the tone of the Christian Priest kissing the Muslim Sheikh or the image of the Church and Mosque embracing ... Our cause is extremely sensitive. We should learn from the past, or the current conditions will reflect badly on us, and thus we will prove to the world that we are undeserving of life. We should always be ready to convince anyone who wants to get rid of us that their attempts will only fail. They tried to get rid of us on many occasions, but failed to do so, and in 1958 they also tried but failed. We will prevent the state [1943 model] to stand on its feet, because it will only lead to our ruin. The root of all evil was this State, long before the problem was Muslim vs Christian.[101]

Walid Joumblatt's sentiments were not very different; he made it abundantly clear that Lebanon had been moulded to please the Maronites and that the war in Lebanon would not end until true reform – in other words, de-Maronification – was achieved.[102] Joumblatt agreed with Bashir that the crux of the problem rested in the pact itself and that the following was needed to resolve the current crisis:

> a new non-sectarian pact which is different from the sectarian one concluded in 1943. Once we get to this new pact, perhaps this war might stop. To achieve this goal we need to empower the current state institutions and to pass some constitutional amendments which place all people on equal footing before the law.[103]

Figure 3.10 Kamal Joumblatt with his rebel fighters in the courtyard of the Palace of Moukhtara in 1958 (PSP Archives).

All my interviewees stated that the events of what was popularly called 'the 1958 revolution' in a multi-faceted way contributed to the shaping of not only their own, but also their communities' collective memories. Age is an extremely important factor for the formation of collective memory. Social scientists have concluded that historical events either witnessed by or related to the same cohort are usually remembered well. Studies conducted by Rubin, Wetzler and Nebes have concluded that individuals between the ages of thirteen and twenty-five are the group most likely to retain and pass on memory.[104]

Hassan al-Beaini, a retired Lebanese Army officer and commander of the PSP Military Police, vividly recalled his father's exploits during the 1958 revolution. Beaini specifically remembered how his father had to 'walk to the Lebanese-Syrian border to get weapons for the village and how, upon his father's return, he brought him to the village square and made him fire a weapon in the air'.[105]

The Slaying of Na'im Moghabghab

Halim Bou Fakhraddine, a physician and the PSP representative to the Soviet Union during the civil war, remembers in detail his father's leading role in the 1958 events. Halim's father was tasked by Kamal Joumblatt to acquire and transport weapons from the United Arab Republic in Syria and to smuggle them through an area known as Deir al-'Ashir. In the days leading up to the confrontation between the 'rebels' and the pro-Chamoun elements, Bou Fakhraddine accompanied his father to the village of Sawfar, where Kamal Joumblatt was meeting his ally, the Shi'ite strongman and former speaker of the house Sabri Hamada. On that day, Halim, then only ten years old, was flabbergasted by the number of fighters who were trickling in from different regions, armed with weapons the likes of which he had never previously seen. These fighters 'commenced to dance and recite the famous war cries known as *hawrabi* as they shouted out pledges of allegiance to Kamal Joumblatt'.[106] Halim admits that, at that young age, he was oblivious to the ideological implications of the conflict, but he remembers quite well the showdown with Camille Chamoun, who wanted to crush Kamal Joumblatt at any cost. However, the most vivid experience imprinted on Bou Fakhraddine's psyche was a murder he witnessed, a murder resulting from the 1958 clashes.

After his election to president, Fouad Shihab decided to vacation in the presidential summer palace in Beit al-Din, the mansion built by the famous Emir Bashir, as it was customary. To welcome him to the Shuf, Joumblatt led a large delegation that soon turned into a political rally, as PSP flags were hoisted and speeches delivered. At first, Halim stood next to his father, but like many children his age, he soon decided to wander around and admire the cars at the venue. He heard a commotion and spotted a man surrounded by a group of Druze who were trying to overpower him. As the muscular man drew his pistol to defend himself, one of the attackers swiftly struck him on the back of the head. The blow caused him to bleed heavily, and thereafter nearly everyone surrounding him proceeded to beat him until he lay in a pool of his own blood.

The dead man was Na'im Moghabghab, a Member of Parliament for the Shuf and a member of Camille Chamoun's National Liberal Party. In addition to serving as one of Chamoun's closest aides, Moghabghab was famous for his heroic act during the 1943 struggle for independence, when he climbed the parliament building under gunfire and replaced the French banner with the newly created Lebanese flag. Moghabghab, who had been elected to parliament twice, in 1952 and 1957, was despised by the Joumblatti Druze for leading the pro-Chamoun police contingent that bullied and harassed their villages during the conflict a few months earlier.[107] It seems that Moghabghab had been curious to see what was happening in Beit al-Din, and so he took his Druze driver Fouad al-Zou'r on a reconnaissance mission; unfortunately, one of the bystanders from his own village recognised him.[108] Interestingly, the life of the Druze driver al-Zou'r was spared, as he was allowed to flee the scene in disgrace. However, the story did not end here for Halim, as his father brought him closer to Moghabghab's body and commanded him to walk over it twice, stepping onto the blood. Halim's brand-new white sandals were ruined, and he remembered how, months later, his gloating father would order him to fetch these blood-stained sandals to show them to visitors in their home. It was obvious to Halim that his father wanted to teach him that 'this would be the fate of anyone who would dare hurt the Druze', a lesson which has stayed with him to this day.[109]

Also present at the same crime scene was retired General Raja Harb. Born in 1945, Harb later assumed the command of the People's Liberation Army, the regular PSP militia during the War of the Mountain; thus, he followed in the footsteps of his father, who had fought with the rebels in 1958, and his grandfather, who had been involved in the 1860 clashes in Deir al-Qamar.[110] Contrary to his father's wishes, Raja followed him to the event at Beit al-Din and also witnessed the brutal slaying of Na'im Moghabghab. Such a traumatic experience at such a young age certainly scarred both Halim and Raja for life and cemented in them their community's collective perception of themselves and of their Maronite enemies.

Such watershed experiences were not limited to Beaini or his community but shared by the Maronites elsewhere. Elie Hobeika, the leader of the Lebanese Forces (LF), whose name was directly associated with the Sabra and Shatila Massacre of 1982, shared a similar experience that scarred him as an adolescent. Hobeika related how in 1970, at the age of fourteen, he witnessed pro-Palestinian elements vandalising his apartment building and

Figure 3.11 Majid Arslan (left) and Na'im Moghabghab (Moghabghab Family Archives).

Figure 3.12 Zalfa Chamoun (left), Camille Chamoun, Majid Arslan and Na'im Moghabghab (Moghabghab Family Archives).

assaulting a Lebanese police officer in his neighbourhood in the heart of eastern Beirut. According to Hobeika, who hailed from a modest family, this was a defining moment in his own life and in the life of his classmates: They felt that they were in immediate danger, which led them to join the Phalangist party and similar factions.[111] One of Hobeika's cohort was Ass'ad al-Chaftari, later executive officer in the LF security and counter-intelligence branch. Despite his middle-class upbringing, he was affected by similar events, as was his commander. After the war, Chaftari became a champion for truth and reconciliation, bravely admitting in his memoirs the hatred that he himself and perhaps others close to him had fostered towards their Muslim compatriots.[112] In 1967, following the Arab debacle, Gamal Abdul Nasser tendered his resignation on live TV, declaring that he was willing to shoulder all responsibility for the defeat. This provoked an outcry from across the Arab world, including the Lebanese Muslims who regarded Nasser as a hero. To Ass'ad, this Muslim reaction was un-Lebanese, since choosing a foreigner as their hero went against his patriotic feelings.[113] This further fortified the image that he had of the Muslims as aspiring:

to build a regional Islamic state, whereas I wanted a free and sovereign Lebanon. They [Muslims] looked towards Arabia and longed to go back to wearing the traditional cloth and ride camels, whereas I looked towards the west and root for modernity . . . I could never get along with these bastards. After the events of 1842 and 1860, the burning of Zahle three times, and the bloody revolution in 1958, it became clear to me that the Christians have always suffered from the Muslims.[114]

Still, these memories by themselves were not sufficient to create conflict; other elements, such as group interests, fuelled and directed these memories in order to mobilise and, in this particular case, militarise the community. On the eve of the Lebanese Civil War, these men and women had been subjected to much indoctrination by various institutions, ranging from their parties and schools, over their families, to their sect. It was against this backdrop that the War of the Mountain unfolded.

Notes

1. Ernest Renan, 'What is a Nation?', lecture delivered at the Sorbonne, 1882. http://www.cooper.edu/humanities/core/hss3/e_renan.htm
2. Ibid.
3. Kaufman, *Reviving Phoenicia*, 21–2.
4. Johnson, *All Honourable Men*, 16.
5. James V. Wertsch, 'Collective Memory', in *Memory in Mind and Culture*, 119.
6. *International Encyclopedia of the Social & Behavioral Sciences* (Oxford: Pergamon, 2001), 2219–23.
7. Richard van Leeuwen, *Notables and Clergy in Mount Lebanon: The Khāzin Sheikhs and the Maronite Church, 1736–1840* (Leiden: E. J. Brill, 1994), 174.
8. Ibid., 175–6.
9. Richard van Leeuwen, 'Monastic Estates and Agricultural Transformation in Mount Lebanon in the 18th Century', *International Journal of Middle East Studies* 23 (1991), 606.
10. Youssef Mahfouz, *Mukhtaṣar Tārīkh al-Rahbanah al-Mārūnīyah* (Kaslik: Kaslik University Press, 1969), 115. Translation mine.
11. Father Karam Rizk, 'Milestones in the History of the Lebanese Maronite Order', Kaslik: University of the Holy Spirit, [n. d.]. http://www.discoverleba non.com/en/panoramic_views/lebanese_maronite_order.php, accessed 5 July 2016.

12. Lebanese Synod, Chapter Six, no. 3 par. 3. Translation from 'The Maronite Church and Education: Academic and Technical', in *The Maronite Church in Today's World*, File III, Text 16.
13. Lebanese synod/council, Chapter Six, no. 1.
14. Rizk, 'Milestones in the History of the Lebanese Maronite Order'.
15. See page 58.
16. Ruhbānīyah al-Lubnānīyah al-Mārūnīyah and Université Saint-Spirite, *Al-Yūbīl al-Mi'awī al-Thālith lil-Ruhbānīyah al-Lubnānīyah al-Mārūnīyah: Turāth wa-Ru'á Mustaqbalīyah = Le tricentenaire de l'Ordre libanais maronite: Histoire et perspectives d'avenir, 1695–1995* (al-Kaslīk: Ma'had al-Tarīkh, Jāmi'at al-Rūḥ al-Qudus, 1996), 318. Translation mine.
17. Randal, *Going All the Way*, 113.
18. Interview with Bulus Na'aman, Kaslik, Lebanon, July 2011.
19. As quoted in Alexander Henley, 'Politics of a Church at War: Maronite Catholicism in the Lebanese Civil War', *Mediterranean Politics* 13, no. 3 (2008), 356.
20. Ibid., 357.
21. Kamal Joumblatt, as quoted in Randal, *Going All the Way*, 113.
22. Ibid.
23. *Al-Masiraa'*, 13 April 1983.
24. Butrus Daw, *Tarīkh al-Mawārinah*, 17, 39–50.
25. During the period in question, two individuals occupied the post of Father Superior of the order, Charbel Kassis (1974–80) and Bulus Na'aman (1980–6).
26. Interview with Bulus Na'aman, 2012. *Bashir: The Series*, BGOH.
27. As quoted in Randal, *Going All the Way*, 141.
28. See page 64.
29. Chaker Abou Sleiman, Najib Dahdah, Jawad Bulus, Fouad Frem al-Boustani, Charles Malik, Said Akil, Edward Honein, Antoine Najm, Charbel Kassis and Bulus Na'aman. For more detail, see André Sleiman, *Vivre ensemble mais séparés? L'émergence et l'évolution des projets de fédération au Liban de 1975 à nos jours* (Lille: Atelier national de reproduction des thèses, 2014), 112.
30. Interview with Bulus Na'aman, 2012, BGOH.
31. Bulus Na'aman, *Al-Waṭan, al-Hurrīyah: Mudhakkirāt al-Abātī Būlus Nuᶜmān* (Lebanon: Sā'air al-Mashriq, 2009), 178–80.
32. Theodor Hanf, *Coexistence in Wartime Lebanon: Decline of a State and Rise of a Nation* (London: Centre for Lebanese Studies, in association with I. B. Tauris, 1993), 232.

33. Fattal's study in French is available in part in Sālim, Būl, Anṭwān Masarrah, Khālid Qabbānī, and Ṣaʻb F. Abū, *Al-lā-Markazīyah al-Idārīyah fī Lubnān: Al-Ishkālīyah wa-al-Taṭbīq* (Bayrūt: al-Markaz al-Lubnanī lil-Dirāsāt, 1996). Moussa Prince, *Hiwar, Hulum, Hal* (Beirut: Joseph Raidy Press, 1980).
34. Phalanges: Pierre, Amin and Bashir Gemayel, Edmond Rizk, Antoine Moarbès, Salah Matar, Ibrahim Najjar. PNL: Camille, Dory and Dany Chamoun, Moussa Prince, Charles Ghostine, Georges Abou Adal. Front national (Frangieh bloc): Sleiman Frangieh, Henri Torbey, Georges Skaff, Jean Naffah. Order of Lebanese Monks: Abbots Charbel Kassis and Bulus Naʻaman, Mgr Michel Hakim, Khayrallah Ghanem, Walid el-Khazen, Victor Ghorayeb. 'Les Intellectuels' (*Ahl al-Mīthāq wal-Qalam*): Édouard Honein, Fouad Ephrem Boustani, Charles Malik, Jawad Bulus, Saʻid ʻAql. Secretariat: P. Thomas Mehanna, Joseph Abou-Khalil (Kataeb), Roger Mraqqadeh, Samir Rohayyem. From Sleiman, *Vivre ensemble mais séparés?* 130.
35. Chamoun, as quoted in Bulus Naʻaman, *Al-Waṭan, al-Hurrīyah*, 153. Translation mine.
36. Ye'or Bat, *The Decline of Eastern Christianity under Islam: From Jihad to Dhimmitude, Seventh-Twentieth Century* (Madison: Fairleigh Dickinson University Press, 1996).
37. Michael Butterand and Maurus Reinkowski, *Conspiracy Theories in the United States and the Middle East: A Comparative Approach* (Berlin: De Gruyter, 2014), 87.
38. http://www.bachirgemayel.org/index.php?option=com_content&task=view&id=50&Itemid=86, accessed 10 July 2016.
39. Hanf, *Coexistence in Wartime Lebanon*, 385.
40. Amin Naji (Antoine Najm), *Lan Naʻisha Dhimmiyyīn* (Beirut: al-Maṭbaʼah al-Ḥadīthah, 1979).
41. Najm, as quoted in Sleiman, *Vivre Ensemble Mais Séparés?* 125.
42. Interview with Antoine Najm, Beirut, Lebanon, 10 February 2016.
43. Ibid.
44. Frank Stoakes, 'The Supervigilantes: The Lebanese Kataeb Party as Builder, Surrogate, and Defender of the State', *Middle Eastern Studies* 11 (1975), 215–36.
45. Ibid., 217.
46. Interview with Joseph Abu Khalil, Beirut, Lebanon, 30 December 2015.
47. Sleiman, *Vivre Ensemble Mais Séparés?* 143.

48. Fouad Ephrem Boustani, *Le problème du Liban: Note succinte, objective, sincère et franche pour servir à comprendre la question Libanaise*, 2nd ed. (Kaslik: C. R., 1978).
49. Anis Obeid, *The Druze and Their Faith in Tawhid* (Syracuse: Syracuse University Press, 2006), 93.
50. The Druze use the term 'born from' (*battein sharia'a*) to indicate that the mother is non-Druze.
51. The number is a moderate estimate, based on the three main Druze communities in the Levant as well in the diaspora.
52. Hazran, *The Druze Community and the Lebanese State*, 27.
53. For more information about the evolution of this rivalry, see page 44.
54. Akarli, *The Long Peace*, 16.
55. Fuad Khūrī, *Being a Druze* (London: Druze Heritage Foundation, 2004), 144.
56. Ṣāliḥ ibn Yaḥyá, Kamal S. Salibi and Francis Hours, *Tārīkh Bayrūt, wa-Huwa Akhbār al-Salaf min Dhurriyat Buḥtur ibn ʿAlī Amīr al-Gharb bi-Bayrūt* (Bayrūt: Dār al-Mashraf, 1969). Ibn Sabāt, *Ṣidq al-Akhbār: Tārīkh Ibn Sabāt* (Ṭarābulus: Jarrūs Bris, 1993).
57. Interview with Rajeh Naim, Beirut, Lebanon, 24 May 2016.
58. On the Long Rebellion and the Druze Ottoman confrontation as discussed by Abdul Rahim Abu-Husayn, see page 41.
59. Interview with Issam Aintrazi (Abu Said), North Carolina, December 2013.
60. Ibid.
61. Ibid.
62. Salibi, *House of Many Mansions*, 125.
63. In Islam, after death the soul is in a state of suspension, awaiting final judgment.
64. Anne Bennett, 'Reincarnation, Sect Unity, and Identity among the Druze', *Ethnology* 45, no. 2 (2006), 88–9.
65. Khuri, *Being a Druze*, 104.
66. Ibid., 105.
67. Bennett, 'Reincarnation, Sect Unity, and Identity', 89.
68. Interview with Imad al-Awar, Beirut, May 2016.
69. Written testimony of Fawaz Dalal, 11 August 2016. Translation mine.
70. Ibid.
71. Obeid, *The Druze and Their Faith*, 171.
72. Ibid., 99.
73. Khuri, *Being a Druze*, 124.

74. Tarif's first visit came on 9 October 1982. *An-Nahar*, 10 October 1982. The Inauguration of the wing took place on 1 July 1990. *An-Nahar*, 2 July 1990.
75. Ibid., 123. For more information, see http://www.alamama.com/index.php?option=com_content&task=view&id=50, accessed 24 July 2016.
76. Judith Harik. 'Shaykh al-'Aql and the Druze of Mount Lebanon: Conflict and Accommodation', *Middle Eastern Studies* 30, no. 3 (1994), 463.
77. Interview with Ali Zeindinne, PSP Oral History Project.
78. The Druze believe *tamimi* to be the embodiment of the universal soul, depicted in green on the Druze flag with its five-pointed star. Obeid, *The Druze and Their Faith*, 97.
79. Kais Firro, 'Reshaping Druze Particularism in Israel', *Journal of Palestine Studies* 30, no. 3 (2001): 50–1.
80. https://www.knesset.gov.il/mk/eng/mk_eng.asp?mk_individual_id_t=422, accessed 3 March 2020.
81. Kais Firro, *The Druzes in the Jewish State: A Brief History* (Leiden: Brill, 1999), 27.
82. Ibid., 30.
83. Farid al-Khazen, 'Kamal Jumblatt, the Uncrowned Druze Prince of the Left', *Middle Eastern Studies* 24, no. 2 (1988), 179.
84. Khalīl Aḥmad Khalīl, *Kamāl Junblāṭ: Thawrat 'al-Amīr al-Hadīth* ([Beirut]: Dār al-Maṭbū'āt al-Sharqīyah, 1984).
85. Ḥizb al-Taqaddumī al-Ishtirākī (Lebanon), *Rubʿ Qarn min al-Niḍāl* (Beirut: al-Ḥizb, 1975).
86. Nasser Kalawoun, *The Struggle for Lebanon: A Modern History of Lebanese-Egyptian Relations* (London: I. B. Tauris, 2000), 4.
87. Caroline Attié, *Struggle in the Levant: Lebanon in the 1950s* (London: I. B. Tauris, in association with the Centre for Lebanese Studies, 2004), 148.
88. Khalīl Aḥmad, *Maʿa Kamāl Junbalāṭ: Shihādah wa-Tārīkh wa-Muqārabah Falsafīyah* (al-Dār al-Bayḍā': al-Markaz al-Thaqāfī al-'Arabī, 2010), 57.
89. Hazran, *Druze Community and Lebanese State*, 161, 163. The Cairo Agreement between the Lebanese state and the PLO gave the latter the legal right to operate from the south of Lebanon and to wage war across the border into occupied Palestine.
90. Joumblatt, as quoted in Hazran, *Druze Community and Lebanese State*, 179.
91. Salibi, *House of Many Mansions*, 200–3.
92. Joumblatt, *I Speak for Lebanon*, 40–1.

93. Bulus Naʿaman, *Al-Waṭan, al-Hurrīyah*, 69. Translation mine.
94. Hazran, *Druze Community and Lebanese State*, 160.
95. Under the provisions of this pact, the Maronites would not seek foreign intervention, but accept Lebanon as an 'Arab'-affiliated country, rather than a 'Western' one, while the Muslims were to abandon their aspirations to unite with Syria. The president of the republic was always to be Maronite, the prime minister Sunni, the speaker Shiʿite, and the deputy speaker of the parliament Greek-Orthodox. All public offices were to be held at a ratio of 6:5 in favour of Christians over Muslims. Leonard Binder, *Politics in Lebanon* (New York: John Wiley & Sons, Inc., 1966), 276.
96. As quoted by Karim Pakradouni, documentary entitled *The War of Lebanon* (*Harb Lubnan*), aired on *al-Jazeera*, 2001.
97. Interview with Antoine Najm, Beirut, Lebanon, 10 February 2016.
98. Antoine Najm, *Dawlat Loubnan al-Ithadiya: Dawlat al-Tanmiyah wa al-Musâwât wa al-ʿAdâlah wa al-ʿAych al-Muchtarak*, (Bayrût: Afâq Machriqiyyah, 1992), 5.
99. Ibid. Translation mine.
100. Ibid. Translation mine.
101. Lecture delivered by Bashir Gemayel, 28 February 1979. Bashir Gemayel Foundation 5-1-1979–31/12/1979: Faith and Cause (Beirut: Muʾassasat Bašīr al-Ǧumaiyil, 1987), 63. Translation mine.
102. *Al-Anbaa*, 18 April 1983.
103. *Al-Moustaqbal*, 20 August 1983. Translation mine.
104. These studies were conducted by David C. Rubin, Scott E. Wetzler and Robert D. Nebes, 'Autobiographical Memory Across the Adult Lifespan', in *Autobiographical Memory*, ed. David C. Rubin (Cambridge: Cambridge University Press, 1986), 202–21.
105. Interview with retired General Hassan al-Beaini, Virginia, USA, February 2010.
106. Interview with Halim Bou Fakhraddine, Beirut, Lebanon, 21 January 2016.
107. Attié, *Struggle in the Levant*, 145.
108. Interview with Halim Bou Fakhraddine, Beirut, Lebanon, 21 January 2016.
109. Ibid.
110. Interview with Retired General Raja Harb, Beirut, Lebanon, 30 December 2016.
111. Elie Hobeika, as interviewed by Ghassān Charbal, *Ayna Kunta fī al-Ḥarb* (Beirut: Riyāḍ al-Rayyis lil-Kutub wa-al-Nashr, 2011).

112. Assad Chaftari, *La vérité même si ma voix tremble* (Beyrouth: Dergham, 2015), 27. I am using the Arabic translation of this book.
113. Ibid., 27.
114. Ibid., 27.

4

THE ROAD TO CONFLICT

Despite their divergent collective identities, the Druze and Maronites were not necessarily destined to clash; however, certain events and junctures led to the gradual escalation of tensions that in the end spilled over into open warfare. The following chapter will highlight these events and reveal how the constructed historical framework of both communities and their constant linkage of current events to an imagined past prevented them from resolving their disagreements and finding a common vision forward.

Harb al-Jabal: 1982–3

Prior to the Israeli invasion, the (Druze) southern parts of Mount Lebanon – that is, the Shuf and Aley – had largely remained outside the scope of the civil war. Most of the fighting during the opening phase, called the 'two-year war' (1975–7) was mainly restricted to the northern part of Mount Lebanon, with sporadic incidents affecting the Maten region north of the Beirut-Damascus highway. This relative tranquility was shattered on 16 March 1977, when the paramount Druze leader Kamal Joumblatt was assassinated by 'unknown' assailants a few miles from his ancestral home, the Palace of Moukhtara in the Shuf. All fingers pointed to the Syrian regime as the perpetrator of the crime, mainly because of Joumblatt's staunch resistance to the Syrian Army's entry into Lebanon to rescue his Maronite enemies, the Lebanese Front, from an impending defeat at the hands of the Lebanese National Movement and their Palestinian allies. Joumblatt never harboured any illusions regarding the nature of the Syrian regime, or its leader Hafez al-Assad, whom he considered nothing more than a petit-bourgeois army officer bent on dominating Lebanon.[1] A year earlier, Joumblatt had visited Damascus, in what would be his last trip to Syria; there, he held a lengthy one-on-one meeting with Assad. Unfortunately, this meeting failed to bridge the gap between the two leaders; rather, it had the opposite effect, pitting them against each other in the raging Lebanese Civil War and creating no consensus on how to put an end to it. According to Abbas Khalaf, the PSP's Vice President for International Affairs, who had accompanied Joumblatt on this trip, the meeting did not go well. In the end, Assad invited Joumblatt to stay the night in Damascus, where they could continue their 'conversation' the next morning. Joumblatt declined Assad's invitation, despite Khalaf's advice to accept it. Khalaf remembered that Joumblatt looked him in the eye and addressed him sternly, in English: 'I have to go back to Beirut, I have work to do'.[2] It was obvious that by now Joumblatt and Assad had crossed the point of no return in an already inimical and arduous relationship and that there was no love lost between the two men. Therefore, when on that warm March day a green Pontiac Firebird with Iraqi plates overtook Joumblatt's car and opened fire on it, no one had any doubt that it was Hafez Assad who had ordered to pull the trigger to eliminate the head of the Joumblatti clan and supreme Druze leader.

That day, Raja Harb was scheduled to meet Walid Joumblatt for lunch at Socrates Restaurant on Bliss Street, a weekly ritual they maintained. He was an eyewitness to the events that transpired the same afternoon. Arriving at the restaurant on time, Harb was extremely alarmed by Walid Joumblatt's tardiness, as the latter was known for his punctuality. Harb immediately called Joumblatt, and he informed him: 'It seems someone has shot at my dad, come by, we need to go up to the Shuf'.[3] Harb proceeded to pick up Joumblatt, and together they drove to the Shuf. When they reached the Ouzai area, the convoy of the *sheikh al-'aql* passed them, flying the Druze flag on the hood. All of a sudden, Joumblatt was assailed by a strange sensation and morosely said to Harb, 'The Arabs will have to wait at least a hundred years or more, before another Abdul Nasser or Kamal Joumblatt comes along. My father is dead'.[4] Upon reaching the Syrian-manned Arab Deterrent Force Checkpoint at Damour, both were briefly detained, and their personal firearms confiscated. Harb tried to explain to the Syrian officer that he was a lieutenant in the Lebanese Army, and that this was his service revolver, but to no avail. Joumblatt arrived at the scene of the crime in the Christian village of Deir Duriet and saw the bodies of his father's two bodyguards, Fawzi Shedid and Hafez Ghousuani, laid out by the side of the road. Upon arriving at the Joumblatts' ancestral palace in Moukhtara, Walid was informed that his father's assassination had unleashed a series of Druze reprisals against innocent Christians across the Shuf and Aley regions, some of whom, ironically, were card-carrying members of Joumblatt's party.

The Druze who had committed these atrocities were most probably driven by two reasons. Despite the obviously Syrian hand in Joumblatt's murder, it was the Maronites or Christians who had requested and 'invited' Syrian military intervention in 1976; therefore, the Maronites were regarded as guilty by association. Secondly, the massacres that the Christians had committed against the Palestinians in the refugee camps of Tal al-Za'atar and Karantina, as well as the so-called 'Black Saturday' massacre during which Christian militias had executed dozens of civilians based on their religious affiliation as stated on their national identity cards had not yet been forgotten.[5] Joumblatt himself, accompanied by the Sheikh al-'Aql Mohammad Abu-Shaqra, went from village to village to stop the bloodshed and save the Christian inhabitants from the retaliation of the Druze. However, the rescue party came too late, as Joumblatt later admitted: 'As soon as Kamal Joumblatt was killed, injustice and ignorance killed tens, no, hundreds, of innocent Christians in the mountains who had no fault other than that they sought refuge with us'.[6] Walid Joumblatt at the time called to his clansmen to 'work together to assure security and stability for all inhabitants of this mountain', but this call fell on deaf ears.[7] Harb has explained the magnitude of this violent and barbaric reaction by citing two main factors. First, while it is certain that the Druze where communally liable for what transpired on that day, the local Druze agents of the Syrian regime had acted as *agent provocateur*, manipulating the wrath of the masses and leading the Druze mobs.[8] Secondly, Kamal Joumblatt was not a mere mortal, at least according

Figure 4.1 Kamal Joumblatt, with his driver, Fawzi Shedid, and bodyguard, Hafez Ghousuani (PSP Archives).

to the Druze. In addition to being a progressive and international persona, 'he was the grandson of *Amud al-Sama* [pillar of heaven, Bashir Joumblatt]', and murdering him was the ultimate sin.[9] Standing on his father's grave, Walid Joumblatt was robed with the traditional mantle of leadership by

Mohammad Abu-Shaqra, who forcefully declared: 'Walid, a worthy successor to a great predecessor'.[10] Despite the efforts of Walid Joumblatt and his party to reassure the Christians and provide them with whatever protection possible, the Druze vengeance prompted a Christian flight from the Shuf and Aley regions on Mount Lebanon to the exclusively Christian regions. A US diplomatic dispatch to the State Department estimated that ninety-one people were killed and 7,000 people fled the mountain, escorted by the Lebanese Interior Security Forces.[11]

Kamal Joumblatt's assassination transformed all of Mount Lebanon, as the Druze-Christian dynamics of coexistence and diversity that since the days of Fakhr al-Din had set the region apart was no more. Remarkably, during the 'two-year war' (1975–7) the Druze and the Maronite were excluded from the senseless violence enveloping the country at the time. Despite their fierce animosity, Kamal Joumblatt and Camille Chamoun had been well aware of the need to keep Mount Lebanon out of the war; thus, they had established back channels to contain and resolve any dispute that may arise between the villagers, so as to avoid bloodshed. Walid Joumblatt confirmed that, 'despite

Figure 4.2 Kamal Joumblatt's car riddled with bullet holes (PSP Archives).

Figure 4.3 Walid Joumblatt (centre), flanked by members of his family and Sheikh Mohammad Abu-Shaqra at the funeral of his father (PSP Archives).

Figure 4.4 Kamal Joumblatt's identity card, party identity card and a picture of his son, Walid, all damaged by bullets (PSP Archives).

being archenemies, the relationship Kamal Joumblatt had with Chamoun was of a different level, we had mutual respect, and during the first mountain war in 1976 there was an agreement to spare the mountain. We fought over the rocks of Mount Sannine, so no one would get killed on the mountain [Shuf]'.[12] Yet, the Joumblatt-Chamoun arrangement was merely cosmetic, as it kept the peace only as long as the two leaders held up their end of the deal. With Kamal Joumblatt gone, the Druze felt no obligation to uphold the pact and therefore felt free to avenge the death of their leader, killing and evicting their Maronites neighbours.

Joseph Abu-Khalil – the Editor-in-Chief of the newspaper *Al-'Amal*, the mouthpiece of the Kataeb party – echoed the frustration and hatred of the displaced Christians towards the Joumblatti faction, especially after 1977. Abu-Khalil, a native of Beit al-Din, confirmed that the Shuf region was spared the turmoil that had engulfed the country starting in 1975. As a Maronite and senior Kataeb member, he felt no physical threat, as in the summer of 1976 he usually drove to his village, where his family was vacationing, at one o'clock in the morning. For Abu-Khalil, the essential historical truth remained that between 1861 and 1958 Mount Lebanon had enjoyed almost a century of tranquility and coexistence between the Druze and the Maronites. However, his sentiments soon changed after he was unable to access his hometown; Abu-Khalil criticised the Joumblatti attempt to establish a Druze canton, which had started with 'Kamal Joumblatt's 1958 coup and continues, to this date, under his son Walid'.[13] Uprooted and defeated, the Christians looked towards their traditional Christian leadership to return them to their villages and homes; yet, by that time these aging leaders had no practical plans to achieve this goal. This situation would soon change with the rise of a young brand of leader who was willing to challenge the traditional Maronite political establishment – a leader who, in the words of Jonathan Randal, 'would be willing to go all the way'.[14]

The Rise of Bashir Gemayel

The manner in which Bashir Gemayel rose to power and the path he charted for himself were very detrimental in the War of the Mountain. Many of this maverick militant-turned-politician's aggressive actions rendered him an existential threat in the eyes of his enemies and the Druze, especially the

Joumblatti faction. In 1975, Bashir was still struggling to make a name for himself within the ranks of the Kataeb. However, this proved to be somewhat difficult as his rebellious ideas clashed with those of his father and his older brother Amin, both of whom belonged to a breed of politicians that Bashir called 'wheelers and dealers'. Bashir's insistence on the notion that 'the old Lebanon [...] is dead'[15] and his image as a military man who preferred violence as first option put him at a disadvantage, with his own community as well as with the Muslims who perceived his statements as a call to war.

In 1976, a sniper bullet killed the Phalangist military high commander, the famous William Hawi, as he toured the front during the siege of the Palestinian refugee camp of Tel al-Za'tar. Consequently, Bashir, as Hawi's deputy, was appointed in his place. His first real test as chief of the Kataeb militia came in the summer of 1978, when they confronted the Syrian Army in Ashrafiyah, east of Beirut. Bashir mistakenly assumed that the West would rush to their aid if they were able to put up a good fight. Bashir's frustration was obvious during his meeting with the German ambassador von Pachelbel, as he had hoped that the Israelis would intervene in the fight, a miscalculation on his part.[16] Over a period of a hundred days, the Syrian Special Forces, who were part of the Arab Deterrent Force (ADF), relentlessly shelled the area and tried to storm it, but to no avail. Ultimately, the hundred-day war cost the Christians a heavy death toll, and the destruction that ensued ravaged nearly the entire quarter. Although Bashir was able to save face by withstanding the Syrian blitz, he later confessed to Abu-Khalil whom he lovingly called *amo* (uncle) that he had miscalculated the situation: 'If I knew Israel would not intervene, I would not have done it [the hundred-day war]'.[17] More importantly, this episode of *realpolitik* proved to Bashir that an exclusively militant approach was insufficient to win the confrontation within his community, as well as against his external enemies.

Almost immediately, Bashir started to transform the image he had previously shaped for himself as a field commander in the early stages of the war. In his public appearances and speeches, his firebrand rhetoric remained unchanged, but privately Bashir started to reach out to the international community, specifically the United States, France and most importantly Israel, in order to convince them of his project. To achieve this aim, Bashir sought out people who could act as his shadow cabinet and provide him with the intellectual and practical packaging needed to make him into a politician and potentially a statesman.[18] All of the fifteen men whom Bashir assembled came from different backgrounds and possessed a different set of skills and talents that Bashir needed to seize power. During their first meeting, a raging

Figure 4.5 Bashir Gemayel (Bashir Gemayel Foundation).

debate concerned how to seize power. Two options were on the table: either to democratically elect Bashir as president, or to appoint him through a military coup. They chose the latter option.

Unity at Gunpoint

This blatant show of Bashir's wish to become president was only possible after he had been able to neutralise all internal threats within the Christian community. One of the most important obstacles that Bashir had to overcome was the disunity of the Christians, whose diversity of political groups and militias was an obstacle rather than an empowering factor. The liberated regions, as the Christians (once again) referred to the areas under their control, were in a state of disarray, as each militia levied its own taxes and tried to enforce its own law. Despite having a unified military command, the members of the Lebanese Forces (LF), which had been established in 1976, continued to operate as separate units, something that Bashir greatly detested.[19] The Kataeb, the National Liberal Party, the Tanzim and the Guardian of the Cedars were the main fighting factions represented on the LF's Joint Command Council, presided over by Bashir al-Gemayel.

In its early years, the LF had struggled to become a true army, as it lacked the funding and the proper equipment which it had to buy from the black market. However, this was to change with the open alliance that the Maronites forged with Israel, which then started to supply weapons and training.[20] Among the main proponents of this open alliance with Israel were Bashir Gemayel and Dany Chamoun, son of former President Camille Chamoun. Both militia leaders had forged a working relationship with the Israeli security and military establishments, and this translated into shipments of guns and military hardware beginning to arrive in the port of Jounieh. Due to its large size in contrast to the other Christian militias, the Kateb was the recipient of the majority of these weapons, while the NLP Tigers were ranked second in this race to arms. Despite its fairly small size, the Tigers militia were well spread out across the 'liberated areas' and had access to weapons that outmatched their demand in numbers; this enabled them to engage in illicit arms trade and drug trafficking – at least according to their Christian allies' claims. It is certain, however, that the NLP Tigers were less disciplined and had a reputation for being mere thugs when compared to the more organised

Figure 4.6 Walid Joumblatt (PSP Archive).

Kataeb. Bashir also suspected that the Tigers, with their various free-lancing warlords, were acting as double agents for the Palestinians and the Syrians. According to Naji Butrus, the LF commander of the 'Ayn al-Remmaneh district and a long-time member of the Kataeb Party, the NLP had two

Figure 4.7 Bashir Gemayel (left), Camille Chamoun and Pierre Gemayel, the leaders of the Lebanese Forces (Wassim Jabre).

types of fighting groups: 'the *Numur* (Tigers) an elite disciplined fighting unit commanded by Dany Chamoun and *al-Ahrar* who were more of a gang rather than a militia'.[21] The NLP and the Kataeb militia had clashed on many occasions, but in the summer of 1980 these sporadic incidents became more recurrent and the channels through which these two factions used to resolve their differences faltered.

Bulus Naʿaman, whom Bashir usually delegated to liaison with the NLP, admitted that his efforts to reconcile Bashir and Dany were an abysmal failure. Over a period of two months Naʿaman met with Rashid al-Khazen, a senior NLP official, to try to mend relations.[22] Bashir also attended some of these meetings, as he was adamant to end this anomalous state of affairs which made the Maronites look weak in the eyes of their Israeli allies. Bashir did not want to resort to violence, primarily to avoid a repeat of the Ehden Massacre, during which Tony Frangieh, the son of the former president, and his family had been brutally gunned down. At Ehden, Bashir had instructed a Kataeb squad commanded by Samir Geagea to storm Frangieh's summer home and arrest a number of his supporters guilty of killing a high-ranking Kataeb member, Joud al-Bayeh.[23] The assumption was that Frangieh would not be present, allowing Samir Geagea and his squad to subdue and apprehend the criminals without a real fight. However, the ensuing gunfight led to a bloodbath, killing everyone in the villa, including the family's pet dog.[24]

On many earlier occasions, Bashir had requested that the NLP militias fall in line with the LF jurisdiction, to refrain from running their own weapons supply line from the port of Tabarja north of Beirut and to keep their troops on a tighter leash. In practical terms, this was not solely about armament, but also about the perception of the liberated regions as a model for the new Lebanon that Bashir propagated. Bashir was unusually patient regarding this matter, until Na'aman informed him that Khazen had confessed to him that he had no real leverage over the militia after 'they had disrespected him and insulted him in public'.[25] Bashir responded to Na'aman: 'You tried your way, now let me try mine'.[26]

Before 'doing it his way', Bashir began to openly declare the need for a radical solution to the lawlessness engulfing the Christin areas. On 27 July 1980, while speaking to the representatives of socio-economic groups in the Kisrwan region, Bashir listed the measures needed to end this internal standoff:

> We believe in political diversity, and we will never abandon this belief; however, we also need to be faithful to the blood of our martyrs and save society in the liberated areas, and this can only be achieved if our forces are united. It is unacceptable for every neighbourhood chief to have his own militia, and for every small shop [meaning faction] to have a tank or a field gun. Practice politics as you please, but let us willingly unite the military, before a lunatic comes along and does so by force.[27]

Eleven days later, this 'madman' appeared and gave Bashir the green light to neutralise with the help of his troops the NLP in all locations, thus ending the debate once and for all. Bashir's men attacked the seaside resort of Safra Marina only after they had made sure that Dany Chamoun had departed. However, Chamoun's men and their families who were sunbathing or napping were not as lucky, and an estimated 150 NLP members were gunned down.[28] This military operation, which Randal has termed 'Day of the Long

Knives',[29] sealed the fate of the NLP militia, forcing them to either dissolve within the LF military structure or flee from the liberated areas to West Beirut.[30] A crucial element that further legitimised Bashir's forceful unification of the 'Christian Gun' was the endorsement of former President Camille Chamoun, who was convinced of the necessity of such a step, even if it came at the expense of his own NLP. The fact that Bashir offered Chamoun a lucrative cut from the National Fund, rumoured to amount to one million US Dollars a month, seemed to appease the ageing politician.[31]

Zahle: Victory in Defeat

Bashir's next challenge was to get his Israeli allies (and by extension the West) to support his bid, not merely in word, but also in deed. To do so, Bashir needed to use his newly united LF in a combat situation and frame this act as a national security concern of interest to his allies. His chance would come in the Battle of Zahle in December 1980, when conflict erupted between the LF and the Syrian army in and around the city. These clashes soon turned into a full-scale war, escalating into the Syrian siege of Zahle, the capital of Catholicism in the Levant. To break this siege, Bashir dispatched his commando units, led by Joe Eddé.

Eddé, the scion of a prominent political family from Byblos, was non-partisan, much like the group consisting of personal friends of Bashir, either from school or university, to which he belonged.[32] In 1977, Bashir commissioned Eddé to organise the LF commando units by solidifying them into an effective and professional outfit, with no allegiances outside the group. Joining Eddé and his men in the defence of Zahle was Augustine 'Tito' Tegho, who had been abroad since 1977. Tegho was a Lieutenant in the Lebanese Army and had fled Lebanon earlier, after his regiment had battled the Syrian army around the Lebanese Ministry of Defense at Fayadieh. Commanded by the legendary Captain Samir Ashkar, Tegho's regiment single-handedly made the decision to respond to the Syrian army's provocation and effectively started the hundred-day war.[33] Sentenced to death *in absentia* for his role in the Fayadieh incident, Tito clandestinely returned to Lebanon on board a commercial boat from Cyprus. Immediately after his arrival, Tito joined Eddé and his men who had made the journey to Zahle on foot, from the ski resort in Faraya and across the snow-capped mountain. Tito, now a retired general who spends his time riding his motorcycle or swimming, spoke to me about the Battle of Zahle with great emphasis. For him and the ninety or so men who joined the people of the city in the defence of Zahle, it was essentially a matter of survival: 'It was not a Christian one but rather a Lebanese Resistance, which fought the Palestinians in 1975 and the Syrians in 1981 in Zahle'.[34]

Zahle was technically under Syrian occupation since 1976 and had no official LF barracks; thus, Eddé had to enter the city with his troops via the rugged trail across Mount Sannine. The LF continued to undertake this long hike until the Syrians used attack helicopters and landed paratroopers to capture the hills overlooking the trail, as well as the city and a strategic military outpost on the mountain peak, known as the 'French Chamber'. The violent Syrian response to Bashir's challenge was expected, given the context and timing of the confrontation. For Syria, the thought of losing Zahle had major military and political implications. In practical military terms, control over Zahle at the mouth of the Beqa'a Valley not only enabled the Syrian army to resupply its troops in Lebanon, but also prevented the Israelis from outflanking them and attacking Damascus by bypassing the Golan Heights that acted as a natural barrier.[35] More importantly, a few months earlier, in October 1980, Syria had signed a Friendship and Cooperation Treaty with the USSR, giving its army the moral and technical confidence to respond to any challenge.[36] This treaty transcended Zahle, as it managed to disrupt the Cold War *status quo* and the the implicit Syrian-Israeli agreement concerning Lebanon.

After the initial Syrian success in Zahle, Bashir gave his men a clear option. Over an open channel that the Syrians could hear, he informed Eddé that they had the option to retreat or risk being stuck in the city:

> without ammunition, without medicine, without bread, and maybe without water; your task will be to coordinate the internal resistance and defend the identity of the Lebanese Beqa'a and the identity of Christian Lebanon, and by that you will give a meaning to our six-year war. I hereby give you full authority to do whatever you see fit. I do not want to theorize. My place should be next to you in Zahle. I wish I could be next to you carrying my gun instead of being in Beirut, waiting to be killed by a random [artillery]

shell, as I prefer to die in battle. If you decide to stay, know one thing, heroes die, and they never surrender.[37]

Eddé and his men had no illusions about their predicament, but retreating was never an option for them, as Eddé responded to his commander with these few simple words: 'We will stay'.[38] They knew quite well that their potential martyrdom would be a sacrifice for the Christians in Lebanon and the Levant. However, the fate of the LF contingents defending Zahle was not sealed, as the Syrian use of aircraft in the Beqa'a Valley had violated the implicit agreement between the Syrians and Israelis, which barred both the Syrians and the Israeli from flying over Lebanon. The Israeli-Syrian Deterrence Dialogue, according to Yair Evron, prevented the Syrians from using aircraft or deploying surface-to-air missiles (SAM).[39] Consequently, the Israeli government under Menachem Begin had acted against the recommendations of the director of the Mossad, the Directorate of Military Intelligence (AMAN) and other members of his administration, when he decided to punish the Syrian transgression.[40] Begin sanctioned an airstrike that destroyed two Syrian helicopters on their landing pad east of Zahle. In the aftermath of this attack, Syria deployed several SAM batteries to curb Israeli enthusiasm about any future attacks. This was the start of what came to be known as the 'Missile Crisis' that required US intervention and the dispatching of Philip Habib, a veteran career diplomat of Lebanese-Maronite stock. As Reagan's Special Envoy to the Middle East, Habib met with all sides concerned, defused the standoff and lifted the siege of Zahle, evacuating the non-native LF fighters from the city, escorted by the Lebanese Police. Waiting for his men at the LF War Council in Karantina, Bashir received the heroes of Zahle, the cream of the LF fighting corps, who had won for Bashir and their community an unprecedented victory, despite evacuating Zahle. Joe Eddé approached and presented the official military salute to his friend and commander Bashir and addressed him with the words 'mission accomplished'.

On that day, the ninety Special Forces fighters, who later received the Medal of Zahle for their bravery and valour, through their heroic stance proved to the world that the Maronite-Israeli alliance was strategic rather than merely logistical. Bashir's words to his men were identical to those of

Figure 4.8 Returning from Zahle, Elias Zayek, Kayrouz Barakat, Bashir Gemayel, Augustine Tegho and Bob Haddad (left to right) (Wassim Jabre).

any leader celebrating a well-deserved victory, as their commander stressed the sacrifices that they had been willing to make to protect Zahle from the invading hordes. However, this speech was more of a political 'coming-out party' and an occasion for Bashir to address the Arab world, as well as the international community. He declared:

> Oh you returning fighters, your triumphant return today indeed crowns your military strength and standing over the course of six months, and in the midst of a reinforced siege, for it has solidified the line of the Lebanese resistance, a line in accordance with the desire of all Lebanese, not in opposition to any Arab or international recommendations or resolution. And on this occasion, it is necessary to thank all Lebanese, Arab and international authorities that undertook a sincere effort in order to end the tragedy of the city of Zahle, and to dismantle its siege and begin the implementation of security measures as part of a comprehensive plan for the future.[41]

It was no mere coincidence that Bashir chose to deliver his speech in Classical Arabic, something he did only three times in his short political career. Selim

Abou, the former President of the Jesuit University, has concluded that Bashir's use of Classical Arabic, customary for politicians and statesmen, was to break away from the military framework in which he was cast and to declare himself fit for the presidency, in addition to making his words heard by Arabs across the world.[42]

The Hundred-Day War complex that had plagued Bashir since 1978 had finally been lifted, as Lieutenant General Rafael (Raful) Eitan, Chief-of-Staff of the Israeli Army, had honoured his earlier promise getting word to him during the Battle of Zahle: 'Do not worry, we will not let you fall'.[43] For the Maronites and their young leader, Zahle proved above all that their cause was worthy enough to result in an international crisis and that their quest to rebuild a new Lebanon, free of the PLO and Syria, was within reach.

The Alliance of Minorities Resurrected

The Israeli decision to publicly and forcefully come to the aid of the Maronites and Bashir in Zahle marked a clear departure from the Israeli state's policy of restraint, a policy that the early Zionist leaders had consciously adopted to avoid being implicated in Lebanon's complicated sectarian feuds. The Israeli-Lebanese encounter predated the establishment of the state of Israel, as the Jewish Agency through its many Arab-Jewish operatives formed an elaborate web of contacts with all the Lebanon factions and leading individuals; however, they made sure to invest heavily in their relationship with the Maronites and their Church. Laura Zittrain Eisenberg's *Lebanon in the Early Zionist Imagination, 1900–1948* traces the evolution of this relationship, which was anchored around the idea of forming an alliance of minorities to protect non-Muslim groups from the hegemony of the Muslim masses.[44] This Zionist fervour was equally reciprocated by their Lebanese counterparts, especially the founders of the Society of Young Phoenicians and leading Maronite figures such as George Naccache, the Editor of the French-language newspaper *L'Orient* and the poet and business tycoon Charles Corm. These Young Phoenicians represented a large segment of Lebanese Christians who believed that Lebanon's and the Maronites' interests were best served in an alliance between the Middle East's minorities. Corm took inspiration from the biblical alliance between King Hiram I (980–947 BC) and King Solomon of Israel, and formed:

> A common front against their principal enemy and that is the Muslim Arab proclaiming pan-Arabism. [The Muslim danger forced] Christian Lebanon to find 'partners in fate' and among them is the Jewish community in Palestine and Zionism in general ... the Jews and the Lebanese must find a way to mutual understanding and regular relations and we are ready for this.[45]

However, Corm and his elitist circles had no real influence over the Maronite political establishment and thus all Zionist efforts to articulate and bring this friendship with the Maronites out into the open failed.

As these Zionist attempts to reach out to the Lebanese were under way, an internal debate within the Jewish Agency occurred, with two schools of thought dominating the discourse: an optimistic school, represented primarily by Haim Arlosoroff, the Head of the Political Department of the Jewish Agency; and a skeptic school led by Moshe Sharett, Arlosoroff's deputy and later successor. Sharett's faction simply looked upon Lebanon's pluralistic nature as an impediment rather than a catalyst towards normalising relations with Israel, and thus saw it futile to invest in this track or allocate funds for it.[46] This skeptic school was reinforced by the actions of the Lebanese themselves, whom the Israelis branded as two-faced and untrustworthy. The National Pact (*al-Mithaq al-Wataniyy*) in 1943 dismissed the possibility of such a Zionist-Maronite alliance, as the Christian leaders preferred to remain neutral *vis-à-vis* the Arab world and considerate of the feelings of the Lebanese Sunni community. Despite their seemingly irreconcilable difference with their Muslim counterparts, the senior leadership of the Lebanese Front – Pierre Gemayel, Camille Chamoun and Suleiman Frangieh – did not renounce the National Pact and preferred to keep their relationship with Israel discrete. Maronite leaders such as Camille Chamoun were always willing and even keen to ask for and receive funds and weapons from Israel but, in reality, they were always trying to please the Arabs and Muslims by being anti-Israeli in public. This Israeli antipathy to Chamoun was palpable in the letter that Israeli Prime Minister David Ben Gurion sent to the UN Secretary General Dag Hammarskjöld during the 1958 crisis; it stated: 'I have no bases to defend Chamoun and in all cases Israel does not interfere in the affairs of any foreign country, but I am truly afraid for the fate of the Middle East'.

He went on by adding: 'I hope that president Chamoun's term in office is short-lived'.⁴⁷

When Moshe Sharrett became Ben Gurion's successor as prime minister in 1963, the skeptic school came to dominate the Israeli cabinet's Lebanon policy, only to change with the election of the right-wing Likud Party and their leader Menachem Begin.

The Likud Party and Bashir

After winning the parliamentary elections in 1977, the Likud Party – headed by Menachem Begin, a veteran politician and hero of the Israeli War of Independence – was tasked with forming the next ministerial cabinet. Begin, who had headed the infamous Irgun militia that had fought both the British mandatory forces and the Palestinians prior to 1948, had all the necessary credentials to lead the Israelis and launch bold and risky initiatives. In 1979, the Camp David Peace Accord that Begin signed with Egyptian President Anwar al-Sadat solidified his position as a political heavyweight. The Begin government devoted more attention to Lebanon and the threat of the PLO on its northern border and consequently enhanced its relationship and cooperation with the LF. In 1978, the LF started to receive serious military hardware such as artillery and tanks as well as the customary small arms and ammunition.⁴⁸ In addition to his political motives, Begin saw in Bashir a younger version of himself, and the fight that the Maronites were waging to liberate their land from the Palestinians was no different from their own struggle in 1948. The few people who sat in on the meetings between Begin and Bashir have confirmed that 'Begin considered Bashir like a son to him'. ⁴⁹ Naturally, this warm, fatherly sentiment reflected on other branches of the Israeli government that had previously detested the LF militia, branding them as 'toy soldiers'.⁵⁰ Bashir and his men were equally influenced by their Israeli allies, as many of them had visited Israel between 1978 and 1982 to receive advanced training courses, some of which were reserved for the elite forces within the Israeli army.⁵¹ These courses included paratrooper training, security, intelligence and infantry training. Elie Hobeika and his men, for example, had been schooled in the latest security and counter-intelligence measures in the *Midrasha*, the famous Mossad Academy near Herzilya. Furthermore, Hobeika and nearly all the senior commanders around Bashir – including Fouad Abu-Nadir, Fadi

Frem and Samir Geagea – had all attended the Staff and Command College in Israel; according to one interviewee, this was 'an intense, fully hands-on course which included top-notch Israeli instructors'.[52] Beyond the military influence, these Maronite warriors were exposed to the literature and rhetoric of the Zionist movement and the various tales of the Israeli struggle for nationhood. When Johnathan Randal first walked into Bashir's apartment, he immediately noticed the memoirs of former Israeli Foreign Minister Abba Eban, a clear political statement illustrating his admiration of Israel. Furthermore, Bashir called the purge of the NLP militia which he himself authorised in July 1980 'Operation Altalena', after the Altalena Affair that had involved the state of Israel and the renegade Irgun militia headed by none other than Menachem Begin himself. In 1948, the Irgun militia had challenged the newly formed Israeli state by trying to land the ship Altalena, which was packed with fighters and weaponry. Following a long standoff between the two sides, the Israeli government ordered the sinking of the ship, confirming that there was only one legitimate Israeli state, much like Bashir did later.[53]

The Likud's parliamentary victory in 1981 saw Ariel Sharon, the hero of the 1973 war, appointed Defense Minister. Known as somewhat of a maverick, Sharon soon found in Bashir a reliable ally who stood apart from

Figure 4.9 Ariel Sharon, Bashir Gemayel and Lieutenant General Rafael Eitan (right to left) (Bashir Gemayel Foundation).

Figure 4.10 Bashir Gemayel meeting with Lieutenant General Rafael Eitan, Chief-of-Staff of the Israel Defense Forces (Bashir Gemayel Foundation).

the traditional ruling class to which his brother and father belonged. In his autobiography, Sharon perceived in Bashir a serious commitment towards 'reconstituting the independent national government that had been buried by the PLO first and then reinterred by the Syrians'.[54]

The End of the Affair: The Killing of Kamal Joumblatt

The slaying of Kamal Joumblatt was a major blow to the Lebanese National Movement and, to some extent, also the PLO, whose alliance with Joumblatt gave it a much-needed political cover to operate. However, the Druze, and certainly the pro-Joumblatt faction among them, were affected far beyond this mere political reality, as they found themselves without a leader and surrounded by Syria and the Lebanese Front, each with their own antagonising plans and goals. By custom of hereditary succession, Walid Joumblatt replaced his father as head of the Joumblatt clan, the PSP and later the Lebanese National Movement. Unfortunately, Kamal Joumblatt had not groomed his only son to replace him, and his untimely death in 1977 brought this untested twenty-eight-year-old to the forefront of his community in extremely perilous times. While his father was the product of the Jesuit educational system, which made him embrace the ideas of the Maronite establishment at least at the beginning, Walid Joumblatt was a graduate of the American University of Beirut, known to be the hub of Arab Nationalism and home to the ideas of the anti-Lebanese establishment. Furthermore, Walid stood in sharp contrast to his father's stoic and philosophical character, as he easily floated in the circles of the intelligentsia, among Western journalist and the revolutionaries of Ras Beirut. In stark contrast to his father, he relished social functions. A US embassy cable profiling Walid immediately after his father's death described his character flaws as well as merits as follows:

> Walid has an eye for pretty women and a sense of humor, according to friends. During college days, he affected 'hippy-like' behavior, dressing in a disheveled manner and roaming Beirut on a motorcycle. Classmates in college and high school found him pleasant, somewhat timid, and of only average intelligence. According to the weekly *Al-Jamhour*, he abhors smoking, but likes reading, photography, and classical music.[55]

However, the author of the same cable warned that Walid Joumblatt should not be dismissed as a lightweight merely because . . .

> It is too early to judge Walid's political abilities. Kamal, before he became head of the Yamani,[56] was supposedly shy, retiring, and unfit for political leadership. Similarly, it is premature to predict with any confidence the political positions which Walid will espouse.[57]

The first major feat of Walid Joumblatt's political career was astonishing and shocking to many of those around him. Forty days after his father's assassination, the period reserved for mourning, Joumblatt made the arduous trip to Damascus to meet the man believed to have murdered his father. Sitting opposite him, Walid listened to the Syrian President Hafez al-Assad as the latter welcomed him and informed him of the new parameters of their future relationship. In a threatening manner, Assad looked at the young Joumblatt and addressed him: 'How much you resemble your father!' This was an obvious reminder of the fate that awaited him if he decided to walk in his father's footstep and continue to oppose the Syrian regime.[58] Joumblatt consciously made this trip because he was fully aware, difficult as that might have been, that reconciliation with Syria was needed to protect the Druze and the PSP; more importantly, it was crucial for the development of his party's military infrastructure.

Figure 4.11 Assad to Joumblatt: 'How much you resemble your father!' (PSP Archives).

Preparing for War

The PSP under Kamal Joumblatt had no regular militiamen, but relied mostly on its Druze irregulars, which could be mobilised when needed. The majority of the PSP members who fought in the Two-Year War (1975–7) had received their military training by joining one of the many Palestinian factions that used to run basic training camps all over Lebanon. The weapons that these fighters used, usually a left-over from the PLO or a regional country, were somewhat basic and in short supply, as Joumblatt had neither the means nor the will to invest heavily in his militia. In November 1976, the PSP founded the People's Liberation Force – the 'Tanoukhi Brigade', a group of young men trained by a Druze medical doctor and former officer in the Mexican Special Forces, Ghazi Karami.[59] The name 'Tanoukhi' clearly indicates Kamal Joumblatt's wish to link his current political venture to that of the early Druze settlers tasked with defending the Lebanese coast against foreign invasions. In any case, this brigade was the basis for many of the fighting units that were formed in PSP-affiliated areas, especially those engaged in combat at this early stage. According to Riyad Taqi al-Din, the former Chief of Staff of the Lebanese Army who was involved in the military activity of the PSP in 1975, the Druze as a people 'were difficult to train and discipline, because they had an intrinsic belief that they were natural born fighters and thus training was unnecessary, a misconception which took a long time to alter'.[60] The decision to form an official fighting body required a long and arduous debate within the PSP. Kamal Joumblatt was not fully convinced of the utility of investing in a military body that would have entailed a tremendous financial burden, as he exclaimed: 'Where would I get the salaries to pay these men?' Nonetheless, some of the military setbacks incurred by the PSP militias, especially in the Battle of 'Araya, a key town on the Beirut-Damascus highway, prompted Joumblatt to sanction this fairly small militia not exceeding 400 fighters.[61] On 3 July 1976, the Lebanese National Movement, in an attempt to relieve their Palestinian allies during the siege of the camp of Tel al-Za'atar, attacked the Christian village of 'Araya, north of the Beirut-Damascus highway. The capture of this strategic juncture could potentially end the camp's siege, or perhaps prompt the Lebanese Forces to redeploy. The PSP were tasked with leading the attack along two main axes, while the other factions (including the Palestinians) were to lead secondary attacks on a parallel axis. Contrary to the set plan, these auxiliary factions faltered, leaving the PSP on its own in an effort to repeal the counter-offensive, which resulted in the death of twenty-seven of their fighters.[62] Raja Harb, who served as First Lieutenant at the time, spear-headed the attack that ended so tragically. To Harb and many of the field commanders, Araya was a wake-up call that victory could only be achieved if the PSP attained military self-sufficiency. Nevertheless, it was not until the death of *al-mouallam* (the guru), as Joumblatt was referred to by his followers, that a process to build a real military structure was set in motion in collaboration with the USSR. Kamal Joumblatt, a recipient of the prestigious International Lenin Peace Prize awarded to the friends of the Soviet Union, maintained a strong alliance with the USSR, and this continued under his son Walid. Kamal Joumblatt, however, never transformed this amity with the Soviets into actionable assets, especially when it came to training and arms.

Halim Bou Fakhraddine, who served as the chief liaison officer to the Soviets after 1978, affirmed that, with the succession of Walid Joumblatt, their relationship with Moscow saw a radical transformation in the modus operandi. The PSP transformed the friendship with the USSR into a more institutionalised form, as large numbers of the Druze and PSP members started to receive scholarships to study at some of the leading Soviet universities.[63] More importantly, on a military level the Soviets took the PSP under their wing and gradually transformed its militia into a proper army, with modern training and unrestricted access to weaponry when needed. Raja Harb spearheaded the transformation of the PSP militia into an organised fighting unit; he confirmed that, from 1978 until its decommissioning in 1990, the PSP militia under his command annually had about 150 men in the USSR, at the two main training facilities in the Odessa and the Simferopol Military Academy on the Crimea.[64] In the winter of 1978, the first group of fifty-two cadets arrived in the USSR, to be exposed to various military courses ranging from the School of Infantry to the more advanced Command and Staff College.[65]

Following their return, these skilled fighters formed the cadres in the PSP training camps, where they transferred the skills they had acquired to a large number of future combatants. Some of these camps featured several Syrian teachers dispatched by Hafez al-Assad to assist his new ally Walid Joumblatt. All these developments allowed Walid Joumblatt to declare on 1 June 1978 the founding of the People('s) Liberation Army (*Jayish al-Tahrir al-Sha'abi*), which eventually grew to include more than 10,000 full-time soldiers, with infantry, mechanised and logistical brigades.[66] The Druze, under the leadership of the young Joumblatt, now had an army capable of confronting any serious challenge, especially the perceived threat that was looming with the rise of Bashir Gemayel and his newly unified LF.

The Missed Opportunity

Despite the widening gap between the Druze and the Maronites, especially after the assassination of Kamal Joumblatt, both sides were determined to find a way to re-establish a working relationship that might possibly pave the way for the Christians' return to the Shuf. One of the earliest attempts was a meeting arranged by the Managing Editor of the newspaper *An-Nahar*, Michael Abou Jawdi, between Walid Joumblatt and Bulus Na'aman. This meeting took place in June 1977, and the main topic of discussion was

Figure 4.12 PSP cadets at the military academy in 1978 (PSP Archives).

Druze-Christian coexistence in the Shuf Mountains and the future challenges that both communities faced.[67] Naʿaman admitted that, while his interlocutor was warm and candid, Joumblatt was not willing to oppose the Syrians or to establish public channels with the Lebanese Front.

In July 1980, shortly after Bashir had neutralised the NLP, Zahi al-

Bustani was delegated to establish contact with Walid Joumblatt. Bustani who sat on Bashir's 'war cabinet' was a native of the town of Deir al-Qamar, and he was aware of the intricacies and dynamics of the Shuf.[68] The lunch meeting in Moukhtara, however, did not yield any serious outcome, even though the message that Joumblatt received was abundantly clear: Bashir was open to suggestions that would secure Druze consent for his project, which would see him elected as the next president of the republic.

Another and more serious attempt to bring the LF and Bashir to terms with Walid Joumblatt was undertaken by the President Elias Sarkis. This initiative was delegated to Colonel Johnny Abdu, Lebanon's military intelligence chief (Deuxieme Bureau), who was on excellent terms with Bashir and his inner circle.[69] The ensuing series of meetings took place at Abdu's house and included Joseph Abu Khalil and Antoine Najm representing Bashir's side, as well as Samir Frangieh representing Joumblatt's side.[70] Shortly after it began, Bashir's emissaries requested that a Druze be added to the opposing side; consequently, Riyad Taki al-Din joined the dialogue sessions. According to Abu Khalil, what facilitated this process was a parallel process which the Syrian regime had launched to parley with Bashir. In the middle of the Battle of Zahle, this process culminated in a meeting between Major-General Muhammad al-Khawli, Chief of Air Force Intelligence, and Bashir, also in the presence of President Sarkis.[71] Syria had always hoped to coax Bashir into abandoning his Israeli allies, in hopes of neutralising and forcing Bashir to join their side. The opinions expressed at the meeting were extremely blunt, but both sides stated their desire to explore ways to re-establish the friendship that had been shattered by the Hundred-Day War. Khawli made this clear to Syria's outspoken critic by declaring: 'I have assured President Assad that you're an upstanding man with whom we can work, and I also told him that your relationship with Israel was out of pure necessity, as you had your back against the wall'.[72]

Samir Frangieh, the scion of a family traditionally on excellent terms with the Assad clan and an active member of the Lebanese National Movement, represented Joumblatt in these talks. His father Hamid had been a leading figure during the post-independence era and a key ally of Kamal Joumblatt in the 1958 war. Frangieh, a close friend of Joumblatt's and a man with leftist inclinations, had been educated at the Jesuit University, where he and other leftists clashed both literally and intellectually with the right-wing factions, particularly with the Kataeb and Bashir Gemayel.[73] According to Frangieh, the meetings with his ideological nemesis were surprisingly positive, despite the fact that they started by hurling accusations related to preceding events at each other; both sides eventually began to exchange fruitful ideas for discussion.[74] It was clear to Frangieh that the Bashir he had known at the Jesuit University in 1968 had matured politically, as the ideas that his delegates were proposing departed from his earlier, more rigid ones. The objective of this series of meetings was to 'agree on common grounds by reaching a written agreement which would pave the way for an eventual meeting between Bashir and Walid that would pave the way to agreeing on a common vision to concoct a formula for the new Lebanon'.[75]

Bashir and Walid had never met before, and much of the information they knew about each other was based on personal impressions relayed by mutual friends or acquaintances. After his only meeting with Joumblatt, Joseph Abu Khalil reported to Bashir his disappointment in the young politician, because contrary to what he thought:

> The man I met today was unimpressive; he does not project self-confidence. He is reserved and paranoid. I thought him to be made of a tougher metal. His logic is very different from ours; he and his allies believe that our aim is the Zionfication of Lebanon. They think us to be more powerful than we are; therefore, I think they fear us. Therefore, I think we are well positioned to negotiate with him.[76]

Walid Joumblatt was equally ignorant of Bashir's persona, and many of the questions he had asked Frangieh about Bashir and the ongoing negotiations were of an inquisitive, yet aloof nature.[77] Joumblatt's ignorance concerning his foe, as well as his hesitancy to meet him, were normal given that he felt disenfranchised within a system dominated by the Maronites. Talking to Alain Ménargues, Joumblatt expressed bare-faced frustration about 'being a Druze, and my children will be as well. We will never become presidents [of the republic], whereas any Maronite, even the stupidest amongst them, can become president just because they are Maronite'.[78]

Despite reservations on both sides, the talks yielded two documents outlining the demands, expectations and responsibilities of each side, in preparation for signing a Memorandum of Understanding (MOU). When placed within their proper context, these documents are a good indication of the mindset of each faction, as well as their immediate and long-term goals. The document submitted by Bashir's team was clearly part of his master plan to seize power, by mustering enough political support to be elected president at the end of Sarkis' term, which was in one year's time. The points raised in Bashir's memorandum about 'liberating the nation from foreigners, reclaiming state sovereignty and changing the political mindset of the country' are a case in point.[79] Bashir and his team wanted to renegotiate the 1943 understanding between the Christians and the Muslims to ensure that the former group would always stay at the helm. This somewhat over-ambitious goal came with practical measures involving the cooperation of Bashir and Walid, leading to the suspension of the constitution, the dissolution of parliament and the absorption of the various militias into the Lebanese Army.[80] The most important element of the document, however, remained that the Joumblatt and the Druze would be elevated from their lowly status and placed second only to the Maronites – practically a return to the pre-1920 situation.

Yet, Joumblatt's document was more akin to a reform plan rather than a road map for political office. Many of its clauses were infused with socialist undertones, as well as demands to abolish the Lebanese sectarian system that 'creates in the Muslims a feeling of inequality and alienation'.[81] Both documents, however, noticeably acknowledge the role that each side was expected to play to warrant the cooperation of their regional and international allies. Neither of the two leaders was swayed by the illusion that their plans would work without the cooperation of Israel, Syria and the PLO. It was the absence of this regional consensus that derailed the negotiation process; by the end of December 1980, it stood only a slim chance of becoming a reality. Early on in the negotiation process, Walid Joumblatt requested that these sessions be conducted in absolute secrecy, for fear that his Syrian allies might construe this move as a challenge to them. Samir Frangieh has maintained that at the last minute 'the Syrians did not allow Walid to proceed with the deal'; the Syrian attempt to open up to Bashir had faltered, and with it the Bashir-Walid dialogue.[82] According to Ménargues, President Assad summoned Joumblatt to Damascus where he was warned not to pursue talks with the Christians and the LF.[83] The story that Ménargues has cited includes a terrifying statement by Assad while addressing Joumblatt: 'It is striking how much you resemble your father, I can see him sitting on the same chair where you are right now, and this was four days before his death. Why didn't he listen to my advice? It's a shame what happened to him'.[84]

This same story has been circulated in different contexts and variations to highlight the high-handed approach that the Syrians employed towards their allies. However, there are reasons to suspect the authenticity of such stories, at least within our current discussion. First, Kamal Joumblatt did not meet Assad four days before his death, as their last meeting took place in the spring of 1976. Second, this story offers Joumblatt the chance to exonerate himself from any blame for abandoning the dialogue with Bashir, framing it not as the result of his personal disposition, but of the Syrian arm-twisting tactics. Shortly before signing the MOU with Bashir, Walid Joumblatt had a change of heart; he travelled abroad and launched a verbal attack against the LF and Bashir's persona, virtually sealing the fate of the MOU.[85] It was no surprise that the talks collapsed almost simultaneously with the beginning of the Battle of Zahle, when a former leader of the purged NLP militia, Elias al-Hannash, instigated a fight with the LF. Believed to be an agent of the Syrian regime, Hannash deliberately provoked the local LF militia to engage in a gunfight, so that the Syrian troops would become involved.

Crossing the Rubicon: Operation Snowball

The regional implications of the Battle of Zahle and the Syrian–Israeli stand-off made it clear that the near future would bring about tremendous change. On 12 January 1981, an Israeli helicopter landed in Zouk, north of Beirut, with the Israeli Defense Minister Ariel Sharon on board, accompanied by high-ranking military and intelligence officers. Sharon was the highest-ranking official to visit Lebanon since the founding of the state of Israel, but the news to be delivered to Bashir and the LF were well worth such a trip.[86] After receiving 'a royal welcome' by Bashir, Sharon and his party were transported to the Mossad office a few miles away; there they met with Pierre Gemayel and Camille Chamoun. Over dinner, Sharon surprised his Lebanese hosts by informing them that Israel would 'rearrange its northern border by launching a major military operation . . . we will not tolerate what is happening and we are adamant to take action'.[87] This declaration, however, was not only to inform the LF, but to ask their logistical and, more importantly, political endorsement of this invasion. The Israeli army would thrust all the way into the outskirts of Beirut, where the LF were expected to get their 'hands dirty', take over and storm the Lebanese capital, which by that time was virtually a PLO bastion. After a long debate, Sharon and the hawkish faction behind him were able to convince Prime Minister Begin of the inevitability of military action in order to protect northern Israel from the artillery and rockets of the PLO and their Lebanese allies. Consequently, Begin had sanctioned Sharon to carry out one of the two plans for the invasion of Lebanon, which was an incursion limited to a range of 40 km into Lebanon, very similar to the operation that Israel had undertaken in 1978.

In 1978, an overland invasion (also known as Operation Litani) by the IDF had pushed the PLO back to the north of the Litani River, 20 miles away from the Lebanese-Israeli border. This operation, however, proved to be unsuccessful, as the activities of the PLO persisted, although with less frequency. After the signing of the Camp David Peace Accord by Israel and Egypt in 1978, as well as an undeclared cease-fire between the PLO and Israel, the right-wing Likud government felt confident enough to put an end to its Lebanon predicament. In effect, Menachem Begin wanted to end the armed Palestinian presence in Lebanon; more importantly, he wanted to 'facilitate the reconstruction of the Lebanese state and political system under the hegemony of Israeli's [Christian] allies' and thus pave the way for signing a peace treaty between the two states.[88] Begin had reshuffled his cabinet and expelled elements that did not fully endorse his outlook. Consequently, Begin had sacked his Foreign Minister Moshe Dayan and Defense Minister Ezer Weizmann, replacing them with Yitzhak Shamir and Ariel Sharon, respectively, one of the most hawkish line-ups to this day. The Israelis, via Sharon, promised Alexander Haig, then US Secretary of State, that their limited incursion into Lebanon would not extend beyond 25 km. According to Philip Habib, Haig, who was well known for his pro-Israeli leanings, gave Sharon the green light by telling him: 'We [the USA] don't think you should invade Lebanon, but it's really up to you to decide that for yourself'.[89]

Sharon had hoped to gain his government's approval for a full-scale invasion which would destroy the PLO's military and civilian infrastructure; however, despite their implicit wish to get rid of the PLO, neither Begin nor

Figure 4.13 Sharon to Bashir: 'We rearrange the northern border by launching a major military operation . . . We will not tolerate what is happening, and we are adamant to take action' (Bashir Gemayel Foundation).

the United States were willing to publicly endorse such a reckless move.[90] Sharon, never known to follow orders, ended up carrying out his original plan and coincidentally also that of Bashir – that is, 'the liberation of Lebanon from the PLO'.

On 6 June 1982, in retaliation for the assassination attempt against its ambassador to the United Kingdom, Shlomo Argov, Israel launched Peace for Galilee, a full-scale invasion of Lebanon that included three months of rigorous fighting and a vicious siege of the capital of Beirut, located 118 km beyond Sharon's initial declared plan. This ended with the evacuation of the PLO and the forced election of Bashir Gemayel as president of the republic. Thus, the stage was set for the bloody events that would eventually unfold between the Maronites and the Druze, adding to the long and turbulent past they had shared over the years.

Notes

1. Jumblatt, *I Speak for Lebanon*, 70–4.
2. Interview with Abbas Khalaf, Beirut, Lebanon, 12 December 2013.
3. Interview with Raja Harb, Beirut, Lebanon, 30 December 2016.
4. Ibid.
5. Interview with Hassan al-Beaini, Virginia, USA, February 2010.
6. http://www.14march.org/news-details.php?nid=MjM0MDkz, accessed 2 August 2016.
7. Walid Joumblatt, as quoted in US Cable, 19 March 1977, Junblatt Assassination-Situation March 19. 01211 191106Z.
8. Interview with Raja Harb, Beirut, Lebanon, 30 December 2016.
9. Ibid.
10. *An-Nahar*, 17 March 1977.
11. US Cable, 19 March 1977, Junblatt Assassination-Situation March 19. 01211 191106Z.
12. Walid Joumblatt, as quoted in Elie Hobeika, as interviewed by Ghassan Charbal, *Ayna Kunta fi al-Ḥarb* (Beirut: Riyāḍ al-Rayyis lil-Kutub wa-al-Nashr, 2011), 293.
13. *Al-'Amal*, 17 March 1983.
14. Randal, *Going All the Way*.
15. Bashir Gemayel, as quoted in Rani Geha, *Words from Bashir: Understanding the Mind of Lebanese Forces Founder Bashir Gemayel from His Speeches* (Lexington: CreateSpace, 2010), 15.
16. US Diplomatic Cable, 24 July 1978, entitled *Lebanon: Views of Bashir Gemayel*. https://wikileaks.org/plusd/cables/1978BEIRUT04178_d.html
17. Interview with Joseph Abu Khalil, *Bashir: The Series*.
18. Charles Malik (former Lebanese Foreign Minister and AUB Philosophy Professor), Zahi al-Boustani (Senior Officer in the Security General), Salim al-Jahel (judge and member of the Supreme Court), Antoine Najm (Kataeb ideologue), Joseph Abu Khalil (editor of Kataeb Newspaper *al-'Amal*), Colonel Michael Aoun, George Freiha (AUB professor), Jean Nadir (head of the Kataeb Ashrafiyah Chapter), Fadi Frem (Deputy Chief-of-Staff of the LF), Fouad Abu-Nadir (LF Commander of Operations), Elie Hobeika (LF Chief-of-Intelligence), Ass'ad Said, Elias al-Zayek and Samir Geagea (LF commanders).
19. Lewis W. Snider, 'The Lebanese Forces: Their Origins and Role in Lebanon's Politics', *The Middle East Journal* 38, no. 1 (1984), 10.

20. Ibid.
21. Interview with Naji Butrus, Makleis, Lebanon, 22 June 2016.
22. Naʿaman, *Al-Waṭan, al-Ḥurrīyah*, 302.
23. Randal, *Going All the Way*, 121.
24. Ibid., 124.
25. Naʿaman, *Al-Waṭan, al-Ḥurrīyah*, 302.
26. Interview with Bulus Naʿaman, Kaslik, Lebanon, 2011.
27. Bashir Gemayel's speech at the Yacht Club of Kaslik, as quoted in Antoine Najm's lecture delivered at AUB, 25 April 2016. Translation mine.
28. Randal, *Going All the Way*, 136.
29. Adolf Hitler's purge of his Nazi SA in 1934.
30. Ibid.
31. Ibid., 139.
32. Interview with Joe Eddé, *Bashir: The Series*.
33. Interview with Augustine Tegho, Beirut, Lebanon, 10 August 2016.
34. Ibid.
35. Alain Ménargues, *Asrār Ḥarb Lubnān: Min Inqlāb Bashīr al-Jumayyil ilá Majāzir al-Mukhayyamāt al-Filasṭīniyah* (Bayrūt: al-Maktabat al-Dawliyyah, 2006), 98.
36. Robert Freedman, *Moscow and the Middle East: Soviet Policy since the Invasion of Afghanistan* (Cambridge: Cambridge University Press, 1991).
37. Bashir, as quoted in Clovis Shuwayfātī, *Ḥarb al-Durūz wa-al-Mawārinah fī al-Jabal* [The Battles of Syria in Lebanon] ([n. p.], 2014), vol. 2, 100.
38. Ibid.
39. Yair Evron, *War and Intervention in Lebanon: The Israeli-Syrian Deterrence Dialogue* (Baltimore: Johns Hopkins University Press, 1987), 95.
40. Ibid., 94–5.
41. Bashir Gemayel's speech entitled 'Return from Zahle', 30 June 1981. http://www.arabmediasociety.com/UserFiles/File/AMS6%20Ajemian%20translations(1).pdf
42. Sélim Abou, *Béchir Gemayel, ou l'esprit d'un peuple* (Paris: Éditions Anthropos, 1984), 94.
43. Ménargues, *Asrār Ḥarb Lubnān*, 107.
44. Laura Zittrain Eisenberg, *Lebanon in the Early Zionist Imagination, 1900–1948* (Detroit: Wayne State University Press, 1994), 28.
45. Corm, as quoted in Laura Zittrain Eisenberg, *Lebanon in the Early Zionist Imagination*, 64.

46. Reuven Erlich, *Al-Matāhah al-Lubnăniyah: Siyāsat al-Ḥarakah al-Ṣuhyūnīyah Tijāḥa Lubnan (1918–1958)*, trans. by Mohammad Bader ([n. p.], 2017), 29.
47. As quoted in Reuven Erlich, *Al-Matāhah al-Lubnăniyah*, 429. According to Erlich, the second part of the letter was edited; hence, this part never made it into the English version of the letter which was signed and sent by Ben Gurion.
48. US Cable, dated 31 July 1978. https://search.wikileaks.org/plusd/cables/1978BEIRUT04345_d.html
49. Interview with Antoine Najm, Beirut, Lebanon, 10 February 2016.
50. Larry Pintak, *Seeds of Hate: How America's Flawed Middle East Policy Ignited the Jihad* (London: Pluto Press, 2003), 40.
51. Kirsten Schulze, *Israel's Covert Diplomacy in Lebanon* (New York: St. Martin's Press, 1998), 106.
52. Interviewee requested anonymity.
53. James Barr, *A Line in the Sand: Britain, France and the Struggle for the Mastery of the Middle East* (London: Simon & Schuster, 2011), 347.
54. Ariel Sharon and David Chanoff, *Warrior: The Autobiography of Ariel Sharon* (New York: Simon and Schuster, 1989), 427.
55. US Cable, dated 22 April 1977. https://search.wikileaks.org/plusd/cables/1977BEIRUT01855_c.html
56. The cable falsely states that the Joumblatts are the heads of the Yemeni factions, while the Arslans are those of the Qaysi. However, the opposite is correct.
57. Ibid.
58. Walid Joumblatt, as quoted in https://www.meforum.org/meib/articles/0105_ld1.htm
59. Bassel Abi-Chahine, *The People's Liberation Army: Through the Eyes of a Lens* (unpublished manuscript), 7.
60. Riyaḍ Taqi al-Din, *Al-Tajribah al-ᶜAskarīyah al-Durzīyah wa-Masāruhā al-Taqaddumī* (Beirut: [n. p.], 1987), 175–6.
61. Interview with Raja Harb, Beirut, Lebanon, 30 December 2016.
62. Taqi al-Din, *Al-Tajribah al-ᶜAskarīyah al-Durzīyah*, 197.
63. Interview with Halim Boufakhereddine, Beirut, Lebanon, 21 January 2016.
64. Interview with Raja Harb, Beirut, Lebanon, 30 December 2016.
65. Ibid.
66. Taqi al-Din, *Al-Tajribah al-ᶜAskarīyah al-Durzīyah*, 220.
67. Naʿaman, *Al-Insān, al-Waṭan, al-Ḥurrīyah*, 176–7.
68. Ménargues, *Asrār Ḥarb Lubnān*, 81–2.
69. See pages 137–8.

70. Abu Khalil, *Qiṣṣat al-Mawārinah fī al-Ḥarb*, 146.
71. Ménargues, *Asrār Ḥarb Lubnān*, 127.
72. As quoted in Ménargues, *Asrār Ḥarb Lubnān*, 127. Translation mine.
73. Interview with Samir Frangieh, Beirut, Lebanon, 12 August 2016.
74. Ibid.
75. Samir Frangieh, as quoted in Abu Khalil, *Qiṣṣat al-Mawārinah fī al-Ḥarb*, 149. Translation mine.
76. Abu Khalil, as quoted in Ménargues, *Asrār Ḥarb Lubnān*, 84. Translation mine.
77. Interview with Samir Frangieh, Beirut, Lebanon, 12 August 2016.
78. Ménargues, *Asrār Ḥarb Lubnān*, 83.
79. Ibid., 446–7. Document dated 20 December 1980, entitled *A Preliminary Plan to Reclaim Sovereignty*, authored by Joseph Abu Khalil and Antoine Najm.
80. Ibid.
81. Ménargues, *Asrār Ḥarb Lubnān*, 448–9. Document dated 30 December 1980, entitled *A Plan for National Agreement*, presented by Samir Frangieh and Riyad Taki al-Din.
82. Interview with Samir Frangieh, Beirut, Lebanon, 12 August 2016.
83. Ménargues, *Asrār Ḥarb Lubnān*, 88.
84. Ibid.
85. Abu Khalil, *Qiṣṣat al-Mawārinah fī al-Ḥarb*, 157.
86. Ménargues, *Asrār Ḥarb Lubnān*, 196–7.
87. Sharon, as quoted in Ménargues, *Asrār Ḥarb Lubnān*, 197.
88. Itamar Rabinovich, *The War for Lebanon, 1970–1983* (Ithaca: Cornell University Press, 1984), 122.
89. John Boykin, *Cursed is the Peacemaker: The American Diplomat versus the Israeli General, Beirut 1982* (Belmont: Applegate Press, 2002), 56.
90. Thomas Mitchell, *Likud Leaders: The Lives and Careers of Menahem Begin, Yitzhak Shamir, Benjamin Netanyahu and Ariel Sharon* (Jefferson: McFarland & Company, 2015), 73.

5

THE POINT OF NO RETURN

Bashir Gemayel's rapid rise to power brought apprehension to his Muslim enemies, but even more so to the Druze Joumblatti opponents, who perceived him as threat to their existence. This perhaps exaggerated fear was bolstered by the collective perception of the majority of the Druze who saw in the overly ambitious Bashir Gemayel an embodiment of Bashir II who had ended the Druze's dominance over the politics of Mount Lebanon, destroyed the Druze *muqatajiya* (tax-farmer) families in the nineteenth century and, most importantly, killed their leader Bashir Joumblatt.[1] Bashir Gemayel's alliance with Israel and the military invasion were also equated with Bashir II's collaboration with the invading Egyptian forces of Muhammad 'Ali Pasha in 1831, which the former used to crush both Christian and Druze opponents. Consequently, in 1982 the Druze felt overwhelmed by the Israeli invasion and the possibility of the LF entering their towns and villages to take revenge.[2] While these fears might have been somewhat exaggerated at first, the sequence of events that followed, as well as the confrontation between the Druze and the Maronites, cemented and reinforced the two communities' perception of each other.

Reclaiming our Rightful Place

On 18 June, twelve days after the beginning of the Israeli invasion, a LF convoy made its way to the Shuf Mountains, effectively starting the chain reaction that was to lead to the War of the Mountain. Before dispatching his soldiers to the mountain, Bashir Gemayel stood on the hood of a jeep at the Kasarjein Barracks in 'Ayn al-Remmaneh and gave his men instructions for the mission ahead. For many of the Christians of the Shuf, the Israeli invasion brought them closer to returning to their villages and homes, which they had left five years earlier when the reaction to Kamal Joumblatt's assassination forced them into exile. George Radi, LF soldier and native of Dar al-Haref in the Maten region, was present that day and listened carefully to the words of *al-qa'id* (the leader). Gemayel, addressing a select group of LF troops, reminded his men of the following:

> May God forgive them [his opponents] for what they did; nevertheless, we will turn over a new page. We are confident that Lebanon's 6,000 years of history will never disappear and that we will rebuild a stronger and a more beautiful Lebanon. Today, a new Lebanon is born and it will not resemble in any way the old Lebanon of 1943, which was based on indifference and dubiousness . . . we need to forget the old institutions, as we will not allow for a weak judiciary or a parliament full of brokers and wheelers and dealers . . . Tomorrow you will return to your villages to find statues commemorating the martyrs of the Communist Party and the Syrian Socialist Nationalist Party [your opponents]. You will also find your houses burnt and demolished. I tell you from now on, your duty is to protect our foes regardless of what they have done to us in the past . . . There are some people we fought for the past eight years all across Lebanon, these people have blown up our houses and desecrated the tombs of our ancestors. But today we have to respect their dead; they might have bombed our houses, but we will protect theirs. They have insulted our rituals, but we will respect theirs, they have expelled us from our homes, but we will keep them in theirs. Now is the time to take back the initiative and to reclaim our rightful place in the *Mashriq* (the Levant) . . .[3]

Also present on that day was ES, a high-ranking LF intelligence officer. Reflecting on Bashir's speech that day, ES believed that the *shabab* (troops)

Figure 5.1 Naji Butrus addressing his troops before their Shuf incursion (LF Archives).

were asked to carry out something that was virtually impossible. Despite Gemayel's conviction that his 25,000-strong militia was a professional and disciplined army, the reality was somewhat different. The LF contingent dispatched to the mountain was composed of two kinds of men. The first group of fighters comprised soldiers native to Mount Lebanon who had been displaced from their homes and villages after 1977 and who had grown up with the collective memory of their ancestors being massacred by the Druze, first in 1860 and then again in 1977, after the slaying of Kamal Joumblatt. The second breed of fighters was totally alien to the mountain but had lost loved ones and comrades and merely wanted revenge. Surprisingly, it was the latter group who aggravated the situation, mainly because they had no understanding or consideration of the particularities of the region and thus committed unspeakable acts against the Druze, such as humiliating them at roadblocks, abducting them and even committing cold-blooded murder. According to ES, Bashir's speech on that day had no 'double meaning'; Bashir literally meant what he said, yet 'the people listening to him had double feelings'.[4] Not only the populace, but also the higher echelons of both the Druze and the Maronite communities were driven by these mixed feelings, including the commander of the LF contingent dispatched to the Shuf, Naji Butrus.

A veteran commander of the 'Ayn al-Remmaneh district, Butrus was one of the participants in the famous 'bus incident' in April 1975, which had triggered the civil war. Although hailing from the southern coastal region of Maten, Butrus was also very familiar with the Shuf and the customs of its people; as a child, he had always spent his summer holiday at his maternal grandparents' house in Deir al-Qamar. Upon receiving his orders, Butrus led a mechanised convoy of 900 fighters (some of whom were support troops) from their barracks in 'Ayn al-Remmaneh to the intersection of al-Damour at the entrance to the Shuf. Waiting for them there was an Israeli General called Beja who escorted the LF troops to their new base in the abandonned Lebanese Army barracks in Beit al-Din.[5]

It seemed that Bashir did not intend to clash with the Druze, but this display of power was sure to provoke a reaction, even though several factors prevented this from happening. First, according to Butrus, the Druze assumed that his advancing troops were Israeli, mainly because their uniforms, arms and vehicles were identical to those of the Israeli Defense Force (IDF). Second, the fact that a high-ranking Israeli general was providing an escort was proof enough that the Israelis would not take lightly to any violent actions undertaken against this deployment. The choice of the Lebanese Army barracks was not coincidental, but a conscious decision by Bashir to avoid provoking the Druze. This decision was partly based on the advice of Antoine Najm, who warned Bashir of the following scenario:

> If you must send your men to the Mountain, make sure to avoid two things. Do not establish your own LF barracks, but rather use the ones that the Lebanese Army uses; second, do not disarm the Druze. If you try to disarm the Druze, they will feel under threat and thus rise in revolt, just as they did in the 1840s when Ibrahim Pasha did so.[6]

From the beginning of the invasion, the Druze refrained from any open military confrontation with the Israeli army. Despite their frustration and shock over the ease and effectiveness of the Israeli advance, not a single bullet was fired at the IDF. Within two days of the invasion, the IDF blitzed through the south of Lebanon with one clear objective – namely, reaching and securing the Beirut-Damascus highway. By securing this objective, the IDF was able to encircle the capital of Beirut and sever the supply line between the PLO and its forces in the Beqa'a Valley. The forces of the PLO, dispersed from the southern border all the way to Beirut, crumbled when faced with a better-trained, properly equipped and organised military force. In his assessment of the 'Palestinian Military Performance in the 1982 War', Yezid Sayigh has underscored the many obstacles and shortcomings of the PLO; he has emphasised that it was the PLO's failure to evolve 'fully from guerrilla units into regular forces using classical modes of operation' that gave the IDF a fairly easy military victory.[7] Regardless of the factors that led to the Palestinian debacle, it is certain that all Lebanese, and especially the pro-Palestinian among them, were shocked about the speed and ease with which the IDF advanced. Sheikh Sharif Abu Hamdan admitted that the sight of the Israeli army blocking the road to his village in the Shuf had 'a tremendous impact on the morale of everyone around him'.[8] Abu Hamdan, a Druze religious judge and an adviser to Sheikh al-'Aql Mohammad Abu-Shaqra, refused to accept the defeat and the occupation that accompanied it:

> Although people at the early stage of the invasion were afraid of the Israeli army and their plans, we, like a good Druze should always do, refuse to appear as vanquished. Upon the instructions of his eminence [Sheikh Mohammad Abu-Shaqra] and Walid Joumblatt, we requested that the people refrain from hoisting any white flags because they were unnecessary to begin with, and to simply act like civilians under occupation and to refrain from talking to the IDF troops or sell them any food and goods they needed.[9]

Walid Joumblatt was very vigilant that the Druze refrain from dealing with the Israelis, to avoid any conflict and, more importantly, to prevent them from becoming willing collaborators with what he perceived as an all-out occupation.

The Druze reality was somewhat different, for as a community the Druze did not view the IDF as an existential threat or a lasting foe. As long as the Druze were allowed to keep their arms, there was no need for them to fight the IDF; the Israelis were simply there to expel the PLO and not to hurt the Druze. For the Druze, their weapons are connected to their existence, as the Druze believe that they are their only means to protect themselves and their lands from historically aggressive surroundings. This attachment to weapons is clearly echoed in Druze popular culture, for when a baby boy is born, he is referred to as rifle, since he will be expected to defend the Druze once he reaches adulthood, much like his ancestors did before him. I vividly remember my late grandfather, who used to recite a Druze proverb emphasising that weapons are an extension of themselves rather than an accessory:

> When a huge fortune comes their way
> A Christian would build a huge mansion
> A Muslim would go to Mecca on pilgrimage
> A Druze would simply buy more weapons

While the IDF seemed to be aware of this Druze dilemma, they still tried to test their limits. On 10 June, an IDF patrol commanded by a captain pulled up to the Palace of Moukhtara, the historical abode of the Joumblatt clan, and requested to search the premises for weapons and fighters.[10] Joumblatt and his military command had anticipated such a scenario and thus refrained from keeping any of the heavy weaponry on the palace grounds; instead, they had smuggled them to other areas of Mount Lebanon. This Israeli demand naturally caused a ruckus, as all persons present (including Walid Joumblatt) confronted the Israeli troops at the entrance and refused to grant them access. According to Suleiman Rashid, the care-taker of the palace, May Joumblatt, Walid's mother, was furious about this blatant invasion of her home.[11] Under normal circumstances and as customary with Arab hospitality, every guest visiting al-Moukhtara would have been served coffee, but when the coffee boy tried to offer coffee to the Israeli soldiers, May reprimanded him by shouting: 'We don't serve coffee to the low-life dogs'.[12] The standoff was defused when the Israeli captain left the palace without completing his task, but the incident did result in a grudge. In response to the Israeli transgression, Joumblatt's close circle sent out calls to neighbouring villages to come to the aid of their besieged leader. In a short amount of time, Druze clerics and laymen started to arrive at the gates of Moukhtara. This small, unarmed crowd quickly turned into an angry mob threatening to capture the Israeli vehicles, causing the Israelis to completely evacuate the area. According to Raja Harb, who was present that day, this was an underhanded attempt by the Israelis to send a message to Joumblatt and the PSP that they were under scrutiny.[13] Shortly thereafter, an Israeli colonel paid a visit to Joumblatt to assure him that the incident was not part of IDF policy, but merely a manifestation of the schism between the different Israeli factions fighting for power.[14] While the Israeli army did enter the Palace of Moukhtara, they never managed to conduct a search or confiscate any weapons.

Yet Joumblatt's position *vis-à-vis* the Israeli invasion was always one of hostility; even when he met with officers or representatives, he made it clear that he was doing so under duress rather than out of conviction. This was the same position that Joumblatt expressed to Nachik Navot, the Mossad officer in charge of Lebanon, when the latter urged him to join a reconciliation committee suggested by President Sarkis.[15] When interviewed by Israeli state TV, Joumblatt announced: 'As a political prisoner I refuse, out of principle, to join any committee while the Israeli tanks are surrounding the presidential palace'.[16] According to Harb, the journalist interviewing Joumblatt asked whether he was a Lebanese Army officer, to which Harb replied: 'I am a Druze and also an officer in the Lebanese Army'.[17] The manner in which Harb identified himself is particularly interesting, since it reflects his own and his communities' frame of mind when threatened, as was the case in that particular moment.

Israeli attempts to reach out to Joumblatt culminated in the visit of Shimon Peres, the head of the Israeli Labour Party, to Moukhtara. Perez, whose party objected to the Israeli invasion as reckless and unnecessary, was dispatched by the president of the Socialist International (SI), Willy Brandt, to check on Joumblatt, one of the two SI Vice Presidents.[18] The Israeli cabinet had been under tremendous internal pressure, as it faced a gale of criticism from the Left, led by Peres who accused Sharon of 'shrouding the whole invasion with a cloak of deceit, and now with the end of the fighting, the immediate aim of the Israeli democratic forces is to topple the government of Begin'.[19] Peres wanted to take advantage of Joumblatt's opposition to the invasion to further discredit Begin, something that Joumblatt made sure to avoid. Joumblatt's hesitant and aggressive stance when dealing with the Israelis was not entirely based on ideology, but rather on *realpolitik*. For Joumblatt, the Israelis had certainly won the military confrontation, but the PLO was still barricaded in Beirut and the Syrian army was still stationed on the Beirut-Damascus highway. On 17 June 1982, Joumblatt left Moukhtara for Beirut, escorted by the American Counselor Ryan Crocker, who drove him through the many Israeli checkpoints around the capital, where he remained until the evacuation of the PLO two month later.[20]

Bashir vs Walid

On 20 June 1982, one day after the LF militia had entered the Shuf Mountains, Gemayel and Joumblatt met at the presidential palace in Ba'abda. The incumbent President of the Republic, Elias Sarkis, convened a so-called 'Salvation Committee', which included representatives of the major sects, to discuss the question of the Israeli invasion and its repercussions. The committee included Prime Minister Shafiq al-Wazzan, Foreign Minister Fouad Butrus, Bashir Gemayel, Walid Joumblatt, Nabih Berri (leader of the Shi'ite 'Amal Movement) and Nasri al-Ma'luf.[21] Joumblatt, who had previously refused to join this committee, finally acquiesced to Sarkis's requests after securing the approval of the Sunni political leaders Saeb Salem and Rashid Karami, as well as the expansion of the committee to include more participants. The two young warlords Bashir and Walid had never met before but had been exchanging messages through a network of interlocutors, at least since 1980. Their latest attempt to reconcile in 1980–81 was supposedly thwarted by Hafez al-Assad, who could not entertain such an idea.[22] Before the committee convened, these two had a preliminary meeting that lasted for about forty-five minutes. According to the classified minutes of this meeting, Gemayel asked Joumblatt for his support in the upcoming presidential elections. In addition, Gemayel requested that Joumblatt help end the military invasion by convincing his allies, the Palestinians, to surrender.[23] In return, Gemayel offered Joumblatt the chance to become the secondmost important man of the republic, answerable only to the president. According to George Freiha, Bashir's Chief-of-Staff, Joumblatt's cooperation was extremely important for the success of the LF project. In fact, Gemayel wanted to reinstate the pre-1840 Maronite-Druze alliance, so that the main centre of power would reside in the hands of the Maronites and the Druze, repsectively.[24] Over the centuries, the Maronites have always harboured some sort of delusion that the Druze shared their Lebanese national aspirations and that, therefore, a return to the Lebanese Emirate was plausible.[25]

Figure 5.2 Bashir Gemayel, President Elias Sarkis and Walid Joumblatt (Bashir Gemayel Foundation).

Figure 5.3 The first and only meeting between Bashir Gemayel and Walid Joumblatt (Bashir Gemayel Foundation).

The blunt manner in which Bashir addressed Joumblatt stems from the fact that, one month before the Israeli invasion, Joumblatt had relayed to Bashir's emissary his willingness to avoid any confrontation on Mount Lebanon. However, the first meeting between the two ended without tangible results. Perhaps Joumblatt would have considered Gemayel's proposal, which would have empowered the Druze politically and granted them a bigger share of the Lebanese state. However, given Joumblatt's political rhetoric during that period, one may presume that the collective memory of the nineteenth century and of his ancestor's conflict with Bashir Shihab in 1825 were not conducive to such a proposal. Any reference to this era evoked images of Maronite treachery and the persecution of Joumblatt's grandfathers, more specifically the above-mentioned Bashir Joumblatt incident. Yet, the Maronites were well aware of this and made it abundantly clear that they would never trust the Druze. Interestingly, a common Lebanese proverb preaches the following line: 'Dine at the Druze house and sleep at the Christian house'. It emphasises that the Druze are treacherous by nature and may kill a guest in their sleep. It is safe to assume that this proverb was neither created nor propagated by the Druze but generated based on the perception of their Maronite counterparts. An article that appeared in the newspaper *Al-'Amal*, entitled 'Walid Joumblatt and the Bashir Gemayel Complex', may serve to underscore this point. This one-page feature stated how Walid Joumblatt, ever since his tribal appointment to the helm of the Joumblatti clan, harboured resentment against the Maronites and particularly Bashir Gemayel, a sentiment that Joumblatt had inherited from his father. However, the most important point that the author 'Walid', so Nabil Khalefh's pen name, stated is the following:

> The name 'Bashir' has always been problematic to the Joumblatt family because it reminds them of the end of their feudalism and Bashir II. Now the Maronites, under the leadership of Bashir Gemayel, have proven that they can transform into a fighting Spartan community and not only remain businessmen and men of letters.[26]

The Battle of Qoubbei' al-Krayeh: The First Spark

On 27 June 1982, seven days after their meeting, Bashir's proposal fell through. In addition to the LF forces dispatched to the Shuf, a smaller contingent was sent to the Aley-Maten region, where it was stationed in the Mar Elias Monastery in the village of Kahlouniyeh, a few miles west of the Beirut-Damascus highway. The LF troops had taken advantage of the Israeli presence in the area and consequently started to patrol some of the surrounding villages, searching the houses for weapons. From the very beginning of the invasion, the PSP military command had issued instructions to all its units to refrain from openly carrying arms and to maintain vigilance, especially at night. However, the continuing LF transgressions, especially the search for weapons and the questioning of people, was sure to provoke a violent Druze response. At dawn, the Druze keeping guard in the village of al-Krayeh noticed some movement from the LF barracks, as troops started to head in the direction of their village. Most of my informants who fought in the battle that day confirmed that, when the LF – to which they commonly referred as Kataeb – entered their village, they were caught completely off guard. The main reason for this surprise was simply that they had assumed that these troops were Israeli, because the LF uniforms and vehicles were identical to those of the IDF. The LF started to search the houses and round up some of the villagers in the town square, which the Druze perceived as an ominous sign of a potential massacre. The Druze were particularly weary of a repeat of the 1976 scenario in the village of Salima where, in retaliation for the death of some of their own Christian fighters and using as cover the presence of the Syrian army, the LF had raided the settlement and killed a number of Druze. Shortly after the IDF had entered their region, the people of Maten delegated Jihad Bou Fakhraddine, a PSP military commander, to convey to the Israelis their fears, as well as their complete refusal of any LF presence within their areas:

> We will not allow you to enter our villages if the Kataeb [LF] militants come in after you use your forces as cover to gain entry to our areas. If you do so, we will be forced to fight you. Instead, you make sure to prevent the Kataeb from setting up checkpoints and posts. If you opt not to, you will enter the Maten only over our dead bodies.[27]

Kamel Daou, a 79-year-old Druze cleric, was detained in the village square and, along with the rest of his village, forced to sit there for more than eight hours; then, they were forced to go home and remain under house arrest for the entire six days of the battle. Insulted and annoyed by his detention, Daou addressed one of his captors: 'We are not used to sitting like this for [eight] hours'. The LF militiaman angrily replied: 'Shut up, you [Druze] have made us sit on the ground for over eight years'.[28] The manner in which the soldier responded reflects how, despite Bashir's clear instructions, many of them were guided by revenge rather than political ideology. A native of Qoubbei', Halim Bou Fakhraddine, recalls how, a few days before the LF stormed his village, he had had an altercation with an LF fighter at the hospital in the city of Aley. Following a short gunfight between the PSP and the LF, one Druze fighter was transported to the hospital with serious injuries, and as Halim started to attend to his wounds, several LF fighters stormed into the Emergency Room to arrest the patient. As a physician, Halim stood up to these men and their leader, an aggressive young man with a beard and a handgun. Emmanuel Gemayel, Bashir's nephew, addressed Halim threateningly: 'Listen, Doctor. We are the [Lebanese] State here, our way of doing things will prevail, you need to get used to it'.[29] Halim did not recognise the man at the time, but would encounter him again a week later while examining his dead body a few steps from his house.

You're Back? . . . We Have to Fight

The main response to the invasion of the village of Qoubbei' al-Krayeh came from their relatives and neighbours in the adjacent village of Qoubbei', who were equally surprised by the appearance of the LF. Ghanem Tarabay, the senior commander during that battle, confronted the advancing Christian fighters on the outskirts of his village near the mosque that usually catered to the Sunni summer residents in the area. When the Israeli invasion started on 6 June 1982, Ghanem had been in Moscow to receive medical treatment, but he jumped on the first plane to Damascus and then proceeded on foot from the Syrian border all the way to Qarnayal, where one of his comrades met him. Ghanem then drove past the Israeli checkpoints on his way to Moukhtara to meet Walid Joumblatt. Once in Moukhtara, Ghanem had to jump over the fence to gain entry to the palace where Joumblatt and his senior leadership were trapped. As he made his way up the stairs to the main hall, Anwar al-Fatayri, a veteran PSP official, rushed to inform Joumblatt of Ghanem's arrival. Joumblatt rushed to meet Ghanem at the door, addressing him with 'So you are back?' Ghanem inquired about what was to be done and received a clear answer: 'We need to fight'.[30] Ghanem then turned around and went back to his home where he prepared his men for the battle to come. Having undergone extensive training courses in both Lebanon and the Soviet Union, Ghanem harboured no illusions about the Druze's ability to fight, mainly because they were still shocked about the invasion. Some of them were convinced that the LF were better trained and equipped, impossible to beat by a weaker PSP militia. However, this proved to be completely unfounded, because by 1982 the PSP had a fully trained militia capable of defending their areas if needed, as Ghanem confirmed.

Ghanem based his decision to confront the LF on two main considerations. The first was a tactical one, to prevent the LF from linking their forces in the southern parts of Mount Lebanon with their troops in the Christian hinterland in the northern Maten region. For the Druze, such a scenario would have catastrophic military implications, as the entire area would be severed from the PSP's supply lines and thus doomed. Second and more importantly, this battle was simply a fight for our 'existence and dignity', as he reminded his comrades before the battle to 'remember Salima'.[31] For Ghanem, who was twenty-eight at the time, it was clear that the duty at hand was his family's legacy and that he was simply following what his ancestors had done in 1860 and 1958:

> My father, who had fought with the rebels in 1958, died next to me during the battle and so did a number of my cousins . . . We did not clear our decision to engage the Lebanese Forces with the Party [the PSP], but we knew what should be done. I was defending my land and my dignity, just like my father did in 1958 and my great-grandfather before him in 1860.[32]

The LF Chief-of-Staff, Fouad Abu-Nadir, confirmed that his men were acting upon their own initiative, for they had no instruction of any sort to search for weapons or arrest people.[33] Abu-Nadir, Manuel Gemayel's cousin, declared that the entire Battle of Qoubbei' was an 'accident', since the LF field commander, 'in an act of utter stupidity, acted without any instructions which led to two of our men being killed, and as we attempted to retrieve their bodies two more men died, and thus the situation got completely out of hand'.[34] It

Figure 5.4 Massoud 'Poussy' Achkar (far right) and Fadi Frem, Chief-of-Staff of the LF and later its commander (centre) (Wassim Jabre).

Figure 5.5 The Beirut Defense Unit (BDU) (Wassim Jabre).

is perplexing that the troops dispatched to Maten were among the elite of the LF fighting corps, as they belonged to the Beirut Defense Units (BDU), founded by Massoud 'Poussy' Achkar.

Even though he had turned his unit's command over to Joseph al-Zayek, Achkar rushed to Bhamdoun as soon as he received news of the incident. Poussy assumed command of the battlefield and tried to reinforce and extract his men who had been engaged in an intense gunfight with the PSP militia. To his surprise, however, the IDF prevented the LF from suppling their men and even went so far as to prevent them from setting up their mortars to provide support.[35] According to Achkar, the situation became so volatile between his troops and the IDF that a gunfight was imminent, requiring him to personally intervene to de-escalate the situation.

At the LF headquarters in Karantina, the commando units received orders to mobilise and prepare to make the trip to Qoubbei', where the battle had intensified to a great crescendo. Commanded by Ibrahim 'Bob' Haddad, one of the heroes of the Battle of Zahle, the LF commandos assaulted the PSP positions on the strategic hilltop above Qoubbei', but failed to capture it. Nassif Nakhoul, one of Haddad's three platoon commanders, described the task assigned to him and the other commandos as a 'mission impossible'; many of his comrades, he himself and his commander were seriously injured, requiring immediate medical evacuation to Beirut.[36] The PSP equally suffered many casualties, as most of the fighting fell on a dozen or so local fighters with fairly limited resources. Slowly, as word spread, these fighters were joined by their relatives and fighters from neighbouring villages. Leading a group of ten fighters from the village of Bmariam was Fawzi Abi-Chahine, also known as Abo Mot'aib (father of mischief). Abo Mot'aib regarded the battle he fought in 1982 as identical to the one that the Druze of Syria had waged in the village of al-Krayeh under the leadership of Sultan Pasha al-Atrash against the French occupation:

> That day we were around eighteen fighters on board one vehicle trying to make our way to the battlefield. The Kataeb were using all sorts of weapons and artillery in preparation for storming Qoubbei' and consequently the whole Maten. But as you are aware, the *shabab* [fighters] and the people of the Mountain have more faith and are more resilient than people who

come from Kisrwan or mercenaries from Egypt,[37] who are here to rule over a people [Druze] who answer to no one but God almighty.[38]

The LF completely dismissed the fact that their enemy consisted of local fighters but insisted that they were a façade for larger and more notorious factions. On the second day of the battle, the newspaper *Al-'Amal* reported that the IDF in Qoubbei' were engaged in an open gunfight with 'a 2,000-strong group comprised of Iranian, Palestinian and Jordanian recruits who are acting upon Syrian instructions'.[39] The report further explains that the PSP and these 'recruits' ignored the wishes of the local Druze clerics, who requested that they evacuate their village and refrain from engaging with the Israelis. Strangely enough, the Kataeb mouthpiece never made any mention of the fact that many of its men were fighting, or the fact that the grandson of Pierre Gemayel had died in combat. Responding to these allegations, Ghanem pointed out the irony of the Christians never recognising that it was the Druze who fought them, as they always sought to blame an external party. They always maintained that '[i]n 1860 it was the Ottomans, in 1958 it was Abdul Nasser and in 1982 it was the Palestinians and the Syrians. They [Maronites] do not accept that a small group such as the Druze could defeat them'.[40] Be that as it may, the Maronites certainly perceived themselves as facing a much larger plot, as Bashir's rhetoric clearly reflected in 1976:

> It must be clear for the international public opinion that the war we are conducting now is absolutely not a war between the Christians and the Muslims. It is even not a war between the Palestinians and the Lebanese. It is mainly a war between the Lebanese system, the Lebanese personality; the Lebanese identify against the extreme left groups, against the anarchist groups, against those who do not believe in democracy, in freedom, in liberty – and those people are trying to take advantage of the Palestinian cause and the Palestinian presence in Lebanon, in order to sue them to do what they are doing against Lebanon.[41]

Therefore, for Bashir or any member of the LF, limiting their confrontation with the Druze to a sectarian and tribal framework would mean to trivialise the entire confrontation and to abandon the struggle for a 'New Lebanon'.

Stuck in this quagmire, Bashir reached out to his allies within the Druze community, the Yazbaki faction led by Emir Majid Arslan. Arslan, a hero of Lebanese Independence, was seventy-four at the time, and his deteriorating health prevented him from performing the normal duties of leadership. Consequently, the burden of command fell on Arslan's eldest son Faisal, who was on excellent terms with the LF and its leader Bashir Gemayel. On the second day of the battle, Bashir met with a Druze delegation from Ras al-Maten, one of the largest towns in the Maten region, at the Kataeb chapter in Kahaleh, south of Aley. Following this meeting, Gemayel issued a public statement stressing the 'commitment to enhancing the cohesion between the Druze and the Maronites and other segments of Lebanese society'. Gemayel also asserted to his Druze guests that 'the Lebanese Forces want to achieve freedom, security and equality for all Lebanese, and that the LF merely wants to temporarily provide security and to prevent acts of vengeance until the Lebanese state can take over'.[42] Beyond this customary political rhetoric, the primary reason for this meeting was to agree on a cease-fire that would allow the LF to evacuate Qoubbei'and retrieve the body of Emanuel Gemayel. Bashir was very careful not to position himself as an enemy of the Druze, for he needed every single vote he could muster from the still surviving 1972 parliament, to be elected president. Gemayel was fully aware that any attempt to punish the Druze or harm their areas would also harm his presidential aspirations. While some Druze factions appeased and cooperated with Bashir, Walid Joumblatt continued his all-out attack on Bashir and what he called the Kataeb-Israeli plot to subjugate the mountain and Beirut. On the very day that the LF collected Emanuel's remains, Joumblatt warned his enemies that 'we [the Druze would] not permit the settling of the scores of 1860' and that the Druze would never accept disarmament under any circumstance.[43]

For Ghanem and his men, the battle had been won, despite the great casualties and damages, as they had proven to the skeptics amongst the Druze that the LF with their formidable training and equipment could be beaten. Beyond its local implications, however, this confrontation exposed both the Druze and the Maronites to the rules of engagement *vis-à-vis* the IDF. Despite their strategic alliance with the LF, Israel was not willing to take sides, nor to allow their Lebanese allies to use them to impose their will on

Figure 5.6 Mir Majid welcoming Bashir Gemayel into his home in Aley (Bashir Gemayel Foundation).

Figure 5.7 Faisal Arslan, Bashir's Druze partner (Bashir Gemayel Foundation).

Figure 5.8 Charles Malik (left), Bashir Gemayel and Faisal Arslan, following the tallying of votes that elected Gemayel President (Bashir Gemayel Foundation).

the Druze. During the battle, Ghanem had requested from one of the Druze village elders, a sheikh who had participated in the 1958 events, to take his World War II-era rifle and to walk to the Israeli post in Bhamdoun. Once there, this sheikh did nothing but keep company with the Israeli officer who was following the events via his field binoculars. This symbolic gesture was an implicit message understood by both sides, conveying that 'we mean you no harm' and that the Druze were only carrying arms for purposes of self-defence.[44] Ironically enough, the Syrian Army was also monitoring the developments of the battle from their outpost in Sawfar, where according to the LF leadership they were also providing the Druze with men and ammunition, as well as fighting support.[45] This last claim, however, remains unsubstantiated and is highly unlikely, because any Syrian intervention would have provoked a response by the IDF, something that did not occurr at that stage of the invasion.

The Assassination of Bashir

Despite this military setback in Qoubbei', Bashir remained undeterred. On 21 August 1982, as part of the settlement brokered by the US Special Envoy to Lebanon, Philip Habib, the PLO began its evacuation of the besieged capital. Two days later, the Lebanese Parliament convened under the protection of the Israeli army and elected Bashir the seventh President of the Lebanese Republic. Bashir's election, at least according to the Maronites, was not just a political conquest; rather, it was the reclaiming of a strong Lebanon capable of protecting the Christians of the East.

More importantly, Bashir's presidency was the culmination of the resistance that had started in the seventh century with the Mardaites, thus fitting perfectly within the framework of the Maronites' collective memory. Bulus Na'aman saw in Gemayel's election the realisation of a long-awaited dream that had spanned many generations.[46] This was the case because to many Maronites, including Na'aman, Bashir was not only a politician, but also a symbol of power for the Lebanese and the Christians of the Levant. This dream, however, was short-lived, as on 14 September the President-Elect was assassinated, and with him the 'dream of Lebanon'. Bashir's death took his community completely by surprise, for the bomb planted by Habib Shartouni, a pro-Syria member of the Syrian Socialist National Party (SSNP), not only killed Bashir the man, but the project that Bashir represented. His rise to power and his commitment to the ideas he preached gave people hope that a strong Lebanon might emerge from the rubble of the old. Thomas Friedman, then *New York Times* correspondent in Lebanon, witnessed Bashir's rapid ascent, as well as his tragic demise. In his landmark narrative of that period, *From Beirut to Jerusalem*, Friedman has placed Bashir, as well as other actors, as part of a regional and international poker game – a game guided only by the consideration to what extent the player is willing to use violence. No one could beat Hafez al-Assad's hand at that game. Assad, who had destroyed the Syrian city of Hama to crush the mutiny of the Muslim Brotherhood, was certainly not going to spare Bashir, or the Israelis:

> All summer long, Syria's President Hafez Assad had been losing his shirt in Lebanon. With Bashir's election, it looked as though Assad was going

to have to resign himself permanently to an Israeli victory. But in Middle Eastern poker when the pot is at stake, the rules go out the window. The only rules become Hama Rules and Hama Rules are no rules at all. On the last hand of the summer, Assad topped the Israelis' four kings with an ace, which he pulled right off the bottom of the deck. The Israelis cried for the sheriff, and Assad just laughed. 'Around these parts', he told them, 'I am the sheriff'.[47]

The LF capitalised on the martyrdom of Bashir in order to generate a new chapter in the Maronite community's memory, so that his death could be used as a launching pad for rather than the end to the Maronite political project. Several coincidences helped to make this memorial construction process less arduous. At the time of his assassination, Bashir was in his early thirties, the same age as Jesus Christ when he was crucified. On the day of his death, which happened to coincide with the Day of the Exaltation of the Holy Cross, Bashir visited the Monastery of the Holy Cross, where his sister Arzeh was a nun. Standing underneath a large cross, he delivered what was to be his last sermon, in which he stressed that Lebanon would never be subjugated. Moreover, that time was considered the resurrection of Lebanon. In addition to Bashir's image as a pious and ardent warrior, these factors helped to canonise and even deify him in his supporters' collective memory. As Michael Johnson has remarked, this 'process transformed the Lebanese Forces to a monastic order comparable to the Knights Templar, the warrior monks of the Crusade'.[48]

The LF's self-perception as an ideologically driven military outfit is clearly exhibited in its members. For example, George Radi boasted that the LF had superior arms, as well as the 'most expensive military uniform in the world'.[49] Interestingly, the LF received arms and equipment from the IDF, which were indeed of good quality, but not necessarily of the highest grade, whereas the Druze's arsenal was composed of arms made in the Soviet Union or the Eastern bloc, which the LF mistook for being of inferior quality. Furthermore, the LF fighting doctrine did not restrict them to a certain geographical location within Lebanon; therefore, an LF soldier originally from the north could serve in the south of Lebanon and *vice versa*, and this differentiated tem from the other factions fighting for local gains. Furthermore, Radi's perception

Figure 5.9 Bashir Gemayel in his last photograph, at the Monastery of the Holy Cross (Bashir Gemayel Foundation).

greatly resembled that of Crusader knights, who believed that their western armour and bravery surpassed that of their Muslim opponents. In reality, the Maronites – who were Western, non-Arab and Christian – were far more superior to their Eastern, Arab and Muslim foes.

Although Bashir's assassin, Habib al-Shartouni, was a Maronite and a member of the Syrian Socialist National Party (SSNP), the LF decided to avenge Bashir in a murderous bloodbath, and their brutality set them apart from other factions. Two days after the assassination, facilitated by the Israeli Army, Elie Hobeika, the LF's Chief of Intelligence, ordered militiamen under his command to enter the Palestinian refugee camps of Sabra and Shatila in West Beirut. As early as 1969, the Lebanese Right had demonised the Palestinians, openly accusing the PLO of trying to deport the Christians of Lebanon and establishing a surrogate Palestinian home. For example, the Guardians of the Cedars, an ultra-nationalist militia who joined the ranks of the LF in 1980, promoted the following slogan: 'The duty of every Lebanese is to kill one Palestinian'. Years of hatred, augmented by the frustration over the death of *al-Bashir* ('The Bashir'),[50] were directed against the innocent civilians in the refugee camps. After two days of carnage – which included the brutal murder of infants and the mutilation of some refugees' sexual organs – the murderous party evacuated the camps, leaving behind more than 1,700 dead civilians. Although the LF denied any involvement in the massacre, this episode tarnished the image of the pious Christian warriors that they had tried to uphold. More importantly, this massacre damaged the already turbulent relationship with the Druze who now felt that a similar fate would await them.

The loss incurred by Israel was indeed great, as both Begin and Sharon had wagered on Bashir to lead his country into a post-PLO Lebanon that would sooner or later have followed in Egypt's footsteps and signed a peace treaty with Israel.[51] With Bashir gone, both the Maronites and Israelis were doomed, as Bashir himself had predicted; shortly after his election, he had warned: 'If I die and 60,000 Bashirs don't replace me, then damn you and the cause'. Bashir's ominous warning would soon come true, as the next stage brought the Druze and the Maronite even closer to conflict.

Long Live the King

Almost a month after Bashir's death, parliament reconvened under similar circumstances, with the Israeli army providing security, and elected Amin Gemayel as President of the Lebanese Republic. Amin, the eldest son of Pierre Gemayel who had founded the Phalangist party, greatly differed from his younger brother Bashir. As a member of the Lebanese Parliament, which his brother Bashir had described as an assembly of wheeler-dealers, Amin fully espoused the 1943 formula. According to George Freiha, Bashir's chief-of-staff had agreed to support Amin's candidacy, if he honoured Bashir's commitment – namely, to sign a peace treaty between the two countries. However, Amin did not abide by this promise, and this was to have terrible repercussions on the Maronites, as will be discussed below. These factors placed him at odds with the so-called 1958 generation, which comprised most of his community, including the 25,000-strong LF.

Once Bashir was elected president, the leadership of the LF passed to Fadi Frem, the former head of its military operations and husband of Bashir's niece. Frem's mission was clear: to prepare the LF for its full incorporation into the Lebanese state, so that it would act as the backbone for a 100,000-strong army capable of protecting the entire area of Lebanon – that is, its entire 10,452 km^2.[52] However, the demobilisation of the Christian militias required the full cooperation of the Lebanese state, as these troops would form an elite unit that would answer only to the President of the Republic, Bashir Gemayel. With Bashir dead, the LF had to adjust its plan and deal with his successor, his older brother Amin. It was public knowledge that the two brothers were bitter rivals, as Amin stood in complete contrast to his brother. Amin's political career and rhetoric were the anti-thesis of the LF's new vision for the republic. While Amin was a staunch supporter and guardian of the 1943 National Pact, Bashir had wanted to destroy it.

Amin announced his intention to run for the presidency during his brother's funeral. Delivering the family eulogy, Amin seized the chance to step up to the plate:

> Comrades of Bashir Gemayel in the Kataeb or the Lebanese Forces, our oath to you is that Bashir Gemayel is still alive in his creed, he is still alive in

his determination to bring back the spirit of Lebanon . . . Our oath to you, oh great heroes, heroes of the Lebanese Forces! Some of you died defending Lebanon. Any conspiracy [to destroy Lebanon] will shatter; they were able to kill Bashir's body but they will never be able to vanquish the spirit of Bashir, nor his will to liberate and unify . . . the journey will persist until the goals for which Bashir died have been achieved.[53]

Amin would repeat the pledge 'to walk in his brother's footsteps' on two other separate occasions. The first was to Fadi Frem and the LF central command – consisting of Elias al-Zayek, Elie Hobeika and Fouad Abu-Nadir – when he hosted them for a dinner at his house in Bikfaya. To the LF officers around the dinner table, their fears and hesitation to support Amin were not totally unfounded. Nicknamed *al-ᶜanid* ('the stubborn one'), Amin had always resisted subjecting the Maten region to the rule of the LF and refused to surrender his hold over the many businesses and racketeering organisations he operated. Amin ran the area under his command as his own fiefdom, with a standing army answerable to him, a think-tank called *House of the Future* and a newspaper, *Le Reveil*, to promote his own line.[54] Bashir's war cabinet, which was now leaderless, met and deliberated about the upcoming presidential elections, primarily about their position *vis-à-vis* Amin's nomination. Following a heated two-hour session, the group consented to Amin's nomination after he vouched to implement Bashir's governance and reform plan.[55]

Amin would reiterate this pledge on 20 September, three days before his election, to an Israeli delegation that he hosted at the *House of the Future* in Antelias. Sitting opposite the Israeli Foreign Minister Yitzhak Shamir, Ariel Sharon and David Kimche, former Deputy Director of the Mossad and Director-General of the Ministry of Foreign Affairs, Amin confirmed that, if he were elected, he would honour Bashir's earlier commitments.[56] Menachem Begin and his hawks had to adjust to the reality of losing Bashir; however, they hoped that their original plan to evict the PLO and sign a peace treaty with Lebanon was still attainable. Amin had contacted the Israeli state as early as his brother and Dany Chamoun had done, but he always made it a point to suppress this fact and instead portrayed himself as a clean-cut politician unattached to any militia. Alain Ménargues has maintained that Amin was in fact far more brutal than his brother Bashir, since he had personally led the

Figure 5.10 Amin Gemayel, Pierre Gemayel and Bashir Gemayel (LF Archives).

Kataeb forces on the battlefield; however, the major difference resided in the fact that, while Bashir publicised his involvement in such actions, his older brother did the exact opposite.[57] Despite his contact with Israel, Israeli intelligence agencies always viewed Amin with suspicion, mainly due to his good relations with the Assad regime and the PLO. Furthermore, Amin was one of the main advocates for the Syrian army's entry into Lebanon in 1976, to aid the forces of the faltering Lebanese Front. In September 1982, however, the forty-year-old Gemayel told his Israeli guests what they wanted to hear:

> You are most welcome! I am very delighted to receive you at the House of the Future . . . we cannot describe the amount of grief we as a family, party and a nation are experiencing due to the loss of Bashir; above all, he was my brother. Bashir has done tremendous work for the country and the Lebanese people, so we have to continue what he has left behind and try to persist in the same direction. I have read some of the minutes of your meetings with Bashir. Our relationship has been ongoing since 1958, and I believe it can be developed into a real peace treaty between the both of us.[58]

Shamir was mesmerised by this tune, and the mere mention of peace caused him to bestow the presidency on Amin, by addressing him with the following symbolic statement: 'Mr. President, we are saddened by the loss of

Bashir, but we are glad that your movement and your people have found a leader to continue the road towards independence. We are confident that tomorrow you will be elected president'.[59] Towards the conclusion of this fateful meeting, Sharon in his usual brutish, blunt manner grabbed Amin by the shoulders and declared: 'The king is dead, long live the king'.[60] True to the Israeli promise, the members of parliament voted for Amin to become the seventh president of the Lebanese Republic. Shortly thereafter, upon the initiative of US President Ronald Reagan, the multi-national peace-keeping forces comprised of American, French and Italian divisions landed in Beirut, with the 'declared' mission of 'prompting the withdrawal of Israeli, Syrian and Palestinian forces from Lebanon and to strengthen the ability of the government of Lebanon to defend its sovereign territory'.[61]

The Druze recognised neither the legitimacy of the new president, nor the fact that he did not necessarily share his brother's political vision. The PSP media outlets launched an all-out attack against Amin and accused him of trying to establish a monarchy. *Sawt al-Jabal* (Voice of the Mountain), the PSP's radio station, constantly referred to Amin as 'the Shah of Ba'abda' and to the Lebanese Army under his command as 'the Army of the Ruling Family'.[62] This perception of Amin Gemayel as a despot and extension of his brother was embedded in the Druze collective psyche, adding to their resentment of the Maronites and making it impossible for the Joumblatti Druze to reconcile with their Maronite foes. More importantly, an examination of the Druze rhetoric during the period from the fall of 1982 to the fall of 1983 clearly demonstrates their fear of annihilation at the hands of a people whom they considered as 'neo-Crusaders'. Walid Joumblatt's interview with *Newsweek Magazine* summarised this fear and the lengths to which the Druze were willing to go in order to prevent it from becoming a reality:

> We are now in a state of war with the Isolationists [Lebanese Forces] who are responsible for the massacres of Sabra and Shatila and Tel al-Za'tar, among others. They want to do the same thing to the Druze. However, I will not allow at any cost my people to be butchered at the hands of the Phalangist.[63]

The Sabra and Shatila Massacre had grave repercussions for both the IDF and their Lebanese allies, especially within the context of the Druze–Maronite conflict. First, it internationally discredited the current Israeli leadership, especially Begin, Shamir and Sharon, for not honouring their promise to the United States not to enter Beirut. Second, it placed the responsibility for the carnage on the LF's shoulders, as they had perpetrated an act of blind vengeance. These were the conclusions of the 'Commission of Inquiry into the Events at the Refugee Camps in Beirut', set up by the Israeli government shortly after the massacre and headed by the Supreme Court Justice Yitzhak Kahan. The Kahan Commission placed the responsibility on the Israeli political elite, blaming them for neglecting their duty and refraining from taking appropriate action. However, immediate blame was clearly placed on the LF who had entered the camp under the supervision and with the assistance of the IDF, as this had permitted their Lebanese allies to commit the most heinous of crimes:

> Our conclusion is therefore that the direct responsibility for the perpetration of the acts of slaughter rests on the Phalangist forces. No evidence was brought before us that Phalangist personnel received explicit orders from their command to perpetrate acts of slaughter, but it is evident that the forces who entered the area were steeped in hatred for the Palestinians, in the wake of the atrocities and severe injuries done to the Christians during the civil war in Lebanon by the Palestinians and those who fought alongside them; and these feelings of hatred were compounded by a longing for revenge in the wake of the assassination of the Phalangist admired leader Bashir and the killing of several dozen Phalangists two days before their entry into the camps.[64]

This condemnation demonised the LF both locally and internationally, as this gruesome act lacked any basis of self-defence, a concept that Bashir had previously used as pivotal anchor of his political project. It also placed the LF on a collision course with President Amin Gemayel, who shortly after his election refused to meet with any Israeli officials and failed to honour his earlier commitment to stay on his brother's charted path. The LF had become a political liability for Amin Gemayel who was keen to re-establish political and economic relationships with the Gulf States and, ultimately, with Syria.

Notes

1. Traboulsi, *History of Modern Lebanon*, 230.
2. Interview with Sheikh Sharif Abou Hamdan, PSP Oral History Project.
3. *An-Nahar*, 19 June 1982.
4. Interview with ES, Beirut, January 2010. The interviewee requested anonymity. He said this *verbatim*.
5. Interview with Naji Butrus, Makleis, Lebanon, 22 June 2016.
6. Interview with Antoine Najm, Beirut, Lebanon, 10 February 2016.
7. Yezid Sayigh, 'Palestinian Military Performance in the 1982 War', *Journal of Palestine Studies* 12 (1983), 8.
8. Interview with Sheikh Sharif Abu Hamdan, PSP Oral History Project.
9. Ibid.
10. Interview with Raja Harb, Beirut, Lebanon, 30 December 2016.
11. Interview with Suleiman Rashid, PSP Oral History Project.
12. Ibid.
13. Interview with Raja Harb, Beirut, Lebanon, 30 December 2016.
14. Ménargues, *Asrār Ḥarb Lubnān*, 243. The rank of the officer is not confirmed, due to two contradictory sources; however, he certainly was a high-ranking field commander.
15. Ibid., 249.
16. As quoted by Ménargues, *Asrār Ḥarb Lubnān*, 250.
17. Interview with Raja Harb, Beirut, Lebanon, 30 December 2016.
18. Ménargues, *Asrār Ḥarb Lubnān*, 250.
19. Peres, as quoted in Ménargues, *Asrār Ḥarb Lubnān*, 250.
20. Interview with Suleiman Rashid, PSP Oral History Project.
21. See *An-Nahar*, 20 June 1982.
22. See page 155.
23. Interview with an LF official who requested anonymity.
24. Interview with George Freiha, Beirut, Lebanon, 11 January 2010.
25. Salibi, *House of Many Mansions*, 205.
26. *Al-'Amal*, 4 July 1982, 'Walid Joumblatt and the Bashir Gemayel Complex: A reading into Joumblatt's political stances based on a psycho-sociological historical interpretation.' The article also featured a relatively small picture of Walid Joumblatt with the subtitle 'The remnant of old Lebanon', while in the centre above it was a large picture of Bashir Gemayel with the subtitle 'The new face of Lebanon'.

27. Interview with Jihad Boudine, PSP Oral History Project.
28. Interview with Sheikh Kamel Daou, PSP Oral History Project.
29. Interview with Halim Bou Fakhraddine, Beirut, Lebanon, 21 January 2016.
30. Interview with Ghanem Tarabay, Qoubbei', Lebanon, 23 June 2013.
31. Interview with PSP Military Commander who requested anonymity, Beirut, December 2009.
32. Ibid.
33. Interview with Fouad Abu-Nadir, Beirut, Lebanon, 23 February 2016.
34. Ibid. According to Druze sources, the LF's local commander who consequently died during the battle was Ibrahim al-Tawil, but this fact has never been verified.
35. Interview with Massoud Achkar, Beirut, Lebanon, 7 June 2016.
36. http://www.lebanese-forces.com/2015/03/28/nassif-nakhoul-kunna-hounak/, accessed 21 August 1981.
37. This is a reference to Pierre Gemayel's family who took refuge in Egypt for fear of Ottoman persecution.
38. Interview with Fawzi Abi Chahine, PSP Oral History Project. Translation mine.
39. *Al-'Amal*, 28 July 1982.
40. Interview with Ghanem Tarabay, Qoubbei', Lebanon, 23 June 2013.
41. Bashir Gemayel's Interview with ITN, 21 August 1976. http://www.itnsource.com/en/shotlist/RTV/1976/08/21/BGY510070259/?s=%22Lebanon%20first%22%20bashir
42. *Al-'Amal*, 29 July 1982.
43. *Al-'Amal*, 1 July 1982.
44. Interview with Ghanem Tarabay, Qoubbei', Lebanon, 23 June 2013.
45. Interview with Massoud Achkar, Beirut, Lebanon, 7 June 2016, and Fouad Abu-Nadir, Beirut, Lebanon, 23 February 2016.
46. Antoun Saad, *Man, Country, Freedom: The Memoirs of Bulus Na'aman* (Beirut: Entire East Publications, 2009), 469.
47. Thomas Friedman, *From Beirut to Jerusalem: Updated with a New Chapter* (New York: Picador, 2012), 157.
48. Michael Johnson, *All Honourable Men: The Social Origins of War in Lebanon* (Oxford: Center for Lebanese Studies. 2001), 66. Bashir's speech can be viewed in full on http://www.youtube.com/watch?v=I-AFsC_AUkU&feature=related.
49. Randal, *Going All the Way*, 17.
50. Following the death of Gemayel, his name started to appear in LF media outlets as well as in their rhetoric as 'The Bashir', to glorify his martyrdom.
51. Ibid., 144.

52. Ménargues, *Asrār Ḥarb Lubnān*, 394.
53. Amin Gemayel's eulogy at Bashir's funeral, as reproduced in *Al-'Amal*, 16 September 1982.
54. Randal, *Going All the Way*, 133.
55. Ménargues, *Asrār Ḥarb Lubnān*, 45–6.
56. Ibid.
57. Interview with Alain Ménargues, Kaslik, Lebanon, 30 December 2015.
58. Amin Gemayel, as quoted in Ménargues, *Asrār Ḥarb Lubnān*, 54. Translation mine.
59. Yitzhak Shamir, as quoted in Ménargues. *Asrār Ḥarb Lubnān*, 2, 55. Translation mine.
60. Interview with George Freiha, Beirut, Lebanon, 11 January 2010.
61. National Security Decision Directive (NSDD), 64.
62. The Voice of the Mountain radio station, one-year anniversary of *Harb al-Jabal*.
63. As quoted in *Al-Anbaa'*, 6 June 1983. It is interesting that Joumblatt refers to the Druze as 'my people' rather than 'my sect'.
64. Kahan Commission, 8 February 1983. http://www.jewishvirtuallibrary.org/jsource/History/kahan.html, accessed 3 March 2020.

6

THE WAR OF OTHERS VS DRUZE–MARONITE COLLECTIVE ANIMOSITY

The devastating outcome of the Sabra and Shatila Massacre reflected badly on the LF, beyond their political and legal condemnation. The Kahan Commission further punished the LF, as it recommended to Begin to sack his Minister of Defense, Ariel Sharon, reminding Begin of his prerogatives 'under Section 21-A(a) of the Basic Law to remove a minister from office'.[1] Begin refused to adopt this recommendation at first, but finally bowed to local public opinion; ultimately, he settled on the removal of Sharon's portfolio and kept him in his cabinet as a minister without portfolio.

The Israeli Tide Shifts

Replacing both Sharon and the IDF Chief-of-Staff Eitan were Moshe Arens and Lieutenant General Moshe Levi, respectively, who, according to David Kimche, 'were made of a different fiber'.[2] Kimche, the veteran spymaster and former deputy director of Mossad, was known for his zeal concerning the Maronite-Israeli alliance, which he himself as the head of the Mossad's Lebanon operations had solidified after 1975. Naturally, Kimche saw Sharon's removal and his replacement with the more sober and pragmatic Arens as having dire consequences on the Israeli-Lebanese political process. At the time, Kimche was leading the Israeli team that engaged in the peace negotiations between the two countries, which later came to be known as the 17 May Agreement. Obviously, his main priority was for these talks to succeed. Both Arens and Levi, however, shared one priority: 'to redeploy their troops to reduce casualties, and to cut the size of the army committed to the Lebanese front so that the training programs could be resumed'.[3] Therefore, any earlier commitments that their predecessors had made to their Lebanese allies had to be secondary to their current policy.

Walid Joumblatt and the Druze were equally aware of this new shift in policy, as the Israeli cabinet and the IDF began to slowly abandon their clear bias towards the Maronites. At the beginning of the Israeli invasion, Joumblatt and the PSP constituted the main allies of the PLO; this naturally placed them at a disadvantage and led the IDF to approach them with suspicion. While adopting a clearly anti-Zionist rhetoric, the Druze of Lebanon never committed any acts hostile to the invading Israeli forces. It was the elders of the Druze community who imposed this attitude, rather than the consensus of the Druze political leadership, which was divided concerning its view of the invasion. The Yazbaki faction led by Faisal Arslan was fully committed to Bashir Gemayel and his quest for the presidency, while the Joumblatti faction felt stifled by the defeat of their PLO allies.

Amidst this schism, the Druze *mashayikh* (clerics) would determine the parameters of the relationship with Israel. While it would have been politically embarrassing for the PSP and its supporters to establish contact with the IDF, the Druze clerics felt no shame in contacting their fellow Israeli Druze across the border. However, their initiative had no direct political implications, nor did it entail any normalisation of relations with the Israeli state. The clerics restricted their interaction with the Israeli Druze as much as possible, commonly referring to them as 'the Arabs of 48' – a thinly veiled expression to avoid calling them 'Israeli'. Early on, with the IDF's entry into the Shuf and following several incidents that included gunfire on some Druze villages and rumours of the Israelis' intention to confiscate their weapons, the clerics initiated contact with the head of the Israeli forces in the area. Upon the request of the eminent Sheikh Abu Mohammad Jawad Walieddine of Baakline, Sheikh Muhana al-Btadini, accompanied by his brother and another member of his family, marched to the Israeli base in their village of Kfarnabrkh. After an hour's wait, the three Druze clerics were granted an audience with the Israeli General. With the help of a translator, Btadini addressed his host: 'We, the Druze, preserve our dignity and our honour and our land. We have not fought you [Israelis]; we have only fought those who have harmed us, and our weapons are to be used for this purpose alone'.[4] The Israeli general was extremely cooperative, as he assured Btadini and his companions that they could keep their weapons, provided they were kept concealed and that they informed the IDF of the existence of any 'saboteurs', as Palestinian fighters were commonly called. Before the Druze cleric and his companions departed, they requested that the general provide them with a document that attested his promises, after which they headed back to Baakline to inform Sheikh Abu Mohammad Jawad of their feat.[5] With the restrictions on travel to and from Israel lifted, the Druze from both sides of the border, and especially the clerics among them, started to exchange social and religious visits. This naturally rekindled the relationship between the two communities, which had been severed by the creation of the state of Israel in 1948. Yet, this resumption of relations did not translate into practical measures, since until the assassination of Bashir Gemayel the IDF had treated the Druze of Lebanon with borderline hostility. This was even evident in the behaviour of several Druze officers within the IDF, particularly Colonel Said Abdul-Hak, who later commanded the exclusively Druze Herev (Sword) Battalion. The Druze of Israel had always occupied a privileged status in comparison to other non-Jewish communities; they were drafted and allowed to enlist in the IDF, both as service men and officers. By the 1980s at least, their allegiance to the state of Israel was no longer in doubt, as they had served in many wars and spilled blood defending the Jewish state.[6] Furthermore, the head of the community, Sheikh Amin Tarif, was recognised as the spiritual leader of the Druze by the state of Israel and awarded all the legal and political prerogatives that came with this post. For the IDF's Druze soldiers dispatched to Mount Lebanon in 1982, including Abdul-Hak, the mission was clear: to neutralise the Palestinian threat while limiting civilian casualties and collateral damage.[7] Abdul-Hak was rather unbrotherly when dealing with many of the Lebanese Druze, especially members of the PSP, earning himself the nickname Abdul-Mahiq (the Dwindling Slave). Raja Harb, who on a number of occasions experienced altercations with Abdul-Hak, accused him of having anti-Joumblatti sentiments, as he went out of his way to harass and restrict their movements. However, Abdul-Hak's aggressive attitude towards the Joumblatti clan was an isolated example, as the majority of the Israeli Druze were untouched by the Joumblatti-Yazbaki schism and essentially only interested in supporting their Lebanese Druze brethren.

The Druze Follow-up Commission

Zeidan Atashi was the first Druze to serve on the Israeli Knesset (Parliament) and the first Druze to enter the Israeli Foreign Service, having occupied a number of posts, including the Israeli Permanent Mission to the UN. On 29 June, Atashi participated in a tour of Lebanon organised by the Knesset to demonstrate the progress of the IDF, which was laying siege to the capital of Beirut.[8] During this tour, Atashi visited the Druze town of Aley, where he heard of his fellow Druze's protests over the continuing IDF cover and support for the LF and their intolerable infractions.[9] According to his book *Druze and Jews in Israel*, Atashi's first of many trips to Lebanon was extremely revealing for this Israeli Druze lawmaker, as 'this was my first encounter with Druze on Arab soil and it was not pleasant to see the IDF, in which I also served, participating in acts of cruelty against my Druze brothers'.[10] After his return home, Atashi initiated a series of actions that would greatly aid the Lebanese Druze in their looming confrontation with the Maronites. Tobias Lang, in his study *Die Drusen in Libanon und Israel* (The Druze in Lebanon and Israel), has explained how Atashi's endeavour required one specific key element to succeed – that is, the support of Sheikh Amin Tarif.[11] Tarif was not merely the *sheikh al-'aql* of the Druze of Israel; his stature exceeded this legal framework, as he also occupied a spiritual role in Israel and beyond. According to Atashi, however, Tarif and his immediate circle were extremely hesitant to extend their support to the Lebanese Druze, because this would naturally entail directing criticism towards the Israeli state, something that Tarif refused to do, especially during wartime. Faced with considerable pressure from within his community, Sheikh Tarif finally conceded and blessed the activities of Atashi's group. Consequently, the Israeli Druze community set up a lobby group that approached Menachem Begin to voice their disapproval of the IDF actions *vis-à-vis* the Druze of Lebanon. In response to the Druze disgruntlement, Begin promised 'that he would not permit that a hair should fall from the head of any Druze in

Lebanon'.[12] Begin's attitude towards the Druze might have been supported by a number of factors, as the Druze essentially represented a segment of the Likud Party's electorate; thus, he was compelled to answer them in this fashion. The second and more plausible reason lies in the fact that this issue was tackled by the Office of the Prime Minister's Adviser on Arab Affairs, whose duty it was to ensure that the affairs of the non-Jewish minorities, among them chiefly the Druze, were always addressed. While some voices within the community objected to the Druze's conscription to and service in the IDF, the majority of the Israeli Druze were extremely supportive of the state and its policies. According to Atashi, the invasion of Lebanon was the first time in the community's history that the Druze stood in stark opposition to their state.[13] This position was the crux of the committee known as 'Druze Follow-Up Commission on behalf of the Druze of Lebanon'(*Lajnat al-Tawasil*(, formed by leading activists, each with their own background and network of connections.[14] The activities of the *Lajnat al-Tawasil* consisted of a two-pronged approach: the first was to address Israeli public opinion with an orchestrated media campaign, and the second was to lobby the Israeli government as well as key officers of the IDF. The main argument that Atashi and his associates utilised to influence the Israeli public was to frame the Israeli invasion led by Sharon and the hawks as deceptive in nature; he stressed that the LF failed to honour their promise – namely, joining the battle against the PLO as 'the [Israeli] soldiers found themselves fighting the Phalangists' war for them'.[15] Moreover, by crossing the forty-kilometre range originally assigned to the operation, Sharon had violated the trust of the Israeli government and its people. Furthermore, the IDF troops deployed across Mount Lebanon badgered the Druze of Lebanon, thus 'acting beyond the declared operational targets'.[16] Atashi admitted that the main leverage that allowed them to effectively voice their protest consisted of the rights awarded to them as 'full' Israeli citizens, but, perhaps more importantly, they had officers and soldiers placed throughout the IDF and various state agencies.[17] Many active and retired IDF Druze servicemen were asked to approach their comrades-in-arms and simply ask the following questions: 'Why is the IDF supporting the Maronites who are killing our Druze brothers in Lebanon, and what have the Lebanese Druze ever done to hurt Israel?'[18] This simple yet powerful message slowly made its way across

Mount Lebanon, as the IDF abandonned the measures they had formerly adopted against the Druze and curbed the LF's hostilities against them.

However, the activities of the Follow-Up Commission went a step further by providing the Druze of Lebanon with moral support for more practical military measures, which proved vital when the conflict reached its climax. Atashi and other members of the commission started to make regular trips to Lebanon, where they would secretly meet with senior members of the PSP's political and military arm. The commission was mindful of the importance of keeping their support to their coreligionists as covert as possible, to avoid embarrassing them in front of their Muslim compatriots, as well as broader Arab circles.[19] On the Druze side, secrecy and a good amount of reservation cloaked this relationship with the Druze of Israel, as none of the members of the PSP publicly acknowledged that these meetings took place, nor that these meetings consequently fostered friendship. The only name that the Lebanese side acknowledged in public was that of Atef Salloum, a pediatrician and graduate of the American University of Beirut who had launched his career in Beirut before relocating his practice to Aley. Salloum was instrumental in coordinating the activities of the Follow-Up Commission on the ground. According to Avner Yaniv, Salloum acted as Joumblatt's *quasi* foreign minister, as he made frequent trips to Israel where he met prominent members of the Druze community, as well as high-ranking state officials.[20] Yaniv related that on 31 July 1983 Salloum was scheduled to meet the Deputy Prime Minister David Levi, but for reasons unknown this meeting was canceled in the last moment.[21] Salloum unequivocally denied Yaniv's allegation, stating that such a meeting was fictitious and that the relationship with the Israeli side was never one of a diplomatic or political nature, as some might assume; rather, it emerged from the need to 'coordinate with the IDF, the force that was occupying our region at the time, so the Druze could have a semblance of normalcy in their everyday life and have proper access to food, freedom of movement and above all access to weapons'.[22]

The choice to have Salloum handle the coordination with the Follow-Up Commission is very revealing of how Joumblatt and his group approached their contacts with Israel. Atef Salloum never was a card-carrying member of the PSP, nor had he ever occupied any political post that could be traced to Joumblatt and his party.[23] Despite working closely with Kamal Joumblatt at the outset of the civil war on matters pertaining to medical and healthcare issue, Salloum always stayed out of the limelight, a fact on which Walid Joumblatt later capitalised. Joumblatt could simply deny any involvement in these activities and disregard any of Salloum's commitments towards the Israeli side. The essential reason for Walid Joumblatt and his Druze constituency to keep their association with the Israeli Druze underground was not merely consideration towards the feelings of their Muslim compatriots, but rather a self-serving existential aim. The Druze collective self-perception – that is, being descendants of the early Arab settlers defending the Syrian coast against Crusader attacks – clashed with that fact that they were neutral towards or even collaborating with the Zionist state. Just as the Druze have suppressed the fact that their Buhturid ancestors collaborated with the Crusaders or that the great Druze Emir used the Italian city-states to rebel against the Ottomans, they did not want this episode to figure in their community's history.[24] Be that as it may, Salloum was not merely acting in favour of the Joumblatti clan; rather, his actions were directed by a wider social and religious compass interested in the well-being of the Druze community as a whole. He did not see in his actions anything harmful to the self-perception of the Druze, nor to their regional standing.

Admitted to the Druze *'uqqal* at a young age, Salloum had the full support of his ecclesiastic brethren who commissioned him to act as a liaison with the Druze political elite, the Lebanese state and later the Israeli occupation. Initially, Salloum had been summoned by Sheikh Abu Mohammad Jawad Walieddine and informed that the Druze *'uqqal* wished for him to act as their representative, as they did not wish to be involved in worldly political matters. This appointment was further confirmed by Sheikh al-'Aql Mohammad Abu-Shaqra, Emir Majid Arslan and Walid Joumblatt. Thus, Salloum's contact with the Israeli side, of which the Syrians were coincidentally informed, was not as secretive as assumed, but the endeavour was carried out discretely to ensure its full success.[25]

Be that as it may, the Follow-Up Commission was able to gain traction and slowly influence Israeli public opinion. On 19 October 1982, upon the call of the commission, around 1,500 people demonstrated outside the office of Prime Minister Begin. Atashi communicated to the government the demands of the mob, which amounted to a virtual threat:

The government of Israel must choose between the alliance with the Druze of Israel – which has proved itself – and the dubious collaboration with the Phalanges. This is an hour of testing and decision, and we have had enough un-kept promises. Israel must know that the Druze have never bent their knee in the to stand history of the Middle East and will continue strong and upright as surety for their brothers.[26]

By stating that the Druze were in an alliance with Israel, Atashi was virtually revoking his people's Israeli citizenship for a far more important consideration, one that was at the core of his community's faith. According to Atashi, the whole endeavour he led simply constituted his religious duty as a Druze, because by 'safeguarding his brothers and sisters (*hifiz al-ikhwan*), he was doing the 'proper thing', which any other Druze in his position would do'.[27]

To safeguard their Lebanese brothers, the Follow-Up Commission set several practical goals that would rid them of their Maronite enemies:

- To remove all roadblocks erected by the Phalange under IDF cover.
- To secure the release of all Druze prisoners detained on the initiative of the IDF forces or as a result of Phalangist incitement.
- To find ways and means of transferring essential weapons from place to place with the aid of locals or Druze IDF soldiers serving in various locations.
- To raise funds among the Druze of Israel, to be remitted to the Druze leadership in Lebanon, in order to help purchase combat weapons and clothing and rations for the combatants.
- To affect a gradual modification of the attitude of the IDF officers and commanders responsible for the Druze villages and to attempt to foster understanding for the Lebanese Druze and the actions of the Israeli Druze on their behalf.
- To ensure that the Follow-Up Commission confined its contacts to the Druze spiritual leadership in Lebanon, and elements representing the PSP headed by Walid Joumblatt, the militia in charge of Druze defence and security.
- To refrain from interfering in the internal Druze dispute between the Joumblatts and the Arslans.

- To unambiguously refute the claims of the Phalangists who falsely accused the Druze of Lebanon of giving asylum to thousands fleeing Palestinians in front of the IDF commanders and policy-makers.[28]

To achieve these difficult goals, the Follow-Up Commission needed the help of the IDF officers and troops deployed across Mount Lebanon. Many of these troops started to slowly realise that they were entangled in a primordial conflict between the Druze and the Maronites. According to Thomas Friedman, General Amnon Lipkin-Shahak, the supreme commander of the IDF in the Shuf, discovered that things in Lebanon were never what they appeared to be and that he certainly 'lacked the imagination Beirut and Lebanon required'.[29] Lipkin-Shahak, a hardened solider who later assumed the post of chief-of-staff, found himself caught between the Druze and the Maronites, each of them demonising the other in hopes of gaining the support of the IDF. Like many of his comrades, Lipkin-Shahak arrived at the conclusion that he 'was in the middle of a game I did not understand'.[30] This feeling was more amplified within the ranks of the Druze IDF officers, chiefly among them Amal As'ad, whose paratrooper battalion was the first to enter the Shuf Mountains in 1982. As'ad, who was the first enlisted Druze to join the prestigious paratrooper brigade, admitted that he was at first influenced by the LF's misinformation concerning the Druze of Lebanon. According to As'ad, 'as Druze officers we never cared about the politics involved, but slowly after we entered Shuf we realised that the Kataeb had lied to us'.[31] The Maronites, so As'ad, were using the IDF as cover to commit unspeakable acts against his people; therefore, he felt obliged to act. Consequently, As'ad made sure that all the IDF posts and roadblocks had a Druze soldier posted to it, so as to intervene on behalf of their Lebanese brothers. As'ad commanded respect among the elite IDF units, and he explained that their support of the Lebanese Druze was never driven by logic, but deeply rooted in their psyche.

During one of the gunfights, As'ad and his men were caught in the village of Qabr Chamoun; there, he saw an elderly Druze woman approaching his position, accompanied by a small girl who appeared to be injured. As'ad has admitted that, as he stood in front of the woman wearing the traditional white *mandil* (veil), something inexplicable happened: 'It was as if I were looking into the eyes of my mother'.[32] Immediately, As'ad ordered his men to stop shooting and proceeded to address the woman in Arabic, asking her how he could be of assistance. The woman was taken aback by the fact that Asʿad spoke Arabic; he jokingly replied: 'Auntie, I am a calf like you, I am a Druze, don't worry'.[33] In a similarly emotional situation, Asʿad was informed that the Druze religious shrines of Sit Shaʿawani in the West Beqaʿa Valley had sustained some direct hits, but that their contents were still intact. Consequently, with permission from Sheikh al-ʿAql Muhammad Abu-Shaqra, Asʿad commandeered more than seventeen IDF trucks and evacuated the entire contents of these shrines to the shrine of Sheikh al-Fadil in the region of Wadi al-Tayem. This gesture on Asʿad's part might not carry any real practical military implications, but within the context it was a resounding affirmation of Druze identity and Druze attachment to land and traditions.

As the confrontations between the Druze and the Maronites escalated, the Druze IDF soldiers adopted a more pro-active role, even participating in combat on the side of the PSP. The soldiers' participation provided moral support, as it reaffirmed their belief that 'the Druze are like a copper tray; if you hit it on one side, the whole tray resounds'.[34] While the IDF command allowed some of these transgressions, one should not assume that it was their policy to support the Druze and the PSP. Many of the Druze IDF soldiers who disobeyed orders were court-martialed and even imprisoned; such was the case of Amal Asʿad's brother, who spent some time in the military stockade.[35] Many of these Druze transgressions were permitted by the IDF, as long as 'no Israeli blood is spilled on Druze land', a pledge which the Follow-Up Commission was able to extract from their PSP contacts.[36]

The Follow-Up Commission played a very important logistical and military role, as the Israeli Druze bribed their fellow Jewish soldiers deployed across Mount Lebanon to facilitate the movement of PSP logistics. Salloum has admitted that a small fortune was spent on pursuing these goals, as all arms shipments sent to the Druze from Syria had to go through checkpoints manned by Israeli soldiers, soldiers who received envelopes filled with cash, as Salloum conveniently ensured. Perhaps more importantly, Salloum also had a monthly allocation of 15,000 USD, which was paid to the Druze in Israel for translation service rendered to the Hebrew Israeli press, since the Lebanese Druze were carefully following the internal debate about the Israeli invasion and the pressure on the government to quickly bring it to an end.[37]

On the eve of the Israeli withdrawal from Mount Lebanon, Salloum was able to obtain a treasure trove of military information, as the Israeli Druze – equipped with 100,000 USD provided by a Lebanese Druze philanthropist – obtained the full Israeli withdrawal plans with detailed maps, something that proved to be vital in the ensuing battle.[38]

The arrangement brokered by the Follow-Up Commission allowed Walid Joumblatt to assert his command over the Druze even more strongly. Despite having the support of a clear majority over his Yazbaki opponents, Joumblatt still lacked the legitimacy and the experience that his father and his ancestors had possessed. Furthermore, the Druze Yazbaki faction at the time was at its political apex, with its leader Faisal Arslan granting Bashir Gemayel's project his full support. The election of Bashir, as it was rumoured at the time, would soon guarantee Faisal Arslan an appointment in the next cabinet, where he would naturally assume one of the key portfolios. Following Bashir's election, Faisal led a large delegation of his own supporters to the hometown of the president-elect, Bikfaya, to congratulate his friend and ally on the resounding victory. Arslan's congratulatory party, which included a noticeable majority of senior Druze clerics, intended to serve two goals: to assert Arslan as the paramount leader of the Druze, and to declare that, contrary to the Joumblatti allegations, Bashir was indeed a friend of the community. Bashir had always found the Arslans 'more Lebanese', as opposed to the Joumblatts whose international and regional affiliations, particularly with the Palestinians and the international Left, were not located within the same ideological framework. In addition to Faisal Arslan, Joumblatt was also challenged by other elements within the Yazbaki faction, as well as the community at large. His challengers included Fadlallah Talhouk (Aley MP), Bashir Awar (Maten MP), Malek Wahab, Salim al-Daoud, Hussein Talhouk, Kamal Abou Hamdan, Raouf and Wahib Abdul Samad, Kahtan Hamada and Farid Hamada. Essentially, this anti-Joumblatt front genuinely believed that it was in both their personal as well as the Druze's interest to support the Maronite bid for power.[39]

Farid Hamada, the son of the last Yazbaki Sheikh al-'Aql Rashid Hamada, in his opposition to the Joumblatti faction went so far as to coordinate with Bashir Gemayel to form his own Druze militia that would challenge the PSP militia if needed. George Rouhana, one of the veteran Kataeb military

Figure 6.1 Farid Hamada (Wikimedia Commons).

instructors who had trained the first cohort of fighters in 1975, admitted that 'Sheikh Bashir sent me twenty men from the Hamada family to train in our camps, but he gave me strict instructions that none of our comrades should know that they were Druze'.[40] According to Rouhana, who referred to the matter in a humourous tone, 'luckily enough, these Druze trainees were blond with colourful eyes, and thus it was feasible to have them pass as foreigners'.[41] According to Alain Ménargues, Hamada's military outfit, the Druze Jihad Organisation (*Majd*), was also funded and trained by the French external intelligence agency (DGSE), which used *Majd* as an information-gathering tool.[42] Hamada's French connection was very evident; it continued long after the end of the war, when he was given asylum by the French authorities after the Syrian army entered East Beirut where he had been exiled since 1984. The anti-Joumblatt faction headed by Hamada attempted to reach out to the Druze clerics whose support was instrumental for Walid Joumblatt's survival. Consequently, Hamada, the scion of a family that had produced three sheikh al-'aql, during the feud with the LF reached out to the Druze clerics of the religious seminary in Khalwat al-Bayada and the surrounding region, trying to convince them of the futility of supporting Joumblatt.[43]

The Unification of the Druze

Faced with the threat that both the LF and the Yazbaki faction posed, Joumblatt was still struggling to win over the majority of the Druze who were either too afraid to act, or traditionally hostile to the Joumblatt household. To unify his community, Walid Joumblatt had to employ a method other than the one utilised by Bashir Gemayel, who applied brute force to get his way. Within the tribal structure, any spilling of Druze blood would polarise and further divide the community; therefore, Joumblatt and his veteran PSP staff deliberately avoided any public attacks on their Yazbaki opponents so as not to turn the confrontation into a political tug-of-war. According to Hisham Nasreddine, a member of the PSP Politburo and during the War of the Mountain the head of the party in the district of Aley, the decision to avoid Druze bloodshed was a conscious and practical decision that the party leadership firmly implemented. Nasreddine, a key adviser to Joumblatt, warned him that 'under no circumstance should the PSP suppress their Druze rivals by utilising violence, because spilling Druze blood would have dire consequences on the unity of the community and consequently on its ability to fight the Kataeb'.[44]

Nasreddine confessed that his advice was rooted in the history of the Druze, particularly in the confrontation between Sheikh Bashir Joumblatt and the Abu Nakad family in the nineteenth century, which ultimately weakened the Druze and later prevented them from forming an effective front against Emir Bashir.[45] Instead of adopting a Bismarckian approach to unifying the Druze, the PSP appealed to their non-partisan Druze network to discredit and refute the Yazbaki claims, and to expose the existential threat that the LF posed for all the Druze, regardless of their political inclinations. The PSP subsequently conceded some of its political roles and allowed other Druze elements to lead the confrontation against the Maronites. These elements included both religious and secular Druze, who were equally apprehensive about the Maronite infiltration into their areas. Despite its essentially secular doctrine, the PSP allowed the Druze sheikhs to assume a more active military as well as political role, by including them in the meetings that the PSP regularly held with either the LF or the IDF. Sheikh Kamal Ghanam (Abu Saleh) was delegated by the Druze clerics to participate in the various meetings which Toufic Barkat, head of the PSP Shuf district, and Naji Butrus, the LF Shuf commander, held to negotiate cease-fires or secure the release of hostages. Butrus recalled how aggressive Abu Saleh always was in their meetings, as opposed to Barkat who was always willing to entertain his demands and suggestions.[46] The PSP, and subsequently the Druze, adopted this tactic in their many rounds of negotiations with the LF. This strategy included Barkat giving Butrus the impression that he was willing to accept his demands, upon which Abu Saleh would then interject and take a more militant stance. This front, which the PSP wanted to maintain, gave them a strategic advantage, by allowing them to use the entire Druze community as cover. Moreover, this strategy relieved them from any blame due to potential setbacks, while still being able to take credit for any future victories or gains. Just like their Buhturid ancestors had done at the battle of 'Ayn Jalut, the PSP did not want to shoulder the responsibility for their entire community, because a defeat could mean their displacement and ultimately their demise.[47] This stance reflects the Druze tendency to never concede defeat, but to adapt to the outcome, whatever it may be, with the intention of preserving the community. As the story goes, the Druze would never make a move or declare their real intentions until the result of any situation was known, so as to avoid having to concede defeat. Consequently, the Druze are famed for saying: 'The matter can no longer wait, we need to congratulate them or go offer our condolences'.[48]

The PSP similarly sought legitimacy for their project from the office of *mashayikhit al-'aql* and Sheikh Muhammad Abu-Shaqra, whose staunch opposition to the LF's entry into Mount Lebanon was extremely palpable throughout the conflict. Contrary to the traditional Druze narrative, however, the support of the sheikh al-'aql was neither rudimentary, nor easy to acquire, as Abu-Shaqra was not willing to fully adopt the PSP's plan of action *vis-à-vis* the LF or President Amin Gemayel. Elected to office in 1949 on the initiative and with the support of Kamal Joumblatt, Abu-Shaqra had previously conformed to all Joumblatti policies, especially when his faction was challenged. In 1958, during the brief conflict between Joumblatt's men and Camille Chamoun's forces, Abu-Shaqra had taken a firm stand behind his political patron, 'all for the good of the Druze community and as a living symbol of the community's religious foundation, unity and steadfastness'.[49]

In 1982, however, matters were different, as Abu-Shaqra's blind obedience to the Joumblatti factions changed. First, Abu-Shaqra was no longer competing with a Yazbaki contender, since the death of Sheikh Rashid Hamada had virtually unified the post. Second, Abu-Shaqra saw himself as more experienced in Druze affairs, as he himself had placed the symbolic mantle of leadership on the shoulders of the young Walid Joumblatt in 1977; therefore, he assumed a *quasi* mentor role for the young Joumblatt, and not the other way around. The Maronite political establishment also tried to further empower Abu-Shaqra with the intention of weakening Joumblatt, whom they wanted to portray as unfit to lead the Druze. Abu-Shaqra had responded to this positively, but restricted his interaction with Amin Gemayel, who, despite Joumblatt's objections, ultimately was the elected president of the republic. During the conflict in 1983, Gemayel ordered the installation of a direct telephone line between himself and Abu-Shaqra, to be used for deliberations as well as emergencies.[50] Naturally, this special relationship between Abu-Shaqra and Gemayel was not welcomed by the PSP; nevertheless, no public denunciation was ever issued on their part. Most of the senior PSP officials whom I interviewed spoke of their uneasy relationship with Abu-Shaqra, but they remained cordial towards him. To overcome this challenge, the PSP used a method similar to the one employed by the Israeli Druze to convince their own Sheikh al-'Aql Amin Tarif to cooperate with them. Consequently, Joumblatt and his circle never challenged or questioned Abu-Shaqra's authority in public, but at their private meetings with him included implicit threats would he ever fail to conform to their plans. The PSP's success in finally reigning in Abu-Shaqra was facilitated by the fact that in many parts of Mount Lebanon the Druze were subjected to random acts of violence by some elements of the LF contingent at their various checkpoints. Fouad Abu-Nadir has admitted that some of his men violated orders by insulting the Druze and especially their clerics, and going so far as to shave moustaches and pull down the sheikhs' traditional baggy trousers to humiliate them.[51] Such transgressions made it impossible for Abu-Shaqra to continue his lukewarm support of the PSP; perhaps under moral duress, he soon began to coordinate with Walid Joumblatt before issuing political statements, especially during the months before the final military confrontation with the LF. Sheikh Sharif Abu Hamdan, political aide to Abu-Shaqra, remarked that 'it was the courageous and synchronised position of the great patriotic leader Walid Joumblatt, and his eminence Sheikh Muhammad Abu-Shaqra which helped the Druze survive'; he added that the Druze 'never fear death nor shy away from war, as they had fought Ibrahim Pasha and the Egyptians, the Ottomans, the French and any future aggressor'.[52] Naturally, the Druze religious and political establishment wanted to portray such an image of internal cohesion, even though this so-called unity was lacking for most of the period in question.

In a further attempt to strengthen their legitimacy, the PSP tried to widen the scope of support within the Druze community by appealing to a segment of the community that usually remained neutral in the Joumblatti-Yazbaki strife. This group of Druze notables had all achieved success in their own respective fields, and they had the necessary wealth or stature to speak on behalf of the Druze. These individuals were also active in several Druze NGOs and associations, mainly based in Beirut. Sensing the need for media outlets and political representation in Beirut, these individuals had established the Permanent Bureau of Druze Associations (PBDA), which offered a platform through which the Druze could lobby for local and international public opinion.[53] While the PSP did possess the resources and the expertise to create their own media and to recruit people, they could not adopt an explicitly denominational undertone, which the PBDA could do without reserve. Anwar al-Fatayri, a veteran PSP activist, was appointed Commissioner for Mobilisation, a Soviet-inspired post, which was created at that time. A great orator and polemicist, Fatayri was tasked with strengthening the resolve of the PSP's members and supporters across Mount Lebanon; however, his scope remained restricted to this circle and thus was insufficient by itself. Hisham Nasreddine, who assisted Fatayri by going from village to village to lecture and rally support for their cause, admitted that 'on the Beirut scene, however, we [the PSP] lacked the media presence, and therefore the PBDA was needed to fill this void'.[54]

According to Akram Saab, a founding member of the PBDA, their initial task was to ensure that the Druze point of view regarding the events of *Harb al-Jabal* was heard by the general public. This task was further augmented once Walid Joumblatt left Lebanon for Jordan, after his life was at serious risk in the winter of 1983. Consequently, the PBDA compensated for his absence by flooding the local and international media with articles and news emphasising

Figure 6.2 Akram Shehayab, Anwar Al-Fatayri, Raja Harb, Sharif Fayyad and Hisham Nasreddine (left to right) (PSP Archives).

the defensive nature of the Druze's military actions.[55] As the fighting escalated, the PBDA became part of the military effort and established the Emergency Fund, which raised funds worldwide to serve a variety of needs, ranging from purchasing weapons and ammunition to basic medical and relief efforts, and even food and supplies for both civilians and combatants.

Sheikh Halim Takieddine, a member of the PBDA's executive board and the head of the Druze religious courts, was a regular contributor to this information war, as his articles and commentaries appeared in the daily press, either responding to allegations by the Maronites and their Druze allies, or simply illustrating to the public the fears of his own people. Takieddine, who came to be the voice of the PBDA, would travel far and wide to spread information and explain the ongoing conflict. On one of his trips to Brazil, Takieddine was invited to address the Brazilian prime minister and an assembly of Druze and Arab expatriates. In his address, he stated:

> The whole idea of Lebanon was the creation of the Prince of the Druze, the Great Ma'an, when the Shuf was the heart of Lebanon and the base of

the principality ... in your quest today we have not attacked any of our Lebanese brothers [Maronites], and we have neither challenged nor provoked them because this is simply not part of our principles and customs ... the Druze have never assaulted anyone, and if any attack occurs, they would object to it and demand justice for the victim. They [Druze] also have never allowed anyone to attack them, and if this attack did happen, their reaction would be brutal and more violent, for in peacetime they are loving, loyal and neighbourly, and in times of war they are brave, chivalrous and noble.[56]

The theme of self-defence was a staple of nearly all Druze political rhetoric, and especially so of the literature of the PBDA, which provided reasons for the Druze's use of excessive force against the LF and civilian Maronite targets. The PSP and the Druze religious authorities had warned their followers against targeting civilians, but these warnings naturally fell on deaf ears. This was mainly due to the traditions within the rural tribal structure of Mount Lebanon, dictating that violence would always be met with violence. This led Halim Takieddine to issue a statement at the height of the clashes, urging the religious authorities on both sides to take a firm stance against the killing, abduction and torture of civilians, the destruction of places of worship and the looting of homes. Takieddine went so far as to declare that violators of these 'commands' would be subjected to excommunication.[57] Takieddine's threat did not deter the Druze from what they considered a preemptive and defensive strike against their Maronite enemies, as they committed horrendous acts of violence that further bolstered their reputation as bloodthirsty and ruthless.[58]

On 8 November 1982, the Christians of Kfarnabrkh in the Shuf were burying the victim of an encounter with the Druze, when their funeral procession was ambushed; seven were killed and several more wounded.[59] The Druze followed this ambush with an attack on the Christian quarter in the village and torched twenty houses and fifteen vehicles, including the house of the Roman Catholic Bishop Mikael Ra'ed.[60] According to Naji Butrus, the IDF prevented him and his men from leaving their barracks in Beit al-Din to come to the aid of the innocent civilians who were butchered by the Druze.[61] The LF had earlier voiced their concerns about the possible collaboration of some of the IDF's Druze troops with the PSP. On the day of the massacre, the IDF contingent stationed in the village had unexpectedly evacuated their positions, leaving the Christians fully exposed to a Druze attack.[62] In a subsequent meeting with the commander of the IDF on Mount Lebanon, Amnon Lipkin-Shahak, Butrus lost his temper and yelled at the Israeli general: 'Who are your friends, us [the LF] or the Druze? Why do you block the entrance of our barracks and prevent us from using our vehicles?' Then he grabbed an ashtray and threw it to the floor. This tantrum was not merely a reaction to the incident at Kfarnabrkh but indicated the overall frustration about the lukewarm support that the IDF had shown the LF over the past months, perhaps an omen of things to come.

The Druze, however, have maintained that the massacre at Kfarnabrkh was not an isolated incident, but the culmination of a series of events that had begun a few months earlier, with the LF's entry under the cover of the advancing IDF forces. A few days prior to the massacre at Kfarnabrkh, three members from the Btadini family were found slaughtered in their house in a secluded rural area on the outskirts of Brih. While the perpetrators of this crime remained anonymous, according to tribal law, the Druze were obliged to avenge their dead; consequently, they decided to open fire at the funeral procession a few days later. This eye-for-an-eye attitude added to the volatility of the situation on Mount Lebanon. A PSP combatant explained why the Druze generally responded with such mercilessness, by referring to the 'anecdote of the cat'.[63] In the villages, it was customary that, before 'a man gets married, he has to yank the head off a cat in the presence of his future wife, to send a message to his wife and all those present that he means business'. This Druze tactic was necessary, because they lacked both numbers and sophisticated weapons at that stage; therefore, 'what we lacked in numbers we compensated for with brute force'.[64]

The Christian drive to arm and militarise their community was a natural reaction to Druze aggression in 1982, as it had been earlier in 1977, after the assassination of Kamal Joumblatt and the massacre of innocent Christian civilians. Joumblatt's murder and the subsequent events led to a feeling of general insecurity within the Christian community. This was especially so among the members who belonged to the parties that rivalled the PSP, leading them to leave their villages and towns, only to return in 1982 with the beginning of the Israeli invasion. Prior to this date, these exiled patrons of the Kataeb, and later the LF, had been organised under the supervision of the Bureau of the Occupied Areas (BOA), which was entrusted to Joe Eddé, the commander of the Battle of Zahle. According to George Eid, one of Eddé's key aides, 'Bashir Gemayel created the BOA to maintain contact with the parts which were under Syrian occupation and in order to recruit its [Christian] youth and train and arm them'.[65] The BOA – which reported to Fouad Abu-Nadir, the head of LF's operations – set up an elaborate and secretive training program for hundreds of LF members who were living in the Shuf and Aley region. Simon Moussallam, a native of the village of Birh in the Shuf, was one of many adolescents who received his basic training through the BOA. He has reported:

> We used to go down to East Beirut where we used to receive basic military and infantry training, and all this was done in secret. Most of these sessions used to take place in the Don Bosco barracks in the Byblos region. We used to assemble each village on its own or sometimes multiple, and when we had thirty members we used to undergo a short training session and then go back home to our villages, without letting our parents know what we were doing. Our main objective was to be prepared to protect our villages if needed; at first, we could not bring weapons to the mountain, so we had to resort to the weapons we already had and use them to guard our villages.[66]

These sleeper cells, which by 1982 numbered in the hundreds, deployed as soon as the IDF reached their villages and unleashed a series of bloody confrontations with the Druze which only grew worse with the passing of time.

Khaled Btadini, a native of Kfarnabrkh and commander in the PSP militia, recalled how the Christians of his village and the area started 'to go to Beit al-Din to receive basic military training, and consequently started to parade in the villages with their guns and in their full Lebanese Forces uniform, provoking the Druze'.[67] Btadini remembers how the mere sight of the LF uniforms would provoke the Druze who at one time attacked a uniformed LF supporter from a neighbouring village and sent him back stark naked. During a more vicious attack, the Druze blew up the gas station in the village of Mas'ar Beit al-Din, after the LF had issued orders that anyone wanting to buy gasoline was obliged to obtain a coupon from their offices.

The Druze, according to Btadini, felt humiliated as they were forced to stand in line, subjected to humiliation and verbal abuse before they could obtain their coupon.[68] Despite these tensions, both the LF and the PSP attempted to avoid future clashes by forming local village committees, which included representatives and clerics from both communities. Fawzi Abu-Abbas, head of the PSP for Arqoub in the Upper Shuf, was a regular attendee at these meetings, which however failed to curb further bloodshed. The main problem, according to Abu-Abbas, was the return of many Kataeb and LF members to their villages, with the clear intention of exerting vengeance for years of displacement.[69] The LF's insistence on assuming the role of the Lebanese state invoked a violent reaction from the Druze who saw the militarisation of their Christian neighbours as threat to their own existence. Both the Maronites and the Druze publicly accused the Israelis of playing a negative role in the events; on one hand, the LF kept demanding that the IDF disarm the Druze and thus defang them, while on the other hand the Druze were demanding the immediate withdrawal of the LF's armed presence from their areas. In fact, the IDF only cared about maintaining the security of their own troops and control over the areas under their command. To achieve this, the IDF would use the carrot-and-stick approach when dealing with both the Druze and the Maronites. The PSP members allowed to arm themselves and to smuggle weapons under the watchful eyes of the IDF, which knew quite well that the source of these weapons was Syria and the USSR. One day, Fouad Abu-Nadir received a call from one of the LF's advanced observation posts on the Beirut-Damascus highway, informing him that the Israelis had allowed the removal of the sand barrier; afterwards, a truck had crossed over. Almost immediately, Abu-Nadir approached the truck filled with weapons and proceeded to follow it on its journey to the town of Aley, where it delivered its payload to the PSP. Abu-Nadir later protested to the Israeli commander of the area, stating that he himself 'had seen the barrel of a mortar protruding from the back of the truck and that the many IDF roadblocks had waved the truck on, fully knowing that it was transporting arms to the Druze'.[70] The IDF commander's shocking reply was: 'Of course, we know where the Druze get their weapons, their arms are Soviet-made, and they have to get them through the Syrians, and for them to do so we have to allow them to pass'.[71]

Hisham Nasreddine showed no restraint in relating this episode of military cooperation with the IDF. For the PSP, arms were vital for their victory; thus, Nasreddine and his comrades resorted to any means necessary to smuggle these weapons across, going so far as to use money, drugs, alcohol and even female prostitutes to bribe the soldiers manning these checkpoints.[72] Nasreddine jokingly narrated how he would gift to the Israeli soldiers who stopped him on his way back from Damascus boxes of *barazek* (Syrian sesame sweets), which they accepted with a smile.

The Battle of Mtolleh

Israeli leniency found its limits when the PSP crossed a red line; punishment was swiftly administered, as the events of the Battle of Mtolleh proved. In an attempt to breach the LF supply lines on their southern flank, the PSP attacked the Christian town of Mtolleh, which divided the Shuf from the Iqlim al-Kharroub, the coastal section of the Shuf. The success of this PSP attack would prevent the LF from reinforcing their troops through the port of Jiyeh, which linked the LF to their heartland. However, the PSP overplayed their hand by carrying out this attack, as they had not realised that this area was not included in the IDF's Jabal sector but belonged to the southern command. Consequently, the LF were successful in repealing the PSP assault after the IDF permitted them to call in reinforcements and artillery cover. The LF Chief-of-Staff Abu-Nadir, accompanied by the LF elite fighting unit al-Saddam, joined these forces the day after he had made the trip to Jiyeh by sea and assumed command on the battlefield. Trained by the Israelis and fashioned after the IDF's Sayeret Matkal unit which carried out the famous Entebbe raid in Uganda in 1976, al-Saddam consisted of experts in close-quarter warfare and proved to be instrumental on the battleground, incurring heavy casualties among the ranks of the PSP.[73]

The PSP had dispatched to the battlefield its best fighting men, most of whom had been trained in the Soviet Union and gained some field experience. Among them was Walid Safi, the youngest PSP officer to graduate from a Soviet military academy at age twenty and the commander of the sector that supported the troops assaulting the LF in Mtolleh and its adjacent area.[74] Safi has denied that the PSP had any intentions or the resources to engage in battle; rather, this confrontation was imposed on his party by the LF and the Israelis. The LF justified their defeat at the Battle of Qoubbei' in a similar

Figure 6.3 Fouad Abu-Nadir (Wassim Jabre).

Figure 6.4 The al-Saddam unit, fashioned after the elite Israeli unit Sayeret Matkal (Wassim Jabre).

tone. The PSP refused to acknowledge any fault in their military tactics or their execution but blamed their failure on the Israelis' direct intervention in the battle. Nearly all of the combatants interviewed by the PSP Oral History Project reiterated this line, adding that part of their battle had been waged directly against the IDF. This clash with the IDF consequently led to the death of one Israeli soldier and the capture of an armoured IDF transport, in addition to a jeep that the PSP then used to transport some of their wounded to the hospital.[75] Mtolleh was a resounding defeat for the PSP, which until that day had kept a fairly successful record in their confrontations with the LF. Alaa Tero, the PSP field commander, was seriously wounded, alongside twenty-nine others, and another seventeen were dead. Some of the bodies could not be retrieved by the PSP until the battle was over.

Interestingly, the LF declared that their victory in Mtolleh was in spite of the Israelis, not thanks to them, as they accused the IDF of aiding the Druze attackers and impeding the movement of their own troops by preventing them from using their heavy artillery. The LF command's bitterness was obvious when they met with General Meir Dagan, head of the Lebanon Liaison Unit (Yakal), shortly after the end of the battle. Dagan, whom Sharon had personally appointed to run Yakal, assured his Lebanese interlocutors that the IDF had indeed dispatched forces to aid the LF, but that those forces had been ambushed by the Druze.[76] Fadi Frem – who in the preceding days had cabled Israel to demand that they declare 'who their friend was and who their foe' – was unsatisfied by Dagan's justification. He repeatedly asked him how it was possible for the Druze to mobilise 500 of their troops without the IDF taking notice. Furthermore, Frem blatantly accused his allies of helping the Druze by supplying the PSP fighters with IDF uniforms, which they used to infiltrate some of the LF lines. The LF senior commanders found it extremely malicious that the Druze had been allowed to use their artillery battery which they had deployed a few miles from the command post of General Lipkin-Shahak in the Aley region, a fact that Lipkin-Shahak himself admitted.[77]

The LF's accusations and fears were not totally unfounded, but a reflection of the political reality that was transpiring in Lebanon and the region. On 6 May 1983, shortly before the Battle of Mtolleh, the Israeli cabinet voted on accepting a peace treaty with Lebanon, one of the top priorities of Prime Minister Begin and a condition that Bashir had promised his allies, a promise that his successor Amin had also pledged to honour. Under the auspices of the Reagan administration, Amin Gemayel hammered out a peace accord between Lebanon and Israel, which was signed on 17 May 1983. Gemayel, who unlike his brother wholeheartedly supported the National Pact, did not want to antagonise the Sunnis whom he considered to be an important pillar of the state. Thus, to use David Kimche's words, he 'could not afford to appear too forthcoming' in their negotiations with the Israeli side.[78] Kimche, who signed the treaty on behalf of Israel, was optimistic that:

> the work we have done together over these past months will have laid the foundations of a strong and lasting bond of friendship between our two countries. This is our destiny, and it will come about despite the contrary words of politicians . . . we are, as you know, an ancient people, conscious of our past heritage which lives on with us. We had, as you know, excellent relations in the past with Hiram, King of Tyre, and with Lebanon

in general. I would like to end my words with a passage from the Book of Kings, which I believe is particularly apt today: 'And the Lord gave Solomon wisdom, as he promised him; and there was peace between Hiram and Solomon; and the two of them made a treaty'.[79]

This Israeli enthusiasm was not reciprocated by Kimche's Lebanese counterpart, as the seasoned diplomat Antoine Fattal, whose main objective was purely aesthetic, remarked: 'For us the wrapping is more important than the content of the parcel'.[80] These were certainly the directives that Fattal had received from Gemayel, who after his election refused to meet with any Israeli officials, but secretly communicated with them via his emissary and school friend Sami Maroun. Gemayel neither honoured nor ever acknowledged in public the talks that Maroun conducted with the Israelis in Beirut and in Tel Aviv.

Amin's passive-aggressive attitude antagonised Begin and Sharon, who had promised the weary Israeli public a swift and decisive victory in Lebanon and, more importantly, a peace treaty. Shortly before being removed from his post as Defense Minister, Ariel Sharon went as far as publicly threatening Gemayel: 'He will end up not as president of Lebanon, or president of Beirut, or the president of Ba'abda. He will end up as president of the presidential palace and nothing else'.[81] While the treaty was indeed signed on 17 May 1983, it was never presented to the Lebanese Parliament for ratification and thus remained in limbo until Gemayel finally abrogated it a year later. Israel's displeasure over Amin's inaction was palpable in their dealings with the LF, as the Israelis made it clear to Fadi Frem that he should denounce their president in public. This, however, was impossible to implement, as the LF as a body was technically a subordinate of the Kataeb and its founder Pierre Gemayel, whose instructions were to always stand behind the state and its president. Amin knew this well, and he used it to further weaken and isolate the LF, which he ultimately wanted to abolish rather than incorporate into the Lebanese state.

One of Amin's most damaging actions towards his Christian comrades was perhaps his political empowerment of their traditional archnemesis, Walid Joumblatt and the PSP. While Bashir Gemayel had never dismissed the idea of cooperating with Joumblatt, it was obvious that he prioritised the

Yazbaki faction within the Druze community. Yet, Amin adopted a policy that not only gave legitimacy to Joumblatt as the leader of the Druze, but also placed the Yazbaki faction in a position that portrayed them as defending the LF who were killing, kidnapping and humiliating the Druze. The predicament of the Yazbaki faction was further exasperated as the PBDA periodically tried to sway Druze public opinion and paint the Yazbaki collusion with the LF as un-Druze-like and therefore disadvantageous to the community as a whole. On 18 March 1983, the PBDA issued a fiery statement attacking the MPs of the 'Aley Independent Bloc', who for a very long time had 'turned a blind eye to the actions of the Kataeb militia, who since their entry into Mount Lebanon, disrupted eight years of peace and harmony which existed between all the different elements'.[82] The PBDA statement further reminded the Druze that their turncoat parliamentarians:

> were harmed by the limited success of the fascists [the Kataeb], for the success of the fascists' 'cultural' project, like their earlier accomplishments in Sabra and Shatila [the massacre], would have left the Druze homeless and landless; perhaps then the Aley MPs would have taken a stand, or perhaps not even then.[83]

The rapprochement that Amin Gemayel had initiated with Joumblatt also further weakened the anti-Joumblatt faction, which gave the latter a clear advantage over his Druze political opponents, who originally had been hopeful that the ascendance of the Kataeb to power would translate into a number of ministerial appointments, something that never transpired under the mandate of Amin Gemayel. Instead, Gemayel empowered Walid Joumblatt by negotiating exclusively with Joumblatt and his inner circle. This naturally provoked a negative reaction from the Yazbaki side which felt deceived and abandoned by their historic allies. Emir Majid Arslan, the head of the Yazbaki party, who had played a pivotal role in the elections of both Bashir and Amin, clearly expressed his growing discontent over the contentious and underhanded approach towards his faction, by stating: 'When will you [the Maronites] honour your promises?'[84] Sheikh Farid Hamada was equally irritated by Gemayel's unipolar approach towards the Druze, as he informed Gemayel's Minster of Foreign Affairs Elie Salam of the need to have 'a full Druze representation in any future national conference'.[85] Naturally,

Hamada used the word 'full' to object to Joumblatt's monopoly over the political hegemony of his community, something facilitated by Gemayel. This frustration over the growing power of Joumblatt and the weakening of his Yazbaki rivals was equally shared by the members of the LF, who regularly met with the Yazbaki faction to try and address this crisis.[86]

On 7 December 1982, a meeting was called at the Mar Antonius Monastery, the headquarters of the Lebanese Order of Monks in Sodeco, to devise a plan to deal with the deteriorating relationship with the Druze community as a whole.[87] Addressing the room, Bulus Na'aman stressed that the Maronites should be aware that the Druze could not be rooted out; thus, a clear plan to deal with and empower their Druze Yazbaki allies was needed. Na'aman went one step further in his diagnosis of the challenge at hand:

> We should have known better how to cooperate with the Arslani leadership, which has been patriotic since the beginning, and to refrain from reaching out to the Joumblattis who always look abroad for support. The policy which we have adopted has estranged both Druze factions. Walid Joumblatt one day told me: 'I am really grateful; you have united the Druze behind me. After Sheikh Amin [Gemayel] was elected president, the Arslani Druze were expecting to play a major role in government but their wait was to no avail.

The urgency of the Maronites to address this Druze predicament arrived exactly one week after Walid Joumblatt had narrowly escaped an assassination attempt that destroyed his convoy, injured his wife and killed one of his bodyguards.[88] The sight of their young leader rushed to the hospital, disoriented and bleeding, further confirmed to the Druze that their existence was indeed at risk and that a political compromise with the Maronites was not an option worthy of consideration. Joumblatt and the PSP never accused the LF of this crime, but instead used this incident to further rally the Druze around Joumblatt as the legitimate and uncontested leader of the community. The LF had arrived at the decision to liquidate Joumblatt after they had lost any hope of containing him or investing in an alternative Druze figurehead. Years later, Elie Hobeika, the head of LF intelligence, would admit to Joumblatt that he had planned and executed several assassination attempts to eliminate him, among them the December 1982 operation.[89]

Several local events and security incidents further reinforced the fears of both communities across Mount Lebanon. After the death of Bashir, the LF started to send reinforcements into the Shuf region to establish military barracks and LF chapters in the different villages, a move that Bashir had intentionally avoided in the past.[90] These actions on the part of the LF were a last and desperate attempt to strenghten their hold on a hostile area that was slowly slipping out of their grasp because of Druze resentment against their presence, in addition to Israeli indifference or cooperation with the Druze.

Notes

1. Kahan Commission, 8 February 1983. http://www.jewishvirtuallibrary.org/jsource/History/kahan.html, accessed 3 March 2020.
2. David Kimche, *The Last Option: After Nasser, Arafat, and Saddam Hussein: The Quest for Peace in the Middle East* (New York: Charles Scribner's Sons, 1991), 173.
3. Ibid., 175.
4. Interview with Sheikh Muhana al-Btadini, PSP Oral History Project. Translation mine.
5. Ibid.
6. It is reported that, until 2015, over 405 Druze IDF members fell in combat. http://www.algemeiner.com/2015/09/24/a-new-book-details-pays-tribute-to-idfs-druze-soldiers/, accessed accessed 3 March 2020.
7. Wilbert E. Thomas, 'Operation Peace for Galilee: An Operational Analysis with Relevance Today', *Naval War College* (1998), 8; https://apps.dtic.mil/dtic/tr/fulltext/u2/a348640.pdf, accessed 3 March 2020.
8. Zeidan Atashi, *Druze and Jews in Israel: A Shared Destiny?* (Brighton: Sussex Academic, 1997), 146.
9. Atashi's visit came on the second day of the Battle of Qoubbei'.
10. Atashi, *Druze and Jews in Israel*, 146.
11. Tobias Lang, *Die Drusen in Libanon und Israel: Geschichte, Konflikte und Loyalitäten einer religiösen Gemeinschaft in zwei Staaten* (Berlin: Klaus Schwarz Verlag, 2013), 85.
12. Begin, as quoted in Atashi, *Druze and Jews in Israel*, 147.
13. Interview with Zeidan Atashi, by proxy, 2 August 2016.
14. Zeidan Atashi, Muhammad Rammal, Fadel Mansour, Ali Qadmani, Dr Jamal Hassoun, Said Halabi, Jihad Azzam, Hassan Hibrawi, Raslan Abu Ruqun and Nawaf Azzam.

15. Atashi, *Druze and Jews in Israel*, 145.
16. Ibid.
17. Interview with Zeidan Atashi, by proxy, 2 August 2016.
18. Ibid.
19. Ibid.
20. Avner Yaniv, *Dilemmas of Security: Politics, Strategy, and the Israeli Experience in Lebanon* (New York: Oxford University Press, 1987), 213.
21. Ibid.
22. Interview with Atef Salloum, al-Abadiya, Mount Lebanon, 15 June 2019.
23. The Progressive Socialist Party archives has no record about Salloum being one of its members.
24. See page 39.
25. Interview with Atef Salloum, al-Abadiya, Mount Lebanon, 15 June 2019.
26. Atashi, *Druze and Jews in Israel*, 154.
27. Interview with Zeidan Atashi, by proxy, 2 August 2016.
28. Atashi, *Druze and Jews in Israel*, 149.
29. Friedman, *From Beirut to Jerusalem*, 22.
30. Ibid.
31. Interview with Amal Asʿad, by proxy, 7 June 2016.
32. Ibid.
33. Ibid. In some sources the Druze have been accused of worshipping a calf; however, this not substantiated in any of their texts or practices.
34. Atashi, *Druze and Jews in Israel*, 152.
35. Interview with Amal Asʿad, by proxy, 7 June 2016.
36. Interview with Zeidan Atashi, by proxy, 2 August 2016.
37. Interview with Atef Salloum, al-Abadiya, Mount Lebanon, 15 June 2019.
38. Ibid.
39. Roger Azzam, *Liban, l'instruction d'un Crime: 30 ans de guerre* (Coudray-Macouard: Cheminements, 2005), 362.
40. Interview with George Rouhana, Beirut, Lebanon, 12 August 2016.
41. Ibid.
42. Ménargues, *Asrār Ḥarb Lubnān*, 272.
43. Azzam, *Liban*, 362.
44. Interview with Hisham Nasreddine, Deir Koubal, Mount Lebanon, 4 September 2016.
45. Ibid.
46. Interview with Naji Butrus, Makleis, Lebanon, 22 June 2016.

47. See page 40.
48. http://10452lccc.com/aaaaanews11a/arabic.april28.11.htm, accessed 3 March 2020. While this link mentions the proverb, it fails to provide an explanation of its origin.
49. Judith Harik. 'Shaykh al-'Aql and the Druze of Mount Lebanon', 472.
50. Interview with Hisham Nasreddine, Deir Koubal, Mount Lebanon, 4 September 2016.
51. Interview with Fouad Abu-Nadir, Beirut, Lebanon. 23 February 2016.
52. Interview with Sheikh Sharif Abou Hamdan, PSP Oral History Project
53. For a more detailed account of the founding of the PBDA, see Chapter 2.
54. Interview with Hisham Nasreddine, Deir Koubal, Mount Lebanon, 4 September 2016.
55. Interview with Akram Saab, Beirut, Lebanon, 14 June 2016.
56. Speech delivered in Sao Paolo, Brazil, 17 January 1982. PBDA Newsletter, 9 February 1983. Translation mine.
57. *Al-Sha'ib*, 18 June 1983.
58. David Urquhart, *The Lebanon (Mount Souria): A History and a Diary* (London: T. C. Newby, 1860).
59. *Al-'Amal*, 9 November 1982.
60. Ibid.
61. Clovis Shuwayfāti, *Ḥarb al-Durūz wa-al-Mawārinah fī al-Jabal* ([n. p.], 2014), 98–9.
62. *Al-'Amal*, 9 November 1982.
63. Interview with PSP combatant, name withheld.
64. Ibid.
65. George Eid, as quoted in Shuwayfāti, *Ḥarb al-Durūz wa-al-Mawārinah fī al-Jabal*, 10. Translation mine.
66. Simon Moussallam, as quoted in Shuwayfāti, *Ḥarb al-Durūz wa-al-Mawārinah fī al-Jabal*, 10. Translation mine.
67. Interview with Khaled Btadini, PSP Oral History Project.
68. Ibid.
69. Interview with Fawzi Abu-Abbas, PSP Oral History Project.
70. Interview with Fouad Abu-Nadir, Beirut, Lebanon. 23 February 2016.
71. Ibid.
72. Interview with Hisham Nasreddine, Deir Koubal, Mount Lebanon, 4 September 2016.
73. See *90 Minutes at Entebbe*.

74. Interview with Walid Safi, PSP Oral History Project.
75. Ibid.
76. Ménargues, *Asrār Ḥarb Lubnān*, 249. In 2002, Dagan was appointed head of the Mossad by Sharon.
77. Ibid., 250–1.
78. Kimche, *The Last Option*, 169.
79. Statements by Director General Kimche at the two ceremonies marking the signing of the Israel-Lebanon Agreement, 17 May 1983.
80. Fattal, as quoted in Kimche, *The Last Option*, 169.
81. Sharon and Chanoff, *Warrior*, 513.
82. *PBDA Newsletter*, 19 March 1983.
83. Ibid.
84. Andary, *Al-Jabal*, 54.
85. *An-Nahar*, 24 August 1983.
86. Andary, *Al-Jabal*, 54.
87. Ibid., 53.
88. *Al-Safir*, 2 December 1982.
89. Ménargues, *Asrār Ḥarb Lubnān*, 106.
90. See page 170.

7

HISTORY MEETS THE BATTLEFIELD

On 6 January 1983, the LF dispatched Samir Geagea along with 200 fighters from their barracks in Qattara in the north of Lebanon to the Shuf Mountains, the heartland of the Druze. Geagea, a former medical student at the American University of Beirut, had acquired a reputation for being both efficient and ruthless during his command of the LF units in the north of Lebanon, as he had led in 1978 the assault on Ehden, which resulted in the deaths of Tony Frangieh and his family.[1] Naji Butrus, originally assigned command of the Shuf, soon found himself replaced by Geagea, whose appointment was part of an internal power struggle among the LF's senior ranks, which after the death of Bashir had started to show signs of disunity. Fouad Abu-Nadir has confirmed that this was indeed the aim of some of the LF's command; however, this appointment was intended to act as a deterrent rather than a dare, urging the Druze to cease their attacks and perhaps negotiate with the LF.[2]

The Maronite Via Dolorosa

Paul Andary, Geagea's second-in-command, has described the perilous task assigned to them as the 'Passing of the Crucifix' on their Via Dolorosa, very similar to the route of grief that Jesus Christ took on his way to the crucifixion.³ Andary and his comrades took command of an area that had already been engulfed by mindless violence which further divided the mixed villages and led to more bloodshed. The morale of the men of the LF deployed to Mount Lebanon was at an all-time low, since they were not only fighting the Druze and the PSP, but they were also entangled in a struggle with their 'allies', the IDF, whose neutrality was frustrating the LF. Despite these challenges, Samir Geagea unreservedly accepted the mission at hand, as he addressed Andary:

> Paul, if we [Christians] are not doing well on the mountain, we will not be fine anywhere else in Lebanon either ... I believe that the struggle of the Christians is interrelated, and it is impossible for the Christians to lose somewhere and yet win somewhere else ... moreover, the Battle of the Mountain is a strategic one; if we win it, we will be able to implement our strategic plan, and if we do lose, a big part of this hope will be lost with it ... we have waited years and years to recreate it [our plan]. The chain of events has shown that we are losing the battle; therefore, it is instrumental that we reorganize ourselves on the mountain'.⁴

Geagea's remarks to his lieutenant were merely a reflection of the policy that the LF senior command had adopted after Bashir's death. In his bid to amass power, Bashir and his group had had two options.⁵ The first was the so-called '10,452 km² option', whereby Bashir would seize power democratically and thus govern the entirety of Lebanon. The second option, called *al-'aryin* (the sanctuary), included taking power by force, but restricting their control to pre-1920 Lebanon which Bashir and his men 'knew well and were confident could serve as a Christian Lebanese homeland'.⁶ Bashir's death and the subsequent demise of the '10,452 km² project' left the LF with *al-'aryin* as their only recourse; however, this placed the Maronites in direct opposition to the Druze, who also inhabited the geographical area referred to as 'the sanctuary'. Under Geagea, the LF broadened its obligatory military service program to all able-bodied Christians between the ages of sixteen and thirty, with the intent to field more fighters and to raise the morale which was at an all-time low. Yet, this program had the opposite effect, as many Christians avoided joining the draft, either by leaving their villages for Beirut or emigrating from Lebanon. According to Simon Moussallam, an LF fighter who originally hailed from the Shuf, 'over 2,200 young men across the mountain received basic military training, over 90 precent of whom deserted and refused to fight'.[7] Several of the Christian villages across the regions of the Shuf and Aley started to lose its young inhabitants, leaving the sick and the elderly who proved to be a liability to the LF, as they needed to be looked after, especially during the harsh winter months.

General Beaufort Resurrected

The Druze–Maronite cycle of violence was mostly driven by reprisals, with each side accusing the other of instigating the killing, abduction and indiscriminate shelling of civilians. In reality, neither of the two sides required a pretext to justify any of their barbarous acts, as they had sufficient historical grievances in their collective perception of themselves and their enemies, enough to transform an already volatile political standoff into a bloodthirsty rampage. Toufic Barkat's PSP Oral History Project interview clearly reflects that the confrontation with the LF went beyond the daily skirmishes and that it was part of an imagined primordial feud going back hundreds of years. Barkat, who served on a joint PSP-LF commission tasked with hostage release and cease-fire negotiations, was enraged when he met one of the LF field commanders in the Shuf, Joseph Abu-Samra, known as Beaufort. Abu-Samra had never harmed or even encountered Barkat, but his *nom-de-guerre* was enough to offend the highly educated PSP official.[8] During a visit to the village of Brih, Barkat asked Abu-Samra about the meaning of his nickname; Abu-Samra replied that it had no real meaning, but that it was the Latin initial B4 which he had acquired while growing up. Unsatisfied by this answer, Barkat snapped back at Abu-Samra: 'You call yourself Beaufort after the General Beaufort d'Hautpoul, who led the expeditionary force in 1860 to punish the Druze, and if you think that you will be able to hurt the Druze, then you are utterly mistaken. We will exact our revenge on the original Beaufort and his descendants [the Maronites]'.[9] Naji Butrus, Beaufort's commanding officer, laughingly dismissed this incident as totally unfounded, as Abu-Samra did not have the intellectual depth to be aware of such a historic figure.[10] Abu-Samra had received the nickname B4, because as a young man he used to play a juvenile game that included shaking a fizzy soda bottle and trying to consume it; B4 thus meant 'the one who shakes the soda bottle'.¹¹ The Druze's paranoia, however, was not unfounded, as some of the LF rhetoric, especially in the months leading up to the final confrontation, plainly framed the Maronite conflict with the Druze as going back to the tenth century AD. While delivering a eulogy for one of the fallen soldiers of the Battle of Mtolleh, Salim Kassab, the Kataeb chief of the al-Zahrani district, declared: 'The battle we [LF] won is part of a struggle dating back 1,300 years'.¹² In practical terms, Kassab saw the Druze as Abbasid frontier warriors who had defeated the Mardaites/Maronite army and occupied land that rightfully belonged to its Christians inhabitants. This same analogy was also shared by the head of the LF women's fighting unit, called *al-Nizamiyat*. Jocelyn Khoueiry also framed the confrontation as going back as far as 1,400 years, if not longer.¹³

The Druze replied to these historic references by illustrating connections between the current conflict and the experiences of their ancestors going back as far as the time of the Prophet Muhammad. This process of moulding the collective memory can also be observed in the PSP's official periodical *Al-Anbaa*; despite the PSP's secular doctrine, the months leading up to the war marked a clear departure from the earlier, more secular practices which avoided connecting the PSP with the Druze community. Several articles with blatant sectarian and confessional undertones, authored by one 'Salman', appeared in *Al-Anbaa*. The author of these articles promoted the unlikely notions that all Druze share a common ancestry and that warfare is the Druze way of life, rather than an anomaly.¹⁴ In response to a call by Fadi Frem urging the Druze to relinquish their support to Joumblatt and the PSP, Salman addressed the Druze as 'Sons of Salman and Soldiers of Abu-Ibrahim', reminding them that they were 'a primordial people as old as the oak trees of this proud mountain'.¹⁵ The choice of oak in and of itself is significant, as it stands in stark opposition to the cedar tree, the symbol of the Maronite church. Beyond its aim to unify the Druze behind Joumblatt, the article also claimed that the Druze were direct descendants of the Prophet Muhammad's companion Salman al-Faris, the champion of the Battle of Khandaq (the trench) in 627 AD. Salman stood by the Prophet during his war against the Meccan infidels; similarly, his Druze successors were resisting the Christian infidels and their Israeli allies.

The Faustian Deal Revoked

The change of the LF field command in the Shuf coincided with the appointment of Moshe Arens as the new Israeli Defense Minister.[16] While Arens was as hawkish as his predecessor, Sharon, he was nevertheless dissatisfied by the political catastrophe in the Lebanon, especially the failure of the Lebanese president to honour his earlier commitments.[17] Consequently, Arens and the IDF command started to look for an exit strategy from Mount Lebanon, for they had no intention of getting caught in a Maronite-Druze shootout based on sectarianism. This new Israeli policy was also evident in the appointment of Uri Lubrani as the coordinator of the activities of the IDF in Lebanon. Lubrani was selected by Prime Minister Begin and Arens, who both felt the need to engage with and appease other Lebanese communities, particularly the Druze and the Shi'ites.[18] Although Lubrani worked closely with the Yakal, who were very fond of the LF, he himself believed that, in order to properly protect the IDF, Israel needed to abandon its unilateral Maronite track. To follow Lubrani's logic, the best way to protect Israel was to establish concentric circles of protection by collaborating with different Lebanese communities, even the most aggressive of them – namely, the Shi'ites. More importantly, Lubrani realised that it was futile to continue to isolate and antagonise Walid Joumblatt and thus invested both time and effort to reach out to and come to an agreement with the Druze warlord concerning the future. While Lubrani's relationship with the Druze remained outside the limelight, the Israelis plainly informed their LF allies of this major shift in policy. In January 1983, Dagan, the head of Yakal, was tasked with breaking the news to the LF leadership:

> We have reached an agreement with the Druze, although it certainly is not as strong as our alliance with you [LF]. We wish Amin [Gemayel] was more reasonable! We wish the Americans did not stick their nose in this. The Druze at the moment are confident that you intend to keep fighting them, and your appointment of Geagea has further provoked them. I am talking to you as a representative of the state of Israel. Do not withdraw your troops from the Shuf! Do not even consider this! We have brought you there, so you have to stay. However, I suggest that you remove your roadblocks and

cease immediately any action which might provoke the Druze. My government's instructions are clear: order must be restored in the Shuf.[19]

Naturally, these policies were not appreciated by the LF, which lacked the inclination and the ability to reach a settlement with Walid Joumblatt and the PSP. Nevertheless, following this ominous Israeli proclamation and upon the insistence of the IDF, the LF tried to reach an agreement with the PSP to put an end to the cycle of violence. Under IDF patronage, the LF and the PSP hammered out a security arrangement that established joint operation rooms including civilian and military representatives from both sides, with a senior Israeli officer present to act as mediator if needed.[20] This agreement was signed by Meir Daghan himself, Nizar Nazarian and Sami Khoueiry of the LF, Salem Reaidi of the Kataeb, Hisham Nasreddine of the PSP and Fadlallah Talhouk, Druze MP for the Aley district.[21] Talhouk was an anti-Joumblatti Druze notable, but the PSP seemed to have included him in these talks for strategic reasons – primarily to weaken Faisal Arslan, and also to fend off any allegations that there was represented only one faction within the Druze community, a faction that was opposing the LF.

The Druze Canton

This agreement soon collapsed, since neither side, including the IDF, honoured their part of the deal; both militias tried to take advantage of the occasional lull in fighting to fortify their positions by moving in ammunition and reinforcements. While the LF ostensibly went along with the Israeli request to appease the Druze, at the same time they launched an attack on Joumblatt, accusing him of trying to establish a Druze canton with the help of the Israeli Druze. In its 15 March issue, the newspaper *Al-'Amal* published a document which it claimed to be circulating among the Druze, stressing the 'unavoidability of establishing a Druze state'.[22] This document initially surfaced through a shady local news agency called *Akhbar al-Yawm* and presented a historical and political rationalisation as to why the Druze must work towards establishing their own state. Driven by *realpolitik*, the documents asked the Druze the following:

> Why should we [Druze] allow the Lebanese Christians who are operating under the protection of the Israel to continue to kill and destroy as they

please? Instead, we should follow suit and establish good relations with the Israelis in order to reverse the situation and consequently take the fight into the Christian heartland and get rid of them [Christians] once and for all.[23]

In the very same issue, Joseph Abu-Khalil directed his accusations towards the PSP and Joumblatt for this separatist scheme, stating even more bluntly: 'We are amazed how this project [the Druze state] or any other like it is being circulated at the moment; because it means that the Joumblatti dominance over the rest of Lebanon has failed'.[24] The LF also reached out to Joumblatt's Druze archenemies, primarily Faisal Arslan, who flooded the local and international media with statements framing Joumblatt and the PSP as serving the Israelis by trying to create an ethnic Druze state. Arslan published a fairly extensive op-ed in *Al-'Amal*, entitled 'The Druze State: A Feeble and Unsustainable Entity'.[25] Arslan and other Yazbaki and anti-Joumblatti figures had been equally affected by Lubrani's shift in policy and thus found it favourable to highlight the Joumblatt-Israeli dealings that would discredit Joumblatt who was using Arab nationalism and anti-Western rhetoric merely as cover. Arslan attacked Joumblatt, without actually naming him:

> As we have said before, the project of the Druze state is not really as tempting as it seems; however, we are afraid of some weak-spirited individuals who do not look favourably at the central Lebanese state because it would weaken their own control of their areas. This has led them to cheer for the Druze state and to convince people of its necessity. Coincidentally, they have gone out of their way to escalate the fighting and to drive a schism with their [Christian] compatriots. This has also led to terrible economic and living conditions across Mount Lebanon, which makes the project of the Druze state a way out of their predicament rather than a willful choice.[26]

Joumblatt responded to the Maronite allegations by issuing an extensive memorandum that included the Druze's demands for reform, underscoring the need for administrative as well as constitutional reform. The 'Druze Memorandum', as it came to be known, endorsed by both Sheikh Muhammad Abu-Shaqra and Emir Majid Arslan, was addressed to President Amin Gemayel, reminding him that 'a strong sovereign state entails all its citizens to be equal in front of the law as well as to be equal in their rights and obligations, for without this equilibrium, the state cannot exist'.²⁷ The memorandum went on to propose amendments to the legislative, executive and judicial branches of government, most important among them the reestablishment of the senate, to be presided over by a Druze.²⁸ These demands were intended to affirm that the Druze had a vested interest in the Lebanese state, provided the Maronite establishment adopted these inclusionary reformist measures, since this would empower the Druze as opposed to making them feel like second-class citizens. The Druze had never flaunted their Lebanese identity in the same manner as their Maronites counterparts, but they always considered themselves both Lebanese and Arab. However, the various stand-offs that Kamal Joumblatt and later his son Walid had with the Maronite political establishment led them to adopt a somewhat reactionary position, which in turn branded Lebanese nationalism as essentially chauvinistic.

This inferiority complex was clearly reflected in much of the Druze's rhetoric and literary production before and during the war with the Maronites. In an article entitled 'Freedoms and Constitutional Rights in Lebanon', Rajeh Naim, the editor of the PBDA newsletter, underscored to what extent the Druze saw the Lebanese constitution as bigoted and unjust towards its non-Christian citizens.²⁹ Naim narrated the following story about a Lebanese professor of law at the Lebanese University: He lectured his students about US President Abraham Lincoln, who in 1865 made the Congress pass the Thirteenth Amendment to the US Constitution, which ultimately ended slavery. The professor then went on to explain how, despite their emancipation, blacks were never treated equally because they possessed five-sixth of the rights that the White Man possessed. According to Naim, 'even though the Negroes 118 years later received their freedom, the Lebanese constitution still only grants the Lebanese Muslims five-sixth of the rights granted to the Christians. Imagine what racist civilisation these people [the Maronites] are flaunting'.³⁰

Israel Exits the Inferno

Despite the many efforts to reconcile the Druze and the Maronites, the slowly unfolding events made the confrontation ever more precarious and imminent. Shortly after the signing of the 17 May Accord, Israeli officials met with the LF on several occasions to inform them of their intention to partially redeploy their troops. On 6 August 1983, Ariel Sharon visited Lebanon and met with Pierre Gemayel and the LF command in Beirut, before moving on to 'Ayn Trez, Samir Geagea's command post on Mount Lebanon. Sharon, equally frustrated by Amin Gemayel's attitude and the Reagan administration's appeasement of Syria, gave his Lebanese allies clear notice:

> My visit today might be the last chance to warn you that we will leave the Shuf soon, I cannot tell you the exact date, but soon. Eight months ago, in January, I warned you that you are putting too much hope on the Americans who are telling you what to do. You have to accept the peace deal between Israel and Lebanon, you should take the road to Jerusalem and stop turning your backs to us.[31]

According to many of the people present at this meeting, Pierre Gemayel was surprisingly certain that Sharon and the Israelis were merely bluffing, and that in reality they would never abandon their most trusted allies, the Maronites.[32] Amin Gemayel also shared his father's view and downplayed these warnings; moreover, he continued to refuse meeting any of the Israeli delegates or even communicating with them through proxies. However, the IDF's intention to redeploy was neither a bluff nor a secret, as it was being circulated in the news, with all senior IDF officers plainly declaring that their Shuf incursion was nearing its end. On 16 August 1983, the IDF Chief-of-Staff Moshe Levy inspected his troops deployed across Lebanon. Following his tour, Levy announced over the IDF radio that 'Israel cannot be held responsible for any violence that might break out between the Maronite and the Druze after our withdrawal, especially if this withdrawal will be very soon'.[33] On the very same day, Arens flew to Beirut to warn the Lebanese government of the need to prepare for the impending IDF evacuation from the Shuf and the events that consequently might unfold. Arens had also expressed his willingness to delay the IDF redeployment, if the Lebanese president officially requested so from the government of Israel.[34] Joined by Uri Lubrani and other senior IDF officers, Arens was on a mission to meet with Amin Gemayel, but having been denied the chance, the Israeli delegation met with Pierre Gemayel, Camille Chamoun and the LF's central command.

The LF command was more pragmatic and saw in Aren's visit a chance to coordinate the IDF withdrawal, and possibly to replace them, especially in some of the vital strategic positions across the Shuf and Aley. The Israelis, however, were not willing to entertain the thought of such a transitional process, granting the LF a clear military advantage over the Druze, who had by then established a military pact with the IDF. According to one of the architects of this understanding with the IDF, the PSP established a solid relationship with Lubrani, who was very aware of the Druze's mental state and the Druze concern about being uprooted from their lands. The PSP leadership was mindful that the IDF would eventually evacuate; therefore, it was not to their advantage to oppose them during their temporary presence on the mountain.[35]

This Druze-Israeli understanding was clear, as echoed at the press conference that Arens held prior to his return to Israel. Arens stated the following points:

- The IDF will redeploy to south of the Litani River no later than 15 September.
- If the Lebanese Army does not deploy on the Mountain, this will leave a big security void.
- Israel will not abandon the Druze of Lebanon.
- The Lebanese government should look for means to reconcile the feuding factions.[36]

Arens regurgitated these points at the meeting with the LF, responding to their multiple requests for weapons and ammunition with the follwoing sober remark: 'It is more proper for you and Lebanon to reach a compromise with the Druze; they are only scared for their lives'.[37] Lubrani was less ashamed of flaunting his pro-Druze sentiments, as he expressed his views to his LF interlocutors concerning what should happen at the next stage:

> They [Druze] want to live in peace and go back to their normal business. They say that you have the option to move to Beirut, whereas they have no other place to go to. They are after their security and existence and not merely supporting Joumblatt. You should negotiate with them, you can either do it harshly or moderately, but you have to do it. Mr. [George] Adwan[38] wants us to discipline them [the Druze] and to tell them what to do. This method is possible with the Syrians, not with the Druze.[39]

Lubrani's realism was not solely based on his own preferences, but also grounded in political reality back in Israel. By the summer of 1983, the Druze in Israel had levelled the playing field for their Lebanese brethren, and Arens was aware of the need to appease the Druze soldiers in the IDF. As the new Defense Minister, Arens visited various Druze villages to offer condolences for their fallen sons who had died in action in Lebanon; he heard their appeals and fears, as well as their requests to support the Lebanese Druze. This naturally gave the Druze further leverage, and this aided Zeidan Atashi and the Druze Follow-Up Commission in negotiating better terms for the Lebanese Druze, especially after the IDF's withdrawal from the Shuf.

The Lebanese Army: One Last Try

Although no official document indicates that the Druze and the IDF had coordinated the partial Israeli withdrawal from the Shuf, one can safely assume that these meetings did take place. The Druze, according to David Kimche, were willing to accept a security arrangement by allowing Lebanese Army troops to replace the IDF's troops, provided the former were preceded by a contingent of the Multi-National Forces (MNF, consisting of US, French and Italian troops).[40] Earlier, the Druze had refused to exclusively allow the Lebanese Army to deploy in the Shuf, unless Amin Gemayel recognised the demand for political reform set forth by the 'Druze Memorandum'. Gemayel, however, completely rejected this Druze bullying which ultimately impinged on state sovereignty. Elie Salem has admitted that Joumblatt's demands were intended to fail, as they were 'impractical' and exceeded the Druze sphere; in fact, they were part of the reform plan of the Lebanese National Movement.[41] Almost a month earlier, on 14 July, Gemayel had tried to dispatch a division of Lebanese Army troops commanded by Colonial Michael Aoun. However, the Druze inhabitants of the area, mobilised by the PSP, attacked Aoun's jeep and refused him entry into town.[42] The PSP used a mob of Druze women, armed with knives and cleavers, to attack Aoun who was on a reconnaissance mission in the area. Although the Israelis had escorted Aoun, they refrained from suppressing the Druze assailants and merely helped to ensure the safe extraction of the stranded soldiers. This incident led Gemayel to stand his ground more belligerently and to discard the notion of a peaceful settlement with Joumblatt and the Druze, who outwardly expressed their intent to do so with all the delegates they had met. Having failed to reach a compromise, Lubrani looked towards Robert 'Bud' McFarlane, Ronald Reagan's Special Representative in the Middle East, to avoid the crisis that the IDF's withdrawal would cause. Lubrani and McFarlane exerted tremendous efforts to reach an agreement sponsored by the Americans, which would prevent the inevitable bloodbath between the Druze and the Maronites. David Kimche, who followed this initiative closely, remarked that the US envoy was keen to deploy the Marines, who were part of the MNF. The Americans had placed high hopes on the Lebanese Armed Forces (LAF), as through his lobbying efforts in both Washington and Beirut Amin Gemayel had led the Reagan administration to commit itself to the Lebanese Army Modernisation Program.[43] This programme, funded with 500 million USD, aimed to create a strong, skilled and well-equipped cross-sectarian army, capable of rebuilding the Lebanese state. Therefore, it was expected that the Americans would support a political settlement that involved deploying the troops in which it had invested so heavily in terms of time and training. On 1 September 1983, a few days before the IDF redeployment, Kimche met with McFarlane to discuss the details of their arrangement; however, contrary to the set plan, the US envoy informed his Israeli counterpart that the US Marines, as part of the MNF, would not participate in any activities in the Shuf. Kimche was taken by surprise, as he had been very optimistic before the meeting, given his earlier meeting at the IDF command post with a Druze emissary, which Lubrani had summoned to go over the last details of the withdrawal. However, US Defense Secretary Casper Weinberger was quick to veto the agreement between Lubrani and McFarlane in order to avoid his troops' participation in any mission that would further implicate them in the Lebanese conflict.[44] Weinberger simply wanted to avoid a repeat of the April bombing of the US embassy in West Beirut, executed by a shady faction calling itself the Islamic Jihad Organisation; the bombing had left sixty-three dead, including seventeen American citizens.[45] The subsequent attack on the US Marine barracks on 23 October 1983, killing 241 US servicemen, further strengthened Weinberger's conviction to avoid confrontation unless strategically mandatory. The Weinberger Doctrine endorsed, among other points, that 'the United States should not commit forces to combat unless the vital national interests of the United States or its allies are involved'.⁴⁶ Obviously, neither the Druze nor the Maronites where of vital national interests to the United States, and therefore the Americans opted out. Crucially, Weinberger's decision was mindful of the fact that Hafez al-Assad had not endorsed such a move and demanded the abrogation of the 17 May Agreement before he would cooperate with Lebanon; therefore, sending US troops into the Shuf would leave them vulnerable to attacks by the Syrians and their PSP allies.⁴⁷

Walid Joumblatt and the Druze had always perceived the Lebanese Army as an enemy; however, this sentiment was further strengthened with the election of Amin Gemayel. The PSP media routinely equated the LAF with both Gemayel and the LF, even going as far as branding it 'the Army of the Ruling Family'.⁴⁸ The PSP had issued a number of statements expressing their rejection of the Lebanese Army's pro-Maronite actions, stating 'no to the [Lebanese] Army. No to the partial security arrangements. Yes for a comprehensive political settlement'.⁴⁹ Furthermore, the PSP saw the LAF as serving 'a Lebanese isolationist scheme which for over a century has tried to subjugate the Druze in order to totally control Lebanon'.⁵⁰ More importantly, according to the PSP, the LAF constituted a tool to help the Maronite political establishment realise an age-old dream:

> A dream which goes back as far as the alliance between Bashir II and Ibrahim Pasha, this alliance has now been renewed by summoning all the nations' armies to crush our [Druze] dream and setting up a racist fascist state, all at the expense of the unity of the people and the land.⁵¹

These anti-LAF sentiments were finally unleashed when the majority of the Druze officers serving in the army mutinied against what they perceived to be a sectarian Maronite Army. A few days prior to the IDF's evacuation, Joumblatt publicly called on the 'patriotic' army officers to refuse to fight alongside the Kataeb and the LF.⁵² Subsequently, these mid-career officers issued a call to all Druze and Muslim officers and soldiers to join them at the army barracks of Hammana which they had occupied earlier. Most of these officers were supporters or clandestine members of the PSP. For example, Raja Harb, who played an instrumental role in orchestrating this rebellion, had been openly engaged in training and leading some of the PSP militia members as early as 1976. By 1983 the situation had changed, as the PSP felt the need to publicly endorse a mutiny that further delegitimised and prevented Gemayel from using the LAF to promote his agenda. In a press conference held in Hammana shortly after the end of the fighting, these officers publicly accused the LAF of collaborating with the LF and perpetrating some of the massacres against the Druze:

> Today, under the same deceitful mottos that call for fighting the foreigners, our towns and villages are being shelled by the artillery and the air force, and our people in Kfarmatta, Abey, Ba'aouerta and Bnaiyye are being driven off their land. Which army are we building, and what country do we want? We see in front of our eyes how the army is being exploited to serve the Kataeb and the Lebanese Forces militia, which has totally controlled it and driven it to commit massacres against our people on the mountain and the southern suburbs of Beirut. How could we continue to follow these military orders, after we the protectors of this nation have been driven to break it apart and to be the knife that slays it?[53]

In practical terms, the Hammana mutiny transformed the LAF from a western-trained and -financed state army to merely one of the many militias engaged in a petty civil war.

The Battle of Bhamdoun

In the late afternoon of 3 September 1983, the IDF started to withdraw its last remaining troops from the Shuf and the Aley region's mountains. The Israeli redeployment left the LF at the mercy of the Druze, who by that time had received ammunition and reinforcements from the USSR via their Palestinian and Syrian allies. According to Raja Harb, by 1983 the PSP had acquired an impressive arsenal as well as the technical skills necessary to use them, something that the LF refused to acknowledge.[54] This LF denial was perhaps rooted in their fighters' belief that their Western/Israeli training and arsenal were far superior to the Soviet weapons that the Druze had at their disposal.[55] However, more importantly, the LF considered their main enemy to be the Syrian regime that was merely 'using Joumblatt and the Druze as cover' to implement its sinister plan to control Lebanon.[56] Fadi Frem constantly referred to their struggle as directed against outsiders, among them the Joumblatti leadership which:

since the nineteenth century has worked against Lebanon as it imported its ideas and directives from abroad, and in 1975 it stood with Palestinian terrorism against Lebanon. The Progressive Socialist Party which is currently headed by Walid Joumblatt has been armed by the terrorist Syrians and the international communists. Its members were trained in the Palestinian camps and the camps of terror, and its officers received military training in the Soviet Union and Syria.[57]

Militarily, the LF under Geagea had reinforced their positions by adding more fortifications and creating new military routes, which were safe from the shelling and ambushes of the Druze. However, the 5,000-strong LF had to cover an enormous area; their supply lines were weak and at times had to pass through or near Druze villages.[58] According to Alain Ménargues, who had served in the French army and had limited military knowledge, the LF were in a very difficult position. First, their ability to maintain their supply lines was always in question; second, their structure as militia constituted a handicap in itself. While the LF were akin to a professional fighting force with a clear structure, the bulk of the PSP forces was composed of recruits who had joined the militia as village units and thus fought alongside their cousins and neighbours. This family structure was at the heart of the Druze fighting tactics that placed blood relations at the forefront; the sheer fact that they would be defending their immediate family members rather than merely fighting for an abstract cause made the Druze extremely ferocious fighters. This naturally excluded the more professional and technical units such as the artillery and the armoured divisions, which were to a large extent very similar to the ones that the LF fielded. Furthermore, it was easier for the PSP to mobilise more men, simply because the theatre of operation was within the Druze hinterland, and thus Druze recruits were expected to serve in a defensive mode most of the time.

Despite this bleak military assessment, the LF had always hoped that Amin Gemayel would eventually send the Lebanese Army to save them from their impending doom. However, the scant mutual respect and trust between Gemayel and the LF had by that time dwindled to next to nothing, as the latter felt that Gemayel wished them to lose this confrontation and thus end Bashir's legacy. Consequently, in the final days before the IDF withdrawal, a growing number of voices within the LF senior command called for overthrowing Gemayel and taking control of the state and the army. One of the most ardent supports of such a move was Antoine Najm, who demanded that Frem take a firm stance. He declared:

> Neither Pierre nor Amin Gemayel are true leaders anymore. The policy of Lebanon is determined abroad. We are going through a very important historic transformation, and I unreservedly stand beside you, Fadi, provided you act with resolve. You are the only hope for the Christians. Go ahead, assume leadership and establish LF offices in both Tel Aviv and Jerusalem.[59]

This wishful *coup d'état* had no chance of succeeding, as the LF had too many factors to deal with, primarily the impending Battle of the Mountain. One of the factors that perhaps nipped this coup in the bud was the promise that Amin Gemayel had given to Geagea when he met him at the presidential palace one week before the IDF's withdrawal. Explaining to the president and his army commander General Ibrahim Tannous the perilous task ahead and the many challenges that awaited him, Geagea was assured by Gemayel: 'Do not worry, do not be afraid'.[60] Gemayel then asked Geagea bluntly: 'What is the maximum time you can withstand the Druze attack before you need me to send the army to intervene?'[61] Geagea replied with an almost identical question: 'How much time you need me to withstand the attack?' After whispering a few words into Tannous's ear, Gemayel answered: 'Twelve hours.' To which Geagea replied: 'Let it be twenty-four hours, but not more'.[62]

Geagea's main concern was the town of Bhamdoun, as it was expected to be the main front for the Druze assault. Located on the Beirut-Damascus highway, Bhamdoun was strategically important, since it constituted the intersection of three different regions on Mount Lebanon – Aley to the south, Maten to the east and the vast Jurd region to the west. The latter intersected with the Druze heartland in the Shuf.[63]

According to Paul Andary who was tasked with defending the Bhamdoun front, the battle was nothing short of a nightmare.[64] With only 250 fighters under his command, Andary was over-extended, while the Druze had been quite successful in mustering the support of the surrounding Druze villages, something that the LF had failed to achieve in Bhamdoun and its vicinity.[65]

Figure 7.1 A PSP map of the Battle of Bhamdoun (Walid Fayyad).

Figure 7.2 PSP tanks rolling into Bhamdoun on 3 September 1983 (PSP Archives).

Figure 7.3 LF fighters manning a 14.5 anti-aircraft gun (Wassim Jabre).

Figure 7.4 LF Infantry heading into battle (Wassim Jabre).

Figure 7.5 Druze sheikh working his land armed with an AK-47 (PSP Archives).

On the eve of the War of the Mountain, Walid Joumblatt, who had left Lebanon after an attempted assassination, addressed the Druze and asked them to prepare themselves for the difficult task ahead. Joumblatt's words were not merely a battle cry, but rather a synopsis of his community's collective memory, as they entered a battle against their historic Maronite foe:

> Our people on the Mountain, sons of *Maruf*, ancestors of *Salman* [al-Farisi], the hour of challenge is upon us. The intentions are clear, and the preparations are under way; it is the time to preserve and protect your dignity . . . it is dignity and your existence at its best. The land is yours, and you are the custodians of history, your sons, your future, your existence, your values and your noble wisdom (*hikma*) are all at stake; either you crush your enemies, as you did time and again over the past years, or be shattered by this new barbarian gale.[66]

Joumblatt's use of religious imagery was a clear departure from his own secular demeanor and that of the party to which he belonged, but it was obvious

Figure 7.6 LF fighter praying to a statute of St Charbel (LF Archives).

that at this moment in time there was a need to invoke the horrors of the past to unite the Druze. Joumblatt went on to remind the Druze of what would await them, if they faltered in the upcoming challenge:

> It is the hour that Kamal Joumblatt described as 'to be or not to be'. Do not be intimidated by their media or the number of their guns; how many times has a small group defeated a bigger foe? History is repeating itself and is harshly and unprecedentedly imposing itself on us; the ability to survive and steadfastness is the only solution. You will defend your honour and our dignity, as no one can uproot you from your homes and force you to leave the soil and the country of our forefathers. We will die with our heads held high. We will die as martyrs convinced of our destiny . . . to the heroic confrontation, to victory, 'Life is the triumph of a people of strong souls, not of the weak in spirit', to a dignified and free life, to the stands of glory which await you on the summits of the mountains. Your strength is in your unity and determination. Your strength is in your allies, friends; your strength is in your right to live.[67]

This rhetoric clearly depicts how the Druze's leaderships reinforced and moulded its community's remembrance process and directed it to serve the communal well-being, which in this case meant boosting the fighting spirit of the Druze before marching into their final decisive battle against the Maronites.

The commanders of both the PSP and LF eagerly awaited the last IDF vehicle to depart, signaling the beginning of the race to capture key positions, especially the bunkers and fortifications that the Israelis had evacuated. As the IDF field commander of Bhamdoun was departing, he looked at Andary and in a blunt and cold manner said: 'Now you can eradicate each other, but first let us get out of the way'.[68]

Over the span of two days (4–6 September 1983), the Druze and the Maronites fought to redeem 123 years of history. On one hand, the Druze aspired to repeat their 1860 victory; while on the other hand the Maronites simply wanted to avoid their ancestors' debacle. Ironically, the 1860 scenario was reenacted in the same brutal manner and involved as much, if not more bloodshed. The Druze, who were better acquainted with the terrain and supported by Syrian and Palestinian logistics and artillery, mowed down the LF, who were only able to hold out for a couple of days. Geagea, true to his word, fought for forty-eight hours, but the reinforcement promised by Amin Gemayel never arrived. The Druze were obviously assisted by the Syrians and their pro-Syrian Palestinian factions, which supplied the much-needed artillery cover, as well as an abundance of fighters that the PSP used to fortify their positions. Also joining the PSP was a hodgepodge of Leftist and Communist factions, chiefly Joumblatt's traditional allies, the Lebanese Communist Party and the Communist Action Organisation. While the Israelis did not interfere in the battle, they had previously warned the Syrians and the PSP that any visible Syrian or Palestinian involvement in the war would be dealt with by force. Consequently, the PSP could not count on the Syrian armoured divisions, and they had to settle for four tanks provided by the pro-Libyan Arab Socialist Union. Ghanem Tarabay, who led the PSP charge from the Maten region, had only one objective in mind – that is, to cut the Beirut-Damascus highway, encircle the LF and link up with the PSP forces in the Jurd region, commanded by Fadi al-Ghraizi.[69] To achieve this goal, Ghanem used the tanks he had commandeered from the Beqa'a Valley to assault the LF fortifications. The two concrete advantages that the Druze fighters possessed were their familiarity with the terrain and the conviction that they were fighting to preserve their land against what they perceived to be a foreign crusader invasion.

Devastated, the LF together with what remained of the Christian inhabitants of southern Mount Lebanon retreated to the town of Deir al-Qamar; this triggered a Druze siege of the town, which lasted for more than three months. According to Raja Harb and other military commanders whom I interviewed, the PSP deliberately created a safe passage to allow thousands of Christian civilians to escape to Deir al-Qamar. While this was indeed the case, the Druze did not spare any of the Christian combatants and civilians who remained in their villages, as Fouad Abu-Nadir has remarked.[70] Abu-Nadir has admitted that his own LF troops targeted Druze civilians and took prisoners of war, whom they later handed over to the Red Cross, something that the Druze did not do, since they simply took no prisoners. Samir Geagea has stated that the decision to fall back on Deir al-Qamar was based on several factors, some purely military in nature, while others were apparently rooted in the Maronites' memory. Because of the 1860 war, this historic town has been of paramount importance in the collective psyche of both the Druze and the Maronites, as it was the second-largest Catholic town in the east and the hometown of the former Lebanese president Camille Chamoun. Therefore, the siege of this town could rally the local and international public support required for the Maronite cause.[71]

Among the besieged was Raji Achkouti, a poet and renowned man of letters, who shortly after the lifting of the siege published his account of *The Siege of Deir al-Qamar*.[72] In the introduction, Achkouti has stated that his book intends to mirror the reality of the people under siege, their feelings, reactions and revolts. The end result yields an ethnography of the entire Christian population of southern Mount Lebanon, who from September 1983 to December 1983 (almost 98 days) were held captive in the above-mentioned town; perhaps, it represents a window into the Maronites' collective memory. An interesting idea reflected in Achkouti's work is the besieged Christians' perception that Joumblatt's victory was a sham:

> ... he will soon face the reality that this so-called victory is fake or with insufficient balance; as they say, history is deemed to repeat itself, and he will end up facing the same fate as his ancestors (in reference to 1860 and

Said Joumblatt).⁷³ Perhaps this was been the same lens through which Samir Geagea saw things when he made his decision to retreat to Deir al-Qamar.

While the Druze emerged victorious in Aley and the Shuf, they were nevertheless dealt a decisive blow in the Gharb region, as their troops were decimated by the LF, led by Fouad Abu-Nadir and supported by the Lebanese Army as well as the US navy gunships positioned in the Mediterranean. The Gharb region was of great strategic importance, since it directly overlooked Beirut and the international airport. More importantly, it protected the southern flank of the presidential palace in Ba'abda, and it connected Aley to the Shuf and the coast (see the map on p. xviii). For the Druze, however, this region was of great historic and religious importance, because it had been home to the Buhturids, the famed defenders of the coast against the Crusaders (see Chapter 3). Moreover, the village of Abey housed the shrine of the famous Druze religious reformer Sayid Abdallah al-Tanoukhi, which the LF later desecrated and razed. The Lebanese Army's intervention in the Gharb proved crucial to the LF's victory; however, Gemayel's reason for involving his troops in this fight was purely self-serving. Gemayel simply wanted to protect the presidential palace, which would have fallen, had the PSP captured the strategic town of Souk al-Gharb overlooking Ba'abda.

The Siege of Deir al-Qamar

Both sides in the conflict perpetrated the most heinous crimes imaginable, targeting civilians, indiscriminately shelling villages and roads, and going as far as to desecrate religious sanctuaries and temples of worship. Nearly all Druze and Maronites combatants I interviewed confessed to committing these acts, but usually followed such confession either with the claim 'it was an act of self-defence', or by simply stating: 'They would not have spared us, if they had the chance'. Walid Joumblatt gave a more truthful, yet bleaker justification for the crimes that his people committed against the Christians. As he saw it, this war as merely part of the Arab tradition of raiding: 'Following the Lebanese and Arab tradition, they simply raided us, and we raided them back, and this is war; whoever said that there is a clean war and that there is a dirty war'.⁷⁴ Shortly after the end of the Battle of the Mountain, Joumblatt also stated what amounts to a *mea culpa*:

> I tried to prevent in the Druze this barbaric tendency of murder and mayhem, but I failed; therefore, on behalf of the Druze I take full responsibility for the massacres that the Druze committed against the other sects and for the blood of the innocent Christians which was spilled, and I demand that I as well as the other leaders of the various communities be brought to justice.[75]

The siege of Deir al-Qamar was yet another episode in which both sides used innocent civilians to serve an immediate political goal. Having been dealt a severe military blow, the LF wanted to repair the image that Bashir had created for them, that of a protector of the Christians in the Levant. Consequently, Deir al Qamar, which overnight became a safe haven for over 40,000 Christian refugees, appeared very similar to the last stand that the Crusaders and their leader Balian of Ibelin took during the siege of Jerusalem in 1187 AD. *Al-Masiraa'*, the LF's bimonthly magazine which started to appear immediately after the assassination of Bashir, made Deir al-Qamar a central theme of its content. One of the early articles was entitled 'Deir al-Qamar . . . The whole title', to underscore that this mountainous town was indeed fighting the battle for Lebanon and its resurrection. It stated:

> Deir al-Qamar, do not be afraid as long as you have men who do not fear death. Today we have become the masters of our own fate; we will reclaim all of our Lebanese land without the help of any side, for liberation to be worthwhile it has to be the product of our own sacrifices and martyrdom, or else we will be a worthless people. Oh, Deir al-Qamar . . . The whole title, to whomever is suffering, think of the one who suffered on the cross before you and keep these joyous words in mind: 'For your pain, oh Lord Jesus Christ'.[76]

After their defeat, the LF's rhetoric clearly took a more religious sectarian undertone, as this article clearly demonstrates. This departure mainly aimed at achieving two goals: to appeal to the Western world, and especially the Catholic Church and Europe, to come to their aid and rescue them from the barbarous Druze who wished to repeat the 1860 massacre; and to portray their stand in Deir al-Qamar as a victory rather than the outcome of their defeat.

The Druze were equally aware of the historical implications of Deir al-Qamar and what the siege signified for them and their besieged enemy. The images of the 1860 massacre at the hands of the Druze were still very vibrant in much of the propaganda that the LF disseminated to the public, both locally and abroad. The LF wanted to draw direct parallels between the atrocities that the forces of Said Joumblatt had perpetrated and what his grandson Walid Joumblatt was accomplishing a century later, by preventing the entry of food and supplies to Deir al Qamar. The PSP, through its Commissioner for Mobilisation, Anwar al-Fatayri, responded to these allegations by accusing the LF of holding the civilian population of the Shuf hostage and using them as human shields.[77] More importantly, Fatayri's main assertion responded to the Druze's historic claims that their use of violence was always based on self-defence, and that the War of the Mountain and the ensuing siege were no different. Walid Joumblatt exhibited a more condescending attitude, as he publicly downplayed the siege of Deir al-Qamar, which '[the Maronites] have transformed it to the Shirt of 'Uthman [a pretext] in a midst of a Crusader global campaign'.[78] Joumblatt went even further by dehumanising his LF opponents, shaming them for the massacres that they had perpetrated in the past against fellow Christians in Ehden and Safra, in reference to the killing of Tony Frangieh and the destruction of Chamoun's NLP.[79] This insistence on the LF's Crusader past also allowed Walid Joumblatt to reassert the image that he upheld for the Druze, depicting them as the descendants of the great Arab warrior tribes whose existential aim was to fend off the attacks of the Crusaders.

The Maronite Exodus

A hundred days after the beginning of the Battle of Bhamdoun and following an arduous negotiation process that required the intervention of the Vatican and other international actors, the siege of Deir al-Qamar was finally lifted. On 6 December, the birthday of his late father, Walid Joumblatt theatrically declared, 'After deliberation with the Sheikh al-'Aql Mohammad Abu-Shaqra we have agreed to allow all the civilians in Deir al-Qamar, including the militia of the Kataeb, to leave the town within the next ten days to allow them to spend Christmas with their loved ones'.[80] While Joumblatt used this occasion to flex his muscles and take the moral high ground by claiming that he had spared their lives, Deir al-Qamar constituted a red line that Joumblatt was not allowed to (nor perhaps ever intended to) cross. While Israel refrained from giving public support to either of the two factions on the eve of its withdrawal from Mount Lebanon, it made it clear to Joumblatt that Deir al-Qamar was not to be breached. The Israelis intended to use the siege to exert more pressure on Amin Gemayel, who was still refusing to honour his earlier promise to ratify the 17 May Accord. Perhaps it was no coincidence that the siege of Deir al-Qamar was lifted shortly after the return of President Gemayel from a stateside visit, during which he met Reagan and other senior members of his administration who promised 'to break the siege and open the road in and out of Deir al-Qamar'.[81]

On 15 December 1983, the 2,500 LF fighters defending Deir al-Qamar assembled in the historic town square in preparation for their evacuation to Beirut. Units from the IDF, commanded by General Daghan, were present to escorts the LF fighters through the Druze lines and the many villages on the way to the port of Jiyeh. From there, a French helicopter carrier transported them to the LF headquarters in Beirut, where the LF senior leadership and Pierre Gemayel gave them a hero's welcome. In an ironic twist of fate, the LF mechanised column, which in June of 1982 had made its way to the Shuf unopposed, was now showered with insults, curses and rocks flung by the Druze militants and civilians who lined up to see their defeated enemies vacate the besieged city. The LF, who coincidentally never admitted their defeat in the War of the Mountain, wanted to use their heroic last stand in Deir al-Qamar in a fashion very similar to the Battle of Zahle in 1981. However, this was impossible to achieve, as Bashir Gemayel was gone and, more importantly, the LF had no plans to implement, with the exception of protecting themselves from Amin Gemayel who was keen to control them. Paul Andary was among those 'survivors who were unloaded by the two massive ships', and he felt utter humiliation and sorrow because the sons of the mountain had been transformed from brave fighters to a people who are treated 'like mere criminals, disarmed and thrown in jail, to the unknown, to oblivion, to Beirut'.[82] Gradually, nearly the entire Christian civilian population of southern Mount Lebanon made the trip down to the coast and into the eastern part of Beirut, where they officially became refugees awaiting their return to over sixty villages, the majority of which the Druze demolished.

The Druze felt that their victory was still incomplete, with the Gharb region and the Iqlim al-Kharroub (coastal Shuf) still under LF control. While both regions were strategically important, the reclaiming of the Gharb, with its historic and religious status, became an obsession for the Druze. Consequently, on 14 February 1984, in what was dubbed 'Operation Sayyid Abdallah al-Tanukhi', the PSP fighters aided by a contingent of Druze clerics, called *Quwwat Abu Ibrahim* ('Forces of Abu-Ibrahim'), were able to infiltrate enemy lines. Some sources claim that members of the Israeli Druze, several on active duty within the IDF, participated in the attack that seized all the LF and Lebanese Army positions in the Gharb and liberated the Mausoleum of Sayyid Abdallah al-Tanukhi. While it has never been substantiated that Israeli Druze took part in this operation, the religious significance of Sayid Abdallah would naturally have enticed them to participate in such an endeavour. The religious and tribal implications of the liberation of al-Gharb were evident in the celebratory rhetoric of the Druze, as it was framed as an act of 'liberation of a pure and sacred land' rather than a merely military victory. Sheikh Sami Abu al-Mona further reinforced this concept in a poem he delivered a few month later, on the Druze holiday of Nabi Shu'ayb (Jethro); the poem radiated with socio-religious Druze imagery reflecting their collective identity. This annual occasion, which the Druze celebrate between 20 and 27 April, makes Druze from all over the Levant flock to Kfar Zeitim in the lower Galilee.[83] Abu al-Mona, who had made the trip from Lebanon, declared to his Druze brethren assembled in the region:

> Oh, Great Spirit of our lord prince [Sayyid Abdallah], rejoice
> We have reclaimed glory in your name, my lord
> To the Gharb we have returned by force
> In the name of the sword and faith and you fresh face
> Whoever survived the battle, be grateful to God, and whoever perished, God has chosen him
> We have returned to tell a story that will become a legend
> We have returned to raise the Druze banner over the rubble of our sanctuary
> We want the whole world to be aware that we are such a people that weapons yearn to be in our hands.[84]

Figure 7.7 Druze cleric fighting with the *Quwwat Abu Ibrahim* ('Forces of Abu-Ibrahim') (PSP Archives).

Beyond the poem's pride and triumphant undertone, it was a reiteration of one of the basic Druze tenets – that is, all Druze are brothers and will come to each other's aid, irrespective of time and space.

As the preceding events have demonstrated, the War of the Mountain was a conflict about which collective identity would triumph and which historical banner prevail. Each battle and each act of violence perpetrated by either side during these bloody confrontations was framed as serving one of these banners, thus either justifying or legitimising the extent to which the combatants were willing to go to avoid defeat and, ultimately, annihilation. However, when the battle ended, the Druze's military triumph left their historical banner somewhat orphaned, especially with their archnemesis, the Maronites, gone. As most of my examples have so far demonstrated, the historical construction of both communities' collective identities required a historical anti-thesis, which ultimately came to define and give meaning to the groups' self-perception. With one of the two opposing sides gone or damaged, the other was at risk, too. While neither the Druze nor the Maronites would ever openly admit it, their strained relationship had given them purpose. The game that both sides had played somewhat resembled that of cat and mouse: the main task of the cat was to chase the mouse, and the latter's role was to evade it.

Notes

1. See Chapter 2.
2. Interview with Fouad Abu-Nadir, Beirut, Lebanon, 23 February 2016.
3. Andary, *Al-Jabal*, 59.
4. Ibid., 60.
5. See page 139.
6. Interview with Fadi Frem, *Bashir: The Series*.
7. Simon Mousallam, as quoted in Shuwayfāti, *Ḥarb al-Durūz wa-al-Mawārinah fī al-Jabal*, vol. 3, 27. Translation mine.
8. Barakat's level of education is evident in many of the examples and analogies he employed throughout the interview, including references to works of history.
9. Interview with Toufic Barkat, PSP Oral History Project.
10. Interview with Naji Butrus, Makleis, Lebanon, 22 June 2016.
11. Ibid.

12. Kassab, as quoted in Interview with Toufic Barkat, PSP Oral History Project.
13. See page 84.
14. *Al-Anbaa'*, 22 May 1983, 30 May 1983.
15. *Al-Anbaa'*, 23 May 1983.
16. See page 198.
17. Hanf, *Coexistence in Wartime Lebanon*, 275.
18. Rabinovich, *The War for Lebanon*, 194.
19. Ménargues, *Asrār Ḥarb Lubnān*, 145. Translation mine.
20. For the full text of the LF-PSP agreement, see Andary, *Al-Jabal*, 77.
21. Ibid.
22. *Al-'Amal*, 15 March 1983.
23. Ibid. Translation mine.
24. Ibid.
25. Ibid., 27.
26. Ibid.
27. The Druze Memorandum.
28. In the 1926, the Lebanese constitution passed by the French Mandate established the senate, which was composed of sixteen senators. This body was suspended barely a year later.
29. PBDA Newsletter, undated [1983].
30. Ibid.
31. Sharon, as quoted in Andary, *Al-Jabal*, 108.
32. Ménargues, *Asrār Ḥarb Lubnān*, 320.
33. Ibid., 325.
34. Andary, *Al-Jabal*, 110.
35. The interviewee, a PSP senior member, requested anonymity.
36. Shuwayfāti, *Ḥarb al-Durūz wa-al-Mawārinah fī al-Jabal*, vol. 3, 32.
37. Arens as quoted in Ménargues, *Asrār Ḥarb Lubnān*, 327. Translation mine.
38. Adwan was a member of the LF War Council, representing the Tanzim organization, an ultra-right-wing faction. Adwan was from Deir al-Qamar and counted among the first to endorse an open alliance with Israel.
39. Lubrani, as quoted in Ménargues, *Asrār Ḥarb Lubnān*, 328. Translation mine.
40. Kimche, *The Last Option*, 174–5.
41. Elie Salem, *Violence and Diplomacy in Lebanon: The Troubled Years, 1982–1988* (London: I. B. Tauris, 1995), 113.
42. Interview with Hisham Nasreddine, Deit Koubal, Mount Lebanon, 4 September 2016.

43. John Rolland, *Lebanon: Current Issues and Background* (Hauppauge: Nova Science Publishers, 2003), 181.
44. Kimche, *The Last Option*, 175.
45. http://www.usdiplomacy.org/history/service/harmsway.php#dillon, accessed 2 October 2016.
46. Kevin Dougherty, *The United States Military in Limited War: Case Studies in Success and Failure, 1945–1999* (Jefferson: McFarland & Company, 2012), 147.
47. Salem, *Violence and Diplomacy in Lebanon*, 113.
48. *Al-Anbaa'*, 3 July 1983, 8.
49. Ibid.
50. Ibid.
51. Ibid.
52. Ibid., 29 August 1983, 10.
53. *Al-Jabal*, 248.
54. Interview with Raja Harb, Beirut, Lebanon, 30 December 2016.
55. Interview with George Radi, Beirut, Lebanon, 12 December 2012.
56. *Al-Masiraa'*, 14 September 1983, 11.
57. *Al-Masiraa'*, 30 June 1983.
58. These are a rough estimate based on many sources I used, including Ménargues, *Asrār Ḥarb Lubnān*.
59. Antoine Najm, as quoted in Ménargues, *Asrār Ḥarb Lubnān*, 359.
60. Samir Geagea, as interviewed by Ghassan Charbel, *Ayna Kunta fī al-Harb?* 170.
61. Ibid.
62. Ibid.
63. See the map on page xviii.
64. Andary, *Al-Jabal*, 85.
65. Ibid.
66. *Al-Anbaa'*, 25 August 1983.
67. Ibid.
68. Andary, *Al-Jabal*, 120.
69. Interview with Ghanem Tarabay, Qoubbei', Lebanon, 23 June 2013.
70. Interview with Fouad Abu-Nadir, Beirut, Lebanon, 23 February 2016.
71. http://www.lebanese-forces.org/hakim/sgremembers/sgremembers.pdf, p 41, accessed 10 May 2010.
72. Raji Achkouti, *Ḥiṣār Dayr al-Qamar* [The Siege of Deir al-Qamar] ([n. p.]: 1984).
73. Ibid., 114–15.

74. Walid Joumblatt as quoted in http://www.aljazeera.net/programs/lebanon-war/2005/1/10/%D8%AD%D8%B1%D8%A8-%D9%84%D8%A8%D9%86%D8%A7%D9%86-%D9%87%D8%B2%D9%8A%D9%85%D8%A9-%D9%82%D9%88%D8%A9-%D8%B9%D8%B8%D9%85%D9%89-%D8%AC11, accessed 3 March 2020.
75. https://www.youtube.com/watch?v=LVenEkHb_Kg, accessed 3 March 2020.
76. *Al-Masiraa'*, 1 October 1983, 21.
77. *Al-Anbaa'*, 8 December 1983, 13.
78. *Al-Nahar*, 5 December 1983.
79. Ibid.
80. *Al-Anbaa'*, 12 December 1983, 2.
81. *Al-'Amal*, 2 December 1983.
82. Andary, *Al-Jabal*, 197.
83. Firro, *Druzes in the Jewish State*, 95.
84. http://www.ormanland.com/forum/showthread.php?t=6901, accessed 14 October 2016. Translation mine.

8

POST-CONFLICT REHASHING AND THE PRESERVATION OF COLLECTIVE MEMORY

As soon as combat ended, both centres of power within the Druze and Maronite communities looked towards active agents to promote their collective identity and to recast and adjust their respective communities' memories. At that particular stage in time, both the PSP and the LF wanted to capitalise on their victories and their failures after coming out of a war that had depleted their resources, including many lives and, in the case of the Maronites, even some land. The post-conflict need to create this feeling of collectivity, as the following chapter will illustrate, was an important ingredient to the process that both groups had experience already in the period leading up to the war itself.

Collecting the Collective

This chapter will draw on two primary examples of active agents used by centres of power to promote collective identity and to recast and adjust the respective communities' memories of themselves and 'the other'. The Maronite periodical *Al-Masiraa* published 'The Story of a Hero called Charbel', a weekly illustrated comic book using the colloquial Lebanese dialect. By using a cartoon format, the LF clearly wanted to win over the younger generation, the age group most susceptible to memory retention. However, these comics are also effective for other age groups and transcend generational barriers. In comparison, the Druze had the works of Taleh Hamdan, a prominent Druze strophic poet. His poems contain many latent examples of the way in which the Druze centres of power wanted their community to remember the war and their supposed enemies, the Maronites.

The centres of power in the Druze and the Maronite communities – that is, the PSP and the LF, respectively – wanted to use the events of the war to recast and perhaps fortify their communities' collective memory of earlier, current and potential future conflicts.

The Story of a Hero Called Charbel

Shortly after the assassination of Bashir Gemayel, *Al-Masiraa'*, the LF's official publication, started to appear as newsletter for internal circulation. According to its founder, Elie Khayat, *Al-Masiraa'* was born out of necessity. Khayat has stated that, after Bashir's assassination, he felt a personal responsibility to remind or refocus the people around him regarding the aim of the LF's cause and the identity of their real enemy. In his capacity as the head of the Fifth Branch (the Media and Guidance Unit of the LF) in the Kfarshima barracks, Khayat was mostly surrounded by fighters between the ages of eighteen and twenty-five, most of whom came from underprivileged families and lacked a high school or university education. Consequently, he felt that they needed some sort of political guidance, in addition to a source of entertainment. This was the main reason why Khayat started to produce what he called *Al-Masiraa'* (The March), initially consisting of an internal newsletter using plain paper and a stencil machine before it was transformed into a publication that catered to a broader audience or readership.[1]

The LF central command soon adopted this newsletter, mainly to use it as a tool to respond to the changing realities after Bashir's assassination. The LF felt the need to reaffirm its main ethos as an institution geared towards defending the Christians and upholding the true values of Lebanon. In its inaugural issue published on 25 October 1982, the opening clearly states this point. Using a very elementary and colloquial dialect, *Al-Masiraa'* proclaimed that its main aim was 'to be the voice of freedom, the voice of the fighters coming from the trenches to the farthest mountains and the seashore'.[2] The need to restate the LF's aim was also partially due to the pressure that the newly elected president Amin Gemayel was exerting on the LF. Immediately after the election of Amin Gemayel, the official Kataeb mouthpiece *Al-'Amal*, in a clear departure from earlier practices under Bashir Gemayel, largely ceased to run news on the LF. As a result, the LF had to create their own print platform to get their message across, whether to supporters or foes. These factors are evident throughout the articles and stories that *Al-Masiraa'* ran: They amounted to rebuttals to attacks from within the Christian community and to Muslims' accusations that they were cold-blooded killers. Immensely damaged by the massacres in the Palestinian refugee camps of Sabra and Shatila, in which the LF had been accused of participating, a media outreach plan was needed to repair their image both locally and internationally. It is against this backdrop and other contributing factors that one needs to see the story of Charbel.

The Story of a Hero Called Charbel, a weekly illustrated comic written in the colloquial Lebanese dialect, started to appear in March 1984, a month after the end of the hostilities in the Gharb.[3] The choice of the name is of extreme importance, as Charbel is the patron-saint of Lebanon and the LF fighters who wore his pendant as a good-luck charm.[4] The LF were quite blatant in this exercise to influence the Maronites' collective memory, proclaiming that a Christian Lebanese hero needed to walk in the footsteps of Charbel:

> This is a story about a hero named Charbel. It is the story of all of our heroes . . . It is the story of a hero who has dedicated his life to protecting his people, his land and his faith. This story we choose to narrate through sketches, so that it will be more expressive and so that every one of us, including *our children*, will remember our real history and never forget it . . . Charbel was born to a mother and a father entrenched in faith in a village near the cedar trees and near the skies . . .

Charbel is a member of the 1958 Generation, as discussed in Chapter 3, who realised that Lebanon with its current political structure was only doomed to fail:

> He remembers his dad carrying a rifle and going away one day [a reference to the 1958 civil war] . . . He grew up with the harsh reality that the [Palestinian] refugees wanted to get rid of us . . . So he joined the LF and

Figure 8.1 Charbel addresses a priest who resembles Abbot Bulus Naʿaman: 'Forgive me, Father, for I have sinned'. To which the priest replies: 'Go in peace, my son, you are forgiven' (LF Archives).

began his training, and he looked up to Bashir who taught him that our existence is tied to our resistance. Subsequently, Charbel graduated to a new man full of vigor and faith and became a LF fighter.[5]

The subsequent episodes of *The Story of a Hero Called Charbel* informed the reader about how this embodiment of a warrior-monk fought in nearly all the battles in which the LF were engaged, including the Battle of Zahle in 1980 and the War of the Mountain, and how, along with his comrades, he refused to retreat before they had ensured the safety of the civilian population, even though they were outnumbered and ill-equipped. After the LF's retreat to Deir al-Qamar, Charbel helped the people under siege, all the while observing his religious duties by regularly attending mass.[6]

Interestingly, the story of Charbel never depicted the Lebanese Muslims and Druze as malicious rivals, but as 'brothers that strayed from the path, preferring to collaborate with the Outsiders [Palestinians and Syrians]'.[7]

In using a cartoon format, the LF clearly wanted to win over the younger generation, the age group most likely to retain memory, as discussed above. The artist constantly used pictures of famous LF leaders, especially Bashir Gemayel, to hammer in the notion that martyrdom and sacrifice were prerequisites for belonging to the Lebanese Christian nation. The example below (Figure 8.2) depicts the famous ceremony that the LF held after the Battle of Zahle in 1981.[8] Bashir is seen pinning the 'Medal of Zahle' – a cultural tool for memory production – on Keyrouz Barkat, the leader of the LF's Special Forces, who fought the better equipped Syrian army to a standstill.

Barkat, a native of southern Lebanon who lost his life in the War of the Mountain, consequently became an object of commemoration for both his brothers-in-arms and the Christian community at large.[9] The fact that Barkat was from the south is extremely important, because it illustrates, at least according to the LF doctrine, that all Christians are obliged to come to the aid of their coreligionists and that the LF militia was the guardian of all Christians in Lebanon and perhaps even the Levant. The same notion was echoed by George Radi, a LF combatant, who confirmed that geography was irrelevant to himself and his comrades: 'We were a professional fighting outfit and would carry out our mission regardless of place and time'.[10]

According to Elie Khayat, *The Story of Charbel* and its *raison d'être* are not as complex as one may think; it was *not* part of a master plan originally devised by the LF's central command to indoctrinate or even spread propaganda. Rather, it was the initiative of a first-year pre-med student by the name of Christian Nasr, who approached Khayat to inquire about ways in which he could lend his support to the cause.[11] Nasr happened to be a talented illustrator, and therefore Khayat came up with the idea of getting these simple messages to the *shabab* ('the fighters') by using a comic book format. Thus, *The Story of Charbel* was born. However, Khayat has stated that he was mainly 'preoccupied with teaching the youth about the history of Lebanon and what had happened recently so they can understand the situation now and for the future'. The seventeen episodes of *Charbel* clearly depict this fixation on history, whether indirectly or through the voice of the narrator, as in the example below.

On more than one occasion, Charbel is pictured on the frontlines reading about the history of Lebanon during his spare time, with a cross shown

Figure 8.2 Keyrouz Barkat (left) receiving the Medal of Zahle from the leader of the LF, Bashir Gemayel (right), and the same image as illustrated in the *Story of Charbel* series (LF Archives).

Figure 8.3 Charbel is studying history when his comrade calls him: 'Charbel, come on, it's time for your shift' (LF Archives).

behind him (Figures 8.3 and 8.4). When his brother-in-arms asks him why he is reading history, Charbel stresses how understanding the history of Lebanon and the Christians in the East is important to better prepare for the challenges ahead.[12] The Maronite obsession with historical instruction utilises Charbel as a tool to frame the future generations' view of the history of the community. The LF also clearly tried to rid themselves of the image of ruthless killers only bent on death and unprincipled destruction, which they had acquired based on recent events. This is was clear in the Charbel series as well as in other articles published in *Al-Masiraa*'.

Charbel attends a LF rally where the newly elected leader, Fouad Abu-Nadir, is reminding his troops that 'any gun that is yielded by a non-believer is in fact being yielded by a killer or a criminal'. The illustration also shows Charbel in the background, silently repeating this phrase (Figure 8.5).[13] By casting the Maronites and the LF as believers, the *Story of Charbel* was in

Figure 8.4 Comrade: 'Brother, put aside the history books and instead tell me what is happening these days.' Charbel: 'We will never understand what is happening today unless we know our history' (LF Archives).

fact branding their enemies, the Druze, as cold-blooded and godless killers. Furthermore, this particular scene, together with the scene in which Charbel confesses to the priest and asks for forgiveness for the sins he committed – that is, for killing while fighting the enemy, among them the Druze – is very revealing, as it attempts to vindicate Charbel and his comrades. The Maronite Christian element essentially is the crux of Charbel's identity, as nearly all comic strips either depict him praying or alternatively feature a crucifix in the background, further underscoring the religious aspect of the conflict (Figure 8.6).

To mark the one-year anniversary of *Harb al-Jabal*, *Al-Masiraa'* published a commemorative issue dealing exclusively with this event. This issue also included a poster that echoed the ethos described above. This poster depicted the difference between believers. A group of LF fighters is shown in full military gear, praying and captioned with the word 'warrior'. Above the group stands a Druze combatant dressed in the traditional clerical cloth, wielding a bayonet and screaming at the camera, captioned with the word 'killer' (Figure 8.7).[14]

Figure 8.5 'Any gun that is yielded by a non-believer is in fact being yielded by a killer or a criminal' (LF Archives).

With such imagery, the LF wanted to reinforce the military ethos within their ranks and to appeal to the younger generation. Khayat admitted that, although the intention was not to target the younger generation, due to its popularity whithin that age group, *Al-Masiraa*'s circulation was boosted from a mere 5,000 to 60,000 copies in the span of a year. Several of my interviewees, mostly Christians who at that time had been between the ages of five and ten, vividly recalled *The Story of Charbel*, which they used to follow regularly.

Beyond its primary goal to form a sense of collective identity, the *Story of Charbel* also served to answer some of the main challenges and questions that were plaguing the Christians at large, especially after their exodus from the Shuf. These questions sought to educate so to avoid the LF's mistakes in their fight against the Druze and, more importantly, how to preserve the legacy of Bashir Gemayel after his passing. In one episode, Charbel and his comrades have been deployed to the front, and one night Bashir Gemayel pays them a surprise visit, dining and spending the evening in conversation with them

Figure 8.6 Scenes from different episodes of *The Story of Charbel*, with the crucifix visible in the background (LF Archives).

Figure 8.7 The killer and the warrior (LF Archives).

(Figure 8.8).¹⁵ The main message that Bashir Gemayel conveys to his men that evening is the following: His ascension to the presidency was not the ultimate goal of the Lebanese Resistance, rather it was 'one more step in our never-ending struggle'.¹⁶ These insinuations reflect the LF's frustration about President Amin Gemayel, who had abandoned his brother's legacy and had, in fact, conspired against the LF during the War of the Mountain.

Despite their resounding military defeat, the LF never conceded this fact, but maintained that their ability to withstand the united assault by the Druze and their Syrian allies was a triumph in itself. The LF upheld this sentiment during and after the conflict, going so far as to issue a commemorative medal to celebrate their victory in the War of the Mountain. This medal, awarded to the fighters who participated in the campaign, depicts an LF combatant leaping forward, weapon in hand, and underneath him the slogan 'Bashir is alive within us' (Figure 8.9).

Despite Khayat's confirmation that the original intention of *Charbel* never was, in his own words, 'to brainwash people', it nevertheless left a visible mark on the collective memory. *The Story of a Hero Called Charbel* promoted nearly all the elements that constitute the Maronite historical identity, as

Figure 8.8 Bashir Gemayel visiting the front lines, where he meets Charbel and has dinner with his men (LF Archives).

Figure 8.9 Medal of the Mountain, issued by the LF in 1983 (LF Archives).

presented in Chapter 3, framed and presented in a vivid manner that appealed to a young audience, yet still served a didactic purpose. Furthermore, the character of Charbel was cast in such a way that it urged the Maronite youth to follow in the footsteps of this simple, honest, faithful and educated warrior, to become a companion of Bashir Gemayel and the future generations who aspired to make Lebanon great again.

This preoccupation with forming or recasting Christian historical memory was not limited to the *Story of Charbel*. Earlier, the Holy Spirit University (USK) had undertaken a very similar project. In 1979, Bulus Naʿaman, the chair of the Department of History at USK, had co-supervised with Professor Kaiser Nasr the publication of *Qissat al-Mawarini* (The Story of the Maronites), a comic book written and illustrated by Antoine and Maiva Bahkus. This two-volume children's book narrates the history of the Maronites in the seventh century AD, on the eve of the Islamic conquest of the Syrian lands.[17] According to Naʿaman, this publication, exclusively written in the Lebanese vernacular, 'aims to introduce the upcoming Christian youth to the history of their forefathers and what they have endured and accomplished throughout the centuries'.[18] The introduction to *Qissat al-Mawarini* emphasises the aim of this project:

> A Maronite's real concern is to live free, to discover, develop his roots and open up to his fellow man. To do so, he has to know himself. The

Maronites have written their history since eternity, however, he remains unsatisfied with this product. A Maronite needs to write his history on a daily basis, not merely on paper, but in real life as well.

Beyond the philosophical points that the publishers of the *Qissat al-Mawarini* tried to convey, this project is better understood as part of the efforts that the Kaslik Research Committee (KRC) was undertaking at that particular time – mainly to lend ideological support and provide material for the Lebanese Resistance as embodied by Bashir Gemayel.[19] The key theme that the KRC wished to promote consisted of the following: the Maronite people or their Mardaite ancestors had inhabited the land of Lebanon since the dawn of time and had fought off many invaders, including the Islamic conquest of the Levant in 638 AD.[20] This purported Maronite pedigree – or, simply put, the question 'who are the *Mawarini*'[21] – is clearly defined at the beginning of the book. It mirrors the Maronite myth as created and propagated by a number of institutions, chiefly among them the Lebanese Monastic Order.[22]

> *Al-Mawarni*, before they were known as such, were a semitic and Indo-European people who settled in the land stretching from Turkey to Mount Lebanon. These many nations were forged into one people whose main quest was to fight persecution and keep their freedom and liberty. They were referred to as Aramaic people simply because they spoke Aramaic, but in times of war they were called the Mardaites or the *Jarajimah*, meaning heroes . . . we are the sons of a civilisation that dates back 5,000 years; they [the Muslims] were born just yesterday; they are crying because this is what newborn babies do, they cry out once they are born.[23]

Similar to the *Story of Charbel*, this story introduces readers to the history of the Maronites by means of two heroes, the brave Mardaite warrior Moran and his son Sema'an (Simon). Despite its countless historical fallacies, this publication was extremely effective in forging the Maronites' collective memory within the context of the current developments unfolding in Lebanon and the broader region. The main protagonist, Moran, is described by both friend and foe as a reckless and persistent man who resembles the rocky Lebanese Mountains from where he hails; he is a seventh-century version of Bashir Gemayel.

Much of Moran's rhetoric throughout the story is directed towards his Christian coreligionists who have failed to live up to the challenge to properly defend their people against the foreign Muslim invaders. Just like Gemayel, Moran was fixated on unifying the Maronites, a prerequisite for defeating their Muslim enemies. In one scene, Moran addresses his fellow Maronites and other Mardaite generals and orders his men to draw a map of the Lebanese Mountain(s) with the corresponding districts and borders. Thereafter, he walks over the map and erases the different borders with his foot, declaring that 'from now on, the mountain is one district and I am its leader. We have to be one body, with one head, or else'.[24] This scene, published in 1979, one year before Bashir Gemayel carried out his plan of the 'Unification of the Christian Gun', is very revealing, because it shows how Bashir Gemayel, with the help of the monks, was striving to unify the community, even if it meant spilling Christian blood.[25] Moreover, just like Moran who collaborated with the monk Youhana Maroun, later the first patriarch of the Maronites, Bashir Gemayel approached the Lebanese monks and through this association symbolically reflected the same fight that their Mardaite forefathers had led centuries earlier.[26] In one of their fictitious encounters, Moran accompanied by Patriarch Youhana Maroun on his journey to Damascus to meet the famous Umayyad Caliph Muʿawiyah I, who was ecstatic about this unexpected visit. This meeting concluded with Moran forcing the Muslim caliph to relinquish the poll tax required from the Maronites and instead pay an annual tribute to them.[27]

Beyond the declared educational aim of both the *Story of Charbel* and *Qissat al-Mawarini*, the Maronite centres of power used these real or imagined historic encounters to draw parallels between their historic, current and future projects and, more importantly, to secure the much needed legitimacy for the success of these ventures. The Druze leadership followed suit by using similar methods rooted in popular culture to interact with their constituency and to keep the Druze collective remembrance process lucid and regulated by the parameters set forth by Joumblatt and the PSP.

Zajal Harb al-Jabal

One such method was the use of strophic poetry (*zajal*) to disseminate and forge the group's memory about the recent Druze victory. *Zajal*, as a popular form of poetry, is deeply rooted within the culture of Mount Lebanon. Both the Druze and the Maronites maintain a tradition of producing and encouraging the composition of *zajal*, once the only available means of disseminating information and creating entertainment. As an art form, it entails many styles ranging from 'Ataba, Mijana, Abu Zuluf and Rouzana to other variants that differ in their poetic meter. More importantly, villages and towns depended on the poet commonly referred to as *qawal* (narrator) to record the history of their community and then transmit and disseminate it orally through the various *zajal* verses he sang during public and private events. *Zajal* became extremely popular as it was institutionalised through competitions that featured two opposing choirs accompanied by a few musical instruments, mostly percussionists. The advent of the radio and later television, which usually transmitted these *zajal* battles, added to the popularity of this form of literary competition. These events, usually attended by an exclusively male audience, included the consumption of copious amounts of a local alcoholic beverage (*'arak*), and the crowd participated by shouting praise and repeating verses. Usually, the *qawal* played the role of a propagandist, by defending his family, tribe or village against those who verbally criticised them through other *zajal*. According to Butrus Gemayel, *zajal* was a predominantely Maronite art form, as between the sixteenth and the twentieth century 192 of the 244 known *zajal* poets were Maronite, followed by non-Maronite Christians (22), Druze (17) and Shi'ite (13).[28]

Kamal Salibi's study on the medieval Maronite historian and Bishop of Nicosia Jibra'il Ibn al-Qila'i reveals how *zajal* was an important form of recording history, which in the case of Ibn al-Qila'i included defending the faith of the Maronite Church against the ideological threat posed by the Jacobites, who had struck deep roots within his community.[29] Ibn al-Qila'i, a native of Lahfid in Byblos (Mount Lebanon), looked towards *zajal* to educate the Maronites on proper Catholic orthodoxy and turn them away from the heresy of the Jacobites.[30] His Catholic zeal was the product of the education he had received at the Maronite College in Rome and his twenty-three-year stay in Italy, which made him an ardent defender of the Maronite Church's union with Rome.[31] Consequently, to achieve his goal, al-Qila'i addressed his people in the most common form known to them, writing nearly all of his liturgical and historical works in *zajal* form. Salibi maintains that Ibn al-Qila'i's works technically cannot be classified as works of history and that, in fact, the author's main intention was not so much to write a history of his people, but to underscore the dangers of the Maronite's digression from the Roman faith.[32] *Madiha 'ala Jabal Lubnan* (Ode to Mount Lebanon), Ibn al-Qila'i's most famous *zajal*, is a case in point: It incorporates historical accounts, some of which are unsubstantiated or contradictory, with Catholic liturgical rhetoric, with the intention to educate both clergy and layman. Later, Maronite scholars influenced by the works of Istfan al-Duwayhi used Ibn al-Qila'i's ideas as basic building blocks to write the history of their community as well as of Lebanon.

According to the Druze, this Maronite account of history intentionally excluded the Druze, the true founders of the Lebanese entity, prompting them to launch their own history project.[33] Among these Druze counter-narratives are the works of Taleh Hamdan, a prominent strophic poet, who clearly depicts the manner in which the Druze centres of power wanted their community to remember *Harb al-Jabal*. A native of the village of 'Ayn Anoub in the Aley region of Mount Lebanon, Hamdan was born in 1944. Hamdan began his career as a member of Zagloul al-Damour's choral ensemble before he branched out and formed his own. While Hamdan was not officially a member of the PSP, his *zajal* entitled *Harb al-Jabal* clearly served the PSP and his community's aim of capitalising on their recent military and political conquests. Long assumed an individual initiative by Hamdan, these *zajal* performances, in fact, were produced upon the recommendation of Walid Joumblatt. Shortly after the end of the Battle of Bhamdoun, Joumblatt summoned Hamdan to Moukhtara and asked him to 'to record the history of this period [the war], just like the great poet Shibli al-Atrash recorded the achievement of the Syrian Revolution with Sultan Pasha al-Atrash and Sheikh Nayef Talhouk, with memorable poetry about the Druze'.[34]

Walid Joumblatt's commission was mainly prompted by his awareness about the history of his family and of his Druze community. In 1860, the Druze military victory over their Maronites was translated into a political defeat, as the Druze were portrayed as aggressors and, ultimately, a number of their leading chiefs were incarcerated, banished and executed – among them Joumblatt's great-grandfather Said. Certainly, Walid Joumblatt wanted to avoid his ancestor's debacle, instead framing his men's excessive use of force as a purely defensive measure against a Maronite foe bent on defeating and annihilating the Druze. Moreover, the Druze victory, at least for Joumblatt, was a chance to recast the history of Lebanon and to acknowledge the Druze's contribution to the Lebanese Idea; Taleh Hamdan's poetry was a means to achieve that goal. Walid Joumblatt's preface to Hamdan's book unequivocally reveals the latter's contentious relationship with Maronite historical scholarship:

> For so long, we have lived as captives of Ibn al-Qila'i, this forged account that historian have used to twist the facts and write the history of Lebanon according to isolationist [Maronite] interests. For the first time, Taleh Hamdan faces the challenge and records the history of the period in which we are living, adding to this history the fragrance and freshness of poetry and his gentle, perhaps unmatched touch.[35]

Joumblatt's direct reference to Ibn al-Qila'i as a distorted source on Lebanese history and his presentation of Hamdan's *zajaliya* as corrective measure places this Druze project of collective identity and memory at the crux of the ideological conflict that continued even after the end of the military conflict.

During and after the war in 1983–4, Hamdan's public performances clearly reiterated the Druze's religious doctrine of fatalism and belief in reincarnation, which partially explains the bravery and fearlessness of their warriors. Furthermore, the choice of location and props for these *zajal* parties constituted statements in their own right, as Hamdan would usually perform surrounded by iconic Druze emblems. Behind Hamdan would hang the Druze flag, the PSP flag, pictures of Kamal Joumblatt, the Syrian rebel Sultan Pasha al-Atrash, Emir Majid Arslan and Walid Joumblatt (Figure 8.10).

This choice of decoration sought to project the image that the Druze were all united under one banner, regardless of their political, ideological or their geographic location. Noticeably, the only missing Druze element was that of the Israeli Druze who, despite their full support to their Lebanese brethren, were deliberately excluded from this display, simply because they did not fit within the pro-Arab tale that Hamdan wished to convey.

Hamdan commenced his recitation or 'singing',[36] as he himself called it, by 'asking God to protect the Druze across the world'.[37] He would then proceed in the customary manner, with a poem known as an *iftitahiyah*

Figure 8.10 Taleh Hamdan (centre), with the PSP flag and pictures of Kamal Joumblatt, Sultan Pasha al-Atrash, Emir Majid Arslan, Walid Joumblatt and the Druze flag on the wall above him (PSP Archives).

('opener'). This long introduction, entitled *Leave Our Precious Mountain*, imparts the Druze interpretation of *Harb al-Jabal* and reaffirms the Druze reading of history overall:

> Leave our precious mountain and leave, you aggressor, you wild thorns don't hurt our precious flowers,
> You are drunk on alcohol and cups of wine, and you left the Druze of the Mountains intoxicated with blood.
> What did you come to do in the land of glory and revolution that was a garden of flowers, you burnt the green meadows and planted agony and sorrow, these were not the teaching of Jesus Christ, who was a humanitarian.
> You have come to uproot a people that bleeds on a land that has time and again drank vessels of their blood.[38]

The Druze's deep attachment to their land is a central theme that Hamdan repeated throughout his recital, stressing that many of the violent reactions of the Druze and the massacres that they committed were in response to the Maronites' attempts to uproot them from the land of their ancestors. In the process, Hamdan boasts about the infinite bravery and valour of all Druze, regardless of gender or age:

> A son would die in front of his sister, just to defend their honour and pride, and so that they can live proud.

> How arrogant if you think you can remove the stars and move mountains unless God wills it.
> You cannot even uproot a Druze child, because this child will cry out: 'My dad has raised me so that I die for this land'.
> Our most gorgeous girls will say: 'I will only marry a Druze man who is willing to fight for honour.
> As a gift I want a rifle instead of a purse . . .'[39]

Hamdan further adds a socio-religious twist by linking the Druze fearlessness to their belief in reincarnation:

> A brother would tell his sister: 'Do not weep for my death,
> I will just change my shirt which has been ruined by a few bullet holes, saving you the trouble of constantly washing my shirts'.

To respond to the Maronite 'distortion of history', Hamdan glorifies his people's myth that Lebanon has always belonged to the Druze, mainly because they have defended it ever since their ancestors settled in the mountains ten centuries ago:

> This land spoke to the Druze and told them that the land of Lebanon was created for your sake.
> You are the most noble of people and the bravest beings ever.
> You have defended Lebanon ever since the Tanukhs and the Arslans,
> even when there were no such things as Byblos and Jounieh and no person existed in the lands of Kisrwan [various regions of Lebanon].
> We [Druze] were born long before the cedar trees were born.
> Lebanon was Druze long before it was Maronite.[40]

These *zajal* performances, repeated over a long period of time, were recorded on tape cassettes, widely circulated and sold in West Beirut by street vendors, and they soon became a feature of male drinking rituals.[41] My own encounter with Hamdan's *zajal* happened at a young age, when my late maternal grandfather played a cassette on our various road trips. Although too young at the time to decipher the verses, the poetry nevertheless instilled a sense of Druze belonging in me. Much of what Hamdan recited in defence of his community was drawn from his own understanding of the political events of the time, coupled with the historical framework he knew from his childhood. While, according to Hamdan, his poetry was the product of celestial inspiration, as 'ideas are revealed to him through a muse', as a poet he made a living delivering eulogies and poems in nearly all Druze villages across the country. This gave him access to the collective fears and concerns of the Druze as a community, and also to their stories, which he later spun into an epic celebrating both myth and reality.

Although his *zajal* recitals might appear very similar in terms of content, one does notice additions or changes that correspond to certain events of that time. This is particularly interesting when analysed in conjunction with Elizabeth Tonkin's work on Africa, as discussed in Chapter 1. Tonkin has argued that oral histories reveal how people read and record their past in juxtaposition with what they hope to achieve in the future; Hamdan's *zajal* poetry exemplifies this argument. Hamdan played a quite interactive role, as he would receive immediate feedback from the audience and effectively had the ability to adjust his poetry from one recital to another.

In a fashion very similar to *The Story of a Hero Called Charbel*, Hamdan's consecutive recitals responded to local developments with more immediate political implications. In his second recording, for example, Hamdan introduced Nabih Berri, the leader of the 'Amal Shi'ite Movement, portraying him as a partner in the Druze war against the regime of Amin Gemayel, thus cementing the notion that the conflict carried an Islamic-Arab subtext. Other adjustments in Hamdan's *zajal* included a response to the United States taking an active role in the conflict, with the battleship *USS New Jersey* battleship shelling Druze villages to prevent the fall of the strategic town of Souk al-Gharb.[42] Consequently, Hamdan composed one of his most memorable melodic poems, *New Jersey*, in which he rebuked all the enemies of the Druze, including the American government:

> The people who dangled a noose for you in all the battles
> would never be intimidated by the [USS] New Jersey or the tanks,
> Even if you ask of [Ronald] Reagan to send you one or even two armies,
> you bombarded 'Ayn Anoub, and no one even blinked.
> Even if you bring down not one but two Souk al-Gharb,
> you would never drink from the water of Aytat [a Druze village adjacent
>   to Souk al-Gharb].[43]

Figure 8.11 'Son of the Mountains' (PSP Archives).

While Hamdan's *zajal* is overwhelmingly charged with sectarian and racial undertones, he nevertheless distinguishes that the main clash was with the LF as aggressors, and not the Christians who, despite their 'inconsequential servant rank throughout history' where friends of the Druze and loyal subjects.[44] In a fashion similar to Charbel, Hamdan, and perhaps the Druze community as a whole, felt the need to leave a door open to reconciliation, however unlikely that may have seemed at the time.

Similarly, the Druze also used posters and graphic illustrations to fortify the Druze collective identity by creating a 'Druze Charbel'. A poster published on 16 March 1984, the anniversary of Kamal Joumblatt's assassination, shows a Druze teenager wielding an AK-47 and captioned 'Son of the Mountains' (Figure 8.11), a clear message that all segments of the community were willing to take up arms in order to defend its existence. The Druze also used the same picture of a Druze cleric waving a dagger, but instead of depicting Sheikh Kamal Ghanam as killer, the caption reads: 'He raised his dagger in front of their faces'. This more positive caption was meant to counter the LF usage of the same image in order to frame the Druze as heartless and bloodthirsty.

Bashir ... We have Returned

On the first anniversary of the War of the Mountain, Walid Joumblatt called for an enormous parade in Beit al-Din to celebrate the Druze victory, as well as the liberation of the Shuf and Aley from the LF aggressor. Designating the palace of Bashir II, the historical foe of the Druze to celebrate the Joumblatti Druze victory was an interesting choice: Walid Joumblatt was avenging the death of his ancestor, Bashir 'the Pillar of Heaven' Joumblatt. The conventional account of the celebrations is as follows: Upon his arrival in Beit al-Din, Walid Joumblatt gazed at Bashir's palace and, in a reenactment of the gesture of the French High Commissioner upon conquering Damascus, proclaimed: 'Bashir ... We have Returned'.[45] While there exists no official documentation of this incident, much of the proceedings of what the PSP dubbed as 'Lighting of the Torch Festival', as well as the concluding speech that Joumblatt delivered on that day in September, support this narrative. The PSP, which earlier had declared the establishment of a civil administration to run the affairs of the districts of the Shuf and Aley, wanted to parade its Soviet-trained and -equipped Popular Liberation Army (PLA) and declare *quasi* independence from the Christian-dominated Lebanese state. In a military display resembling the Soviet Victory Day celebrations, the Beit al-Din Palace was decorated with PSP and PLA flags and featured divisions of PLA soldiers in full parade gear waiting for Joumblatt's arrival. Making his way into the historic palace courtyard, Joumblatt, flanked by three of his generals, proceeded to light the celebration torch, thus signaling the beginning of the ceremony. In a clear *tour de force*, Joumblatt paraded several PLA military divisions, the contingent of Druze fighting clerics (*Quwwat Abu Ibrahim*, or 'Forces of Abu-Ibrahim') and the 'Rebels of 58', a unit who had fought in the 1958 war.

Much of the set-up and many of the details of this event were instrumental for forming the collective memory that Joumblatt and the PSP wanted to impart to the Druze. From the banners hoisted over the German-style military marches that the band played to the high-ranking religious and political attendees, the message was clear: The Druze have avenged the blood of Sheikh Bashir and with it rewritten 159 years of history.[46] More importantly, Walid Joumblatt's speech that day signaled the last chapter in the primordial feud between the Druze and the Maronites, and what the Druze were expected to remember was framed by Joumblatt's powerful delivery:

> This is your flame, my *Mouallam* [Kamal Joumblatt], our greatest martyr, this is the flame of liberty, democracy and socialism; this is your flame, oh Hafez and Fawzi and Jamal, this is your flame, Sheikh Halim [Takieddine]; by killing you they wanted to kill the voice of righteousness, but the voice of justice is much stronger than all of them, and the sword of vengeance is stronger and longer.[47]

The opening of Joumblatt's speech took a more traditional approach, recognising the sacrifices of great men, beginning with his late father Kamal Joumblatt, to his own bodyguard Jamal Saab, who had perished in the assassination attempt that he had narrowly escaped a year earlier. At certain points, Joumblatt moved from his own victory to that of his ancestors in the eighteenth century:

> This is Beit al-Din, this is your Beit al-Din, oh Bashir Joumblatt, for the injustice of history and many generations have gone forever, and here we are now, rebellious, victorious and triumphant; hear this, you hateful monks in the crypts of Kaslik; remember that our God is the God of Righteousness and Justice, and he is the ever capable. This is your flame, oh Bani Maruf [Druze], this is the flame of light and wisdom. This is the flame of [the Prophet] Mohammad, PBUH, this is the flame of al-Miqdad and Salman, this is the flame of Emir al-Bayan [Shakib Arslan] and Adel Arslan.

By reaffirming the Arab-Muslim identity of his sect, Joumblatt located his own struggle and that of his party in a direct line with the struggle of his ancestors, which he linked to the Prophet Muhammad and his companions. By imposing this Arab persona on his people, Joumblatt was, in fact, placing the Druze in stark opposition to the supposed non-Arab Christian Maronite establishment, represented by the Order of Monks. Perhaps Joumblatt's greatest feat was to proclaim himself and the Joumblatti faction as the ultimate designator of the parameters of Druze remembrance; his military victory made certain that the Joumblatti faction was uncontested and remained at the helm of the Druze community.

Figure 8.12 Walid Joumblatt saluting his troops as he enters the parade grounds (PSP Archives).

Figure 8.13 Walid Joumblatt lighting the torch (PSP Archives).

Figure 8.14 Walid Joumblatt flanked by Raja Harb (far left), Anwar al-Fatayri and Sharif Fayyad (PSP Archives).

Despite the cessation of of the military conflict, both sides felt the need to readjust and develop their collective identity to serve their immediate as well as long-term goals. Many cultural tools, among them comic books and *zajal*, are examples illustrative of how the Druze and Maronite centres of power shaped their group's collective memory. This underscores the following: Regardless of the hegemony of these centres of power, memory requires an almost constant framing and readjustment. This process becomes more precarious when collective perceptions are part of a political or cultural project that is exclusionary by nature, or simply fails to allow any counter-narratives to exist. Moreover, many of these collective identity projects that aspire to create one meta-narrative end up not only rejecting the 'other', but also suppressing local elements within the group. The suppression of the Yazbaki and Chamouni factions exemplify such an argument. This reality had major repercussions on the political resilience and on both the Druze's and the Maronites' standing *vis-à-vis* the Lebanese political structure.

Figure 8.15 'Bashir . . . We have returned' (PSP Archives).

Notes

1. Interview with Elie Khayat, Beirut, Lebanon, 21 December 2012.
2. *Al-Masiraa'*, 25 October 1982.
3. *Al-Masiraa'*, 25 March 1984, 37.
4. Joseph Mahfouz, *Saint Charbel Makhlouf: Monk and Hermit of the Lebanese Maronite Order* (Rome: [n. p.], 1976).
5. Ibid.
6. *Al-Masiraa'*, 30 April 1984, 36.
7. *Al-Masiraa'*, 25 March 1984, 37.
8. *Al-Masiraa'*, 13 April 1984.
9. *Al-Masiraa'*, 31 October 1983.
10. Interview with George Radi, Beirut, Lebanon, 12 December 2012.
11. Interview with Elie Khayat, Beirut, Lebanon, 21 December 2012. I tried to reach out to Nasr who is currently a physician at Cleveland Clinic. Although he agreed to give me an interview, his busy schedule did not allow it in the end.
12. *Al-Masiraa'*, 31 July 1984, 34.
13. *Al-Masiraa'*, 30 April 1984, 35.
14. *Al-Masiraa'*, 4 September 1984.
15. *Al-Masiraa'*, 14 September 1984, 41.
16. Ibid.
17. Antoine and Maiva Baḫkus, *Qiṣṣat al-Mawārinī, al-ǧuz' al-auwal* (Kaslik: Holy Spirit University-USEK, 1979).
18. Naʻaman, *Al-Waṭan, al-Hurrīyah*, 245. Translation mine.
19. See page 86.
20. Baḫkus, *Qiṣṣat al-Mawārinī*, 1.
21. The book never uses the formal Arabic name for the Maronites but refers to them by the colloquial term *Mawārinī*.
22. See page 79.
23. Baḫkus, *Qiṣṣat al-Mawārinī*, 9, 11.
24. Ibid., vol. 1, 19.
25. See page 52.
26. Ibid., vol. 1, 39.
27. Ibid., 39–41.
28. Butrus Gemayel, *Zajalyat Ibn al-Qila'i* (Beirut: Dar Lahed Khater, 1982), 69.
29. Salibi, *Maronite Historians of Mediaeval Lebanon*.
30. See page 56.

31. Salibi, *Maronite Historians of Mediaeval Lebanon*, 30.
32. Ibid., 33.
33. See page 28.
34. Interview with Taleh Hamdan, 'Ayn Anoub, Mount Lebanon, 21 January 2016.
35. Taleh Hamdan, *Isu'ālu al-Tārīkh* (Beirut: Al-Dar al-Takadoumi, 1986), 6. Translation mine.
36. Interview with Taleh Hamdan, 'Ayn Anoub, Mount Lebanon, 21 January 2016.
37. *Zajal Harb al-Jabal* Recording, 1. Translation mine.
38. Ibid. Translation mine.

    اترك جبلنا المفدى وفل يا جاني
    يا شوك بري لا تجرح وردنا الجاني
    اذا كنت انت سكران عل كاسات
    ناسي دروز الجبل ع الدم سكراني
    شو فيك تعمل ب ارض المجد والثورات
    لِكانِتْ جنينة زهر للزهر حلياني

39. Ibid. Translation mine.
40. Taleh Hamdan's Poetry, *Harb al-Jabal* Recordings.
41. https://www.youtube.com/watch?v=5rS8XyPf1a8, accessed 24 October 2016.
42. *New York Times*, 9 February 1984.
43. شَعْبٍ لْعَأْقْلَك مَرْسي بْكل العركات
    لا بْتهمو نيوجرسي ولا الدبابات
    مِن ريغن لولا طْلَبتو جيش وجيشِن
    تا عين عنوب ضْرَبتو ما رِمْشِت عين
    ومش سوق الغرب نْجبتو نْجبتو الغربين
    شربنا الدم وما شربتو مي بْعَيْتات

44. *Zajal Harb al-Jabal*, vol. 1.
45. The story goes that Henri Gouraud kicked the tomb of Saladin and shouted: 'Awake, Saladin! We have returned.'
46. Bashir Joumblatt was killed in 1825.
47. Video recording of Walid Joumblatt's speech at Beit al-Din, 2 September 2016.

CONCLUSION

Post-war Lebanon: The Quest for Reconciliation

The War of the Mountain may have ended in 1984, yet the Lebanese Civil War continued for another seven years, until regional developments – primarily the Palestinian Intifada and the looming prospect of a war in the Gulf – dictated a cessation of hostilities in Lebanon. In 1989, the different Lebanese political factions involved in the conflict, represented by the surviving members of the 1972 parliament, met in the Saudi city of Taif and passed the National Reconciliation Accord, commonly referred to as the Taif Accord. This constitutional arrangement theoretically addressed some of the key grievances that originally had led to the outbreak of the civil war in 1975, primarily concerning the issue of Muslim participation in the government and legal equality with their fellow Christians. The Taif Accord succeeded in 'silencing the guns' and bringing peace to almost all parts of Lebanon, except for the south which remained under Israeli occupation until May 2001. In line with this post-war arrangement, parliament passed an amnesty law for crimes perpetrated prior to 28 March 1991, after which various militias (including the PSP and the LF) were decommissioned and most of their members integrated into the Lebanese armed forces. This law was intended to pave the way for an open national dialogue, which would allow the warring factions to air out their grievances. However, instead of opting to establish a truth and reconciliation commission similar to the South African model, the Lebanese political establishment ignored the old rivalries that existed between the warring parties, along with the memories of what had occurred during the civil war. This course of political action deprived both victims and perpetrators of the 'right to memory, which would create spaces for the nation to confront its memories of a horrific past, and in so doing provide the potential for dialogue to occur'.[1] This deliberate avoidance of addressing the thorny issue of the civil war was due to a number of factors, some of them local in nature, others purely external.

One of the most important and contributing factors was the Syrian military presence in Lebanon, legitimised by the provisions of the Taif Accord, which gave Syria a mandate over Lebanese political affairs. In 1976, under the rule of Hafez al-Assad, Syria had decided to intervene in the Lebanese Civil War. Initially, Syria entered the war on the side of the Maronites, before switching over to the Druze side. Naturally, the Syrians did not want among the Lebanese a public debate that would ultimately implicate Syria. To achieve this, the Syrian regime collaborated with their Lebanese allies in order to ensure that Syria remained outside the realm of criticism and instead be depicted as an element of stability. Consequently, there surfaced a rhetoric promoting the idea that the Lebanese Civil War had been a 'war of others' who had used Lebanon as the venue. As a result, the Syrian-Lebanese ruling establishment spun a master narrative blaming the civil war on Israel, the Palestinian armed presence and the sectarian political system that had been installed by the French mandate. In a recent study, Sune Haugbolle has concluded that this 'war of others rhetoric dominates public culture throughout the post-war period as an attempt to externalise collective guilt, and as a means to break with the past and pave the way for a new political culture'.[2]

However, this externalisation of guilt did not pave the way for a new Lebanese governance structure; instead, it resurrected the 1943 system with one major change. The Maronites who had held the ultimate power in pre-war Lebanon were relegated to sharing power with the Muslims. Perhaps the only challenge to this perpetual political amnesia materialised from within Lebanon's civil society, mostly from Leftists. Subsequently, several NGOs launched 'never-again' campaigns to force the government to jump-start a public debate on the civil war. These NGOs also tried to lobby the Lebanese parliament to erect a civil war memorial. This memorial would transcend its physical significance, because it could be used as a tool to deconstruct the different collective memories of the war and to compose a unifying national narrative. The late Samir Kassir, a historian and columnist, encouraged the writing of the history of the civil war; according to him, this process was extremely important because remembrance can serve as tool for creating a collective identity, which the Lebanese currently lacked.[3] He also viewed as counter-productive and extremely dangerous the undeclared policy of amnesia that successive Lebanese governments had adopted following the end of the war. To address these issues, Kassir and a group of civil society activists established an NGO with the name 'Memory for the Future'. Although the Syrians were still in control in Lebanon, this NGO was able to organise its first conference in March 2001.[4] These efforts, however, never received the much-needed popular support due to several factors. To begin with, these annual activities, usually organised on 13 April, remained an elitist exercise, as the masses never participated. Second, the ruling establishment, with its different religious sects, did not allow the NGOs access to their communities to address their collective memory, so as not to weaken their grip over their constituency.

While the Taif Accord introduced a number of structural amendments to the 1943 National Pact, one of its more practical provisions was to deal with the 847,000 persons displaced by the war that had erupted in 1975.[5] Among these displaced were the 240,000 Christians of Mount Lebanon, who had been driven out by the Druze in 1984. To respond to this challenge, the Taif Accord included the following article:

> The problem of the Lebanese evacuees shall be solved fundamentally, and the right of every Lebanese evicted since 1975 to return to the place from which he was evicted shall be established. Legislation to guarantee this right and to ensure the means of reconstruction shall be issued.[6]

Consequently, in 1993 the Lebanese parliament passed Law 193, establishing a Ministry for the Displaced (MoD) tasked with 'funding the housing and the return of the displaced to all the regions across Lebanon and improving their social and economic conditions by rebuilding or renovating homes or paying money to ensure the fulfillment of this return'.[7] In an ironic twist of fate, the first minister appointed to carry out this objective was no other than Walid Joumblatt, the warlord largely responsible for displacing the Christians of the Shuf and Aley districts. With the help of some of the individuals who had formerly made up the cadres of his militia, Joumblatt launched a series of meetings to pave the way for the Christians' return to their villages. Among those tasked to lead this reconciliatory mission was the newly appointed Director-General of the MoD, Hisham Nasreddine, who repeatedly met with the same people he had confronted in 1983, but this time in order to discuss the steps needed to resolve the many obstacles hindering the return of the displaced. These facilitators' main challenge rested in their ability to reconcile the Druze and Maronite inhabitants of the villages and towns that had witnessed some of the worst atrocities. According to the tribal traditions of Mount Lebanon, spilled blood could be addressed in three ways: killing the perpetrator or another member of their immediate family, permanent exile of the killer's family from the village, or the more practical option of paying the victim's next-of-kin a hefty sum of money, called *diyya* ('blood money'). Following lengthy negotiations with the different Christian and Druze village committees, the MoD was able to accomplish a number of reconciliation pacts, slowly promoting the return of several Christians to their villages. This return, however, was made possible only after the Lebanese state, via the MoD, paid both sides enormous sums of money to compensate for the loss of lives and to help with the reconstruction of the villages, some of which had been razed to the ground.

Shortly after the end of hostilities in 1984, Joumblatt and the Druze were left struggling with an enormous dilemma: What to do with the many vacant houses that the Christians had left behind? While some were confiscated by the Druze that had also been displaced by the fighting, this was not enough to populate these Christian ghost towns. The PSP devised a practical plan, systematically demolishing many of the vacant villages and towns. While this might appear as just another sinister and vengeful scheme on the part of the Druze, this act, in reality, revealed the Druze's anxiety and the future implications of the Christian flight from Mount Lebanon. According to one of the senior PSP commanders who supervised and personally carried out part of these demolitions, the Druze had in fact dynamited these towns to prevent non-local elements, particularly the Shiʻites displaced from southern Lebanon, from moving in and occupying these vacant houses.[8] Despite the cruelty of this act, it showed that the Druze did not fully dismiss the eventual return of their primordial enemy to their homes. In fact, even before the end of the civil war and the adoption of the Taif Accord, Joumblatt had attempted to start his own reconciliation process, which at that time had been unsanctioned by his Syrian allies and thus ultimately doomed to failure.

On 8 February 1989, upon the instructions of Joumblatt, Anwar al-Fatayri and Toufic Barkat, and with the help of the Mayor of Deir al-Qamar, George Dib Nehmé and Fouad al-Saad organised a meeting in Deir al-Qamar, bringing together the Druze and the Maronites with the intended aim of discussing ways to jump-start the return of the displaced to Mount Lebanon. Soon after the end of this meeting, Fatayri proceeded to the adjacent villages of Jahliye and Serjbal, where he was scheduled to meet with the Druze residents. However, Fatayri failed to make it to his appointment, as he and his bodyguard were gunned down by a native of Jahliye who had lost one of his family members during the War of the Mountain.[9] While this killing was cast as having been perpetrated by a mad Druze keen on revenge, many signs at the time indicated that this was an implicit warning to Joumblatt from the Syrians' side and that Syrian consent was required for any settlement, especially one that involved empowering the Christians. Nevertheless, both examples hint that, despite the Druze's' utter contempt for their Christian enemies, they still wanted them to return to Mount Lebanon, for without the latter the entire region under Druze control amounted to nothing more than a ghetto. This divide was neither reflective of the diversity of Mount Lebanon with its variegated sectarian and political composition, nor economically sustainable in the long run, because the Druze alone were demographically and financially incapable of sustaining a healthy local economy.

From 1993 onwards, many of the displaced across Lebanon started to return to their homes and villages. In the case of Mount Lebanon, the Christian response was shy, as many of the displaced had begun new lives elsewhere and thus found it impractical to relocate. Moreover, many regions across Mount Lebanon had fallen behind in terms of infrastructure and social services, as its primitive schools, hospitals and other essential services could not cater to the potential returnees. Despite the many reconciliation efforts carried out by the MoD and Joumblatt, neither side discussed the events that had taken place during the fighting. More importantly, no one asked: 'Why did these neighbours engage in a mindless bloodbath that left both the Maronites and the Druze orphaned and weaker than they used to be?' This obvious disregard of the importance of public remembrance continued with the Maronite patriarch's famous visit to the mountain in 2001 in order to reconcile with the Druze, which was insufficient to initiate the process at the grassroots level. This visit in the summer of 2001 saw the Maronite Patriarch Nasrallah Butrus Sfeir exercising his political capacity by visiting the Shuf and Aley regions, where Walid Joumblatt received him. The political rhetoric that surfaced as a consequence of this 'historic visit' remained limited to the political actors who agreed on facing the challenges ahead, without discussing the real reasons and the violence that had occurred between them.

Even though he is fully convinced of the need to retain and foster these positive elements between the Druze and the Maronites, Ghanem Tarabay has maintained that a major step is still necessary. Ghanem spent his adult life fighting for and defending his community, but has never been given the chance to sit down and discuss and exchange stories with the Christians whom he fought and to air out the grievances that originally prompted him to take up arms in 1975.[10] This is also true of many Maronite combatants I interviewed as part of my research, as only those who remained politically active within the senior echelons of the PSP or the LF engaged in any serious dialogue. Hence, this exercise was limited to the senior figures within the PSP and LF and, important as it is, has never trickled down to the lower party ranks, nor touched the many non-partisans who experienced the war as both combatants and victims. The importance of public testimony *vis-à-vis* violence and civil conflict resides not in merely remembering the past, but in serving as as a tool for 'remembering for the future'.[11] By admitting and implicitly condemning the atrocities of the past, the agent of remembering is in fact expressing to their listeners their intention to share not only their past, but also their future. More importantly, if performed correctly, this testimony has the potential to render previously weaponised frames of collective memory harmless, as it will prevent various factions from mobilising their community by using the methods highlighted throughout this study.

On the three main occasions during which the Druze and the Maronites clashed, the outcome was downright devastating, resulting in the death and displacement of thousands of people on both sides. Yet, as this book has demonstrated, the most damaging effect is the persistence of bitterness between the two sides, something made possible by the ruling elite's refusal to allow relevant collective memories to be exposed as part of the post-conflict settlement. On both sides, the centres of power have been content with the political settlement and preferred not to air out any differences that might expose responsibility, but more importantly render the weapons of collective memory useless.

In 1860, the Druze dealt their Maronites foes a humiliating military defeat. Soon, however, the Druze saw themselves subject to an international punitive campaign led by France, which resulted in the arrest, summary trial, imprisonment, fining, exiling and even execution of the Druze traditional leadership. With the help of the French expeditionary force that had landed on the Lebanese coast, this arrangement helped the Maronites regain face and slowly return to their destroyed villages and towns, to rebuild them with financial assistance from the international community, primarily France. The 1860 war ended with the introduction of the *Mutasarrifiya* system, which gave the Maronites a clear disadvantage over the demographically weaker Druze, an arrangement that seemed to satisfy the two warring sides at least for the time being.

In 1958, the showdown between the Druze and the Maronites was surely less bloody and violent; yet, it drove both sides to even further distrust the National Pact which they had already aimed to abolish. Fully aware of the limitations of the system and the realities of the Cold War, Kamal Joumblatt and Camille Chamoun both accepted whatever gains they could achieve and decided to wait for another occasion to engage in conflict, ultimately resulting in the 1975 civil war and the War of the Mountain.

The Taif Accords in 1989 and the ensuing period permitted the different warring factions, exhausted by fifteen years of conflict, to divide the resources of the Lebanese state and shed their warlord attire, swapping it for a seat in parliament. Naturally, this post-war regional settlement brokered by the international community came at a heavy price, as the Lebanese were now answerable not to their state, but to Hafez al-Assad who retained a political mandate over Lebanon. This political reality would persist for the next fifteen years, until the Syrians were forced to evacuate their troops from Lebanon following the assassination of former Prime Minister Rafik Hariri, the primary architect of the Taif Accords.

The eighteen different sects that constitute Lebanon perceive their communal memories as part of a self-defence mechanism and, hence, a prerequisite for their survival. This study has restricted itself to exploring the collective memory of the Druze and the Maronites; however, the other Lebanese sects are no different, as each of them holds collective perceptions that are as dangerous as those discussed above. The examples of projects promoting collective identity, as discussed in the preceding pages, are extremely valuable because they allow for a better understanding of the real essence of the conflict and how the respective centres of power form and utilise collective memory.

A proper and complete reconciliation in Lebanon still awaits certain prerequisites, among them chiefly the unpacking and public discussion of the different communities' collective memories. This unpacking process can prevent sectarian power centres from using the violent past(s) as active agent to mould their group's collective memory. The failure of the Druze and the Maronites to discuss their problems in public in 1860 and 1958, respectively, permitted them to form a certain collective remembrance that proved to be a recipe for disaster, especially when threatened by internal or external challenges.

In May 2008, a series of local and regional events pitted the pro-government Druze against the anti-government Hezbollah militia. The Druze under the leadership of the now veteran Walid Joumblatt used the very same process as the one detailed here to mobilise their ranks to confronted and defeat the invading Shi'ite Hezbollah fighters. In 1982, the Druze demonised their Maronite opponents in order to unify their ranks in support of Joumblatt and the PSP. In 2008, the Druze merely substituted the words 'Maronite' and 'Lebanese Forces' with 'Shi'ite' and 'Hezbollah', respectively, and once again were able to achieve the desired effect of total mobilisation. I believe that the above-described process of collective memory formation, with some variation, also exists in other communities in Lebanon, and perhaps beyond. The conflict in the city of Tripoli between the Sunni inhabitants of Bab al-Tabani and the Alawites of Jabal Mohsen is one such example. These two communities, which clashed in 1985 and on multiple occasions after 2008, have exhibited symptoms and tendencies similar to those of the Druze and the Maronites over the years of conflict.

Much of the rhetoric and the manner in which these groups exchanged words and blows were reminiscent of the way in which the Druze and the Maronites fought. At the macro level, the process of collective memory formation can also be applied to the ongoing apocalyptic Sunni–Shi'ite conflict in the region. This allegedly primordial hatred that these two Muslim sects currently harbour towards each other employs an elaborate and intricate doctrinal and religious discourse which, in fact, is an invention constructed in later centuries. In reality, the history of most Lebanese groups is one of extended periods of cooperation and amity, rather than of conflict and animosity.

The enduring legacy of this state-sponsored amnesia pertaining to Lebanon's violent past, whether concerning the Druze–Maronite conflict or any other community, can only set the stage for further conflicts in the future. As long as the Lebanese state and the oligarchs who run it continue to adopt this reluctant attitude towards remembering the civil war, the specter of memory will always haunt the common people. Such an attitude also presents extreme danger, should a new wave of violence be unleashed, for it will find a ready-made platform upon which it can build. Many have worked towards creating a common history text book for Lebanon, one that various schools across the country can use, to bring together the sons and daughters of the 1958 Generation and to make them feel part of one nation that shares a common path. Yet, even this somewhat primitive approach to nation-building has not garnered the necessary consensus of the various sects who continue to carry out their own uninterrupted collective memory projects. A real breakthrough may not lie in creating one super-narrative, but in allowing these differing narratives to grow side by side and identifying the very elements that may potentially weaponise these collective perceptions by transforming them into a foundation for future conflicts instead of diversity and pluralism.

Kamal Salibi has adapted the title of his ground-breaking work on Lebanese history, *A House of Many Mansions*,[12] as a descriptive term signifying not only the diversity of Lebanese society, but also the basis on which historians could or should write the history of Lebanon. In this house of many chambers, each group can occupy its own room or even multiple rooms where they maintain their collective identity and historical narratives. Yet, the common space in this mansion will preserve a common history or histories that incorporate these conflicting collective perceptions and historical banners, while seeking to deconstruct them in a manner that creates a common vision of Lebanon's future, if not necessarily its past.

Notes

1. Paul Haupt, 'Between Memory and Hope: The Role of Memory in the South African Truth and Reconciliation Commission', in *Memory for the Future*, ed. Amal Makarem (Beirut: Dar An-Nahar, 2002), 135–6.
2. Haugbolle, 'The Politics of Remembering in Post-War Lebanon', 303.
3. Samir Kassir, *La Guerre du Liban: De la dissension nationale au conflit régional, 1975–1982* (Paris; Beyrouth: Karthala; CERMOC, 1994).
4. The proceedings of this conference were published in Amal Makarem, ed., *Memory for the Future* (Beirut: Dar An-Nahar, 2002).
5. Carole Dagher, *Bring Down the Walls: Lebanon's Post-War Challenge* (Basingstoke: Palgrave, 2000, 84.
6. https://www.un.int/lebanon/sites/www.un int/files/Lebanon/the_talf_agreement_english_version_.pdf, accessed 13 October 2016.
7. http://www.ministryofdisplaced.gov.lb/Cultures/ar-LB/Programs/cfd/Pages/Law193.aspx, accessed 13 October 2016.
8. Interview with PSP senior commander, name withheld.
9. Dagher, *Bring Down the Walls*, 88.
10. Interview with Ghanem Tarabay, Qoubbei', Lebanon, 23 June 2013.
11. Sue Campbell, Christine M. Koggel and Rockney Jacobsen, *Our Faithfulness to the Past: The Ethics and Politics of Memory* (Oxford: Oxford University Press, 2014), 172.
12. John 14:2 of the King James Version (KJV) of the Bible: 'In my Father's house are many mansions: if it were not so, I would have told you. I go to prepare a place for you'.

APPENDIX
TABLE OF INTERVIEWS

Interviewee	Affiliation	Place	Date
Abbas Khalaf	Vice President of the PSP (1977)	Beirut, Lebanon	12 December 2013
Akram Saab	Board Member of PBDF	Beirut, Lebanon	14 June 2016
Alain Ménargues	Radio France Internationale	Kaslik, Lebanon	30 December 2015
Amal As'ad	(Retired) General of the IDF	Proxy	7 June 2016
Antoine Najm	LF	Beirut, Lebanon	10 February 2016
Atef Salloum	Member of the Follow-Up Commission	al-Abadiya, Mount Lebanon	15 June 2019
Augustine Tegho	(Retired) General of the LAF	Beirut, Lebanon	10 August 2016
Bulus Na'aman	Head of the Maronite Order of Monks	Kaslik, Lebanon	July 2011
Elie Khayat	LF, Founder of the magazine *Al-Masiraa'*	Beirut, Lebanon	21 December 2012
Fouad Abu-Nadir	LF Commander (1984–5)	Beirut, Lebanon	23 February 2016
George Freiha	Chief-of-Staff to Bashir Gemayel	Beirut, Lebanon	11 January 2010
George Radi	LF Fighter	Beirut, Lebanon	12 December 2012
George Rouhana	LF Fighter	Beirut, Lebanon	12 August 2016

Interviewee	Affiliation	Place	Date
Ghanem Tarabay	Field Commander of the PSP in Maten	Qoubbeiʻ, Lebanon	23 June 2013
Ghazi al-Aridi	PSP	Beirut, Lebanon	8 July 2016
Halim Bou Fakhraddine	Physician and PSP-USSR Liaison	Beirut, Lebanon	21 January 2016
Hassan al-Beaini	(Retired) General of the LAF	Virginia, USA	11 February 2010
Hisham Nasreddine	PSP Politburo	Deir Koubal, Mount Lebanon	4 September 2016
Imad al-Awar	PSP Combatant	Beirut, Lebanon	6 May 2016
Issam Aintrazi (Abu Said)	Field Commander of the PSP in Beirut	North Carolina, USA	21 December 2013
Joseph Abu Khalil	Editor-in-Chief of Kataeb Newspaper	Beirut, Lebanon	30 December 2015
Massoud Achkar	Field Commander of the LF in Beirut	Beirut, Lebanon	7 June 2016
Naji Butrus	Field Commander of the LF in ʻAyn al-Remmaneh	Makleis, Lebanon	22 June 2016
Paul Andary	LF Deputy Field Commander of the Mountain District	Adma, Lebanon	28 January 2010
Raja Harb	(Retired) General of the LAF	Beirut, Lebanon	30 December 2016
Rajeh Naim	Editor of the PBDA Newsletter	Beirut, Lebanon	24 May 2016
Samir Frangieh	Lebanese National Movement	Beirut, Lebanon	12 August 2016
Taleh Hamdan	Druze poet of *zajal*	ʻAyn Anoub, Mount Lebanon	21 January 2016
Zeidan Atashi	Druze Member of the Israeli Knesset	Proxy	2 August 2016

BIBLIOGRAPHY

Archives

American University of Beirut, Lebanon (AUB)
National Archives and Records Administration, College Park, Maryland (NARA)

Newspapers & Periodicals

Al-'Amal, Al-Kataeb's Newspaper
Al-Anbaa', Progressive Socialist Party's Publication
Al-Masiraa', Lebanese Forces' Magazine, 1982–4
Al-Nahar, 1982–4
Al-Safir, Daily Newspaper, 1982–4
Al-Sha'ib, Newspaper.
Permanent Bureau of Druze Associations (PBDA) Newsletter

Primary Sources

Bashir: The Series. Mercury Media Production. Beirut, 2016. Full, unedited transcripts.
Oral History Interviews with combatants, politicians, and journalists.
Progressive Socialist Party Oral History Project.
Radio Free Lebanon Archive – Lebanese Phalangist Party.
Voice of the Mountains Archive – Progressive Socialist Party.

Secondary Sources

Arabic

Abou Khalil, Joseph. *Qiṣṣat al-Mawārinah fī al-Ḥarb: Sīrah Dhātīyah.* Beirut: Sharikat al-Maṭbūʿāt lil-Tawzīʿ wa-al-Nashr, 1990.

Abu Shaqra, Arif. *Al-Harakāt fī Lubnān ila 'Ahd al-Mutasarrifiya.* Beirut: Dar al-Farabi, 1982.

Abu Salah, Abbas and Sami Makarem. *Tārīkh al-Muwaḥḥidīn al-Durūz al-Siyāsī fī al-Mashriq al-ᶜArabī.* Beirut: Manshūrāt al-Majlis al-Durzī lil-Buḥūth wa-al-Inmā', 1980.

Al-Jabal: Difaʿān 'an al-Wujud wal Karamah. Published by the Civil Administration in the Shuf, 1984.

Al-Shidyaq, Tannous. *Kitāb Akhbār al-Aʾyān fī Jabal Lubnān.* Beirut: Lebanese University Publications, 1970.

——. *Akhbār al-Aʾyan fī Jabal Lubnān.* Beirut: Lebanese University Publications, 1970.

Achkouti, Raji. *Ḥiṣār Dayr al-Qamar.* [n. p.]: 1984.

Andary, Paul. *Al-Jabal: Haqīqah lā Tarḥam.* [n. p.]: 1983.

Baḥkus, Antoine and Maiva. *Qiṣṣat al-Mawārinī, al-ǧuz' al-auwal.* Kaslik: Holy Spirit University-USEK, 1979.

Būl, Sālim, Anṭwān Masarrah, Khālid Qabbānī, and Saʿb F. Abū. *Al-lā-Markazīyah al-Idārīyah fī Lubnān: Al-Ishkālīyah wa al Taṭbīq.* Beirut: al-Markaz al-Lubnanī lil-Dirāsāt, 1996.

Charbal, Ghassān. *Ayna Kunta fī al-Ḥarb.* Beirut: Riyāḍ al-Rayyis lil-Kutub wa-al-Nashr, 2011.

Daw, Butrus. *Tarīkh al-Mawārinah al-Dīnī wa-al-Sīyāsī wa-al-Haḍārī.* Beirut: Dār al-Nahār, 1977.

Erlich, Reuven. *Al-Matāhah al-Lubnāniyah: Siyāsat al-Ḥarakah al-Ṣuhyūnīyah Tijāha Lubnan (1918–1958),* trans. by Mohammad Bader. [n. p.], 2017.

Ibn Yaḥyá, Ṣāliḥ, Kamal S. Salibi, and Francis Hours. *Tārīkh Bayrūt, wa-Huwa Akhbār al-Salaf min Dhurriyat Buḥtur ibn ᶜAlī Amīr al-Gharb bi-Bayrūt.* Beirut: Dār al-Mashraf, 1969.

Gemayel, Butrus. *Zajalyāt Ibn al-Qilāʾī.* Beirut: Dar Lahed Khater, 1982.

Hamdan, Taleh. *Isuʾālu al-Tārīkh.* Beirut: Al-Dar al-Takadoumi, 1986.

Khalīl, Khalīl Aḥmad. *Kamāl Junblāṭ: Thawrat al-Amīr al-Hadīth.* Beirut: Dār al-Maṭbūʿāt al-Sharqīyah, 1984.

Khūrī Ḥarb, Anṭwān. *Al-Mawārinah: Tārīkh wa-Thawābit.* [Beirut]: al-Rābiṭah al-Mārūnīyah, 1998.

Mahfouz, Youssef. *Mukhtaṣar Tārīkh al-Rahbanah al-Mārūnīyah.* Kaslik: Kaslik University Press, 1969.

Ménargues, Alan. *Asrār Ḥarb Lubnān: Min Inqlāb Bashīr al-Jumayyil ilá Majāzir al-Mukhayyamāt al-Filasṭīniyah.* [n. p.], 2006.

———. *Asrār Ḥarb Lubnān: Min Madhābiḥ Ṣabrā wa-Shatīlā ḥattá Riḥlat Amīn al-Jumayyil ilá Dimashq.* [n. p.], 2012.

Naʿaman, Bulus. *Al-Waṭan, al-Hurrīyah: Mudhakkirāt al-Abātī Būlus Nuʿmān.* Beirut: Sāʾair al-Mashriq, 2009.

Najm, Antoine. *Dawlat Loubnan al-Ithadiya: Dawlat al-Tanmiyah wa al-Musâwât wa al-ʿAdâlah wa al-ʿAych al-Muchtarak.* Beirut: Afāq Machriqiyyah, 1992.

Naji, Amin (Antoine Najm). *Lan Naʾīsha Dhimmiyyīn.* Beirut: al-Maṭbaʾah al-Ḥadīthah, 1979.

Prince, Moussa. *Hiwar, Hulum, Hal.* Beirut: Joseph Raidy Press, 1980.

Ruhbānīyah al-Lubnānīyah al-Mārūnīyah and Université Saint-Spirite. *Al-Yūbīl al-Miʾawī al-Thālith lil-Ruhbānīyah al-Lubnānīyah al-Mārūnīyah: Turāth wa-Ruʾá Mustaqbalīyah = Le tricentenaire de l'Ordre libanais maronite: Histoire et perspectives d'avenir, 1695–1995.* al-Kaslīk: Maʿhad al-Tārīkh, Jāmiʿat al-Rūḥ al-Qudus, 1996.

Ṣafi, Izzat. *Ṭarīq al-Mukhtārah Zaman Kamāl Junblāṭ.* Beirut: Dar Nahar, 2007.

Salibi, Kamal. *Ṭāir ʿalá Sindiyānah: Mudhakkirāt.* ʿAmmān: Dār al-Shurūq, 2002.

Shuwayfāti, Clovis. *Ḥarb al-Durūz wa-al-Mawārinah fī al-Jabal.* [n. p.], 2014.

Taqi al-Din, Riyaḍ. *Al-Tajribah al-ʿAskarīyah al-Durzīyah wa-Masāruḥā al-Taqaddumī.* Beirut: [n. p.], 1987.

French

Sélim Abou, *Béchir Gemayel, ou l'esprit d'un peuple* (Paris: Éditions Anthropos, 1984)

Azzam, Roger. *Liban, l'instruction d'un Crime: 30 ans de guerre.* Coudray-Macouard: Cheminements, 2005.

Boustani, Fouad Ephrem. *Le Problème du Liban: Note succinte, objective, sincère et franche pour servir à comprendre la question Libanaise.* 2nd ed. Kaslik: C. R, 1978.

Chaftari, Assad. *La vérité même si ma voix tremble.* Beyrouth: Dergham, 2015.

Kassir, Samir. *La Guerre du Liban: De la dissension nationale au conflit régional, 1975–1982.* Paris; Beyrouth: Karthala; CERMOC, 1994.

Najm, Bulus. *La Question du Liban: Étude d'histoire diplomatique et de droit international.* Paris: A. Rousseau, 1908.

Sleiman, André. *Vivre ensemble mais séparés? L'émergence et l'évolution des projets de fédération au Liban de 1975 à nos jours.* Lille: Atelier national de reproduction des thèses, 2014.

Tuwayni, Ghassan. *Une guerre pour les autres.* Paris: J. C. Lattes, 1985.

English

Abi-Chahine, Bassel. 'The People's Liberation Army: Through the Eyes of a Lens'. Unpublished manuscript.

Abu-Husayn, Abdul Rahim. 'The "Lebanon Schools" (1853–1873): A Local Venture in Rural Education'. In *The Syrian Land: Processes of Integration and Fragmentation: Bilād Al-Shām from the 18th to the 20th Century*, ed. Thomas Philipp and Birgit Schaebler, 205–20. Stuttgart: F. Steiner, 1998.

———. *The View from Istanbul: Lebanon and the Druze Emirate in the Ottoman Chancery Documents, 1546–1711.* London: I. B. Tauris; Oxford: Centre for Lebanese Studies, 2004.

———. 'The Shihab Succession (1697): A Reconsideration'. *Archive Oreintalni, Supplementa* VIII, 1998.

———. 'The Junblats and the Janbulads: A Case of Mistaken identity'. In *Acta Viennensia Ottamanica*, ed. Markus Köhbach et al., 1–6. (Vienna: Selbstverlag des Instituts für Orientalistik, 1999).

———. 'The Ottoman Invasion of the Shuf in 1585: A Reconsideration', *Al-Abhath* 33 (1985): 13–21.

———. 'Rebellion, Myth-Making and Nation-Building: Lebanon from an Ottoman Mountain Iltizam to a Nation State'. In *Studia Culturae Islamica* 97. Tokyo: ILCAA, Tokyo University of Foreign Studies, 2009.

Abu Izzeddin, Nejla. *The Druzes: A New Study of Their History, Faith, and Society.* Leiden: Brill, 1993.

Akarli, Engin. *The Long Peace: Ottoman Lebanon, 1861–1920.* Berkeley: University of California Press, 1993.

Allen, Barbara, and William Lynwood Montell. *From Memory to History: Using Oral Sources in Local Historical Research.* Nashville: American Association for State and Local History, 1981.

Allouche, Adel. *The Origins and Development of the Ottoman-Safavid Conflict, 906–962/1500–1555.* Berlin: Klaus Schwarz, 1983.

Andary, Paul and Rani Geha. *War of the Mountain: Israelis, Christians and Druze in the 1983 Mount Lebanon Conflict Through the Eyes of a Lebanese Forces Fighter.* Lexington: CreateSpace Independent Publishing Platform, 2012

Andrew, Christopher M. and A. S. Kanya-Forstner. *The Climax of French Imperial Expansion, 1914–1924*. Stanford: Stanford University Press, 1981.

Atashi, Zeidan. *Druze & Jews in Israel: A Shared Destiny?* Brighton: Sussex Academic, 1997.

Attié, Caroline. *Struggle in the Levant: Lebanon in the 1950s*. London: I. B. Tauris, in association with the Centre for Lebanese Studies, 2004.

Barr, James. *A Line in the Sand: Britain, France and the Struggle for the Mastery of the Middle East*. London: Simon & Schuster, 2011.

Beiser, Frederick. *The German Historicist Tradition*. Oxford: Oxford University Press, 2011.

Bennett, Anne. 'Reincarnation, Sect Unity, and Identity among the Druze'. *Ethnology* 45 (2006): 87–104.

Binder, Leonard. *Politics in Lebanon*. New York: John Wiley & Sons, Inc., 1966.

Blatz, Graig and Michael Ross. 'Historical Memories'. In *Memory in Mind and Culture*, ed. Pascal Boyer and James Wertsch, 223–37. Cambridge: Cambridge University Press, 2009.

Boykin, John. Cursed Is the Peacemaker: the American Diplomat Versus the Israeli General, Beirut 1982 Belmont, CA: Applegate Press, 2002.

Campbell, Sue, Christine M. Koggel and Rockney Jacobsen. *Our Faithfulness to the Past: The Ethics and Politics of Memory*. Oxford: Oxford University Press, 2014.

Choueiri, Youssef. *Breaking the Cycle: Civil Wars in Lebanon*. London: Stacey International, 2007.

Dagher, Carole. *Bring Down the Walls: Lebanon's Post-War Challenge*. Basingstoke: Palgrave, 2000.

Dougherty, Kevin. *The United States Military in Limited War: Case Studies in Success and Failure, 1945–1999*. Jefferson: McFarland & Company, 2012.

Eisenberg, Laura Zittrain. *Lebanon in the Early Zionist Imagination, 1900–1948*. Detroit: Wayne State University Press, 1994.

Evron, Yair. *War and Intervention in Lebanon: The Israeli-Syrian Deterrence Dialogue*. Baltimore: Johns Hopkins University Press, 1987.

Farah, Caesar. *The Politics of Interventionism in Ottoman Lebanon, 1830–1861*. Oxford: Centre for Lebanese Studies, 2000.

Firro, Kais. *The Druzes in the Jewish State: A Brief History*. Leiden: Brill, 1999.

——. 'Reshaping Druze Particularism in Israel'. *Journal of Palestine Studies* 30 (2001): 40–53.

——. *Inventing Lebanon: Nationalism and the State Under the Mandate*. London: I. B. Tauris, 2003.

Fawaz, Leila. *An Occasion for War: Civil Conflict in Lebanon and Damascus in 1860*. London: I. B Tauris, 1994.

———. *A Land of Aching Hearts: The Middle East in the Great War*. Cambridge, MA: Harvard University Press, 2014.

Fentress, James and Chris Wickham. *Social Memory*. Oxford: Blackwell, 1992.

Frazee, Charles. *Catholics and Sultans: The Church and the Ottoman Empire, 1453–1923*. London: Cambridge University Press, 1983.

Freedman, Robert. *Moscow and the Middle East: Soviet Policy since the Invasion of Afghanistan*. Cambridge: Cambridge University Press, 1991.

Friedman, Thomas. *From Beirut to Jerusalem: Updated with a New Chapter*. New York: Picador, 2012.

Funkenstein, Amos. 'Collective Memory and Historical Consciousness'. *History & Memory* 1 (1989): 5–26.

Geha, Rani. *Words from Bashir: Understanding the Mind of Lebanese Forces Founder Bashir Gemayel from His Speeches*. Lexington: CreateSpace Independent Publishing Platform, 2009.

Hakim, Carol. *The Origins of the Lebanese National Idea, 1840–1920*. Berkeley: University of California Press, 2013.

Hanf, Theodor. *Coexistence in Wartime Lebanon: Decline of a State and Rise of a Nation*. London: Centre for Lebanese Studies, in association with I. B. Tauris, 1993.

Harik, Judith. 'Shaykh al-'Aql and the Druze of Mount Lebanon: Conflict and Accommodation'. *Middle Eastern Studies* 30 (1994): 461–85.

Harris, William. *Lebanon: A History, 600–2011*. New York: Oxford University Press, 2012.

Mishaqah, Mikhail. *Murder, Mayhem, Pillage and Plunder: The History of Lebanon in the 18th and 19th Centuries*. Translated from the Arabic by W. M. Thackston, Jr. Albany: State University of New York Press, 1988.

Hathaway, Jane. *A Tale of Two Factions: Myth, Memory, and Identity in Ottoman Egypt and Yemen*. Albany: State University of New York, 2003.

Haugbolle, Sune. 'The Politics of Remembering in Post-War Lebanon: Civil War, Memory and Public Culture'. Ph.D. diss., Oxford University, 2006.

———. *War and Memory in Lebanon*. New York: Cambridge University Press, 2010.

Haupt, Paul. 'Between Memory and Hope: The Role of Memory in the South African Truth and Reconciliation Commission'. In *Memory for the Future*, ed. Amal Makarem, 133–48. Beirut: Dar An-Nahar, 2002.

Hazran, Yusri. *The Druze Community and the Lebanese State: Between Confrontation and Reconciliation*. London: Routledge, 2014.

Henley, Alexander. 'Politics of a Church at War: Maronite Catholicism in the Lebanese Civil War'. *Mediterranean Politics* 13 (2008): 353–69.

Hodgson, Marshall G. S. 'Al-Darazî and Ḥamza in the Origin of the Druze Religion'. *Journal of the American Oriental Society* 82 (1962): 6–20.

——. *The Venture of Islam: Conscience and History in a World Civilization*. Vol 2. Chicago: University of Chicago Press, 1974.

Hoffman, Alice, and Howard S. Hoffman. *Archives of Memory: A Soldier Recalls World War II*. Lexington: University Press of Kentucky, 1990.

——. 'Memory Theory: Personal and Social', in *Thinking About Oral History: Theories and Applications*, ed. Thomas L. Charlton, Lois E. Myers and Rebecca Sharpless, 33–54. Lanham: Altamira Press, 2008.

Iggers, Georg. 'The Role of Professional Historical Scholarship in the Creation and Distortion of Memory'. In *Historical Perspectives on Memory*, ed. Anne Ollila, 49–67. Helsinki: Hakapaino Oy, 1999.

International Encyclopedia of the Social & Behavioural Sciences. Oxford: Pergamon, 2001.

Johnson, Michael. *All Honourable Men: The Social Origins of War in Lebanon*. Oxford: Centre for Lebanese Studies, 2001.

Joseph, John. *Muslim-Christian Relations and Inter-Christian Rivalries in the Middle East: The Case of the Jacobites in an Age of Transition*. Albany: State University of New York Press, 1984.

Joumblatt, Kamal and Philippe Lapousterle. *I Speak for Lebanon*. London: Zed Press, 1982.

Kalawoun, Nasser. *The Struggle for Lebanon: A Modern History of Lebanese-Egyptian Relations*. London: I. B. Tauris, 2000.

Karpat, Kemal H. *Ottoman Population 1830–1914*. Madison: University of Wisconsin Press, 1985.

Kayalı, Hasan. *Arabs and Young Turks: Ottomanism, Arabism and Islamism in the Ottoman Empire, 1908–1918*. Berkeley: University of California Press, 1997.

Kaufman, Asher. '"Tell Us Our History": Charles Corm, Mount Lebanon and Lebanese Nationalism'. *Middle Eastern Studies* 40 (2004): 1–29.

——. *Reviving Phoenicia: The Search for Identity in Lebanon*. London: I. B. Tauris, 2004.

Khalidi, Walid. *Conflict and Violence in Lebanon: Confrontation in the Middle East*. Cambridge, MA: Center for International Affairs, Harvard University, 1979.

Kerwin, Lee Klein. 'On the Emergence of Memory in Historical Discourse'. *Representations* 69 (2000 = Special Issue: Grounds for Remembering): 127–50.

Khazen, Farid. 'Kamal Jumblatt, the Uncrowned Druze Prince of the Left'. *Middle Eastern Studies* 24 (1988): 178–205.

——. *The Breakdown of the State in Lebanon, 1967–1976*. Cambridge, MA: Harvard University Press, 2000.

Khuri, Fuad. *Being a Druze*. London: Druze Heritage Foundation, 2004.

Kiersch, Theodore. 'Amnesia: A Clinical Study of Ninety-Eight Cases'. *The American Journal of Psychiatry* 119 (1962): 57–60.

Kimche, David. *The Last Option: After Nasser, Arafat, & Saddam Hussein: The Quest for Peace in the Middle East*. New York: Charles Scribner's Sons, 1991.

Lang, Tobias. *Die Drusen in Libanon und Israel: Geschichte, Konflikte und Loyalitäten einer religiösen Gemeinschaft in zwei Staaten*. Berlin: Klaus Schwarz Verlag, 2013.

Lebanese Synod, Chapter six, No. 3, Paragraph 3. Translation from 'The Maronite Church and Education: Academic and Technical', in *The Maronite Church in Today's World,* File III.

Leese, Peter. *Shell Shock: Traumatic Neurosis and the British Soldiers of the First World War*. New York: Palgrave, 2002.

Leeuwen, Richard van. *Notables and Clergy in Mount Lebanon: The Khāzin Sheikhs and the Maronite Church (1736–1840)*. Leiden: Brill, 1994.

——. 'Monastic Estates and Agricultural Transformation in Mount Lebanon in the 18th Century'. *International Journal of Middle East Studies* 23 (1991): 601–17.

Lewis, Bernard and Buntzie Ellis Churchill. *Notes on a Century: Reflections of a Middle East Historian*. New York: Viking, 2012.

Mahfouz, Joseph. *Saint Charbel Makhlouf: Monk and Hermit of the Lebanese Maronite Order*. [Rome]: [n. p.], 1976.

Makarem, Amal. *Memory for the Future*. Beirut: Dar An-Nahar, 2002.

Makdisi, Ussama. *The Culture of Sectarianism: Community, History, and Violence in Nineteenth-Century Ottoman Lebanon*. Berkeley: University of California Press, 2000.

Maktabi, Rania. 'The Lebanese Census of 1932 Revisited: Who are the Lebanese?' *British Journal of Middle Eastern Studies* 26 (1999): 224–52.

Malinowski, Bronislaw, and Robert Redfield. *Magic, Science and Religion: And Other Essays*. Garden City: Doubleday, 1954.

Mitchell, Thomas. *Likud Leaders: The Lives and Careers of Menahem Begin, Yitzhak Shamir, Benjamin Netanyahu and Ariel Sharon*. Jefferson: McFarland & Company, 2015.

Moosa, Matti. *The Maronites in History*. Syracuse: Syracuse University Press, 1986.

Nasr, Salim. 'Backdrop to Civil War: The Crisis of Lebanese Capitalism'. *MERIP Reports* 73 (1978): 3–13.

Novick, Peter. *The Holocaust in American Life*. Boston: Houghton Mifflin, 1999.

——. *That Noble Dream: The 'Objectivity Question' and the American Historical Profession*. Cambridge: Cambridge University Press, 2007.

Obeid, Anis. *The Druze and Their Faith in Tawhid*. Syracuse: Syracuse University Press, 2006.

Patel, Abdulrazzak. *The Arab Nahdah: The Making of the Intellectual and Humanist Movement*. Edinburgh University Press, 2013.

Phares, Walid. 'The Historical Background of the War of the Mountains'. *Al-Masiraa*, 4 September 1984, 51.

Pintak, Larry. *Seeds of Hate: How America's Flawed Middle East Policy Ignited the Jihad*. London: Pluto Press, 2003.

Porath, Yehoshua. 'The Peasant Revolt of 1858–1861 in Kisrawan'. *Asian and African Studies Annual* 2 (1966): 77–157.

Portelli, Alessandro. 'On the Peculiarities of Oral History'. *History Workshop* 12 (1981): 96–107.

——. *The Battle of Valle Giulia: Oral History and the Art of Dialogue*. Madison: University of Wisconsin Press, 1997.

Randal, Jonathan. *Going All the Way: Christian Warlords, Israeli Adventurers, and the War in Lebanon*. New York: Vintage Books, 1984.

Renan, Ernest. 'What is a Nation?' Lecture delivered at the Sorbonne, 1882. Available at http://www.cooper.edu/humanities/core/hss3/e_renan.htm

Riccoeur, Paul. *History and Truth*. Trans and intr. by Charles A. Kelbley. Evanston: Northwestern University Press, 1965.

Reich, Bernard. *Political Leaders of the Contemporary Middle East and North Africa: A Biographical Dictionary*. New York: Greenwood Press, 1990.

Rizk, Father Karam. 'Milestones in the History of the Lebanese Maronite Order'. Kaslik: University of the Holy Spirit, [n. d.]. Available at: http://www.discoverlebanon.com/en/panoramic_views/lebanese_maronite_order.php, accessed 5 July 2016.

Rodogno, Davide. *Against Massacre Humanitarian Interventions in the Ottoman Empire, 1815–1914: The Emergence of a European Concept and International Practice*. Princeton: Princeton University Press, 2012.

Rolland, John. *Lebanon: Current Issues and Background*. Hauppauge: Nova Science Publishers, 2003.

Rubin, David C., Scott E. Wetzler and Robert D. Nebes. 'Autobiographical Memory Across the Adult Lifespan'. In *Autobiographical Memory*, ed. David C. Rubin, 202–24. Cambridge: Cambridge University Press, 1986.

Saad, Antoun. *Man, Country, Freedom: The Memoirs of Bulus Naʿaman*. Beirut: Entire East Publications, 2009.

Salameh, Franck. *Language, Memory, and Identity in the Middle East: The Case for Lebanon*. Lanham: Lexington Books, 2010.

Salem, Elie. *Violence and Diplomacy in Lebanon: The Troubled Years, 1982–1988*. London: I. B. Tauris, 1995.

Salibi, Kamal. 'The Buhturids of the Garb: Mediaeval Lords of Beirut and of Southern Lebanon'. *Arabica* 8 (1961): 74–97.

——. *Crossroads to Civil War: Lebanon, 1958–1976*. Delmar: Caravan Books, 1976.

——. *A House of Many Mansions: The History of Lebanon Reconsidered*. London: I. B. Tauris, 1988.

——. 'The Maronite Church in the Middle Ages and Its Union with Rome'. *Oriens Christianus* 42 (1958): 92–104.

——. 'The Maronites of Lebanon under Frankish and Mamluk Rule (1099–1516)'. *Arabica* 4 (1957): 280–98.

——. *Maronite Historians of Medieval Lebanon*. With a preface by Bernard Lewis. Beirut: Paris Naufal, 1959.

——. *Syria Under Islam: 634–1097*. 2nd ed. Beirut: Dar Nelson, 2009.

Sayigh, Yezid. 'Palestinian Military Performance in the 1982 War'. *Journal of Palestine Studies* 12 (1983): 24–65.

Schacter, David. *The Seven Sins of Memory*. Boston: Houghton Mifflin, 2001.

Schulze, Kirsten. *Israel's Covert Diplomacy in Lebanon*. New York: St. Martin's Press, 1998.

Setton, Kenneth. *A History of the Crusades*. Madison: University of Wisconsin Press, 1969.

——. The *Papacy and the Levant, 1204–1571*. Vol. III. Philadelphia: American Philosophical Society, 1976.

Sharon, Ariel and David Chanoff. *Warrior: The Autobiography of Ariel Sharon*. New York: Simon and Schuster, 1989.

Snider, Lewis W. 'The Lebanese Forces: Their Origins and Role in Lebanon's Politics'. *The Middle East Journal* 38 (1984): 1–32.

Spagnolo, John P. *France and Ottoman Lebanon*. London: Ithaca Press, 1977.

Stoakes, Frank. 'The Supervigilantes: The Lebanese Kataeb Party as Builder, Surrogate, and Defender of the State'. *Middle Eastern Studies* 11 (1975): 215–36.

Thomas, Wilbert. 'Operation Peace for Galilee: An Operational Analysis with Relevance Today'. *Naval War College* (1998). Available at: https://apps.dtic.mil/dtic/tr/fulltext/u2/a348640.pdf, accessed 3 March 2020.

Thompson, Paul. *The Voice of the Past.* Oxford, New York: Oxford University Press, 2000.

Tonkin, Elizabeth. *Narrating Our Pasts: The Social Construction of Oral History.* Cambridge: Cambridge University Press, 1992.

Traboulsi, Fawwaz. *A History of Modern Lebanon.* London: Pluto Press, 2007.

Urquhart, David. *The Lebanon (Mount Souria): A History and a Diary.* London: T. C. Newby, 1860.

Volk, Lucia. *Memorials and Martyrs in Modern Lebanon.* Bloomington: Indiana University Press, 2010.

Walker, Paul. *Caliph of Cairo: Al-Hakim Bi-Amr Allah, 996–1021.* Cairo: American University in Cairo Press, 2009.

Wertsch, James V. 'Collective Memory'. In *Memory in Mind and Culture*, ed. Pascal Boyer and James V. Wertsch, 117–37. Cambridge: Cambridge University Press, 2009.

Wright, Patrick Devine. 'A Theoretical Overview of Memory and Conflict'. In *The Role of Memory in Ethnic Conflicts*, ed. Ed Cairns and Micheal Roe, 9–33. Basingstoke, New York: Palgrave Macmillan, 2003.

Yaer, Bat. *The Decline of Eastern Christianity under Islam: From Jihad to Dhimmitude, Seventh-Twentieth Century.* Madison: Fairleigh Dickinson University Press, 1996.

Yaniv, Avner. *Dilemmas of Security: Politics, Strategy, and the Israeli Experience in Lebanon.* New York: Oxford University Press, 1987.

Zamir, Meir. *The Formation of Modern Lebanon.* Ithaca: Cornell University Press, 1988.

INDEX

Abdu, Johnny, 69, 157
Abdul-Hak, Said, 200, 201
Abdul Nasser, Gamal, 109, 122, 132, 182
Abu-Husayn, Abdul Rahim, 41, 42, 44–7, 71–3, 75, 126
Abu Nadir, Fouad, 149, 163, 179, 191, 196, 212, 217–19, 228, 230, 251, 252, 258, 260, 268
Abu-Shaqra, Muhammad, 104, 105, 132, 134, 135, 171, 204, 207, 211–13, 236, 254
Achkar, Massoud, 180, 181, 196
Achkouti, Raji, 251, 260
Adwan, George, 259
Aintoura, 108
Aintrazi, Issam, 97, 126
al-Aridi, Ghazi, 20, 22
al-Assad, Hafez, 86, 129, 131, 152, 153, 155, 157, 160, 174–86, 192, 242, 292, 297
al-Atrash, Sultan Pasha, 95, 181, 278–80
al-Beaini, Hassan, 118, 128, 163
al-Boustani, Fouad Ephrem, 93, 124, 126, 163
al-Chaftari, Ass'ad, 122, 129

al-Farisi, Salman, 233, 248
al-Fatayri, Anwar, 178, 213, 214, 254, 287, 295
al-Halabi, Abbas, 27, 34
al-Krayeh, 176, 177, 178, 181
al-Majmu' al-Lubnani, 80
al-Saddam, 219, 221
al-Zayek, Elias, 163, 181, 191
al-Zou'r, Fouad, 120
Andary, Paul, 13–15, 24, 32, 229–31, 245, 250, 255, 258–61
Aoun, Michael, 163, 240
Arafat, Yasser, 83, 115
Arens, Moshe, 198, 199, 234, 238–40, 259
Arlosoroff, Haim, 148
Arslan, 37, 72, 95, 105, 165 183–5, 199, 208, 235, 281, 285
  Faisal, 183–5, 199, 208, 235, 236
  Majid, 69, 105, 122, 183, 184, 204, 224, 236, 279, 280
  Shakib, 37, 95, 285
As'ad, Amal, 206, 207
Atashi, Zeidan, 201–5, 226, 227, 240
'Ayn al-Remmaneh, 140, 168, 170

Baakline, 111, 199, 200
Barakat, Keyrouz, 266, 267
Barakat, Toufic, 211, 232, 258, 259, 295
Baʻabda, 223
Beaufort, Charles de, 60, 232
Begin, Menachem, 145, 149, 150, 161, 166, 173, 189, 191, 194, 198, 201, 204, 222, 223, 226, 234
Beit al-Din, 48, 69, 119, 120, 136, 170, 215, 217, 284, 285, 290
Bhamdoun, 181, 185, 243, 245, 246, 250, 254, 278
Bin al-Qilai, Jibra'il, 52, 57, 277
Bou Fakhraddine, Halim, 119, 120, 128, 154, 178, 196
Btadini, Khaled, 217, 218, 228
Buhturid, 39–41, 70, 71, 103, 204, 211, 252

Chamoun, Camille, 89, 109, 110, 119, 122, 125, 134, 139, 141, 143, 148, 160, 211, 238, 251, 297
Chamoun, Dany, 125, 139, 142, 191
Cheiko, Louis, 64
Corm, Charles, 64–6, 75, 76, 87, 147, 148, 164
Council for Druze Studies and Development, 27, 28

Daghan, Meir, 235, 255
Deir al-Qamar, 14, 50, 85, 110, 120, 157, 170, 251–5, 259, 260, 265, 295
Duwayhi, Istfan, 52–4

Eddé, Joe, 143–5, 164, 217
Eid, George, 217, 228
Eitan, Rafael (Raful), 147, 150, 151, 198
Entebbe, 219, 228

Fatimid, 36, 38, 94
Frangieh, 125, 141, 142, 148, 158, 254
  Samir, 157, 159, 166
  Suleiman, 125, 148
  Tony, 141, 230, 254
Freiha, George, 163, 174, 190, 195, 197

Frem, Fadi, 124, 150, 163, 180, 190, 191, 222, 223, 233, 243, 245, 258

Geagea, Samir, 141, 142, 150, 163, 230, 231, 234, 238, 244, 245, 250–2, 260
Gemayel, 1, 2, 21–5, 69, 90–3, 141, 146, 148, 150, 151, 155, 158, 160, 162–4, 167, 168, 169, 174–6, 178, 179, 182–5, 186, 188, 192–7, 199, 200, 208, 210–12, 222–5, 240–5, 252, 263, 266, 267, 272–7, 289
  Amin, 21, 88, 92, 125, 137, 190, 191, 192, 193, 194, 197, 211, 212, 222, 223, 224, 225, 234, 236, 238, 240, 241, 242, 244, 245, 250, 255, 264, 272, 282
  Bashir, 23–5, 69, 73, 80, 86–8, 90, 97, 98, 110, 113, 116, 117, 119, 124, 125, 128, 133, 136–47, 149–51, 155–60, 162–4, 167–70, 174–6, 182–96, 199, 200, 208–10, 217, 222–4, 226, 230, 231, 242, 253, 255, 258, 263–7, 270, 272–6, 284, 285, 288, 290
  Manuel, 179
  Pierre, 1, 86, 91, 92, 125, 141, 148, 160, 182, 190, 192, 196, 223, 238, 245, 255
Gurion, David Ben, 148, 149, 165

Habib, Philip, 145, 161, 186
Haddad, Bob, 146, 181
Halbwachs, Maurice, 5, 7–9, 31
Hamada, Farid, 208, 209, 224, 225
  Marwan, 34
  Sheikh Rashid, 105, 212
Hamdan, Taleh, 5, 171, 195, 208, 212, 228, 263, 278–83, 290
Harb, Raja, 120, 131, 132, 154, 155, 163, 165, 172, 173, 195, 200, 214, 242, 243, 251, 260, 287
Hariri, Rafik, 298
Hasbaya, 50, 102
Hawi, William, 137
Hazran, Yusri, 110, 114
Hoayek, Elias, 67, 76
Hobeika, Elie, 120, 122, 128, 149, 163, 189, 191, 225

Ibrahim Pasha, 42, 49, 60, 170, 213, 242
Irfan, 105
Irgun, 149, 150

Jacobite, 56, 74, 277
Jarajimah, 36, 51, 275
Joumblatt, 26–30, 44, 46–50, 60, 61, 71, 72, 73, 95, 96, 99, 108–19, 124, 127, 130–6, 151, 160, 167, 169, 171–6, 178, 183, 197, 199, 203–5, 208–13, 216, 223–5, 233–7, 239, 240, 242–4, 248, 255, 276, 278–80, 284–7, 294–8
    Bashir, 47, 48, 49, 50, 97, 98, 110, 113, 133, 167, 176, 285, 288, 290
    Kamal, 29, 37, 84, 88, 99, 100, 104, 105, 108, 109, 112, 113, 114, 115, 118, 119, 130, 132, 133, 134, 135, 136, 151, 152, 153, 154, 155, 157, 160, 168, 169, 203, 211, 216, 237, 249, 279, 280, 283, 285, 297
    Said, 252, 254, 278
    Walid, 26, 29, 30, 33, 68, 69, 112, 113, 116, 117, 131, 132, 133, 134, 135, 136, 140, 151, 152, 154, 155, 157, 158, 159, 160, 163, 165, 171, 172, 174, 175, 176, 178, 183, 193, 195, 199, 204, 205, 208, 209, 210, 212, 213, 223, 224, 225, 234, 235, 242, 244, 248, 252, 254, 261, 278, 279, 280, 284, 286, 287, 290, 294, 296, 298
Joumblatti-Yazbaki, 44, 62, 105, 201, 213

Kahan Commission, 194, 197, 198, 226
Karami, Rashid, 153, 174
Kaslik (USK) 82, 84, 86, 87, 123, 124, 126, 164, 197, 274, 275, 285, 289
Kaslik Research Committee, 87, 88, 90, 93, 275
Kassis, Charbel, 83, 124, 125
Kataeb, 1, 2, 4, 5, 84, 88, 91–3, 125, 136, 137, 139–42, 158, 163, 177, 181–3, 190, 192, 206, 208, 210, 217, 218, 223, 224, 233, 235, 242, 243, 254, 264
Kfarmatta, 243
Kfarnabrkh, 199, 215, 216

Khalaf, Abbas, 131, 163, 301
Khalwat al-Bayada, 102, 103, 107, 209
Khayat, Elie, 33, 263, 266, 270, 272, 289
Khazen, 2, 6, 54, 80, 108, 125, 127, 141, 142
Khoueiry, Jocelyn, 84–6, 233, 235
Kimche, David, 191, 198, 222, 223, 226, 229, 240, 241, 259, 260
Kissinger, Henry, 90

Lammens, Henri, 53, 64, 66, 67, 75
Lebanese Monastic Order (al-Rahbanah al-Mārūnīya), 79, 80, 81, 82, 83, 84, 123, 187, 275
Likud, 149, 150, 161, 166, 202, 310
Lipkin-Shahak, Amnon, 206, 216, 222
Lubrani, Uri, 234, 236, 238, 239, 240, 241, 259

Ma'an, 41, 42, 47, 68, 214
    Ahmad, 44
    Fakhr al-Din, 43, 44, 45, 46, 55, 67, 98, 111, 112, 134
    Korkmaz, 42, 43
Malik, Charles, 87, 124, 125, 163, 185
Maradites, 52, 275
Ménargues, Alain, 158, 159, 164–6, 191, 195, 197, 209, 227, 229, 244, 259, 260
Moghabghab, Naim, 119, 120, 122
Monothelitism, 56
Mossad, 145, 149, 160, 173, 191, 198, 229
Moukhtara, 33, 37, 60, 61, 70, 96, 114, 118, 130, 132, 157, 172–4, 178, 278
Mtolleh, 219, 221, 222, 233
Muhammad 'Ali Pasha, 48, 49, 167, 278, 279, 280
Mutasarrifiya, 51, 61, 62, 63, 66, 67, 297

Na'aman, Bulus, 83, 86, 87, 90, 113, 124, 125, 128, 141, 155, 164, 186, 196, 225, 265, 274
Naim, Rajeh, 29, 34, 72, 96, 120, 126, 237
Najm, Antoine, 25, 66, 90, 91, 93, 116, 124, 125, 128, 157, 163–6, 170, 195, 245, 260

Nasreddine, Hisham, 210, 213, 214, 218, 219, 227, 228, 235, 259, 294
National Pact, 68, 69, 89, 91, 92, 116, 117, 128, 136, 148, 190, 222, 293, 297
Nizamiyat, 84, 233
Nujaym, Bulus, 66, 67, 82

Palestine Liberation Organisation (PLO), 2, 83, 86, 88, 90, 110, 112, 113, 127, 147, 149, 151, 153, 159, 161, 162, 171, 173, 174, 186, 189, 191, 192, 199, 202
Peres, Shimon, 173, 195
Permanent Bureau for Druze Associations, 28, 213
Phalangist, 1, 23, 122, 125, 137, 190, 193, 194, 202, 205, 206
Progressive Socialist Party, 4, 16, 25, 108, 113, 227, 244

Qaimaqamiyya, 59
Qaramita, 38
Qaysi-Yemeni, 43, 44, 55, 62
Qoubbei, 33, 176, 178, 179, 181–3, 186, 196, 219, 226, 260
Quwwat Abu Ibrahim, 106, 256, 257, 284

Rashaya, 99, 100
Reagan, Ronald, 145, 193, 222, 238, 241, 255, 282
Renan, Ernest, 77, 78, 123
Rome, 53, 56–8, 74, 79, 80, 277, 289

Saab, Akram, 213, 228, 301
Sabra and Shatila, 120, 189, 193, 198, 224, 264
Safra, 142, 254
Saint Joseph University (USJ), 63, 64, 84
Salazar, António, 21, 22
Salibi, Kamal, 3, 5, 6, 34–6, 38–41, 49, 52–5, 58, 70–5, 126, 127, 195, 277, 289, 290, 299
Salloum, Atef, 203, 204, 207, 208, 227
Sawfar, 119, 185
Sayeret Matkal, 219, 221
Sharett, Moshe, 148, 149

Shamir, Yitzhak, 161, 191, 192, 194
Sharon, Ariel, 150, 151, 160–2, 165, 166, 173, 189, 191, 193, 194, 198, 202, 222, 223, 229, 234, 238, 259
Shartouni, Habib, 186, 189
Shehayab, Akram, 214
Sheikh al-'Aql, 103, 104, 105, 127, 131, 132, 171, 201, 204, 207, 208, 209, 211, 212, 254
Shihab, Bashir, 46, 47, 48, 49, 50, 58, 80, 97, 98, 110, 113, 119
Soviet Union, 114, 119, 154, 155, 164, 179, 187, 219, 243, 244, 284
Syrian Socialist National Party (SSNP), 113, 186, 189

Takieddine, Halim, 34, 214, 215, 285
Talhouk, 72, 278
  Fadlallah, 208, 35
Tannous, Ibrahim, 245
Tanoukhi, 153
Tarabay, Ghanem, 16, 17, 19, 33, 178, 196, 250, 260, 296
Tarif, Amin, 103, 200, 201, 212
Tegho, Augustine, 143, 146, 164, 301

Unitarian, 28, 36, 105

Voice of the Mountain (Sawt al-Jabal), 20, 21, 193, 197

Walieddine, Abu Mohammad Jawad, 199, 204
Weinberger, Caspar, 241, 242
Weizmann, Ezer, 161

Yazbaki, 44, 47, 48, 50, 69, 95, 103–5, 183, 199, 208, 210, 212, 224, 225, 236, 287
Yemeni, 44, 54, 165

Zahle, 50, 123, 143, 144, 145, 146, 147, 157, 160, 164, 181, 217, 255, 265, 266, 267
Zeindinne, Ali, 127
Zionism, 66, 107, 147, 148, 150, 204

EU representative:
Easy Access System Europe
Mustamäe tee 50, 10621 Tallinn, Estonia
Gpsr.requests@easproject.com

www.ingramcontent.com/pod-product-compliance
Lightning Source LLC
Chambersburg PA
CBHW071828230426
43672CB00013B/2784